JAINISM

THE WORLD OF CONQUERORS

VOLUME 1

The
World
of Conquerors

History has witnessed many conquerors.
There have been conquerors of regions, lands,
kingdoms and great empires. In contrast to the military conquerors such as Alexander the Great, Julius
Caesar or Clive of India, the modern world has presented
opportunities to some to carve out great empires in
business and in property. Others metaphorically 'conquer'
areas of scientific research, of sport, of entertainment and
other such worldly matters.

These are, in a sense, external conquests. Often they prove to be
fleeting and temporary. Great empires, like those of the Romans
or the British, rise up only to pass away. Business achievements
and sporting prowess are overtaken by events.

In our personal lives, too, happiness and fulfilment often seem
to elude us. It is in this realm of the personal that the Jain
religion holds out both a challenge and a way forward. 'Jain'
means conqueror. A conqueror of the self. In this work, we
shall explore the world of those who have striven to achieve
victory over the self and to gain the rewards which flow
from it. These rewards are not of the fleeting,
contingent, material sort. The happiness achieved is
independent of material circumstances and events.

Any person, irrespective of language, religion,
circumstances or physical attributes, can
follow the Jain path and find peace and
happiness – and in doing so
contribute to the well-being of all
life in the world.

CONTENTS

FOREWORD

By His Excellency
DR L. M. SINGHVI
High Commissioner for India in the UK

'A magnum opus of a lifetime' is how Dr Natubhai Shah's two volumes on *The World of Conquerors* deserve to be described. I consider it a privilege to be invited to write this Foreword to these two volumes, which I regard as a welcome contribution to the understanding of the Indic heritage in the perspective of our time.

A remarkable example of painstaking erudition and inspired dedication, these two volumes by Dr Shah provide an integrated and comprehensive framework and deal in depth with different dimensions of Jainism, Jain beliefs, Jain social and cultural ethos and milieu, and the contemporary relevance of Jainism. They are written in a simple and lucid style and are greatly enhanced by excellent illustrations. The distinguished author of these two volumes seeks to communicate the essence of Jainism, philosophically, ethically, historically, culturally and socially. He has succeeded in providing in the space of these two volumes a macro-level perspective on Jainism as well as its particular facets, and this he has achieved by a methodical and inclusive approach. Metaphorically speaking, he manages to see for himself and share with his readers a view of the forest as well as the trees and the pathways in the forest without losing his way in the jungle. He provides to his readers an excellent route map, a reliable compass, an illuminating awareness and an intimate vantage view of what he calls 'the world of conquerors', a world of inner and outer space waiting to be conquered not by warlike weapons unleashed by greed, malice, domination, violence and exploitation but by peaceful conquerors following principles and practice of Right Faith, Right Knowledge, Right Conduct, and Right Austerities based on reverence for life, compassion, non-violence, equanimity and a sense of mutual interdependence.

Dr Natubhai Shah's work *The World of Conquerors* seeks to encompass the vast range, wide extent and profound depth, which are the hallmarks of Jainism. In these eminently readable volumes, those hallmark qualities of Jainism are reflected and condensed in a compendium. It is remarkable that nothing that a scholar or an average student may ordinarily want to know about Jainism is left out. These volumes will, I hope, receive the attention and study they deserve at the hands of the younger generation of Jains and non-Jains alike. They could serve a larger segment of the population in India if translated into some of the Indian languages. I would like to express the hope that these books will also be translated into some of the major international languages.

The first volume is devoted to the antiquity of Jainism, Jain history (including the historical perspective relating to the *Tirthankaras*, prominent *Aacaaryas*, the Jain *Sangha*, the schisms and migration of Jains abroad), Jainism in the twentieth century, the Jain community, popular Jainism and Jainism in the modern world. In the second volume, Dr Shah gives an elaborate account of Jain sacred literature and modern Jain literature, Jain cosmology, Jain philosophy, Jain logic, science and Jainism, Jain heritage (including Jain art and architecture, Jain temples and places of pilgrimage and Jain institutions) and other faiths. Each volume contains its own appendices, bibliography, glossary and inclusive index. Each chapter is comprehensive and is a model of clarity and brevity. The entire work is a bridge between past, present and future and is animated by conscientious social activism and contemporary concerns of modern life.

I commend Dr Natubhai Shah's magnum opus and welcome its publication. Dr Shah's message for the Jains and his views on Eastern and Western faiths embody a vibrant meaning and a clarion call for all Jains. It takes us to the heart and soul for all Jains. Like the beautiful Jain temple in Leicester, in the construction of which Dr Shah had a pivotal role, these two volumes on Jainism will remain an outstanding and abiding contribution to Jainism for many decades to come.

September 1997
London

PREFACE AND
ACKNOWLEDGEMENTS

Jainism is regarded by its followers as the world's oldest religion, which was revived by the *tirthankara* Mahavira more than 2,500 years ago, in Bihar, northern India. He addressed himself to the mass of the people, delivering his teachings in *Ardha Magadhi*, then the language of the ordinary people of Magadha (Bihar). It is Mahavira who is credited with founding one of the distinctive features of contemporary Jain society and religion: the four-fold organisation of ascetics, female ascetics and male and female laypeople. Throughout its long history, Jainism has seen periods when it has flourished and others when it has declined, but for thousands of years it has remained a living religion and a way of life in India. It has exerted profound influence on many Indian civilisations, on cultures and on the lives of millions of people, through its teachings, through the conduct of its followers, and through its examples of its art and architecture. These concrete expressions of the Jain heritage are now counted among the greatest of the treasures which India has given to the world.

Inevitably, given the immensely long history of Jainism, some changes have taken place over time. However, Jainism's principles and teachings have remained remarkably constant, while allowing freedom and growth in its practices and rituals. The three most important expressions of Jain teaching are the 'Three Jewels': Right Faith, Right Knowledge and Right Conduct. For followers of Jainism, the most important outward practices are *ahimsaa*, 'non-violence and reverence for all life', *aparigraha*, 'non-attachment to worldly possessions, power or position', and *anekaanta-vaada*, 'relative pluralism' or multiplicity of views.

Jainism can be seen as a microcosm of Indian society, yet its concepts have a direct relevance to many issues currently of concern to many in the West as well as in the East. In the vibrant societies in which Jainism flourished, philosophical debates ranged widely, touching upon the entire range of human experience and understanding. Although all Jains shared a common fundamental outlook, differences of interpretation were bound to arise and these were responsible for a variety of rituals and worship, which led to the emergence of the four major sects of Jainism: Svetambara, Digambara, Sthanakvasi and Terapanthi.

These sectarian differences seem less relevant outside India and the experience of Jain migration in East Africa and to the West has created new opportunities for seeing Jain identity in a fresh light. In the work I undertook in creating the Jain Centre in Leicester, I had contact with and received the blessing and support of both lay leaders and ascetics from all the major sects of Jainism. While the Jain Centre in Leicester embodies the ideal of Jain unity, becoming a place of worship and pilgrimage for all Jain groups, by its nature it could influence only a relatively small number of people. I therefore conceived the idea of writing a book which could express something of the meaning of Jainism to Jains and non-Jains alike. And, indeed, it was the establishment of the Jain Academy which gave focus to my writing this work.

I have tried to give readers not only a feel for Jain beliefs and philosophy, about which there are many works in print, but also an insight into the lives of ordinary Jain devotees. To my knowledge, little has been written on the practical aspects of Jainism. This work is in two volumes, and while each volume stands on its own, the two have been conceived as one integrated work. A brief look at the figures in volume 2, before tackling volume 1 in earnest, will reward the reader with a necessary conceptual acquaintance with the Jain idea of the Universe, the cosmic cycle, the eight types of *karma* and the fourteen stages of spiritual development. It will help place the chapters of volume 1 in a developmental and overarching context. The appendices of both volumes contain useful and practical information. The appendices of volume 1 contain information for those wishing to take up the practical aspects of Jain vegetarianism.

I acknowledge my gratitude to those who have helped me, directly or indirectly, in the completion of this work. I must thank the many authors, mentioned in the bibliography, whose work has been a source of inspiration. I learned much from the leaders of the Jain community, especially the Jain Samaj Europe and the Jain Academy. I would like to express my sincere gratitude to Dr Paul Marett for reading the entire manuscript and suggesting improvements, to Dr Nandlal Jain who worked with me for nearly three months procuring information from many scriptural and textual sources, and Robert Ash who helped in the practical editorial work, and to my secretaries Diana and Christine who typed the initial drafts. I am sincerely grateful to Dr L. M. Singhvi, the High Commissioner of India, and a scholar of Jainism, for sparing his valuable time to write the foreword to this work.

My special thanks are due to my wife Mrs Bhanumati Shah for her inspiration, sacrifice and her untiring work in entertaining all who helped me to complete the book. I am grateful to my daughter Leena and my son Samir and their families for the constant inspiration to finish the work. While I have tried always to check the accuracy of the text, I take full responsibility for any inaccuracies or mistakes unknowingly appearing in this work. I would appreciate comments and suggestions from readers on how the work might be improved for future editions. It is my sincere hope that this work will serve both as an accessible introduction to Jainism for the general reader and as a spur to the scholar to undertake further study and research into this ancient faith.

Dr Natubhai Shah
July 1997
London

TRANSLITERATION AND PRONUNCIATION

The languages of the Jain communities which produced the scriptures and the languages spoken in modern times by most Jains are very different from English. There are difficulties in conveying to readers through print alone how words sound in other languages. I have transcribed words from ancient and modern Indian languages in a way that seemed most likely to give modern English-speaking readers an approximation to the original sounds.

In the case of personal and place names and of well-known words, such as *brahmin*, I have retained the spellings widely used in English, but which do not necessarily express the pronunciation accurately.

Readers may assume that transliterated words sound approximately as they do in English except for:

aa the double a indicates a long vowel sound
dh this combination of letters sounds like th in 'the'
c in most instances, the consonant c sounds like ch as in 'chair'
s in most instances the consonant s sounds like sh as in 'share'

Letters such as t, th, d, l and n are not pronounced as in 'standard' versions of English, but may, sometimes, require a prolonged or emphasised sound. Interested readers are requested to seek expert help.

ks and **jn** indicate two sounds which are unknown in English and an attempt to convey these accurately through transliteration would be unhelpful.

JAINISM
THE WORLD OF CONQUERORS

VOLUME 1

Religion itself is an island, a resting place, strength and the best shelter for living beings swept away by forceful currents in the form of old age and death.

(Uttaraadhyayana 23: 68)

All those who are totally attached to the body, complexion and beauty in thought, words and deeds are ultimately creating miseries for themselves.

(Uttaraadhyayana 6: 11)

Material pleasures are like thorns. Material pleasures are like poison. Material pleasures are like a poisonous serpent. People seeking pleasures get into an unhappy state of rebirth, without getting any of the pleasures.

(Uttaraadhyayana 9: 53)

Look at human life in this world! It may be over either early in youth or after a hundred years. You should know that this life is an abode for very short duration. However, the greedy people still remain engrossed in worldly pleasures.

(Sutra Krutaanga 1: 2: 3: 8)

Chapter 1

INTRODUCTION

THE MEANING OF LIFE

Let me introduce you to Jainism by greeting you in a Jain way, *Jai Jinendra*. This greeting literally means: 'honour to those who have conquered themselves'. By this, Jains mean honour to those who have conquered their inner impulses, whether good or evil, and who exemplify the path of self-conquest and happiness to all other living beings.

Life is dear to us all—human beings and other living beings, happy individuals as well as miserable ones. Many questions about life arise in our minds. Who has given us life? Who takes it away when we die? Why are there injustices in life? Why are some born into poor families and others born into wealthy ones? Why are some born as humans and others born as animals? Why one as male and another as female? Why do some live a long life and others a short one? Why are some born with great intellectual gifts, while others are less well endowed? Can we explain why some are born with physical attributes, which are prized, such as beauty, while others lack these? Why is one person healthy and another full of suffering? Why do some achieve popularity and fame yet others are unpopular or even notorious? Why do some people have great wealth, while others cannot make ends meet?

The more we think, the more questions come into our inquisitive minds. Do our lives have meaning? Do they have purpose? Can we achieve permanent happiness and bliss? Who are we? Where have we come from? And what are we here for?

For endless centuries these questions have puzzled all thinking people, philosophers, theologians, scientists and the intelligentsia. They have sought answers, postulated theories and have attempted to find the truth about these great mysteries and the nature of the universe. Some believe it is the will of the Almighty 'Supreme God', the creator, the sustainer and the dispenser of justice. Others maintain that the universe is eternal and the mysterious phenomena of nature, justices and injustices, are the results of karmic bondage of the soul. Our own actions in the past, whether good or bad, cause this karmic bondage, which we will discuss in detail in volume 2, chapter 4.

Jain Tradition

Indian civilisation has produced many philosophies and religions. Among them is Jainism, one of the oldest religions of the world. Jainism is a religion, a philosophy, a way of life taught and preached in the past by countless jinas (and which will be taught in the future by other jinas). Although historians have made various speculations about its origin, the origin of Jainism remains untraceable. Jains believe it to be an eternal religion. The name Jainism comes from jina, meaning 'victor' in the classical Indian language Sanskrit. Jinas are the victors of the self, have achieved liberation from karmic bondage and they have attained the true characteristics of the soul such as infinite faith, infinite knowledge, perfect conduct, infinite bliss and eternality by their own efforts. They are called *tirthankaras*, persons who lead us towards the path of the eternal life of perfection. Tirtha means (spiritual) path, or the order, which follows this pathway. Each tirthankara establishes four orders of society (caturvidha sangha) consisting of monks (*saadhus*), nuns (*saadhvis*), male lay followers (*sraavakas*) and female lay followers (*sraavikaas*).

The *tirthankara* leads the above four orders of society towards the path of spiritual perfection by teaching the truth about the universe and its nature, the meaning of life and the ethical path to be pursued. When we say that Jainism is a religion preached by the *jinas*, we mean Jainism expresses the eternal truths of life and spirituality taught by pure souls, who are victors of themselves, with perfect knowledge and understanding.

Jainism believes the universe to be eternal, its constituents such as living and non-livings things may change form, but they are basically eternal. Time rotates in a cycle, like a wheel moving clockwise, descending and ascending. In each half of the time cycle (aeon), descending and ascending, twenty-four *tirthankaras* establish the four-fold order and teach the path of happiness and perfection to all the living beings of the world. The first *tirthankara* in this aeon was Risabhdeva and the twenty-fourth (and last) was Vardhamana Mahavira who lived, according to generally accepted dates, from 599 to 527 BCE.

Revival of Jainism

The last *tirthankara* Mahavira is not the founder of Jainism, but he revived it and expounded the religious, philosophical and ethical teachings of previous *tirthankaras*. Jainism belongs to the non-Vedic, *sramana* tradition of Indian culture and is reputed to be pre-Vedic, antedating in its origins the coming of the Aryan peoples to India.

Over a period of nearly a century after Mahavira's liberation, Jainism produced a series of omniscients. These were followed in succession, for more than two centuries, by scriptural omniscients and later on by prominent ascetic-scholars. These knowledgeable ascetics evolved Jainism into a complete religious system, with its own philosophy, ethics, rituals and mythology. They produced a vast sacred literature covering all aspects of human life and the situation of other living beings in the universe.

The four-fold order developed into a highly organised society of monastic orders and laypeople. Jains have created beautiful temples, *upashrayas* (monasteries and places of meditation), and preserved most of their sacred literature. They have established institutions of education, social welfare and animal welfare. 'Live and help to live' is their motto and their way of life is based on the teachings of Mahavira.

Mahavira was a contemporary of the Buddha. Both preached religions that stemmed from the *sramana* tradition. They believed sacrifices and other religious practices conducted by brahminical priests not only unnecessary, but a hindrance to the goal of salvation. The way to salvation, they claimed, was through self-discipline, meditation and ascetic practices. The similarities between the Jain and Buddhist religions and especially the fact that Mahavira and the Buddha lived at the same time in the same region caused confusion among Western scholars for a long time. There are basic differences in the beliefs of Jainism and Buddhism, which we shall discuss in volume 2, chapter 8. Jainism is a highly original system of thought containing ancient material. The two religions, though similar in origin and approach, evolved along different lines and each gathered a vast number of followers. But Jainism, unlike Buddhism, spread little beyond the frontiers of India. Its hold over its adherents in India, however, continued to be strong throughout the ages and it was able, therefore, to counter the strong forces of the Hindu revivalists. Buddhism, on the other hand, could not withstand these pressures and consequently virtually disappeared from the land of its origin. Jainism, though restricted to a minority, continues to be a living tradition in India today. Owing to recent migrations, Jain followers are now to be found in most countries of the world.

Mahavira was very practical in his approach. He divided society into male ascetics and female ascetics, who can follow his teachings rigorously, and laymen and laywomen who can pursue the path of his teachings to the best of their abilities in the light of their worldly duties. Jainism does not demand unquestioning faith from its followers, but encourages understanding before acceptance.

Jain Teachings

The Jain way of life is not at odds with normal everyday life. It is an ethical doctrine with self-discipline as its core. It does not recognise an almighty god or a Supreme Being. It believes in godhood that can be attained by most of us, provided we follow the path of the teachings of *jina* and liberate our souls. Jains do not depend on 'divine grace' to attain liberation, but attempt to achieve it through individual initiative and effort. They worship *tirthankaras* as examples and do not ask for any favours.

Jainism is an open religion. Persons born in the Jain community have to be Jains by following the teachings of the *jinas*. They have a better environment to be true Jains. Jainism believes, irrespective of labels attached to us by birth or otherwise, any person who follows the path of the *jinas* is a Jain.

Jainism teaches that the universe consists of living and non-living things. It is the attachment of non-living substances to living things, the soul, which causes suffering, an unending process of birth, death and rebirth. The Jain way of life consists of the co-ordinated path of the 'Three Jewels': Right Faith, Right Knowledge and Right Conduct. Right Faith is belief in the teachings of the *jinas*, Right Knowledge is a proper grasp of the nine real entities making the universe as found in the teachings of omniscient *jinas* and Right Conduct is the ethical code, behaviour and actions laid down by the teachings of the *jinas*.

The universe consists of six substances: the soul, matter, the medium of motion, the medium of rest, space and time. The soul is the living being *(jiva)* and the others are non-living substances *(ajiva)*. Both *jiva* and *ajiva* are interdependent and everlasting. Living beings can be categorised into two types: those who are liberated, that is who have successfully freed themselves from the cycle of birth, death and rebirth, and those who are still enmeshed in that cycle (worldly). Whenever the worldly *(sansaari)* soul appears on earth it is born as either a mobile or an immobile being. The immobile being has only one sense, that of touch. The simplest example is a plant. Mobile beings have the sense of touch and, in addition, one or more of the remaining four senses, taste, sight, smell and hearing. The five-sensed living beings are further subdivided into those that have a mind, such as human beings, and those that do not have a mind, such as most animals. This produces a classification like that in table 1.1 (It should be remembered that the traditional divisions may not accord exactly with those accepted by modern biology.)

Causes of the Mysteries of Worldly Life　In the worldly life, living beings have been attached to non-living *karma* since eternity and this bondage is responsible for birth, death, sufferings, pain and illusory pleasures of a temporary nature. Karmic bondage is described in detail in

Table 1.1 Types of *Jiva*

	JIVA		
Liberated (siddha)		Worldly (samsaari)	
Immobile with one sense, e.g. plants		Mobile	
2 senses e.g. worms birds, fish,	3 senses e.g. lice	4 senses e.g. bees	5 senses (with or without mind) e.g. animals, humans, heavenly being, hellish being

volume 2, chapter 4. It is the result of our own actions, physical, verbal or mental. The moment the *karmas* are totally shed, the soul becomes liberated and is able to live with its full potentials of infinite bliss, knowledge, faith and spiritual energy, and perfect conduct eternally along with other liberated souls. When one dies, the soul leaves behind the body, which is made of matter, but takes the *karma* attached to it. The type of *karma* forces the soul to create another body according to the characteristics of its particular *karma*.

Jainism describes *karma* as subtle matter of sub-atomic particles, not perceptible to the senses, found everywhere in the cosmos and having the property of penetrating the soul and clouding its characteristics. The activities of mind, body and speech make vibrations in these particles and attract them towards the soul. Intense activities cause severe vibrations, causing these particles to penetrate the soul and stick to it tightly. The influx of karmic matter occurs all the time. Benevolent acts cause good *karmas* (merit), while sinful acts cause bad *karmas* (demerit). The result of merit is good body, good destiny and family, and material happiness; the reverse is the case with demerit. Both merit and demerit keep the soul in the worldly cycle, they do not cancel each other out. Karmic particles penetrate the soul and form karmic body around the regions of the soul. For liberation from the cycle of birth and death, all karmic particles, whether of merit or demerit, have to be shed.

The quantity, the size, the type and the density of karmic particles determine the form that the soul will assume in forthcoming births. it is the karmic body which causes the living being to have inherent passions such as greed, anger, deceit and pride. Of course, external environments affect these passions, increasing their severity in a complementary way, but Right

Conduct including ethics, meditation and austerities can prevent this complementary effect.

After the effect of the deeds, good and bad has been worked out in the soul; the *karma* matter is shed. If this were to continue uninterruptedly then the soul eventually would shed all the *karma* matter. Unfortunately, this is not possible because while a being is shedding old *karma* matter, it is simultaneously attracting new, through different actions of mind, body and speech. Thus the soul remains in bondage of karmic body and transmigrates in the worldly cycle.

Liberation of the soul from karmic bondage can be achieved only through an active shedding of all existing *karma.* Jainism describes this as a two-stage process. The first stage is the stoppage of all channels through which *karma* flows into the soul. This requires rigorous self-control and freedom from worldly attachments by cutting oneself off from worldly ties and occupying oneself in meditation. Once the ingress of *karma* has been plugged, then begins the second stage of shedding the particles of karmic body by austerities until the *karma* is destroyed. When this finally occurs, after countless lives and long spiritual development, the soul, released from its bondage, reverts to its true natural state of pure perfection and attains liberation. It ascends to the apex of the universe where it dwells in *siddha silaa* a, a liberated soul without material body, enjoying infinite bliss, infinite knowledge, detachment and equanimity.

The theory of *karma* explains almost all the questions raised in the beginning of this chapter, such as the injustices in this world, the type of body which one occupies, the misery and unhappiness, and the cycle of rebirth. We will discuss *karma* in more detail in volume 2, chapter 4. The answer to the question, 'What am I?' becomes a little clearer. I am a soul, which occupies different types of bodies, which may be heavenly, human, subhuman or hellish depending upon the *karma* attached to it. It is because of karmic bondage that I cannot enjoy the true characteristics of the perfect soul: infinite bliss, knowledge and peace, and my aim of life is to achieve it.

Like dirt mixed with gold particles, karmic bondage with the living being is there from limitless time. It is the objective of human life to remove this bondage, achieve self-realisation and restore the soul to its natural state of eternal bliss and unending calm.

Most beings of the world have not understood the true meaning of life. They are on the wrong quest, seeking the so-called ways to happiness through wealth, property, position, power and external objects. The pleasures brought by these material things are temporary, dependent on outside influences and substances that produce more and more desires, greed, pride, egoism, attachment and ultimately unhappiness. Ignorance, uncontrolled desires and activities of mind, body and speech are the causes of the bondage of the soul. The path towards self-conquest is gained if one controls the mind, develops detachment towards external objects, concern for the welfare of living beings, and contemplation on the soul. The path, the Jain way of life, is described in later chapters. The happiness, which comes from within by self-conquest is not dependent on any external objects but is self-generated and permanent. To utilise the body for self-realisation and self-conquest is the true meaning of life. Life becomes blissful if one has friendship to all and malice to none. Let me end this section with a Jain prayer.

Sivamastu sarva-jagatah; Parahita-nirataa bhavantu bhuta-ganaah,
Dosaa prayantu naasam; Sarvatra sukhi-bhavantu lokaah.
(Let the cosmos be blissful; Let all living beings be devoted to the welfare of others; Let worries, sickness, dejection and miseries be destroyed; Let every human being be happy everywhere.)

THE ANTIQUITY OF JAINISM

There is nothing in my saying that Jainism was in existence long before
the *Vedas* were composed.
(Dr S. Radhakrishnan, President of India, 1962–7)

India is a land of religious people. In the West people see religion as a mental and spiritual activity but in the East people think of it as activity concerned with all aspects of mind, body and speech, so that every person, irrespective of his or her outlook, is a religious person. In India, the word usually translated by the English word 'religion' is *dharma*, but *dharma* has a wider connotation, it involves the individual's duties and functions, physical and spiritual, throughout life. It is a way of life, thought and action, unlimited in scope. However, traditionally, the *dharma* is defined as those activities, which lead one to total happiness and self-realisation. It is this meaning of *dharma* that we shall use throughout this book.

In the Jain view, the ideal religion would be capable of being a universal religion having the widest possible appeal. However, we know from history and our own experience that the world's major religions such as Hinduism, Buddhism, Sikhism, Jainism, Christianity, Islam and Judaism have so far been of limited or qualified appeal. Some of these religions are named after a historical figure, Christ or Buddha, some after a nation or its lands, Hind or Judah, and others after particular qualities, Islam (submission to God). Jainism falls into the latter category, taking its name from Jina (self-conqueror). Jainism sees self-conquest as a goal to which all human beings should aspire. It is in this that modern Jains see its potential for universality.

The Republic of India is a secular state, though this was by no means always true in the history of the many states, which existed from ancient times in the sub-continent. The Indian sub-continent has long been a land of many religions: today Hinduism, Islam, Christianity, Sikhism, Buddhism and Jainism are all important living religions. Though the 1981 census shows a fairly small number of Jains, around three millions, the number of people who follow the Jain way of life, whether consciously or not, is many times more, not only in India but also throughout the world. Jain organisations in India estimate that the number of *de facto* Jains may be as high as twelve million.

There has long been confusion, among scholars as well as ordinary people, regarding the history, origin and status of Jainism. It is only in the last hundred years that Eastern and Western scholars have studied this religion and the results of their researches have done something to clear the clouds of confusion which long veiled Jainism. Scholars such as Dr Radha Krishnan, Hiralal Jain, Zimmer, Jacobi, Vincent Smith, and Furlong have studied Jainism and the results of their researches have cleared the clouds of confusion which long veiled Jainism. These scholars have confirmed that it is without doubt one of the oldest religions of India, distinct in its own right from Buddhism (with which it was long confused in Western eyes) as well as from other Indian faiths. In the *Majjhima Nikaya* (*Mahasimhanada Sutta*: 1,1,2), it has been noted that the Buddha was *Sramana* and practised rigorous ascetic practices such as pulling one's hair and fasting; these practices are similar to those of the disciples of Parsvanatha. Both Dharmananda Kosambi and Pandit Sukhlal claim that the Buddha did adopt the practices of Parsva tradition, the four-fold practices of conduct, before he developed his system. According to the historian Radhakumuda Mukharjee, the Buddha developed his way of life after attempting Jain and the Vedic practices; it has been confirmed by Mrs. Rhys Davids in her book, Gautama, the Man (pp. 22–5).

It is surprising that today, when reverence for life is a public issue in the West (reflected in the prominence of issues such as environmentalism and animal welfare) many have not heard about this ancient faith which lays great stress on non-violence. The path to which Jainism points consists of the highest spiritual progress achieved through the individual's own efforts. Most of its principles and practice accord well with modern scientific thinking. Its philosophy is logical. Its teachings are relevant to the world of today. This book is an attempt to show Jainism in its true perspective.

Much scholarly work has been devoted to tracing the early history of Jainism, though the origins of the religion lie far back in prehistory and beyond scholarly reconstruction. Jain writings have preserved an extensive and consistent legendary history. In contrast to this traditional account, modern scholarship has reached widely varying conclusions, though confirming in some parts the traditional view. The study of history never had the importance in India, which it has had in the West or in China and much of the early history of India, and not only of Jainism, is still obscure. Research in the 19th and 20th centuries has increased our knowledge of India before the time of Alexander the Great.

It is possible to look at the early history of Jainism through sources of four kinds: (i) Literary, (ii) Archaeological, (iii) Scientific-Geological and (iv) Philosophical. These have been studied by, among others, J. P. Jain in *Jainism, the Oldest Living Religion* (Varanasi 1988), to which the reader is referred for further details. The main characteristics of Jainism do exhibit a primitive and prehistoric substrate, though dynamic in its development.

(i) *Literary Sources* It must be emphasised that many of the conclusions regarding early Jainism drawn from early literary sources are highly speculative, depending often on the individual interpretations of particular scholars regarding chance reference in the sources studied, the *Vedas*, *Puraanas*, and also in other historical records. Thus it is said that Jainism was in existence at least in the period of the *Mahabharata*, the great Indian epic. A copper plate inscription discovered in Kathiawar (Gujarat) in 1935 recording a grant to a king of the Sumera tribe who built a temple of Neminatha, the twenty-second Jain *tirthankara*, at Rasvataka (Girnar), is adduced as confirmation. The *Rigveda*, said to be the earliest book still extant and reputed to date in part from as early as 4,500 BCE, though reaching its final form around 1,500 BCE, includes hymns referring to the first *tirthankara* Risabhdeva. It describes him as a great man in the *sramana* (that is, Jain) tradition and refers also to the twenty-second *tirthankara* Neminatha. The ancient writings known as *Puranas* follow the *Rigveda* and even gave Risabhdeva the status of one of the incarnations *(avataaras)* of the god Vishnu. Later Indian literature contains references to the same effect. It is said that the traditional name for India, Bharat, has been derived from that of Risabhdeva's son, Bharat. The historicity of the twenty-fourth *tirthankara*, Mahavira, and his predecessor Parsvanatha, some 250 years earlier, has been proved beyond doubt.

(ii) *Archaeological* The epoch making discovery of the prehistoric Indus Valley Civilisation (*c.*4,500 to 1,500 BCE) at Mohenjodaro and Harappa (now in Pakistan) has provided material on the basis of which some have concluded that Jainism existed already during this ancient civilisation. The evidence is capable of many interpretations: here, for what they are worth, are the main pointers. Nude figures in standing posture have been interpreted as Jain *yogis* in the relaxed standing meditational *(kaayotsarga)* position widely found in Jain iconography. Similar figures appear on some of the seals excavated at these sites. Seals have been found bearing the image of a bull, the emblem of Risabhdeva. Hooded figures may represent the seventh *tirthankara* Suparsvanatha, whose main iconographic characteristic is a hood formed by seven snakes. Attempts to interpret the Indus Valley script have been largely unsuccessful, though the historian Pran Nath Vidyalankar has read the inscription of seal No. 449 as *jineshvar* or *jinesha*, possibly representing the *jina* or self-conqueror, a term used for the *tirthankara*. He also seems to have deciphered the incantation *srim hrim klimek*, used (but not exclusively) by the Jains. If one accepts the interpretation of this, admittedly problematic, evidence, the existence of Jainism can be traced back to pre-Aryan, pre-Vedic times, and to the original Dravidian inhabitants of northern India, perhaps as far back as the seventh millenium BCE.

(iii) *Scientific–Geological* It appears that the last ice age ended about 8,000 to 10,000 years BCE. In the succeeding post glacial age it is thought that Aryan peoples began moving south towards India. They found a good level of civilisation at the borderline between the neolithic, or new stone age, and the chalcolithic age when copper and stone implements were in use side by side. This is the period when the civilising work of the first *tirthankara*, reputed in Jain tradition to have introduced humanity to the new useful arts, could have taken place.

(iv) *Philosophical Evidence* Certain Jain philosophical or cosmological principles suggest great antiquity. Three examples may make this clear.

(a) The concept that life exists in all things, except the limited range of purely material matter, is characteristic of Jain thought and seems to be of ancient origin.
(b) The concept of cyclical time is found in Buddhism and in other ancient religions.
(c) Buhler has referred to the third concept supporting the antiquity of Jain thought. It is the identity or non-difference between a substance and its attributes. This has been modified by the later concept of 'relative pluralism' *(anekaantavaada)*. It is a characteristically Jain way of regarding all facts to see them from multiple viewpoints.

Undoubtedly, the Jain religion is of great antiquity. The simple fact is, however, that given the present state of our knowledge, any attempts to trace or date its early history are speculative.

There is one eternal place on the summit of the occupied cosmos where there is no old age, death, disease or pain. But it is very difficult to reach there.

(Uttaraadhyayana 23: 81)

One becomes a *saadhu* by equanimity; a *braahmana* by practising brahmacaya; a *muni* by acquiring knowledge and a *taapasa* by penance.

(Uttaraadhyayana 25: 32)

They are called disciplined pupils, who obey the orders of their teacher, always stay with their teacher and are capable of reading the thoughts and expressions of their teacher.

(Uttaraadhyayana 1: 2)

If a person follows the course of conduct which conforms to religion and which has always been pursued by the wise, one will never be blamed.

(Uttaraadhyayana 1: 42)

Chapter 2

HISTORY

THE ORIGINS OF JAINISM AND THE FIRST
TIRTHANKARA — RISABHDEVA

Jainism, like every religious and cultural system, has a traditional account of its origins. In Jain belief the sermons of an omniscient *tirthankara* were delivered in a divine language, which were rendered by the chief disciples into scriptures and preserved over many centuries, at first as memorised by the ascetics and only later as texts. This vast sacred literature, of the primary canon and subsidiary texts, contains accounts of the origins of Jainism, lives and teachings of the *tirthankaras*, cosmology and the cycles of time.

The Jains believe that their religion is eternal and non-revealed, that knowledge is realised through the awareness of the true self, typified by the experiences of the *tirthankaras* and their chief disciples, known as the heads of ascetic lineage *(ganadharas)*. They existed in a cosmic cycle of time, which is described using the image of the single rotation of a wheel (see figure 3.4 in volume 2, chapter 3). We are living in the fifth phase of the descending cycle, which is 21,000 years long; so far, more than 2,500 years have passed in this phase. According to Jain tradition, Risabhdeva was destined to be the first *tirthankara* in the present descending cosmic cycle.

Due to the lack of generally available English translations of many traditional Jain texts, we outline here some of the mythological material relating to the cosmic cycle. The first phase of the current cosmic cycle *(susamaa-susamaa)* was a period of great pleasure, of the utmost happiness for people; their lives were without strife or want; all their needs and desires were abundantly satisfied by ten miraculous wish-fulfilling trees. In this period men and women exhibited great love towards each other and spent all their time together in a faithful relationship akin to marriage; both were destined to die simultaneously and, at the very moment of death, to give birth to twins, a boy and a girl. These twins, in turn, lived as husband and wife until it was time for them to die when they gave birth to another set of twins.

The second cosmic phase *(susamaa)*, was also one of pleasure, of happiness, although not of utter bliss. In the third phase *(susamaa-dusamaa)* happiness became tinged with unhappiness and, as this phase drew to close, the power of the wish-fulfilling trees diminished.

The Age of Fourteen Patriarchs (Kulakaras)

The texts go on to tell how at suitable intervals in the descending era fourteen Patriarchs were born, who played a significant role in assisting people to cope with the declining condition of the world and explained the many changes that would follow as the cosmic cycle continued on its downward course.

The first startling change was that the sun and the moon became visible in the sky, until that time the brilliance of the radiant wish-fulfilling trees had obscured the light of all celestial bodies, but now, as the intensity of the former dimmed, the latter shone forth. The appearance of the sun and the moon aroused fear and suspicion in the minds of the people and it became the task of the first Patriarch to calm their apprehension by describing how these celestial bodies had become visible. As the light from the radiant wish-fulfilling trees faded further, twinkling stars manifested themselves in the skies. The second Patriarch described the nature of this phenomenon, discussing the different stars, the constellations, and the movements of the planets, and the causes of solar and lunar eclipses. He also prepared men and women for forthcoming changes such as the rising and setting of the Sun, which would lead to a separation between day and night on earth.

In the time of the third Patriarch, the texts recount that people were astounded to see animals such as lions and tigers, which had hitherto been harmless, turn into fierce attacking beasts. The third Patriarch told them not to expect the animals to be docile any longer, and he warned them to avoid all animals which possessed fangs, claws or long horns, with the exception of domesticated cows and buffaloes. For the protection of the people, the fourth Patriarch instructed them in the use of weapons and other means of legitimate self-protection.

As the descending era advanced, the power of the wish-fulfilling trees declined still further until even basic necessities, such as food, became scarce, which caused serious dissent among the people. The fifth Patriarch therefore assigned the wish-fulfilling trees to specified territories and encouraged everyone to share whatever resources were available, but some individuals made sly incursions into the areas of others, which resulted in bitter and violent quarrels. The sixth Patriarch was compelled by this situation to demarcate territorial boundaries by means of hedges. The seventh Patriarch taught people how to ride upon animals such as horses and elephants. As described earlier, the traditional texts inform us how in the initial phases of the cosmic cycle, parents had no occasion to see their offspring, because they died the instant their children were born. This began to change during the rule of the eighth Patriarch, as at that time parents began to catch fleeting glimpses of their children. Thereafter, the advent of each further Patriarch coincided with a lengthening of the time which parents and children could spend together. At first this was only for a few minutes, then a few hours, then a few days until, finally, the term of family life extended over many years.

The texts continue with stories from Patriarchal times: an account of how familiar geographical features, such as hills and streams, were formed, and how the twelfth Patriarch taught people the skills necessary to deal with these changes, such as building boats and cutting steps into the slopes of hills. The thirteenth Patriarch introduced a major social change: exogamy (out-marriage), henceforth individuals could choose marriage partners from other social groups or clan; formerly, brothers and sisters had cohabited, a practice well documented among ancient Egyptian pharaohs. The *Rigveda* acknowledges this form of cohabitation, and there is a reference to Yama's rejecting the amorous advances of his sister Yami.

The fourteenth and final Patriarch was Nabhiraja, who is also known as Manu, and this text links Jain tradition to other Hindu mythology. In Hindu mythology, there are fourteen *manus* who correspond in some ways to the fourteen Patriarchs of the Jains; for example, in the *Shrimad Bhagavata*, the most celebrated of the eighteen Hindu texts known as the *puraanas*, Nabhiraja is claimed as the great-grandson of the first *manu*, Svayambhuva. By the time of the fourteenth Patriarch, people had learned to work, the world had deteriorated and became a place where it was necessary to work in order to survive, and new challenges arose for the Patriarch to resolve.

Risabhdeva—the First *Tirthankara*

According to Jain tradition, Risabhdeva lived at the end of the third cosmic phase. He is also known as Adinatha (the 'First Lord'). He was said to be the son of the fourteenth Patriarch Nabhiraja and his wife Marudevi; his family took the name Ikswaku, because, according to the 9th century CE Jain scholar Jinasena, Risabhdeva was the first to teach people how to extract the juice of sugar cane (in Sanskrit, *ikshu*). The age in which Risabhdeva lived is described in the texts as a transitional period when old traditions were fading and new values were yet to assert themselves. People lived, as it were, in mid-stride with one foot still in the past and the other ready to step into the new social environment yet to be consolidated. The earlier nomadic way of life had ended, but family and social stability were yet to become established. The population was slowly increasing, yet natural resources and social structures appeared to be inadequate, As a consequence, human greed arose, and with it a tendency for criminality. It was therefore necessary to draw up codes of conduct for the betterment of society and in order to facilitate the establishment of a stable social order, the fourteenth Patriarch, Nabhiraja, organised people into a social polity. His son Risabhdeva became the first king and exercised political authority, establishing the capital of his kingdom at Vinitanagara (modern Ayodhya) and producing the first laws for the governance of his people. Although historians are, not surprisingly, sceptical about the traditional accounts of the lives of the twenty-four *tirthankaras*, it may well be that Risabhdeva was an actual prehistoric figure around whose real life much legend has gathered over time. Other civilisations look back to their founding ancestors, often embellishing their biographies with legend: the early Emperors of China or the Patriarchs of the Bible are but two examples of this, and historians will perhaps never completely succeed in separating myth from historical fact.

Jain tradition says that the most important task facing Risabhdeva was to provide food, shelter and protection for his subjects; he taught his people agriculture, further military skills, as well as introducing the skill of making earthenware pottery and fire for cooking. Education was not neglected and he taught the seventy-two traditional arts for men and the sixty-four for women. Jinasena also notes the six main arts and sciences of Risabhdeva's time: (i) the use of weapons *(asi)*, (ii) writing *(masi)*, (iii) agriculture *(krusi)*, (iv) education *(vidya)*, (v) trade and commerce *(vanijya)*, and (vi) art and architecture *(silpa)*. Risabhdeva's sons and daughters received instruction in economics, social science, dancing, singing, painting and mathematics. During his reign animals were first domesticated: cows, horses and elephants. His daughter Brahmi was taught the alphabet and literature, and so the early script, the precursor of the *devanaagari* system (in today's Hindi and other north Indian languages) called *braahmi*. Risabhdeva is therefore seen as the pioneer of education and the arts of civilisation, and he taught that the status of women was equal to that of men.

Risabhdeva was the first to divide the people into three classes *(varna)*: warrior *(ksatriya)*, merchant *(vaisya)* and manual worker *(sudra)*, based purely on the division of labour, not on birth, which contrasts with the situation in the later Indian caste system. The aim of caste divisions was to utilise the capabilities of different people in an efficient manner in order to bring about economic prosperity, and Risabhdeva himself taught the use of weapons and the art of warfare and may thus be considered a *ksatriya*. He travelled far and wide in his kingdom and encouraged the *vaisyas* to build up trading links, he argued that all people should do their duty wholeheartedly and serve the people in the capacities best suited to them. The triple division of society did not in any way suggest the superiority or otherwise of one class in relation to the others; all were equal in the eyes of law and society. In the time of Risabhdeva's son, Bharat, a fourth class was introduced, that of intellectuals *(braahmana)*, and this additional distinction was introduced not because the *braahmanas* were superior by birth but because it was found necessary that some of Bharat's subjects who had intellectual ability should specialise in learning and teaching. Thus the teachers, and those engaged in meditation and the search for knowledge, were to be considered *braahmanas*, and the three *varnas* of Risabhdeva's time became four under Bharat, but the system remained, however, purely functional and unrelated to an individual's birth.

Thus King Risabhdeva brought social and economic benefits to his people and to their welfare. He is credited with being the first king of ancient times, and is depicted as an inspired guide to his subjects, ruling with justice and charity, with malice to none and showing compassion to all. By the standards of the ancient world, his was seen as an enlightened age.

Risabhdeva ruled for a long period with justice and equanimity, but his heart was not content only with worldly matters. His efforts for the betterment of society reflected a hunger and thirst after spiritual rather than temporal matters. While he desired good for his people and strove to develop his kingdom for the prosperity of all, he yearned within himself to look beyond and seek, with a detached mind, the goal of spiritual perfection.

One story tells how on a spring day his court was filled with courtiers and subjects, watching the dance of an etherial dancer named Nilanjana (see Kalghatgi 1988: 21). The dance was exquisite and the audience was entranced, Risabhdeva was engrossed, however in the middle of the dance Nilanjana collapsed and, according to the story, her body disappeared. But Indra, lord of the heavenly beings, instantly introduced a 'replica' of Nilanjana and the dance continued apparently without interruption. The audience knew nothing of the collapse of Nilanjana and the introduction of the substitute. However, with his clairvoyant knowledge, Risabhdeva saw through the substitution and, in doing so, became intensely aware of the transience of the world. His mind turned to contemplation of the meaninglessness of this world and its activities. He began to long for the realisation of the spirit, which is more permanent than involvement in worldly affairs. He decided to renounce the world. He handed over most of his kingdom to his eldest son Bharat and distributed the remaining parts to his other sons. He gave to his son Bahubali the kingdom of Poudanapura. Risabhdeva left Ayodhya and, in a garden called Siddharta-Udyana on the outskirts of the city, sitting beneath an *asoka* tree, he discarded his clothes and ornaments, plucked out his hair, and became a ascetic on the eighth day of the dark half (when the moon was waning) of the month of *Caitra*.

The incident of Nilanjana may have a mythological content but it has great psychological significance, as such occasions express the inner yearning for renunciation provoking the non-attached to action. With sufficient intuitive insight a person distinguishes the real from the appearance. For thousands of years people have seen objects fall to the ground, but it was Newton who saw in that simple fact the law of gravity. It was the everyday occurrence of seeing an old man, a sick man and a dead body that led the Buddha to embark upon his quest for the meaning of life. Similarly, Risabhdeva's enlightenment arose from his own reflection upon a mundane enough scene, a dance.

Risabhdeva spent one year in the practice of asceticism and meditation. People offered him gifts appropriate for a king, but he declined them. He did not seek food from others and he fasted for almost thirteen months. (Jain ascetics accept appropriate food only when it is offered). During this time some four thousand people had joined him as disciples,but they eventually found it too much of a strain to live such a severely ascetic life. Gradually they departed to set up their own 'schools' with an emphasis on the middle way between indulgence and austerity.

After thirteen months, on an auspicious morning on the third day of the bright half (when the moon is waxing) of the month of *Vaisak*, Risabhdeva entered the city of Gajapura (modern Hastinapura). The ruler of the city, King Sreyansa approached the ascetic with great respect and offered him some sugar-cane juice and on this occasion, as the food was appropriate for an ascetic, Risabhdeva accepted the gift offered. According to tradition, this was the first sustenance he had taken since becoming a ascetic. To-day, many Jains follow Risabhdeva's example and fast (on alternate days) for a year; they break their fast at Hastinapura on the auspicious day known as the 'Immortal Third' *(aksaya tritiya)*. This austerity is called the year long penance *(varsi tapa)*.

For a long period after this Risabhdeva practised penance and meditation, and during his wanderings he visited many places. One day, it is said, he was sitting under a banyan tree, lost in meditation, it was the eleventh day of the dark half of the month of *Phalguna*. In the early hours of the morning he reached the highest state of transcendental meditation and was absorbed in the realisation of the self; he became free of all obscuring *karma* and reached the state of perfect knowledge, omniscience. He was one who had conquered all passions and became a *jina*, an *arihant*, an enlightened one and a *tirthankara*. In a sermon he is recorded to have said: 'The aim of life is not indulgence in pleasure but self-restraint and sacrifice for the sake of others. Life is not for attachment but is for detachment for the sake of self-realisation. Do not fall prey to instincts and impulses but make efforts towards the realisation of the self.'

Tirthankara Risabhdeva preached the five major vows to the ascetics and the twelve minor vows to the laity. Having listened to his sermons Bharat, with his brothers and his sister Sundari, accepted the rules of conduct for the laity expounded by Risabhdeva. He is reputed to have established the four-fold structure of Jain society, which is recognised to-day, a society of monks, nuns, laymen and laywomen. Risabhdeva travelled widely, preaching the message of non-violence and non-attachment to possessions, which have remained basic principles of the Jain religion; he explained Jain philosophy, cosmology, *karma* theory and other basic tenets. His sermons emphasised the practical path for self-realisation and permanent happiness.

In its efforts to spiritual heights, Jainism does not ignore the secular life, as the cardinal view of the Jain is to give due weight to the spiritual without ignoring secular values. Jainism is quite aware that, to borrow an analogy from Christian scriptures, we must render unto Caesar what is Caesar's and to God what is God's. A story told about Risabhdeva's son Bharat may serve to illustrate this point.

Bharat ruled his kingdom with justice and an exemplary regard for the highest values in life, his people were happy, his capital city, Ayodhya, was prosperous. An interesting aside to the story is the fact that the country, which Bharat ruled, modern India, stretching from the Himalayas to the southern seas is today called Bharat by its inhabitants after its erstwhile ruler. One day King Bharat received three pieces of news: the first was the news of Risabhdeva's enlightenment, the second was the news that his son was born, and the third was of an amazing event in the royal armoury. A miraculous weapon, a sharp edged discus (a weapon known as a *cakra*, widely used in ancient India) had suddenly appeared in the armoury. Bharat interpreted the significance of these events quite differently: Risabhdeva's enlightenment he saw as belonging to the world of religion (*dharma*): the birth of his son he saw as a worldly matter, belonging to the realm of desire (*kama*); and the event in the armoury was a matter belonging to the realm of political authority (*artha*). Accordingly, Bharat paid his respects to Risabhdeva, left his newborn son and went out on a military campaign of conquest armed with the miraculous *cakra*.

Bharat interpreted the appearance of the *cakra* to mean that he should set out to conquer the (known) world, to become the first World Emperor (*cakravarti*). He campaigned successfully to the east and the rulers there accepted his authority, likewise he conquered the south, west and north. On his triumphal return to Ayodhya, the miraculous *cakra* would not enter the city. The wisest of his advisers said to the king: 'O king, this sign means that you have yet further conquests to make. Your brothers have not yet paid homage to you. Your brother Bahubali should come to pay homage.' The king sent messengers to summon his brothers to pay homage, but his brothers were upset at this summons and with the exception of

Bahubali, they went to Risabhdeva and offered to renounce the world and become ascetics. Bahubali is said to have been strong, handsome and upright of character. He said to Bharat's emissary: 'O noble one, you have brought a message from the king, Bharat. If your *cakravarti* had sent for me as brother to brother I would gladly have gone to meet him. But your *cakravarti* is an ambitious man and ambition knows no bounds. He wants me to surrender to him. Go and tell your master that I would rather meet him on the battlefield; ask him to be prepared for the fight.'

The two armies met outside Poudanapura. To avoid the huge loss of life, which would inevitably, result from a pitched battle, advisers on both sides suggested a single combat between the two kings. The duel began and during a bout of unarmed wrestling, Bahubali lifted his brother clear off his feet and was about to throw him, when it dawned on him how disrespectful it was to treat an elder brother in such a way, just to become an emperor into the bargain. He therefore let him down gently to the ground. The traditional account says that Bharat found this act humiliating and, contrary to the rules of a fair duel flung the *cakra* at his brother, but instead of striking Bahubali, which would have been fatal, the *cakra* circled around him harmlessly (the *cakra* never harms a family member) and then returned to Bharat. This had a profound effect upon both men. Bharat felt ashamed of his cowardly act of anger. Bahubali realised the futility and emptiness of all that had happened. He announced to his brother that he was giving up his former life to become an ascetic.

Accordingly, he left his kingdom and went into the forest to perform penance, to live an ascetic life and to meditate. He meditated in a standing position. A massive statue at Sravanbelgola in southern India, one of the most famous places of Jain pilgrimage, depicts Bahubali deep in meditation, heedless of the creepers growing over his limbs. For a year he practised austerities, but failed to gain enlightenment. His pride in his spiritual practices and envy of his brothers who had earlier achieved enlightenment were an impediment to his own progress. Eventually, with the help of his sisters Brahmi and Sundari, he was able to attain self-realisation and enlightenment.

For the Jains the story of the struggle between Bharat and Bahubali is significant. For example, the story exemplifies the Jain attitude of 'relative pluralism' *(anekaantavaada)*, the principle of seeing things from all possible points of view. Bahubali won the duel in one sense, but when he considered what had taken place he was overcome by a sense of the futility of his actions.

As for Risabhdeva, he lived for many more years, moving from place to place preaching the tenets of Jainism. There are many legendary accounts of his life. When the third phase of the descending cycle of time was three years and eight months from its conclusion, Risabhdeva and ten thousand disciples went to the Astapada Mountain where on the thirteenth day (or fourteenth, according to some) of the dark half of the month of *Maagha*, he attained final liberation.

THE LATER *TIRTHANKARAS*

In Jain tradition the twenty-four *tirthankaras* are born in each half of the cycle of time. We are currently in the regressive half-cycle *(avasarpini)*, when it is steadily becoming more and more degenerative. Risabhdeva, the first *tirthankara* of the present half-cycle, lived during the latter part of the third phase of this half-cycle, when life was on balance rather happier than unhappy. His successors, the other twenty-three *tirthankaras*, lived during the fourth phase when unhappiness prevailed but did not completely exclude happiness. The twenty-four *tirthankaras* and their iconographic symbols are set out in table 2.1.

Table 2.1   The twenty-four *tirthankaras* and iconographic symbols

Tirthankara	Symbol	Tirthankara	Symbol
1. Risabhdeva	Bull	13. Vimala	Boar
2. Ajita	Elephant	14. Ananta	Hawk
3. Sambhava	Horse	15. Dharma	Thunderbolt
4. Abhinandana	Ape	16. Shanti	Deer
5. Sumati	Partridge	17. Kunthu	Goat
6. Padmaprabha	Lotus	18. Ara	*Nandyavaata*
7. Suparsva	Swastika	19. Malli	Water jar
8. Candraprabha	Moon	20. Munisuvrata	Tortoise
9. Suvidhi	Crocodile	21. Nami	Blue lotus
10. Sitala	*Srivatsa*	22. Nemi	Conch shell
11. Sreyansa	Rhinoceros	23. Parsva	Cobra
12. Vasapujya	Buffalo	24. Mahavira	Lion

Note: the suffix —nath(a) or —swami meaning lord or protector is commonly added to many of these names.

The succession was not continuous: there were long periods between one *tirthankara's* leaving the world and another's appearance to teach the faith to the people. The Jain scriptures relate the extraordinary attributes, dimensions and longevity of these teachers. We are on the verge of history, albeit still shadowy, with the twentieth *tirthankara* Munisuvrata, said to have been a contemporary of Rama, the hero of the great epic, the *Ramayana*, but who is also prominent in the Jain biographical literature,

Plate 2.1   Image of Shantinatha at the Jain Centre, Leicester, England. Note the iconographic symbol of a deer

the *Padmapuraana*. Neminatha, the twenty-second, is described as a cousin of Lord Krishna who figures so prominently in the *Mahabharata* and if Krishna is accepted as an historical figure, then we can probably argue that Neminatha was also historical. With Parsvanatha there is little doubt as to his historicity: according to the traditional dating he lived and preached in the 8th century BCE, 250 years before Mahavira and, of course, there can be no serious challenge to the historical existence of Mahavira. In this chapter we shall look briefly at the lives and teachings of the last two *tirthankaras* before Mahavira—Neminatha and Parsvanatha. The life of Mahavira, who was certainly not the founder of Jainism, though he can have some claim to be considered as the founder of the modern Jain faith, as we know it today, will be considered later in this chapter.

It is well to be aware that the non-Vedic *(sramana)* schools of thought have been relatively neglected by scholars in comparison with the Brahminical 'orthodoxy'. This is hardly surprising, given the numerical preponderance to adherents of Hinduism in the Indian sub-continent and the multiplicity of philosophical and religious traditions embraced within that indefinable term. The *sramanic* schools, represented particularly by Jainism and Buddhism, have tended to be regarded as a revolt against the orthodox Vedic tradition with its sacrifices and rituals, rather than as independent traditions. There has been little study of the lesser *sramana* currents of thought. Buddhism has certainly had its full share of attention but a great deal of its history has lain outside the geographical bounds of India, Jainism has produced over the centuries many distinguished scholars but until fairly recently the Jain tradition was introspective and little known outside a limited circle.

Neminatha

Neminatha (or Aristanemi) is referred to on four occasions in the *Rigveda* as well as in the *Samaveda*. In the *Yajurveda* three *tirthankaras* are noted: Risabhdeva, Ajitanatha and Neminatha. Some scholars have suggested that Angirasa Ghora who appears in the *Candogya Upanishad* may be identified as Neminatha. Indeed the path to self-realisation, which Angirasa Ghora taught to Krishna, bears a striking resemblance to the five great vows, which Mahavira was later to expound. Angirasa Ghora spoke of honesty, asceticism, charity, non-violence and truthfulness. In the *Mahabharata* Neminatha is described as teaching the way to salvation *(moksa)* to King Sagara. The dating of the different parts of the *Mahabharata* is very uncertain in spite of modern scholarship, and since *moksa* was a relatively late concept in orthodox Brahminical thought, this must represent an early example of *sramanic* teaching. The identification of Neminatha with a Scandinavian or Chinese deity, propounded by some, may be regarded as fanciful. Leaving aside Jain tradition, the evidence for the historical existence of Neminatha may be regarded unproven, though there is no reason to reject him totally as an historical figure, but the traditional accounts of his life are both interesting and inspiring.

Neminatha's birthplace is given as Shauripur, near the modern city of Agra in Uttar Pradesh and at that time the capital of a small state where two princes ruled, Vasudeva and Samudravijaya; Krishna was the son of Vasudeva, and Neminatha was the son of Samudravijaya. Neminatha grew up as a handsome, dark complexioned, strong youth, endowed with unprecedented knowledge. Krishna loved and respected him. There are tales of his great strength even as a boy, his spinning of the great *cakra*, the discus, on the tip of his finger, or, also from the armoury, swinging with ease a mighty club. He could also blow the conch-shell bugle so loudly that it frightened the people of the whole town.

The story of Neminatha as given in numerous Jain works is seen as one of the most inspiring examples of non-violence *(ahimsaa)*. When he was old enough Neminatha was betrothed to a beautiful princess, Rajamati, the daughter of King Ugrasena of Bhojakula. A great wedding feast was arranged and the sheep that were to be slaughtered and cooked for the meal were brought in and penned up ready for the butchers. Neminatha set off in great style for the wedding, splendidly clothed and bejewelled, mounted on a magnificent elephant and surrounded by a huge escort and many musicians. On the way he saw the animals in their pens, frightened and miserable, bleating piteously. He asked what was the meaning of this and was told that these were to form the wedding meal for all those present. Neminatha was touched with sadness at this news that the feast would be provided for the guests at the cost of the lives of all those innocent creatures, and that he himself, as the person for whom the celebration was to take place, must take responsibility for the slaughter. He ordered the sheep to be released and, profoundly affected by the incident, he decided to renounce the world and seek salvation as a homeless mendicant ascetic. Not surprisingly, his bride-to-be was very upset but after a period of grieving she realised the value of Neminatha's renunciation and she too followed his example and renounced the world.

After taking his decision Neminatha discarded his jewels, gave them to a servant and left his possessions to be distributed to the poor. He left his hometown and, once more in a great procession, though different from his marriage, went to a park or garden called Revatika. There he gave up his princely clothes, plucked out his hair, and took the vow of renunciation. His cousin Krishna was full of admiration. It was after a period of fifty-four days and nights, indifferent to worldly things and deeply meditating, that he attained supreme knowledge, omniscience *(kevala jnaana)*, on the day of the new moon, the first day of the bright half, of the month of *Asvin*.

Then he preached the way of salvation to a great assembly of people, and thousands of devotees, including royalty, joined him and took the vow of renunciation.

Krishna especially celebrated Neminatha's achievement of omniscience with great dignity and splendour. Later on, Krishna's chief queen, Padmavati, also took the vow of renunciation and his other wives took lesser vows of self-restraint. Krishna went to Neminatha and asked him why he himself could not make up his mind to take the path of renunciation. 'O Krishna,' he replied, 'you are in the world and your services are needed by society so you cannot become a ascetic'. Nevertheless, he predicted from his omniscient knowledge that in a future age, Krishna's soul would be reborn as the eleventh *tirthankara*, in a city called Shatadvara, and his name will be Amama. There is a Digambara tradition which believes that after the destruction of Krishna's capital city Dwaraka, as narrated in the *Mahabharata* and, after the death of Krishna, his kinsmen the Pandavas, who played a prominent role in the famous epic, realised the impermanent nature of things of the world and took the vow of renunciation and ultimately achieved liberation *(moksa)*.

After his enlightenment, Neminatha travelled around Saurastra preaching the principles of non-violence *(ahimsaa)* and non-attachment to material things *(aparigraha)*. In the course of time (after a phenomenally long life, according to the old traditions) Neminatha finally, on the eighth day of the bright half of the month of *Asadha*, passed away. As the *Kalpa Sutra* records, he passed beyond the bounds of *karma*, was uplifted after having left the world, cut asunder the ties of birth, old age and death, and became perfected and liberated; this occurred on Mount Girnar in Saurastra (Gujarat), a place of pilgrimage to this present day.

Parsvanatha

If the life of Neminatha lies on an uncertain boundary between legend and history, there is little good reason to doubt the historical existence of Parsvanatha, the twenty-third *tirthankara* of the present age. As he is said to have lived some 250 years before Mahavira, taking the traditional dates of Mahavira's life would place Parsvanatha in the 9th to 8th centuries BCE. He preached a four-fold code of conduct involving non-violence, truthfulness, and abstinence from taking what is not given and, fourthly, non-attachment to material possessions. It is said that this four-fold code was enjoined by all the twenty-two *tirthankaras* after Risabhdeva, with only Risabhdeva and Mahavira including the fifth vow, chastity, among the great vows. Other sources, however, attribute the five-fold code to Mahavira alone. (It has been argued that chastity was simply implicit in the other four vows and did not need separate mention). The last sermon delivered by Mahavira *(Uttaraadhyayana Sutra)*, has an interesting discussion between Kesi, a follower of the way of Parsvanatha, and Indrabhuti Gautama, the chief disciple of Mahavira, in which Gautama dispels the doubts of Kesi on the articles of faith, including the five-fold vows, which mark the way preached by the twenty-fourth *tirthankara*. There is a reference to the 'four-fold rule' in the *Tripitaka*, the Buddhist collection of scriptures. It is suggested by the Buddhist scholar, Dharmananda Kosambi that the Buddha accepted the practices of Parsvanatha tradition for sometime. The Jain tradition of non-violence, exemplified in the first rule of Parsvanatha's code of conduct, may have been the basis for the revulsion at the practice of sacrifices, which appears in the *Upanishads*.

Parsvanatha, the twenty-third *tirthankara*, was born in Varanasi (Benares) traditionally in 877 BCE and died at the age of 100. His father, Asvasena, was the ruler of the Kashi kingdom, of which Varanasi was the capital, and his mother was called Vamadevi. Needless to say, the sources describe Parsvanatha as handsome and strong, but much is made, however, of an incident showing his compassion. When he was out with his friends in the forest he saw an ascetic named Kamath who was enduring self-inflicted pain by exposing himself both to the blazing sun and to blazing fires. In one of the logs of wood, which the man was putting on the fire young Parsvanatha noticed two snakes and he implored the ascetic not to burn those living creatures. The ascetic had not seen the snakes and Parsvanatha had to get someone to split open the log to reveal them and set them free. The two snakes were severely burnt and in their dying moment Parsvanatha recited the *Namokara Mantra* to them, and because of this, the two snakes were reborn in their next lives as Dharanendra, King of the Nagas, the serpent deity, and Queen Padmavati. Kamath was reborn as a demon called Meghamali. The lives of these remained intertwined for, later, when Parsvanatha was an ascetic, the demon Meghamali assaulted him in various ways, and when the assault took the form of a fearful storm, Dharanendra protected him with a cobra hood above his head. This is why Parsvanatha's recognised symbol is a cobra and his images are depicted with a cobra hood.

It was seeing a picture of Neminatha, which is said to have directed the mind of Parsvanatha as a young man to renouncing the worldly life. Accounts differ as to whether he was married before he became an ascetic, the Digambara tradition makes no mention of it whilst according to the Svetambara he was married to the daughter of King Prasanjit, Prabhavati. At any rate, at the age of thirty he distributed his property and, to the rejoicing of crowds customary on these occasions, took his mendicant vows on the eleventh day of the bright half of the month of *Maagha* on the outskirts of Varanasi. After some four months of severe austerities he attained omniscience *(kevala jnaana)*, becoming an *arhat*, a *kevali*.

Thereafter for seventy years he travelled around preaching and gathering converts to the faith. He was well respected and many people of all classes came to greet him and to pay their respects. His followers were great in number and he organised them in the same way as Neminatha, before him, into four-fold order. He had eight, or ten, principal disciples, and the first of these was Svayambhu. The leader of the female ascetics was Sulocana. Parsvanatha revived the teachings of the earlier *tirthankaras* and taught the shape and eternity of the world in the way, which was later to be shown by his successor Mahavira. He had great influence, not only in his own time but long after: his teachings were still followed two and a half centuries later when Mahavira was born. His emphasis on non-violence may well have been a cause of the discontinuance of the cruel Vedic sacrifices.

After seventy years as a wandering mendicant Parsvanatha's life on earth ended. Realising that final liberation *(moksa)* was at hand, he went with thirty-three ascetics to the mountain Sammeta Sikhara, in modern Bihar, and there, after a month of austerities, the last remaining *karma* destroyed, he achieved liberation from birth and death. The mountain where Parsvanatha attained *moksa* is still a place of pilgrimage.

VARDHAMANA MAHAVIRA

It is often observed that 'the period from the eighth to the sixth centuries BCE was particularly rich in charismatic religious personalities. In Israel during this period there were the prophets Amos, Hosea, Micah, Isaiah and Jeremiah, to name the more outstanding; in Persia there was Zarathustra, and in India the Buddha and Mahavira' (Ling 1968). This was an age of intellectual ferment across the world: In Greece, we see such figures as Thales, said to be the father of geometry, and, towards the end of the century, the Sophists, itinerant teachers rather than philosophers. While the great age of Greek learning was still a century in the future, with Socrates and Plato still to arise, the 6th century was a time when the great minds were already studying the world and the meaning of life. On the other side of the world, in China, Confucius (traditional dates, 561 to 479 BCE) laid the foundations to a world outlook and social system that survived for two thousand years.

India too, one of the pioneers of civilisation, witnessed during this period enormous ferment and movements in the intellectual and social fields. Many philosophers, seeking to disseminate their ideas, roamed across north-eastern India, the area which may be regarded as the cradle of Indian culture. An ancient Jain scripture, the *Sutra Krutaanga* gives descriptions of the philosophical theories prevailing then, with a view to refuting them: the *Kriyaavaadis* claimed that the individual is responsible for his actions, good or bad; the path of the *Akriyaavaadis* lay in non-action, indifference to good or bad actions; the Agnostics or *Ajnaanavaadis* held that the nature of truth was unknowable; and the *Vinayavaadis* claimed that truth couldn't be easily analysed. A famous and popular Buddhist scripture, the *Suttanipata* described no fewer than sixty-three *sramana* (non-Vedic) schools of thought which existed in the 6th century BCE. The multiplicity of 'schools' of philosophy created intellectual confusion among the intelligentsia,.but all these views are condemned as inadequate when compared with the many-sided Jain view of truth.

In the social sphere there was uncertainty: Vedic ritualism was attempting to re-assert itself; sacrificial rites, the offering of animal victims to the gods, had reappeared. People were passive spectators exploited by a sophisticated priestly class who professed to be a link between gods and humanity, leading the worshippers to heaven through ritualised sacrifices. The priestly class saw itself as the custodian of spiritual and secular good and felt superior to all others, and claimed a monopoly in the preservation of culture. The lowest of the classes was the *sudra*. Women were regarded as inferior to men. As the caste system became consolidated, it legitimised inequality. There is a story in a Buddhist text *Majjhimanikaya* of an incident in which a *sudra* was beaten and tortured because he stepped in front of a high caste girl while on the way to his house, as it was consdered to be inauspicious to a person of high caste. In the Jain scriptures, a disciple of Parsvanatha the twenty-third *tirthankara*, Kesi Kumara, is depicted as saddened by the ignorance of the people and their exploitation by the higher classes. It was in this situation that two contemporaries, Siddhartha Gautama, known as the Buddha, and Vardhamana Mahavira, the twenty-fourth and last *tirthankara*, set out to remove suffering and show the path which would lead to perfection. Jain scholar Kalghatgi, expresses the contribution of Mahavira beautifully: 'out of dust Mahavira made us into men and he lifted us to be angels' (Kalghatgi 1988: 63).

At that time a large confederation of clans, the Vajjis whose capital was at Vaisali (near Patna in Bihar), had a king Cetaka. His sister Trisala, and her husband Siddhartha, ruler of Kundalpura, were followers of the religious tradition preached by Parsvanatha, the twenty-third *tirthankara*, some two and a half centuries earlier. To them a son was born on the thirteenth day of the bright half (when the moon was waxing) of the month of *Caitra* and according to tradition, this was the year corresponding to 599 BCE. He was named Vardhamana, meaning 'increasing prosperity' as the prosperity of his father's realm steadily increased after his conception, but he is known to history as Mahavira, the Great Hero.

There are many stories about his bravery as a youth: once some children were playing in a mango grove when they encountered a huge snake. They ran for their lives but Vardhamana coolly took the serpent in his hand and carried it away to safety. Another popular story tells of the children playing a game in which the forfeit for the loser was to carry the winner on his back for some distance, but a heavenly being joined in the game, assuming the form of young boy, and purposely lost the race. When Vardhamana sat on the back of this 'boy', he started running and grew in size until he had taken the form of a giant. But Vardhamana, far from being frightened, punched the giant so hard that he was taken aback at the youngster's enormous strength. This is the popular account of how he came to acquire the name 'Mahavira'. A story is told which demonstrates Vardhamana's sharpness of intellect at an early age: someone asked Vardhamana's parents where the boy was, his father said he was downstairs while his mother said he was upstairs when, in fact, he was on the middle floor. Afterwards he explained that both his parents were right: from the standpoint of the upper floor he was downstairs, but from the bottom floor he was upstairs. This is an early example of a key concept of Jain philosophy, 'relative pluralism' (*anekaantavaada*), the notion that contradictory statements may both be right when looked at from different viewpoints.

These anecdotes were intended to portray the physical and mental superiority of Vardhamana in a manner that is familiar in the biographies of heroic figures of the past. Whatever the facts, they portray the youth as history was to remember him. Jain scriptures claim that Vardhamana Mahavira possessed the extra-sensory perceptual capacity of clairvoyance (*avadhi jnaana*), in addition to the normal sensory experiences of sense perception (*mati jnaana*) and reasoning (*sruta jnaana*). All *tirthankaras* are credited with these capacities from birth. We need not be sceptical about clairvoyant powers: modern psychical research has not ruled out extra-sensory perception.

At the age of eight, when it would have been time for a child such as Vardhamana to begin a formal education with a teacher, his intellectual capabilities were so far above those of other children that it was realised that such a conventional education would hamper his development. Regarding his marriage, two major sects of Jainism, Svetambara and Digambara, are not agreed. Svetambara texts claim his having a wife, Yasoda, and a daughter Priyadarsana, while Digambara Texts State that Mahavira took his ascetic vows while still a bachelor (Kalghatgi 1988:66). In any event, Mahavira sought the spiritual life and wanted to renounce the world to seek the way of happiness for all living beings, however, he was prepared to wait while his parents were alive, as it would hurt their feelings. When he was twenty-eight years old his parents died and two years later, with the permission of his elder brother, Nandivardhana, he entered upon the life of an ascetic. In contrast with the story of the Buddha, who abandoned his family, Mahavira, and subsequently all Jain ascetics, seek the consent of their families before their renunciation.

The news of a prince giving up his wealth and position to become a
recluse was a remarkable event. Throngs of people gathered to bid him
farewell. An old man, Harikesi, ran towards him to touch his feet and pay
his respects. The crowd shouted 'do not let Harikesi go near Mahavira, he
is an outcaste.' Mahavira said, 'Please do not stop him, let him come', and
he embraced Harikesi and bade him goodbye. Harikesi was overwhelmed
with gratitude and reverence for Mahavira, and with tearful eyes he paid
his respects. This incident is significant in the context of the different social
revolutions which Mahavira and the Buddha unleashed, both of which
emphasised equality between men and women. In a garden called
Khandavana on the outskirts of his hometown, sitting beneath an *asoka*
tree, Mahavira took the vow of renunciation, he shed his princely title to
become a simple *sramana*, a homeless mendicant ascetic. (The word
sramana is both the religious tradition of those, principally Jains and
Buddhists, who did not follow the Vedic orthodoxy as well as the mendicants of those traditions.)

His Ascetic Life

Many Jain scriptures recount the story of Mahavira's ascetic life, including
the *Kalpa Sutra*, one of the most widely read and popular of these texts,
however, there is little available in English. The scriptures tell how he had
to make superhuman efforts to attain total knowledge, omniscience, which
is the highest spiritual achievement.

His ascetic life began with a two-and-a-half day fast, after this he put on
the simple clothing of a mendicant and plucking out his hair, he left his
home forever. To begin with he had clothing but he gave half his robe to a
poor Brahmin, and when the other half became entangled in a thorn bush
he abandoned it and remained thereafter without possessions. When
people gave him food he simply took it in the hollow of his hand. For more
than twelve years he accepted all hardships, without regard for his body,
suffering without concern for pleasure or pain, totally chaste, circumspect
in speech and movement, overcoming pride, deceit and greed, he cut all
earthly ties. In the eight months of summer and winter, outside the rainy
season, Mahavira never spent more than a single night in any village and
five nights in any town. He regarded everything with complete detachment: the scent of sandalwood or the stench of decay was alike to him. Free
from all passions, he meditated for twelve years on the path to liberation,
which is the reward of truthfulness, self-control, penance and good
conduct. There are many Jain writings that give a chronological account of
the years of Mahavira's mendicant life and the incidents therein. He would
stay a night in a workshop, a village square, a shop or in a straw-roofed
shed, sometimes in a cemetery, an empty house or just at the foot of a tree.

He did not seek sleep for the sake of pleasure, he would sleep occasionally, or lie down in meditation or perhaps he would walk about for an hour in the night. Often he encountered hardships and calamities, attacks and assaults, but always in control of himself and free from resentment he endured these hardships, speaking little and deep in meditation, he progressed on the path to liberation.

In the rainy season, when plant and insect life burgeoned and the likelihood of endangering tiny creatures increased, Mahavira ceased his wandering life and stayed in one place, and this practice is still followed by Jain ascetics to-day. The *Kalpa Sutra* gives the names of the places where he stayed after he first became an ascetic. The authority of the *Kalpa Sutra's* itinerary is ancient and probably reliable, as it gives us a fair idea of the area over which he wandered propagating his faith. When the places can be correctly identified we know that this area roughly covered the modern state of Bihar and parts of Bengal and Uttar Pradesh, but there is a much later tradition that Mahavira disseminated his message in other parts of India, even as far afield as Rajasthan.

Tradition says that Mahavira was born with three types of knowledge: mind-based knowledge, the reasoning faculty and clairvoyance, and at the moment of renunciation he also gained a fourth kind of knowledge, the ability to know the thoughts of all creatures in the world.

The period of twelve years spent in penance and meditation was not fruitless, for in the thirteenth year Mahavira at last attained the supreme knowledge and final deliverance from the bonds of pleasure and pain, and Jain scriptures describe this most important moment in his life. It was the tenth day of the bright half of the month of *Vaisak* when Mahavira, having fasted completely without food or drink for two and a half days, sat in a squatting position with his heels together. He was on the northern bank of the river Rujupalika outside the town of Jrimhikagrama in the field of a householder called Samaga, just north-east of an old temple and near a *sal* tree, with the heat of the sun beating down upon him; and here, with his head bowed, in deepest meditation he attained the complete and full, unimpeded, infinite and supreme form of knowledge and intuition. This total knowledge, omniscience, is *kevala jnaana* and the person who attains it is a *kevali*, an *arhat*, the one who has attained enlightenment. He is also to be described as a *jina*, one who has conquered himself.

Now, as we are told in the *Kalpa Sutra*, the venerable Mahavira was omniscient and comprehending all objects, knowing all the conditions of the world, of heavenly beings, humans and demons, whence they came, where they go, whether they are born as humans or animals, or in the heavens or the hells, their food and drink, their actions and desires, their public and secret deeds, their talk and their thoughts. To him nothing was inaccessible and he knew and saw the conditions of all living beings in the world.

At the time of his achieving omniscience, Mahavira was forty-two years old, and he now entered a new stage of his life, that of a religious teacher. His followers became known as *nirgranthas*, meaning freed from all bonds, and this was the ancient name for the Jains. He went from place to place to propagate his teachings, and his first declaration aroused confidence among his followers that urged them to follow his example in their own lives. According to Buddhist sources, this went as follows: 'I am all knowing and all seeing and possessed of infinite knowledge. Whether I am walking or standing still, whether I sleep or remain awake, supreme knowledge and intuition are with me, constantly and continuously. There are, O Nirgranthas, sinful acts that you have done in the past, which you must now undo by this acute form of austerity. Now that you will be living a restrained life as regards your acts, speech and thought, this will negate the effects of *karma* for the future. Thus, by the exhaustion of the force of past deeds through penance, and the non-accumulation of the effects of new acts, [you are assured] of the end of the future course [of the effects of *karma*] and the resultant rebirths, of the destruction of the effects of *karma*, and from that the destruction of pain, and from that of the destruction of mental feelings, and from that the complete abscence of all kinds of pain.'

Soon after Mahavira attained enlightenment, he travelled some seventy-two miles to the garden of Mahasena at Majjkima Pava. Here a religious gathering took place, at which, after long discussion, Mahavira converted eleven learned Brahmins who had gone there to attend a great sacrifice. King Srenika and his family, including his queen, Celana asked many questions which Mahavira answered to the king's satisfaction.

The Four Orders of the Jain Community

Initially, Mahavira, by his preaching, converted the eleven learned Brahmins who became his chief disciples or *ganadharas*: the first was Indrabhuti Gautama, the others were Gautama's two brothers, Agnibhuti and Vayubhuti, as well as Vyakta, Sudharma, Mandikata, Mauryaputra, Akampita, Acalabharata, Metarya and Prabhasa. One significant fact is that all of them were Brahmins, showing that even among the Brahmins an ideological revolution was taking place, driving them to give up their traditional beliefs and ritualism. Moreover, it was subsequently the intelligentsia, predominantly Brahmins, who helped to spread his teachings.

Mahavira showed a remarkable power of organisation which, with his impressive personality, attracted a large number of people, both men and women, to be his followers. Some could follow his teachings completely and took what came to be known as the five great vows. These were:

ahimsaa (non-violence and reverence for all life)
satya (truthfulness)
asteya (not taking anything without the owner's permission)
brahmacarya (control over the senses, chastity)
aparigraha (non-attachment to worldly things).

Those who could accept these vows and renounce the world became the ascetics, the remainder became the laity, obeying the same vows but with less stringency. Thus there arose the interdependent four-fold community of male ascetics, female ascetics, laymen and laywomen, which survives to this day.

Within thirty years Mahavira had attracted a large following, chief among these were some fourteen thousand male ascetics, who were placed under the charge of Indrabhuti Gautama. For organisational efficiency, he divided the 14,000 ascetics into nine divisions called *ganas*, placing each under the headship of one of the chief disciples or *ganadharas* who were to lead and guide their groups. Even more women than men renounced the world: 36,000 became female ascetics and at their head was the senior nun, Candana.

Mahavira's third order consisted of laymen, *sraavakas*, numbering, it is said, about 159,000, with Sankha Sataka as their leader; and these laymen were householders who could not actually renounce the world but who at least could observe the five lesser vows (called *anuvrata*). The similarity of their religious duties, differing from those of ascetics not in kind but in degree, brought about the close union of laymen and ascetics. Most of the regulations meant to govern the conduct of laymen were apparently intended to make them participate, to a degree and for some time, in the merits and benefits of ascetic life without obliging them to renounce the world altogether. 'The genius for organisation which Mahavira possessed' Dr Sinclair Stevenson rightly observes in her book *The Heart of Jainism* (p. 67), 'is shown in nothing more clearly than in the formation of this and the order of laywomen. These two organisations gave the Jains a root in India that the Buddhists never obtained, and that root firmly planted amongst the laity enabled Jainism to withstand the storm that drove Buddhism out of India.'

The fourth and last order consisted of devout laywomen or *sraavikas*, numbering, it is said, about 358,000, with Sulasa and Revati as the heads. The numbers of members in the four orders of Mahavira's day may be exaggerated, but there is little doubt that Mahavira converted a large number of people to the Jain faith.

Influence on Lay Followers

Mahavira seems to have tried to attract a congregration, who were to form
a large body of lay followers, by prescribing certain rules of conduct: he
made no distinction between people of one caste or class and another, nor
between men and women; and he did not lay down one set of rules for
monks and another for nuns, nor one for male lay followers and another
for females. When he travelled around the country female as well as male
ascetics accompanied him.

Mahavira not only taught his followers to observe penance and live a life
of restraint in all possible ways, but also kept watch over their spiritual
progress, encouraging them in the study of his teachings and developing
their powers of reasoning and arguing. The Buddhist records attest that
there were some able and powerful disputants among the *nirgrantha*
recluses and disciples. The lay followers and supporters of Mahavira and
his four-fold order are all mentioned as persons of opulence and influence.
At the same time they were noted for their piety and devotion.

Royal Patronage

Not only rich financiers and merchants, but even kings and queens, princes
and ministers, became followers of Mahavira. His family connections with
the various rulers were through his mother Trisala and his maternal uncle,
Cetaka, the King of Vaisali; and many royal names are found in the Jain
tradition. Those who joined the four-fold order established by Mahavira
and this royal patronage must have encouraged the spread of the faith. Both
Jains and Buddhists claim most of the contemporary rulers as followers of
their respective religions, as it seems that it was the general policy of the
rulers of these, and indeed later, times to show respect to teachers of
different traditions. The Parsvanatha sect had its stronghold in Rajagriha
and King Srenika's father was a follower, so it was natural that his son
should be attracted to Jainism, and Srenika's son Kunika, in his turn, is
represented in Jain texts as a Jain. According to Jain scriptures, Srenika's
soul, in a subsequent rebirth, is to become an *arhat* and the first *tirthankara*
of the next half-cycle of cosmic time. In Buddhist texts, however, Srenika
and Kunika are known by the names of Bimbisara and Ajatasatru, and are
both described as accepting Buddhism.

Another of Mahavira's converts was a prince Ardraka, who became an
ascetic. He was very much influenced by the teachings of Mahavira and
supported Jainism in disputations with the teachers of other religions. This
Ardraka is identified with a prince of the Persian Emperor Surusha
(588–530 BCE). Both the emperor and the prince are said to have sent gifts
to King Srenika of Magadha and his son Abhayakumara, who sent presents

in return. It is also said that Abhayakumara convinced Ardraka of the truth of Mahavira's teachings so that he became a follower of Mahavira.

Mahavira and the Buddha

The evidence from Buddhist literature *(Anguttha-Nikaya*: 8–2, 1, 7 and *Majjhima Nakaya)* proves that Mahavira and the Buddha were contemporaries, and although they did not meet, there were occasions when they felt interested in knowing and discussing each other's views through intermediaries. These included in particular the Jain ascetics Dirghatapasvi and Satyaka, and, among the Jain laity, the prince Abhaya, the banker Upali and the general Sinha. Even though they are said to have been present at the same times in certain places, Nalanda, Vaisali and Rajagriha, they are not known to have met. Mahavira was older than the Buddha and predeceased him by several years. It is said that the Buddha had great respect for the *tirthankara* and did not openly preach while the latter lived.

Moksa

Mahavira attained *moksa* in 527 BCE according to the traditional dating. It is said in the *Kalpa Sutra* that when Mahavira died the eighteen confederate kings of the neighbouring regions instituted illuminations, saying 'since the light of intelligence is gone, let us make an illumination as a symbol of knowledge..'

As we have seen, Mahavira was not the founder of a new religion. What he did was to reform and elaborate the previous creed handed down through a succession of previous *tirthankaras*. He addressed the various

Plate 2.2 Pavapuri, Bihar, the memorial place of pilgrimage where Mahavira attained *moksa*

problems of the day, such as slavery, the inferior status of women in the family, society and religion, the Brahminical caste system and untouchability, the exploitation of the weak by the strong, the ills of economic inequality, indulgence in carnal desires and passions of the flesh, killing or harming life for the sake of religion or pleasure of the senses; evils which are no less in evidence in the present-day world. He supplied a very firm philosophical basis to the simple creed of non-violence (*ahimsaa*), and reorganised the four-fold order of monks and nuns, laymen and laywomen. This began in the time of Mahavira's predecessors, the twentieth or twenty-first *tirthankaras*, was consolidated during the time of the twenty-second, Neminatha, and the twenty-third, Parsvanatha. It was an accomplished fact by the time Mahavira's terrestial career came to a close.

So, the Master of Thought, the great apostle of *ahimsaa*, the Benefactor of Mankind and the friend of all living beings, ended his bodily existence, attaining *moksa*, on the banks of a lotus lake outside the town now known as Pavapuri, in Bihar, a little before dawn on the fifteenth day of the dark half (when the moon is waning) of the month of Aso. In the Indian chronology the year was 470 years before the beginning of the Vikrama era (which commenced in 57 BCE) and 605 years before the Saka era, that is in the year 527 BCE. This is celebrated today as Dipavali, the festival of lamps, or Divali, symbolising the light of knowledge revealing the truth and illuminating the soul when the master was no longer physically present.

Mahavira was one of the great religious teachers of mankind. He recognised the need for the perfection of the self and prescribed certain practical rules of conduct for its attainment. He did not preach to others what he did not practise himself. He believed that the entire being can achieve blissfulness, but this cannot be bought by the wealth, pomp and power of the world but can certainly be realised through patience, forbearance, self-denial, forgiveness, humanity, compassion, suffering and sacrifice. For this reason he inculcated the doctrine of non-violence (*ahimsaa*) in thought, word and action. Those who came under the influence of his personality renounced the eating of fish and meat and accepted a vegetarian diet. This principle was at the basis of the many humanitarian deeds and institutions which he encouraged.

For Mahavira, distinctions of caste, creed or gender were irrelevant, for him liberation is the birthright of everyone, and it is assured if one follows the prescribed rules of conduct. The doctrine of *karma*, which has the root meaning of 'action' and hence the effects of action, as expounded by Mahavira made the individual conscious of his responsibility for all his actions. It also awakened the realisation that salvation was not a gift or favour but an attainment within the reach of human beings. Mahavira was tolerant in religious matters, there were different conflicting religious views in his time, and in response to this, he formulated the doctrine of *syaadavaada.* This doctrine teaches that assertions are not made absolutely but always remain subject to qualification. It allowed room for the consideration of all views and produced an atmosphere of mutual harmony among the followers of different sects, who began to appreciate the views of their opponents as well as their own.

Mahavira is regarded by Indian traditions, not only by Jains, as the greatest sage the world has known, possessed of infinite knowledge and faith. He explored the condition of all beings, mobile or immobile, high or low, eternal or transient. He saw things in their true light, knew this world and the world beyond, and his perception was infinite.

He was a great reformer. Since many abuses had crept into Jainism he did his utmost to remove them. For this he had to initiate changes even in the traditional religion of Parsvanatha. He added the vow of chastity and emphasised the importance of non-attachment and control over sensual pleasures. Although his teachings were based on the older religion, he created a more systematic arrangement of its philosophical tenets, which point to his great reforming zeal.

Mahavira possessed a great organising capacity and he made the laity participate in the Jain community along with the ascetics. He encouraged a close union between laymen and laywomen, and monks and nuns by advocating similar religious duties for both, duties that differed not in kind but in degree.

The Teachings of Mahavira

As we have seen earlier, Mahavira was not the founder of Jainism but revived the existing faith, his teachings are based partly on the religion taught by his predecessor, Parsvanatha, and partly on his own innovations. Mahavira was able to perceive correctly the root causes of the disorder of those times and of the numerous divisions in society. He understood the factors which led to the aimlessness of the loosely grouped ascetic communities and which had heralded the rise of ritualistic Brahmin practices. He also recognised that the Brahminical ideas of superiority through birth and the priviliged position of the priestly class were unacceptable. He felt impelled to introduce changes to the religion of the people in order to meet the needs of the time. He systematised the beliefs and the code of conduct for each constituent of the Jain order.

In his early sermons he declared that: 'Birth or external appearances do not make one a Brahmin or an ascetic. It is mental purity and right conduct which make a person a real Brahmin or ascetic. Such persons practice equanimity, penance, celibacy, and non-attachment to worldly matters and right behaviour'. He denounced the caste system, which embodied the idea that a person is born into a fixed, unchangeable social status, rather he taught that the social status of a person can be changed, and that the determining factor in a persons life is one's own conduct. Surprisingly, his truthfulness and reforms attracted the very Brahmin intellectuals whom he denounced, and his first eleven disciples were Brahmins. He did not try to find fault in the teachings of others, but instead sought to clarify the thought of the great personages who had preceded him. He expanded the four-fold religion *(cajjuama dharma)*, as preached by Parsvanatha, into a five-fold religion *(pancajama dharma)* by adding celibacy as a separate vow, though some see celibacy implied in Parsvanatha's teaching on non-attachment *(aparigraha)*. The scripture *Uttraadhyayana Sutra* explains the reasons for this additional vow. Jacobi rightly points out the boldness of Mahavira in attempting to rectify the decay in the morals of the order in the period after Parsvanatha. The reasons for adding celibacy to the vows are to promote 'mental purity' and to strengthen the vow of non-attachment. He reformed the ascetic order while keeping doors open to all deserving indiviuals irrespective of class or caste, and thus became a pioneer in the field of spiritual democracy.

Mahavira had a unique method for conveying his 'system' to the people: he always preached to the masses in their vernacular language rather than using the classical Sanskrit, which was not understood by most ordinary people. He encouraged his disciples not to be afraid to seek guidance from him and to ask questions concerning their doubts. The entire *Bhagavati Sutra* is a record of the answers given by Mahavira to his inquisitive disciple Gautama and their relationship as teacher and disciple. The *Uttraadhyayana Sutra* is a continuous sermon given during the last thirty-six hours of Mahavira's earthly life that recounts the fundamentals of his teachings.

THE JAIN *SANGHA*, MONKS AND NUNS, *YATIS* AND *BHATTARAKAS*

The Jain *Sangha*

As described earlier, Mahavira was a superb organiser and the organisation which he developed continues even to-day. He developed the four orders of his community: monks, nuns, laymen and laywomen, and the community is collectively known as the *sangha*, which has supreme authority in all matters. Mahavira gave overall responsibility for guidance and instruction of the *sangha* to eleven chief disciples of which Indrabhuti Gautama was the most senior. They were overall normally in charge of groups *(ganas)* of 250 to 500 ascetics.

To facilitate a smooth administration, the *sangha* conferred leadership responsibility upon the ablest monks who were given the title of *aacaarya*. Other members of the community were given formal titles and responsibilities including: *upaadhyaaya* (responsible for organising education and teaching scriptures to ascetics as preceptor), *sthavira* (responsible as a senior to motivate self-discipline), *pravartaka* (responsible for the promotion and dissemination of the religion), and *gani* (responsible as a group leader for the administration of smaller groups of monks). Monks, who are proficient in *aagamas* and are able to teach, are given the title of *panyaasa*. Deserving female ascetics were given the titles of *mahattaraa* (the great), and *pravartini* (promoter). All these titles are in use to-day. For precise explanation of each term, see the glossary.

Laypersons have a special reverence for the ascetics and are guided by them in matters pertaining to their spiritual welfare. Other social and religious activities are governed by a group of the laity and trustees *(mahaajana)*. The organisation of the Jain community into the Jain *sangha* has enabled it to make a valuable contribution in terms of personal devotion, for e.g. self discipline, and collectively in education, literary activities, the establishment of places of worship, and the promotion of the teachings of Mahavira.

Immediately following the liberation *(moksa)* of Mahavira, Gautama became omniscient, but the Digambara and Swetambara traditions preserve different accounts of his life after achieving omniscience. Sudharma was Gautama's successor as leader of the *sangha* until, after 12 years, he became omniscient. He went on to achieve liberation at the age of 100. The other nine chief disciples obtained liberation in Mahavira's lifetime. Jambu succeeded Sudharma and headed the *sangha* for forty-four years, until he became omniscient. He achieved liberation at the age of eighty.

Then came, in succession, five 'scriptural omniscients', who possessed full and complete scriptural knowledge but could not attain the higher spiritual status of the omniscients. Their leadership of the *sangha* lasted 100 (or 116) years, but after the last, Bhadrabahu, the leadership succession diverged into two sects, the 'white-clad' (Svetambara) and the 'sky-clad' (Digambara).

The early Jain ascetics were very conservative in so far as the writing down of the scriptures, as they feared that the act of creating writing materials involved transgression of their vow of non-violence *(ahimsaa)*. Their vow of avoiding possessions and the rigid rules of asceticism forbade them to reside in any one place for very long or to associate unduly with householders and urban life, and this made it almost impossible for them to pursue literary activities. Moreover, they considered the religious order to be so well organised that it would vouchsafe the integrity of the original teaching of Mahavira, which continued to be preserved orally. Yet, soon after the time of Bhadrabahu, a gradual deterioration in the original canonical knowledge began which was made more pronounced by the break-up of the unified order and the emergance of schism, and the growth of minor differences of dogma, doctrine, traditions, practice and usages.

Attempts were made to rehabilitate the canon and a number of councils were called, including one at Pataliputra (modern Patna in Bihar), to attempt to organise the sacred teachings. This was necessary following famines in Bihar, which had led to the emigration to the south of *Aacaarya* Bhadrabahu and his followers. About the middle of the 2nd century BCE, a council was held at the Kumari Parvata (Udayagiri-Khandagiri hills) in Kalinga (Orissa) at the invitation of the Emperor Kharavela. It appears to have been attended largely by leaders from the south and from Mathura, and members of the council were given responsibility for the redaction of the surviving canon and the production of written literature. In the following two hundred years or so, the efforts begun at the councils led to the compilation of a large number of treatises based on the original teaching of Mahavira. These took on a quasi-canonical status, and pre-eminent among these early writers were Gunadhara, Dharasena-Pushpadanta, Kundakunda and Umasvati. Svetambaras resisted attempts at redaction for many centuries. However, they eventually bowed to the inevitable and about the beginning of the 4th century CE, Svetambara leaders convened two councils simultaneously, one at Mathura and the other at Valabhi (in Saurastra). Yet it was only about the middle of the fifth century CE that they, under the leadership of Devardhigani, in a council at Valabhi, finally redacted an acceptable canon. These pioneering activities, involving both Digambara and Svetambara scholars and stretching over many centuries, encouraged an exegetical literature and numerous independent works on diverse subjects, religious as well as secular, written in a number of languages, which has continued for the last two thousand years.

With the passage of time, both Digambara and Svetambara communities have continued to develop, almost independently of each other, into a number of sects, sub-sects, divisions and subdivisions, evolving their respective rituals and practices. Yet, there are no fundamental ideological differences between these two principal sects. Most of the places of pilgrimage, festivals and fairs, and several important religious texts, are still held in common, and until roughly the beginning of the medieval period of Indian history (about the 10th century CE) temples and images were almost similar. The ascetic orders have no doubt differed in some of their outward practices, but so far as the laity is concerned there has hardly been any noticeable distinctions.

Modern historians, who accept the historicity of Parsvanatha, also believe that Jainism may have existed before his time, although they usually date the beginning of Jain history to the time of Mahavira. Even if missionary activities of Mahavira were limited to Bihar and the surrounding area, adherents of the religion following the earlier *tirthankaras* existed in other parts of India. When circumstances such as natural calamities or persecutions caused mass emigrations of Jain ascetics from Magadha or Ujjain to Gujarat, Kalinga, the Deccan, Karnataka and other parts of southern India, they found a welcome among their co-religionists. There is evidence indicating that as early as the beginning of the 4th century BCE, flourishing Jain communities existed in Sri Lanka, but in time Jainism spread throughout India as the Jain philosophy and its ascetic discipline attracted many people. The strength of the four-fold order enabled Jainism to survive and keep its integrity to this day.

For some centuries after the liberation of Mahavira, the internal history of Jainism is characterised by schismatic tendencies, growing complexity in the *sangha* organisation, gradual decline in the effectiveness of the collective memory of the ascetics, and the development of religious dogmas. In those centuries, Jainism spread slowly from Magadha to the west and south.

Monks (Saadhus)

In early centuries, the leadership of the *sangha* was in the hands of a succession of ascetics who had 'perfect knowledge', whom we describe below. According to both older and current texts, the first eight omniscients and 'scriptural omniscients' after Mahavira are, other than Gautama:

Sudharma (*c.* 607 to 506 BCE)   Sudharma entered the order of ascetics at the age of fifty, was the chief disciple of Mahavira for thirty years, and succeeded Mahavira, attaining omniscience at the age of 92 and liberation at the age of 100.

Jambu (*c.*543 to 449 BCE)   Jambu was Sudharma's successor and the last ascetic to achieve omniscience and liberation in this descending era.

Prabhava (*c.*443 to 338 BCE)   Prabhava succeeded Jambu 64 years after Mahavira's liberation; remarkably, he was a leading bandit before his conversion by Jambu. He had come to burgle Jambu's palace on Jambu's wedding night, but his experience of meeting Jambu changed his life.

Shayyambhava (*c.*377 to 315 BCE)   Prior to becoming the head of the *sangha*, Shayyambhava was a respected Vedic scholar, but after initiation as a Jain ascetic, he mastered the fourteen pre-canonical texts *(purvas)* through Prabhava. He is remembered for composing the *Dasavaikalika Sutra* in 340 BCE.

Although Shayyambhava was a married person and his wife was pregnant, he decided to renounce and became an ascetic. After he was initiated into the order, his wife gave birth to a son, who was named Manaka. When Manaka was eight years old, on learning that his father was Shayyambhava, he desired to be his father's disciple. Shayyambhava initiated the boy, but by means of his prognostic knowledge Shayyambhava perceived that Manaka would die within six months. For the sake of his son, Shayyambhava condensed the essence of the sacred scriptures into ten lectures, which Manaka learned and then died as predicted.

Yasobhadra (*c.*351 to 235 BCE) After Shayyambhava's death, Yasobhadra became his successor and the head of the *sangha*.

Sambhutavijaya (*c.*347 to 257 BCE) and *Bhadrabahu* (*c.*322 to 243 BCE) After a most exemplary life of an ascetic and as a teacher, Yashobhadra died leaving the management of the *sangha* to his two principal disciples Sambhutavijaya and Bhadrabahu. This saw the beginning of the two lineage with two heads in the *sangha* and it was a period when royal patronage became significant in the development of Jainism.

Kunika became the King of Magadha in Mahavira's time. Because of the sad associations of his deceased father's capital at Rajagriha, Kunika moved the capital to Champa. When he died his son Udayin, out of a similar sadness caused by the memories of his late father, established yet another new capital at Pataliputra. In the centre of this city a fine Jain temple was built by the order of the King, who was a devout Jain. Sixty years after Mahavira's liberation, the childless Udayin was murdered by the agent of a rival king. Following this incident, Udayin's ministers proclaimed Nanda as the King. Nanda's chief minister was Kalpaka, a devout Jain, who became famous for his practice of non-violence, and he is said to have sacrificed his life for peace.

Sthulabhadra (*c.*297 to 198 BCE) Nanda's dynasty lasted another seven generations. Kalpaka's descendants were appointed successive chief ministers. Sakadala became the Chief Minister of the last Nanda. Sakadala had two sons: Sthulabhadra and Sriyaka. Sriyaka became the personal bodyguard of the king, whose confidence and love he had gained. Sthulbhadra fell in love with a royal dancer Rupkosa, and lived with her for twelve years. He was so much in love with her that he ignored the feelings of his family and requests to return home. His father, Sakadala, was a popular, well-respected and faithful chief minister. However, on one occasion, through the scheming of Varichi, a political opponent of Sakadala, the King believed that Sakadala was manufacturing weapons in order to take over the kingdom. In fact, the weapons were intended as a gift to the King on the joyous occasion of a forthcoming royal wedding. To spare the whole family from the king's anger, Sakadala told his son, Sriyaka, to chop off his (Sakadala's) head, when he was bowing down before the King. Sriyaka reluctantly did as his father ordered. To save Sriyaka from the sin of killing his own father, Sakadala had already taken a poisonous pill, ensuring his death. The King was shocked when he eventually learned the truth about the weapons. He offered Sriyaka the seal of the Chief Minister, but he refused it in favour of his elder brother Sthulabhadra. So the same offer was made to Sthulabhadra, who said that he would consider the matter. The king pressed him to make up his mind without delay. Then Sthulabhadra's reflections took an unexpected turn; he recognised the vanity of the world and resolved to give up its empty pleasures. He plucked out his hair and told the king of his resolution to become an ascetic, and became a disciple of Sambhutavijaya.

After twelve years of resolute ascetic life, Sthulabhadra mastered his passions and became detached from worldly surroundings. He considered encouraging Rupkosa to adopt the spiritual life and sought the permission of his guru to spend four months of the rainy season at Rupkosa's home. While he was there, Rupkosa used all her dancing skills and allurements to try to attract him back to his former life, but she could not break his determination. Seeing his resolve, she overcame her pride and took the vows of a laywoman from him. When Sthulabhadra returned to Sambhutavijaya, the guru applauded him by saying *'Duskar, Duskar'* (most difficult task done). It is said that the following year another ascetic, thinking that staying with a royal dancer was an easy undertaking, persuaded Sambhutavijaya to permit him to spend the rainy season at Rupkosa's home. But within a few days he could not control himself. It was Rupkosa who brought this ascetic to his senses by swift action.

Jain seers appreciate the remarkable control of Sthulabhadra over himself. Along with Mahavira and Gautama, Jains venerate Sthulabhadra in their daily prayers The Jain scriptures state that Sthulabhadra will be remembered for 84 half-cycles of time (*tirthankaras* like Risabhdeva and Mahavira will be forgotten in a few cycles).

At the insistence and order of the *sangha*, Bhadrabahu, who was in Nepal, became the teacher of Sthulabhadra. After mastering ten pre-canons, Sthulabhadra tried to demonstrate his knowledge to his sisters (this is regarded as vain and a misuse of knowledge). Following this incident, Bhadrabahu refused to teach him further. When Sthulabhadra prayed for forgiveness and, under pressure from the *sangha*, he consented to teach the last four pre-canons to Sthulabhadra on condition that Sthulabhadra would not teach these to anyone else. On Bhadrabahu's death, Sthulabhadra became the head of the *sangha*. He was the last scriptural omniscient.

His disciples Mahagiri and Suhasti succeeded Sthulabhadra. We will continue their history and history of other prominent *aacaaryas* later in this chapter.

Nuns (Saadhvis)

In the four-fold order created by Mahavira, women make a significant contribution to the maintenance of Jain traditions, playing leading roles as ascetics and as lay followers. Female ascetics have always outnumbered males by at least two to one ever since the time of Mahavira. Among Indian religions, the institution of female ascetics is unique to Jainism, demonstrating the equal status of women. Women have realised all the positions that men can attain, for example, Candana was the leader of the female ascetics in Mahavira's time and an important figure in the *sangha*, and Svetambara texts note some female ascetics attaining omniscience.

We have little in the way of historical record about female ascetics. Among the Svetambaras there were three types of female ascetics: group leader *(mahattaraa)*, 'promoter' *(pravartani)*, and ordinary female ascetic *(saadhvi)*. Sthanakvasis, a non-image-worshipping sect, call their female ascetics 'great sacrificers' *(mahaasatis)*, the word used for a female ascetic among the Terapanthis is *saadhvi*, while the principal female ascetic is called the *saadhvi pramukha*. Digambaras recognise two levels of female ascetic. The lower level, which is still generally a householder, though celibate, is known as *brahmacaarini*. The senior level female ascetic is a group leader called the *aryika ganini*. In the present day, there are more than six thousand Svetambara female ascetics, while Digambara female ascetics probably number only a few hundred.

The reasons why female ascetics outnumber ascetics are complex: it may be that the traditional female role in the household, with responsibility for care of the family, in some ways inclines women to be more 'religious'; women also have more daily contacts with the ascetics; and they have also played a traditional role in promoting Mahavira's teachings among the family. Whatever the reasons behind the choice of the ascetic life by women in the past, in modern times female ascetics have widened their sphere of activity. In addition to performing their ascetic and teaching duties, they are involved in modern education and contribute to Jainological research and literature.

Many female ascetics have published books and have earned high academic qualifications. They play an important role in motivating laymen and laywomen to carry out temple rituals, to perform incantational recitations and to observe the minor vows. Their example and encouragement lead many to be initiated as ascetics. Female ascetics are highly respected in the community for their simple life and their promotion of the Jain way of life and culture.

In recent years there are many examples of female ascetics being in forefront to promote Jainism. *Mahattaraa* Mrugavati, was a key founder of the Vallabh Smarak (a magnificent temple dedicated in the memory of her guru Vallabh) and the B.L. Jain Institute at Delhi, and was active in numerous other institutions in Northern India. *Ganini* Jnana Matiji, was the key personality in motivating the construction of the *Jambudvipa* model at Hastinapur. She is the author of more than 150 books. *Mahaasati* Shardabai was a well-known commentator on Mahavira's teachings and an outstanding orator. *Saadhvi* Sanghmitra is a foremost Digambara group leader and has written many books.

Yatis and *Bhattarakas*

There have been a number of periods in history in which the Jain community has been inordinately wealthy, which is not, in itself, either beneficial or harmful. Sometimes, however, it has had consequences, which have proved to be detrimental to the well being of the community. One such period occurred in the 12th and 13th centuries. At that time, unsurprisingly, a substantial part of the wealth of the community found its way into temples and associated institutions such as schools and libraries. Jain ascetics became increasingly involved in the administration of these resources and became, their critics argue, corrupted by the wealth with which they came into contact. As this scenario developed, the power of these self-appointed 'administrators' increased and they asserted control over temple rituals and, through this, over the lives and conduct of laypeople. Both the main Jain groups, the Svetambaras and the Digambaras, experienced this unwelcome development in the role of monks. The Svetambaras called such 'former' monks as *yati*, while the Digambara equivalent was known as a *bhattaraka*, meaning venerable. The institution of *bhattaraka*s survives today, but the modern *bhattaraka*s are highly respected figures, celibate but not monks in the strictest sense. The institution of *bhattaraka*s was first established at Delhi in the middle ages, and later at other places in India, such as Sravanbelgola and Mudabidre in Karnataka; Punugonda and Kaanchi in southern India; Nandani, Kolhapur, Nagpur, Karanja and Latur in Maharashtra; Idar and Sojitra in Gujarat; and Gwalior, Jaipur and Dungarpur in Rajasthan.

The *yati*s and *bhattaraka*s filled a role midway between ascetics and laypeople; a kind of semi-ascetic. Their social and religious roles made them respected, but also powerful in the local areas. Today, *bhattaraka*s administer a wide range of the needs of the community, temporal and spiritual, acting as spiritual guides and religious functionaries for rituals in temples and homes. They officiate at consecration ceremonies of temples and images and deliver religious discourses. Among Svetambaras, ascetics officiate in consecration ceremonies and deliver sermons in place of the *yati*s. Social, pastoral functions are discharged by laypeople.

The corruption of the ascetic order contributed to the weakening of the entire *sangha* and, eventually, Jainism suffered. Fortunately, over the course of several centuries, reformers succeeded in restoring the original ascetic ethos of the orders, which had always been one of the great moral strengths underpinning the *sangha*. The Jain laity play a not inconsiderable part in holding ascetics to their vows, for a backsliding monk or nun loses all respect in the community.

PROMINENT *AACAARYAS*

The *aacaaryas* were, and still are, responsible for the management of the Jain *sangha* and the dissemination of Jain teachings and practices. *Aacaaryaship* is conferred by the *sangha* to suitable ascetics who are highly proficient in the scriptures, and who display qualities of leadership, skills in public speaking, maturity and wisdom.. There are very few texts available in English, which give detailed accounts of their lives as recounted in the Jain tradition. While it is impossible to give details of all great *aacaaryas* in this book, we will mention some who have played a major part in the spread of Jainism either through their literary work or by their leadership. Historically, they have played a major role in the success of Jainism and its diffusion throughout India.

We have given an account of the lives of prominent ascetics up to the time of Sthulabhadra in the 4th century BCE. Our account now continues with his disciples; again, it must be remembered that traditional dates in the early years of Jain history are uncertain.

Mahagiri (*c.*268 to 168 BCE) and *Suhasti* (*c.*222 to 122 BCE)   Mahagiri and Suhasti were disciples of Sthulabhadra, from whom they learned ten pre-canons. Eventually, Mahagiri handed over the charge of his own disciples to Suhasti and lived as an ascetic, modelling his conduct on the example of the *jina*, Mahavira.

The Emperor Samprati, grandson of the famous Emperor Ashoka, had great faith in Suhasti and as a consequence of his influence the king became a devout Jain, and showed his zeal by commissioning Jain temples, which were built throughout India, some of whose images survive. The example of Samprati induced subordinate rulers to patronise the Jain faith, so that not only in his own domains but also in adjacent countries, Jain ascetics could practise their religion. He was instrumental in arranging for missionaries to be sent out to spread the message of Jainism. Suhasti was followed by an unbroken succession of *aacaaryas*.

Shyamaacaarya (*c.*247 to 151 BCE)   He is also known as Kalakacharya I and was the composer of the famous work the *Prajnaapana Sutra*, which is an encyclopaedia of Jain tenets. He is also acknowledged as the first person to expound the doctrine of the existence of a micro-organic world of 'one sense beings'.

Vajraswami (c.31 BCE to 47 CE)   He was known for his leadership and capability as an organiser of the *sangha* as well as for his scholarship and personal austerity; and he is also remembered for his attainment of extra-ordinary powers *(labdhi)*, which he used solely for the benefit of the *sangha*. The texts tell the story of his childhood: before his birth, his father had become a ascetic.; as a baby, he was always crying; and his mother frequently ran out of patience and, out of desperation, when he was three years old, she handed him over to his ascetic father. Vajraswami was happy in the company of ascetics. When he was eight years old, his mother came with a request to have him back, but he refused to go with her. His mother went to the king demanding his intervention, but the king decided to allow Vajraswami to stay wherever he chose. His mother tried to lure him with toys and other desirable things, but he ignored her and stayed with his father. He was initiated as an ascetic at the age of eight years, became profi-cient in scriptures, and taught other ascetics for a long period. He became an *aacaarya* at the age of 52 and led the *sangha* for another 36 years.

Kalakaacaarya II (circa 1st century CE)   Kalakaacaarya II came from the state of Ujjain. He was initiated at a young age, and his sister was initi-ated as a female ascetic soon afterwards. Kalakaacaarya became proficient in prognostics, astrology and other sciences. Because of his leadership qual-ities, he became an *aacaarya* at a very young age. A number of incidents from his life are recorded in the traditions: when King Gardabhilla of Ujjain kidnapped Kalakaacaarya's sister (who was a female ascetic), Kalakaacaarya was able to persuade a neighbouring ruler to attack Ujjain. When this happened Gardabhilla relented and released Kalakaacaarya's captive sister. This use of violence in the interest of justice and the *sangha* was regarded by many as pardonable.

The annual confession day *(samvatsari)* is the most important day of austerities in the Jain calendar,but the king requested that it be brought forward by one day and, as this was not inconsistent with the scriptures, Kalakaacaarya advised the *sangha* to give its approval; as a result the *sangha* received royal patronage.

Kalakaacaarya was also known as a strict disciplinarian, and when a number of ascetics were getting lax in their daily life and duties, he persuaded them to return to their regime of the Right Conduct. It is said that he was the first *aacaarya* to have travelled abroad for promotion of Jainism, visiting Iran, Java, Borneo and other countries. For an ascetic to travel overseas was something of a minor revolution, but he was always vigilant about his own conduct and would make the appropriate atonement for any transgression, and his example is commended as a model even today. Like his namesake Kalakaacaarya I, he too was an expert on the micro-organic world. He advised ascetics to adapt their conduct according to the prevailing conditions of time and place, and to use robes and bowls,

and was the first *aacaarya* to sanction the writing of sacred literature by
ascetics.

Arya Raksit (*c.*5 BCE to 70 CE)   This *aacaarya* was a systemiser of both
sacred and secular Jain literature. He divided the literature into four groups
depending upon the predominant nature of each composition. His own
works included the *Anuyogadvar Sutra*, a treatise containing a theory of
knowledge and a wide range of teachings on religious topics. His work also
drew upon non-Jain sacred literature, which showed his liberal attitude and
respect for other faiths.

Kundakunda (*circa* 2nd century CE)   This is the first south Indian
ascetic-scholar to contribute towards the literary glory of Jainism. He was
a native of Kundkund in present-day Andhra. He was a prolific writer, but
only a few of his books are available today. His important works include:
the 'Essence of Doctrines' *(Samaya Saara)*, the 'Essence of Ascetic Rules'
(Niyama Saara), the 'Essence of Five Reals' (*Pancastikaaya Saara)* and the
'Essence of Sermons' *(Pravacana Saara)*. A book titled 'Eight Chapters on
the Path of Salvation' *(Astapaahuda)* is also credited to him. He is famous
for expounding the 'absolute stand point' *(niscaya naya)*, and is regarded
as having been a deeply spiritual teacher. In the Digambara Jain morning
liturgy, he is also mentioned in auspicious recitations along with Mahavira
and Gautama.

Umasvati (*c.*240 CE to 340 CE)   He is one of the scholarly *aacaarya*s
revered by both Svetambaras and Digambaras for his masterly work, the
'Manual for Understanding the Reals' *(Tattvartha Sutra)*. This is the first
authentic Sanskrit text on Jain tenets giving a complete survey of Jain
beliefs in terse and pithy aphorisms. This text is so popular that more than
twenty-five commentaries and translations have appeared in different
languages, including English and German, and a notable new English translation was published in 1993 (see Bibliography). Another great work
credited to him is *Prasamarati*, a guide for the aspirant on the path of peace
and liberation from karmic bondage.

Devardhigani (*c.*400 CE to 480 CE)   He hailed from Saurastra (Gujarat)
and was a *ksatriya* by birth, initiated as a Jain ascetic by Aacaarya
Dusyagani and is known in Jain texts as one of the most respected *aacaarya*
under whose auspices the last council, where the oral canon was redacted,
took place in 460 CE at Valabhi (Gujarat). Following the work of two
earlier councils at Pataliputra and Mathura, the canon was organised and
put into written form. Over 500 ascetics attended this council, which lasted
nearly fifteen years. Each ascetic was given an opportunity to recite the oral
canon and the final product is the possible correct scripture in the written
form and this was a great tribute to Devardhigani.

Samantabhadra (*c.*450 CE to 550 CE)   This southern ascetic-scholar,
lived during the Cola dynasty. He was a poet, logician, eulogist and accom-

plished linguist. His works include: the 'Critique of the Enlightened' *(Aptamimansa)*, the 'Discipline of Logic' *(Yuktyaanusasana)*, the 'Eulogy of the Tirthankaras' *(Svayambuhstotra)* and the 'Jewels of Conduct for the Laity' *(Ratnaakaranda Sravaakaacaara)*. It is said that he also composed a commentary on Umasvati's *Tattvartha Sutra*. He is credited with performing many superworldly feats for the promotion of Jainism. During his time Jainism became widespread in southern India.

*Siddhasen Divakar (c.*500 CE to 610 CE)   This Brahmin scholar was initiated as a Jain ascetic by A*acaarya* Vruddhavadi. He founded the Jain system of logic and was instrumental for the popularity of Jainism in more than eighteen kingdoms of central, southern and western India. His works cover a range of literature: eulogical, logical, and religious; his 'Descent of Logic' *(Nyaayavtaar)*, the 'Logic of Right Wisdom' *(Sanmati Sutra)*, the 'Eulogy on Welfare' *(Kalyaana Mandir Stotra)* and many hymns, each of 32 verses *(dvatrisikas)*, played a crucial part in the development of the later literature. His brilliance and accomplishments brought to Jainism royal patronage from many rulers.

*Pujyapada (c.*510 CE to 600 CE)   This Karnataka-born Brahmin scholar became a Jain ascetic out of conviction. He was a poet, philosopher, grammarian and expert on indigenous medicines. He has been credited with many accomplishments, which aided in the promotion of Jainism in the south. He is also noted for his 'Manual of all Reals' *(Sarvartha Siddhi)*, and a commentary on the *Tattvartha Sutra*, popular among Digambaras. His other books include a work on grammar *(Jainendra Vyaakaran)*, the 'System of Meditation' *(Samaadhi Tantra)*, the 'Eulogy on Accomplishments' *(Siddhapriya Stotra)*, the 'Ten-fold Devotions' *(Dasa Bhakti)*, and the 'Sermons on Desirable Practices' *(Istopadesa)*.

*Jinabhadra (c.*500 CE to 593 CE)   This *aacaarya* is noted for composing commentaries on at least fifteen sacred books including the Jain tenets *(Aavasyaka Sutra)*, ascetic conduct *(Jitakalpa)* and the 'Commentary on Jain Essentials' *(Vishesa Vashyak Bhasya)*; and he was a major scholar, expositor and logician.

*Mantunga (c.*600 CE to 660 CE)   This revered *aacaarya* was born in Varanasi during the reign of King Harshadeva (7th century CE), who had a court of noted scholars, including a Jain minister. When challenged to produce a miracle to prove the worth of Jainism, the minister sought the help of the *aacaarya*, who reluctantly agreed to help for the sake of the faith. The king had the *aacaarya* placed in a room, sealed with 48 chains, each of which was individually locked. The *aacaarya* meditated on *Tirthankara* Risabhdeva and composed devotional verses in praise of the attributes of Risabhdeva, and as each verse was completed, one of the locks opened until, eventually, all the 48 locks were unlocked. These verses have come down to us as the famous 'Eulogy of the Immortalisation of the

Devotee' *(Bhaktamara Stotra)*, and are recited by many Jains during their morning prayers.

Akalanka (*c.* 620 CE to 680 CE) This one of the most important Jain logicians and philosophers lived in Karnataka during the Rastrakuta dynasty. He studied Buddhism (clandestinely) and proved himself an able debater against Buddhist scholars. In addition to his reputation as a debater, he is credited with having significantly shaped Jain logic and among his original contributions to Jain literature are works on cognition, the theory of omniscience and the theory of 'Relative Pluralism' *(Anenkaantavaada)*. He composed the outstanding 'Royal Commentary' *(Raju Vartik)* on the *Tattvartha Sutra* and the 'Eight Thousand Verses on Logic' *(Aptamimansa Astasahasri)*.

Haribhadra (*c.*705 CE to 775 CE) He was a shining star among the Jain ascetic-scholars of the 8th century. He was a Rajasthani Brahmin scholar of considerable repute and was proud of his scholarship. He had taken a personal vow to be the disciple of any person whose work proved beyond his understanding. One day while passing a Jain *upashraya*, he heard a verse recited by the Jain female ascetic, *Mahattaraa* Yakini, and could not understand its meaning, so he overcame his pride and went to the female ascetic to ask the meaning, but rather than explain it herself she directed him to her guru Jinabhadra.

As a result of his encounter with Jinabhadra, Haribhadra was initiated as a Jain ascetic. He mastered the Jain scriptures and was awarded the honorific title of *Suri*, which means something like 'sun'. Such was his devotion to Jainism that he mastered Buddhist literature in order to debate with Buddhists and promote Jainism. Of his reputed output of 1,444 books, 88 are extant today. He wrote in Sanskrit and Prakrit on ethics, asceticism, yoga, logic and rituals. He also composed works on satire and astrology as well as novels and canonical commentaries. With his 'Compendium of Six Philosophies' *(Sad Darsana Sammucayas)*, he created a novel style of logic in an era noted for the quality of its philosophical debates. 'The Essence of Religion' *(Dharmabindu)* is a major contribution to the religious life of the laity. Even at a time when Jains were numerically in decline, Haribhadra demonstrated the enduring strength of the faith.

Bappa-Bhatti (*c.*743 CE to 838 CE) He was a 'great soul', who became an *aacaarya* at the age of eleven. He established a reputation as one of the greatest ascetic-scholars and debaters of his time. He was a teacher of his royal patron Prince Amaraj who became King of Kanoj (Uttar Pradesh). Amaraj tested the asceticism of the *aacaarya* by tempting him with royal dancers but Bappa-Bhatti remained unmoved. He was a great orator and author, winning public esteem across India for composing eulogies on the goddess of learning and the twenty-four *tirthankaras*, which remain popular today.

Virasena (*circa* 9th century BC)   This ascetic-scholar had many talents: he was proficient in astrology, grammar, logic, mathematics and prosody. He is noted for his commentary named the *Dhavalaa* on the Digambara pre-canon *Satkhandaagama* (a six-chaptered canon on Jain tenets originating in about 100 CE). He also started the detailed commentary on *Satkhandaagama* called the *Jayadhavalaa*, which was completed by his disciples. He was one of the outstanding minds in the kingdom of Amoghvarsa under the Rastrakuta dynasty, regarded as a golden age of Jain literature and culture.

We are now coming to the aacaaryas of the modern age, the time during which the 'devotional path' (bhakti maarga) of Vaisnavism was spreading, and the Jain aacaaryas had to adopt a more ritualistic worship in order to compete with the popularity of the new cult.

Somadeva (*circa* 10th century CE)   He was a prolific writer of prose and poetry from northern India. Of his three major works, one is on political science, the first by any Jain author, written at the request of the King of Kanoj. The second is a prose novel entitled *Yashastilaka*, said to be stylistically comparable to the best Sanskrit poetry, remarkable for its deep knowledge of Sanskrit grammar, metre and idiom. It deals in part with the conduct expected of the laity, noting that the adoption of local cultures can maintain and preserve the faith. The third work deals with spiritual aspects of Jainism. When the religion faced decline owing to the popularity of ritual movements of other faiths, he adapted rituals to serve the needs of the Jain community.

Abhayadeva (*c*.1057 CE to 1135 CE)   Born in Ujjain, and initiated by Jineshvara Suri, he became a scholar of exceptional ability. It is said that a guardian deity would appear to him in dreams and inspire him to write commentaries on scriptures in Sanskrit. In spite of recurrent health problems he wrote many books, including commentaires on nine scriptural texts, said to total 57,769 verses, which proved so popular that large numbers of the laity volunteered to copy and distribute them throughout India. Tradition attributes that his blessings brought miraculous results; on one occasion when some merchant's ships were in danger of sinking, his blessings saved the ship and crew.

Hemcandra (*c*.1089 CE to 1172 CE)   *Aacaarya* Hemcandra is one of the most esteemed Jain scholars and *aacaarya*s. In his biography by Prabhachandra and Merutung, his key role in enhancing the standing of Jainism through his political, religious, social and academic activities is described in detail. He is considered to be the 'father of the Gujarati language' and, in 1989, the 900th anniversary of his birth was celebrated in many parts of the world.

Hemcandra was the son of a merchant in Dhandhuka (Gujarat); his father was a Vaisnava Hindu and his mother was a Jain, and he was originally called Changadeva. He was an exceptionally intelligent child. Once, when *Aacaarya* Devcandra was passing through his town, he saw the boy and was struck by his facial aura; he sought permission from his mother to initiate the boy as a Jain ascetic,which she reluctantly agreed. The *aacaarya* entrusted him to the custody of Governor Udayan of Cambay (Gujarat) for scriptural study. At the age of nine, he became proficient in all subjects and he was ordained as an *aacaarya* at the age of twenty-one and given the new name: of Hemcandra.

At this time, Siddharaja Jaisinha was the King of Gujarat (1092–1141 CE). He was a sophisticated monarch who appointed the *aacaarya* as his court scholar and historian. Impressed by his scholarship, Siddharaja commissioned him to write a poetic history of his dynasty, the Calukyas, and a Sanskrit grammar. This he did. The king had no son, and his nephew Kumarpala was next in succession, but he did not want his nephew to succeed him, and sent soldiers to kill him. Out of compassion, *Aacaarya* Hemcandra helped Kumarpala by hiding him from the soldiers under piles of his manuscripts. Eventually, Kumarpala succeeded to the throne of Gujarat.

Kumarpala was so impressed by the Jain teachings and by Hemcandra that he became active in promoting Jainism. At the instigation of Hemcandra, Kumarpala issued a proclamation prohibiting the killing of 'mobile' living beings *(amaari pravartan)* in his kingdom, which extended to modern Gujarat and became a vegetarian observing the vows of the Jain laity. Many temples were built during his reign and inscriptions from that period survive in large numbers.

Hemcandra is noted for his literary works, which embrace all the major branches of learning and, because of this great range of knowledge, he is known as the 'omniscient of the contemporary age' *(kali kaala sarvajna)*. On the completion of his Sanskrit grammar, known as the *Siddha Hema Vyaakarana*, elaborate celebrations, commissioned by Siddharaja, and attended by more than 300 scholars from all parts of India, were held. This classic work also included a Prakrit grammar. Hemcandra also composed the first Gujarati grammar. He produced a biography of the sixty-three 'torch bearers' of Jainism and a history of the Jain *sangha*. He also wrote lexicons, poetry and works on logic, the *Yoga Sastra* and prosody.

Jinadattasuri (c.1075 CE to 1154 CE) He is the most celebrated *aacaarya* of the Svetambara sub-sect known as the *Kharataragaccha*. He was initiated as a ascetic at the age of nine years and became an *aacaarya* at the age of thirty-seven. His social, religious and literary activities earned him the title of '*aacaarya* of the era' *(yuga pradhaana)*. He made tremendous efforts to expand the Jain community, both through preaching and through an open, welcoming attitude, and reputedly more than 100,000 joined the Jain community through his influence. So great was his personal influence that the Muslims of Sindh gave land for the use of the Jain community. Like many prominent figures in Jain literature and history, Jinadatta Suri was regarded as possessing supernormal attributes and powers.

His main work was centred on Rajasthan, Gujarat, Maharashtra and Sindh. He was a great scholar of Sanskrit, Prakrit and Apabhramsha, an ancient language used in Gujarat and Rajasthan. His services to the community earned him great reverence and when he passed away at Ajmer, the place of his death was named the 'Garden of Dada' *(Dadawadi)*, *dada* means grandfather and is a term of endearment and respect. As a tribute to his work, his followers have established *dadawadis* or *dadabaris* throughout India, and leading ascetics of this sub-sect are known as *dada gurus*.

*Hiravijaya (c.*1526 CE to 1595 CE)   This prominent *aacaarya* was born in Palanpur (Gujarat). He was initiated at the age of thirteen and he became *aacaarya* at the age of twenty-seven. He was highly studious and intelligent and his work earned him the honorific titles of 'the scholar' *(pandit)*, 'teacher of scripture' *(upadhyaaya)* and 'the orator' *(vaacak)*. According to the book *Ain-i-Akbari* by Abdulfazal, he was one of twenty-one most learned people in the Mogul Empire.

The great Mogul Emperor Akbar invited him to Delhi. He declined the offer of royal elephants for the journey and travelled on foot from Gujarat to Delhi to meet Akbar. He was given a magnificent reception. Akbar was highly impressed by his simplicity, austerity and the learning displayed in his sermons. The *aacaarya*'s teachings on non-violence and reverence for life prompted the emperor to release many prisoners and caged animals; Akbar prohibited the killing of animals on Jain sacred days especially during the sacred period of *paryusana*. Akbar gave up hunting, fishing and even eating meat on many days. Hiravijaya's influence with the great Emperor Akbar earned him the title of 'World Teacher' *(Jagat Guru)*. He left Delhi, leaving his disciples Bhanu Chandra and Vijay Sen Suri as counsellors at the court of Akbar and travelled widely in India.

*Yashovijay (c.*1620 CE to 1686 CE)   There are some ascetics who will not accept the responsibility of being an *aacaarya* as they feel it would not allow them to pursue their literary and spiritual activities to the full. The contribution of such ascetics is unparalleled in Jain history. We have included *Upadhyaaya* Yashovijay in this chapter, as his contribution in literary activity and scholarship is of great significance.

He was born in Kanoda, Gujarat, and showed intelligence as a child. Having listened to the sermons of Muni Nayvijayji, he expressed a wish to become a ascetic, to which his parents reluctantly agreed. In view of his excellent memory and powers of concentration it was thought appropriate to send him to Varanasi to study Indian philosophy, where he became proficient in the subject and defeated a well-known Hindu ascetic (*sanyaasi*) in public debate. This brought him great honour and he became known as an 'expert in logic' (*nyaaya visaarada*), the first Jain ascetic to be honoured in this way in the traditional seat of Hindu scholarship at Varanasi.

In his own religious life, the Jain mystic poet Anandaghana influenced Yashovijay, which resulted in his writings having a concern with inner spiritual values. His guru, *Aacaarya* Vijaydev advised him to put his scholarship to better use in his writing. His prolific literary output includes more than 100 books in four languages, Sanskrit, Prakrit, Gujarati and Rajasthani, ranging from epics, stories and biographies, to ontology, logic, philosophy, yoga, spirituality, and ascetic and lay life. Among his works, his 'Essence of Knowledge' (*Jnaana Saara*) is widely read both by laypeople and by ascetics; also popular is his 'Essentials of Spirituality' (*Adhyaatma Saara*), and four books on yoga practices. The main thrust of his teaching was that liberation is an inner achievement, dependent upon detachment, not upon external material achievement; he also sought to reinforce ritual with deep spiritual significance.

Bhiksu or *Bhikhanji* (*c*.1726 CE to 1803 CE)   He was the founder of the Terapanthi, an offshoot of the Sthanakvasi sect (non-image-worshippers) within the Svetambara tradition. He became a ascetic at the age of twenty-five, but disturbed by what he saw as the laxity in the conduct of Sthanakvasi ascetics and their erroneous teachings, he established a new three-fold tradition for the efficient running of the order. This included having a single head of the order authorised to select his successor, uniform observance, and an ethos of uniformity. During his *aacaarya*hood he initiated 104 persons as ascetics. He composed many books in the Rajasthani language. Bhikshu had a 'holy death' (*sallekhanaa*, the voluntary abandonment of all bodily needs), at the age of seventy-seven.

Amulakh Rushi (1877 CE to 1936 CE)   This Sthanakvasi saint translated the 32 main books of Jain sacred literature into Hindi. He also composed 70 books on many other subjects, which have been translated into Gujarati, Marathi, Kannada and Urdu. In view of his lifelong efforts to spread the holy teachings of Jainism through his translations and writings, his admirers called him the 'destroyer of darkness and ignorance'. Born in Bhopal, initiated at the age of eleven, he became head of the *sangha* at the age of fifty-five. He travelled to many parts of India and had a 'holy death' in 1936.

Vallabh Vijay (1870 CE to 1954 CE)   *Aacaarya* Vallabh Vijay Suri was an influential ascetic of the Svetambara tradition, very much a man of the people and he encouraged many to become active in the welfare both of the

Jain and other communities. He promoted Jain unity and tried to enlist other *aacaarya*s to this end. He was an impressive speaker who emphasised self-sufficiency, strong organisation, education, accessible literature, a caring community, women's welfare and patriotism. He was instrumental in the establishment of the famous Mahavira Jain Vidhyalaya and a chain of other institutions of modern education in the Punjab, Delhi, Uttar Pradesh and elsewhere. Following his guru *Aacaarya* Vijayanand Suri's instructions, his main work remained in Punjab. He promoted the path of Jain values to wider communities. As a result of his work in Punjab, Vallabh Vijaya became known to followers as the 'Lion of the Punjab' *(Panjab kesari)*. For his general work in promoting the Jain values and the welfare of the Jain community he was considered the '*aacaarya* of the era' *(yuga pradhan)*.

During the early period of the British Raj, the Svetambaras held the office of an *aacaarya* in abeyance, and and when conditions were favourable, Vallabh Vijay's guru, Vijaynand Suri was conferred by the *sangha* as the first *aacaarya* after more than a century. Vijaynand Suri was invited to attend the World Parliament of Religions at Chicago in 1893; as Jain ascetics travel on foot, he could not participate, but he motivated a brilliant layman Virchand Raghavji Gandhi to attend. Along with his guru, Vallabh Vijay assisted the preparations of Virchand Gandhi in the task of promoting Jainism and Jain values in the Western World.

A number of miracles are associated with Vallabh Vijay. On one occasion he blessed an installation ceremony of a temple images in a Punjab village, at which more than 15,000 devotees were served full dinner, though the organisers had prepared food for only 5,000 devotees. What should have been insufficient amounts of prepared food became more than adequate in amount due to the blessings of Vallabh Vijay. He defied weather forecasts during religious ceremonies and it is said that rain stopped on many occasions, apparently through his blessings to the *sangha*. He supported the non-violent freedom struggle of India. His interventions saved the lives of many Jains during the disturbed time of the partition of India in 1947. All national leaders of India paid their respects to him for his patriotic and humanitarian sermons. He died in Bombay in 1954. More than 200,000 mourners attended his funeral procession.

Shantisagar (c.1872 CE to 1955 CE)   *Aacaarya* Shantisagar became the first Digambara Jain ascetic after an interval of many centuries. During the Muslim period and most of the period of British Raj, Digambara ascetics were harassed. As a result people did not dare to accept Digambara asceticshood. In the Digambara tradition a layperson who has taken minor vows becomes a 'celebrated laity' *(brahmacaari)*. Spiritual development then leads to the stage of a 'two-garmented laity' *(ksullaka)*, followed by a 'one-garmented laity' *(ailaka)*. Lastly one becomes a 'sky-clad' ascetic.

Born in Karnataka into a family of farmers, he became detached from the affairs of the household and progressed along the spiritual path. He was initiated at the age of forty-eight and given the name 'ocean of peace' *(Shanti Sagar)*. He travelled throughout India, and promoted Jain teachings both to Jains and non-Jains. He observed the *'jina*-modelled' austerities in his personal life, for which his followers honoured him with the epithet of 'king among ascetics' *(muniraj)* and 'ocean of observances' *(silasindhu)*. During one of his times of meditation in a cave, a cobra was seen with its hood raised for many minutes, as if paying respect to this great saint. During the time of the British Raj, 'sky-clad' Digambara ascetics were prohibited from entering major cities. As this restriction, enforced in the name of so-called 'decency', struck at an important element of Digambara belief, Shantisagar undertook a fast at a square near the Red Fort, Delhi until permission was granted for all 'sky-clad' ascetics to roam freely. The British Raj lifted the restrictions and people began to appreciate the austerities of the Digambara ascetic. He had a 'holy death' at Komthali (Maharashtra).

Tulsi (1914 CE–1997CE)   *Aacaarya* Tulsi was the ninth in the line of terapanthi *aacaaryas*. In 1995 he became the first person to be granted the title *ganaadhipati*, superior of all ascetics. He is known as the '*aacaarya* of the era' *(yuga pradhaana)* and 'promoter of minor vows' *(anuvrata-anushasta)*. Born in Ladnun (Rajasthan), initiated at the age of eleven, and ordained to *aacaarya*hood at the age of twenty-three, he was awarded the Indira Gandhi National Award in 1993, for promoting national well being through the 'minor vows' *(anuvrata)* movement. He believed in strong personal discipline, a thorough scriptural education, the global dissemination of Jain values, Jain communal unity and inter-faith harmony.

He was the head of one of the largest organised Jain orders numbering around 500,000 lay devotees and some 200 male ascetics and 500 female ascetics. He was the initiator of many activities of contemporary importance, his literary work includes the preparation and publication of critical editions of Jain scriptures in Hindi and English, canonical lexicons, Jain instructional literature, biographical literature and scientific interpretations of Jain tenets. He encouraged the establishment of educational centres for the newly initiated and the creation of intermediate cadres of 'semi-monk' *(samana)* and 'semi-nun' *(samani)*, allowing them relaxation in the vow of non-violence so that they could travel and promote Jainism to a wider area, especially outside India.

Vidyasagar (1946–)   This Digambara Jain *aacaarya* from Karnataka was initiated at the age of twenty-two and became an *aacaarya* at the age of twenty-six. He is an original thinker and a fine orator, proficient in many languages and motivates his followers to pursue high standards of scholarship. He has written many books of poetry and prose exhibiting a concern with raising moral standards, has made poetic translations of Kundakunda's books and other literature. He wrote a religious novel in Hindi entitled 'silent soil' *(Mook Maati)* which is highly regarded for its style and its content and has been translated into many languages.

He heads a group of about 100 monks and nuns, most of them highly educated. He has initiated a large number of reformist activities, appropriate to modern times, including research institutes, educational centres for new initiates, administrative training centres, annual Jain seminars and discussion groups. He has motivated the renovation of many places of pilgrimage.

This section has covered only a selection of the prominent *aacaarya*s of the past and present. Today many *aacaarya*s are continuing to work to preserve and adapt the Jain heritage in the modern world: work is being undertaken to collect, preserve, and catalogue and publish Jain literature, to build Jain temples and other centres and to serve the *sangha* world-wide.

ROYAL PATRONAGE

Concentrating on things of the spirit, the Jains were never conscious of history. However, many scholars have tried to construct the history of Jainism through the records of royal patronage, existing inscriptions, art and architecture, literary and legendary sources. Royal patronage aided the Jain cause in many ways. The fortunes of Jainism in India have fluctuated over time and a decline in royal patronage has played its part in this. As India is a sub-continent with a history of many kingdoms, royal support was extremely variable. We will briefly describe this process in the different regions of India.

Eastern India

When it came to gaining royal support, Mahavira's birth into a ruling family gave him many useful connections. It is therefore not surprising that Jainism won royal support in the eastern part of the sub-continent. Even before Mahavira, Parsvanatha had travelled widely in the east spreading Jain teachings and creating many followers. Jain ascetics established a solid rapport with local rulers with the result that, according to the *Kalpa Sutra*, Mahavira had over half a million followers in his lifetime. Monarchs such as Srenika (or Bimbisara), Kunika (or Ajatsatru), Udayin, Ashoka, Samprati and the rulers of the Nanda, the Mauryan, and the Maitra dynasty were patrons of Jainism in Bihar before the Common Era. There were some troubled times too, but these usually passed. However, periodic persecution caused the Jains to move out of Bihar to the south and west in two

directions; the first route was through Kalinga (Orissa) and the other via
Ayodhya, Mathura, Ujjain and Gujarat. In all these places early communities of followers and sympathisers of Jainism were strengthened by the
influx of new arrivals.

Candragupta conquered the throne of Nanda. His political mentor
Canakya, who was famous for his intelligence, shrewdness and political
acumen, guided him to conquer Nanda dynasty, 155 years after Mahavira's
liberation. At Canakya's instance he chose Jain teachers as his spiritual
guides. Canakya served Candragupta as his minister and organised the
coronation of his son, Bindusara, following Candragupta's initiation as a
ascetic by Bhadrabahu. Candragupta left his kingdom and went to the
south with his new mentor and ended his life by holy death *(sallekhanaa)*.

Ashoka ascended the throne after Bindusara. Ashoka sent his son
Kunala to Ujjayini to study the political arts. When Kunala was eight years
old, his stepmother tricked him into blinding himself with a hot iron, by
forging a letter from Kunala's father to make it appear that the king wanted
his son to follow this extreme order. His grandson Samprati succeeded
Ashoka. Samprati was a staunch Jain and a powerful monarch. Inscriptions
dating from the reign of Ashoka indicate that Jainism spread as far as
Kashmir. The records of Ashoka's grandson, Samprati, indicate that he sent
Jain missionaries to the south of India and even to foreign lands. His
support for the building of many temples and monasteries, and for the
distribution of images of the *tirthankaras*, suggests that Samprati was a
zealous Jain. Samprati was a strict follower of *Aacaarya* Suhasti and his
deeds of promotion of Jainism are remembered by Jains even today. Many
district names in Bihar, such as Sinhbhumi, Veerbhumi, and the
Parsvanatha hills, have Jain connections and remind us of its former influence in Bihar. The patronage of the ruling class was sustained through to
the 5th century CE, after which it declined.

As an ascetic, Mahavira travelled to Bengal. The *Kalpa Sutra* notes that
he visited Lada and Vajrabhumi. And the fact that one district bears the
name of Vardhamana demonstrates the influence of Jainism in that locality.
Aacaarya Bhadrabahu hailed from Bengal. Many early administrators of
Bengal favoured Jainism, but the religion declined there during the Pala and
Sen kingdoms. However, the records of the Chinese traveller Hiu-en-
Tsang suggest that the influence of Jainism in Bengal continued up to the
7th century CE

Kalinga (Orissa) was a stronghold of Jainism, even before the days of
Parsvanatha. It is said that the eighteenth *tirthankara* Aranatha received his
first alms in Rajapur, the capital of Kalinga. Kalinga has many important
connections with Jain history. Kalinga's most famous King Kharvel and his
queen commissioned Jain inscriptions at Hathigumpha cave temple. The
inscriptions make reference to a council of ascetics, the return of a Kalinga

Jain image from Magadha and the construction of *upashrayas*. Other kingdoms lent patronage to Jains in Kalinga, but this did not last long, although we find that Udyot Kesari was a staunch supporter of Jainism in a later period. The present day *Saraaka* caste (estimated to be more than a million people) of Orissa and Bihar worship Parsvanatha and follow the Jain practices. Many *jina* images of more than 1,000 years old are found in Orissa. It is interesting to note that even the later Saiva kings patronised Jainism in Orissa. However, the spread of Vaisnavism and Jagannatha worship in Orissa forced Jainism into decline. It was in this period that Jainism became syncretistic and adopted many customs and practices of Hinduism, for example in iconography, to maintain its popular appeal. In later times, Orissa became a province ruled by the Rastrakuta dynasty and the influence of Jainism revived. The amalgamation of numerous followers of the *ajivikaa* sects into Jainism helped to strengthen the position of Jainism in the eastern India. Ajivikaa sects began around the 6th century BCE and survived until the 14th century CE.

Western India

Royal patronage of Jainism has a long history in Gujarat. The area once formed part of the kingdom of Samprati. It was a Jain ascetic, Silagunsuri, who was instrumental in the establishment of the Patan kingdom in the 9th century CE. Almost all subsequent kings patronised Jainism, regardless of their personal lineage. The golden age of royal patronage in Gujarat was during the kingdom of Siddharaj and Kumarpala, when not only were temples and *upashrayas* were built, but Jainism permeated the whole culture of Gujarat, an influence that continues to the present day.

Gujarat has always been associated with *Tirthankara* Neminatha, and other leading figures of Jain history such as the Digambara ascetic-scholar Dharasen and Svetambara ascetic-scholar Hemcandra. The great places of pilgrimage, Satrunjay (Palitana) and Girnar are situated in Gujarat and Valabhi, where two councils of ascetics were held, is in Gujarat. Even Muslim rulers and their representatives sought the co-operation and support of Jains. The long history of royal patronage owes much to the honesty and integrity of large numbers of Jain officials, who occupied senior posts in the royal administration. Many such officials, Jain merchants and bankers used their own resources to promote Jainism, and contributed generously to keep the heritage of Jain art and culture alive. This culture flourished under the British Raj because of religious freedom and generous help by the Jain merchants and the wider *sangha*.

Although Maharashtra has no history of royal patronage to compare to that of Gujarat, Jainism flourished there at an early date because of the missionaries sent by Samprati. The language of many Jain writings is today known as Jain Maharastri Prakrit. Maharashtra was, for a time, under the domination of the Calukya and Rastrakuta dynasties and this allowed Jainism to flourish. Some places, such as Kolhapur, still have large Jain population. The 1981 decennial census of India suggested that about 30 per cent of the total Jain population of India lived in Maharashtra.

Southern India

For more than 1,500 years after the time of Mahavira, parts of southern India proved to be strongholds of Jainism, mainly in its Digambara variant. Jain literature claims that Neminatha was in the south when Krishna's city of Dwaraka was burnt. Legend says that a saintly ascetic, who had been repeatedly harassed by some drunken members of the royal household, had put a curse on the city and it may be that the drunken behaviour and brawling of these inhabitants of Dwaraka was the cause of the fire. It is said that there was a Jain temple in Sri Lanka in 400 BCE, if so, this suggests that Jainism might have spread to the south in the time of Parsvanatha. *Aacaarya* Bhadrabahu, the Mauryan King Candragupta and Samprati's missionaries went to the south, suggesting the possibility that Jain civilisation was already in existence in southern India. The Ganga dynasty supported Jainism for some 500 years, as the rulers followed Jainism. It is said that Simhanandi, a Jain ascetic, gave the spiritual guidance and explanation of *ahimsaa* for the rulers, and this helped the establishment of Ganga dynasty. Hoysala rulers, encouraged by a Jain ascetic Sudatta, were also patrons of Jainism.

Many south Indian dynasties supported Jainism. In addition to the Calukyas and Rastrakutas already mentioned, the Kadamba, Pandya, Cola, Kalcuri, Amoghvarsha, Vijaynagar and other dynasties also patronised Jainism. The Rastrakuta period is looked upon as a 'golden era' of Jain literary activities, technical and religious literature, and of Jain art and architecture in the south. After the 14th century CE Jainism declined both numerically and culturally when royal patronage was withdrawn, because of change in the rulers who followed Saivism and Lingayatism. Despite this set backs and some persecution of Jains by Saivites, Jainism still has an appreciable following in Karnataka, Andhra, Madras and Kerala regions.

Northern India

The northern areas of Uttar Pradesh, Delhi, Punjab, Haryana, Madhya Pradesh, Himachal Pradesh, Kashmir and Rajasthan have been associated with Jainism since the days of the first *tirthankara* born in Ayodhya. Many *tirthankaras* were born in the northern India, the last being Parsvanatha, born at Varanasi.

Historically, the north has been divided into many kingdoms, large and small, ruled by various clans and dynasties, some of these patronised Jainism. Mathura and Ujjain developed as great centres of Jainism under the patronage of many rulers stretching over centuries. The evidence of epigraphic remains suggests a strong Jain presence up to the 6th century CE. The Gupta dynasty, though inclined towards Brahminism, patronised Jain scholars. Although Jainism was never as strong in this area as in some parts of the region such as Mathura, Ujjain and Kanoj, it never declined completely, as in some parts of India, because northern rulers were generally sympathetic to it. Even in the Muslim period, many rulers were influenced by Jain ascetics and were sympathetic to the cause of Jainism.

During the Raj, British rule did not actively help to promote Jainism, though indirectly it helped by increasing liberal education and freedom of religion, but the struggle for independence from Britain, in which Mahatma Gandhi so publicly embraced non-violence *(ahimsaa)*, led to a dissemination of Jain values.

In independent secular India, Jainism has revived and the Jain values have been given an impotant place in the life of the nation, and Jainism has been accepted as one of the major religion of India. Under the patronage of the Prime Minister, Indira Gandhi, India celebrated the 2,500th anniversary of Mahavira in 1975. People from all walks of life participated in the head-anointing ceremony of the colossal statue of Bahubali at Sravanabelgola, and many tourists visit Jain temples such as Delwara, Ranakpur and Satrunjay. Some places of pilgrimage have been restored to their formal glory and many new temples are being built throughout India. Jain literature is being made accessible to all through translations into English and Indian languages.

In November 1996 the Prime Minister of the United Kingdom, John Major, visited the Jain Centre in Leicester. These and establishment of Jain Centres in North America are leading to a greater awareness of Jainism outside India. Thus, Jainism is beginning to establish an international dimension, but without active patronage by rulers, in this modern and secular age

POPULAR SUPPORT

Earlier, we described the contribution of ascetics, in the promotion of Jainism. Now we will examine the role played by laymen and laywomen, but there is little historical and biographical material on the lay orders. What follows has been compiled from material scattered throughout Jain literature, but is neither definitive nor exhaustive, and in some instances, the status of individuals mentioned in this section, i.e. whether they were ascetics or laypersons, was not uniformly agreed by the *sangha*.

In the time of Mahavira, Sankha Sataka was head of the laymen's order, and Sulasa and Revati heads of the laywomen. These and many other laypeople strictly adhered to the minor vows and because of their contribution for promotion of Jainism, some, as below, are remembered daily by Jains in the recital of the morning liturgy:

Laymen: Karkandu, Sudarsan Sheth, Vankacul, Salibhadra, Dhanyakumar, Abhaykumara, Ilaciputra, Nandisena.

Laywomen: Sulasa, Revati Manorma, Damyanti, Sita, Nanda, Bhadra, Risidatta, Padmavati, Anjana, Sridevi, Jyestha, Prabhavati, Celana, Rukhmini, Kunti, Devaki, Dropadi, Dharani, Kalavati.

Laypersons have played an important role in building and maintaining temples, *upashrayas*, libraries, welfare institutions and other activities of the *sangha*. They attend to the needs of ascetics and their contribution has kept Jainism vigorous.

The earliest important layperson whom we know by name is *Javadshah*, who, according to the literary record, undertook the thirteenth renovation of the Satrunjay temples in 51 CE. The record is silent for many centuries until we encounter two brothers who were ministers of Gujarat, *Vastupala* and *Tejpa*l. In the 12th century they built the world famous temples of Delwara (Mount Abu), which extended the earlier temple built by *Vimalshah*. These brothers were said to be responsible for building 1,300 temples, 984 *upashrayas*, 700 schools, 3,000 Hindu temples, 700 Hindu monasteries, 64 mosques, 700 *dharmasalas* (boarding houses) for pilgrims and 700 other spiritual centres. They also renovated 2,000 existing temples and provided daily alms to more than 1,500 ascetics. Vastupala's wife *Lalita* and Tejpal's wife *Anupama* were instrumental in motivating the brothers to undertake these works, which demonstrated Jains' care for humanity by the provision of places of worship for all, irrespective of their faith. Their liberalism resulted in a deep friendship with the Muslim ruler of Delhi (Lil-Tutamish). Vastupala wrote many books and 24 honorific titles were bestowed on him. In 1230 CE the brothers undertook a pilgrimage to Satrunjay with 700 Svetambara *aacaaryas*, 100 Digambara *aacaaryas*, 2,100 ascetics and thousands of laypeople.

In the 13th century, under Muslim influence, iconoclastic movements spread through Jain and Hindu communities. This disruption brought misery to many people, which was made worse by a great famine in Gujarat in the reign of king Visaldeva. *Jagdushah*, a wealthy Jain grain merchant, provided food for the entire population during the famine in Gujarat. His generosity also extended to the renovation of many Jain and Hindu temples and the building of a mosque.

Probable contemporaries of Jagdushah, a father and son, *Pethadshah* and *Zanzankumar*, were noted for their devotion to the community, building 84 temples and 74 *upashrayas*. Pethadshah revered the scripture known as the *Bhagavati Sutra* and had it copied and distributed to libraries throughout India. The *Bhagavati Sutra* is a record of thousands of questions put to Mahavira by his chief disciple, Gautama. When this scripture was read publicly Pethadshah gave a gold coin for each question to the *sangha*.

A 13th century minister of King Siladitya of Gujarat, named *Bahadshah*, undertook the fourteenth renovation of the Satrunjay temple with the approval of the king and, after he was wounded in battle, his son *Ambadshah* completed the work.

At this time, Kutubbudin Shah was the Muslim ruler of Delhi. His forces regularly attacked Gujarat, destroying non-Muslim places of worship and encouraging iconoclasm. *Samarsinh*, a Jain, minister in Gujarat successfully co-ordinated the defence of the territory, saving many temples from destruction.

In 1314 CE *Samarashah* carried out the fifteenth renovation of the Satrunjay temple, which had been destroyed by Allauddin Khilji. He undertook five vows (celibacy, eating only once a day, sleeping without a mattress, giving up dairy products and sweet foods, and not shaving). He practised them faithfully until the renovation was completed.

Dharanashah, minister of Rana Kumbha, whose kingdom lay in modern Rajasthan, built the magnificent temple of Ranakpur in 1439 CE. Dharanashah was influenced by the *Aacaarya*s Hiravijay and Somasundar. The temple of Ranakpur is one of the wonders of Jain architecture. It has 1,444 hand-carved sandstone pillars and is one of the best examples of Jain temple building and a major centre of pilgrimage. Extensive renovation has been carried out in the second half of the 20th century by the *Anandji Kalyanji Pedhi* (a trust established to care for the temples and to promote the Jain way of life), under the supervision of *Kasturbhai Lalbhai* of Ahmedabad, a leading Jain philanthropist and expert on Jain heritage. Great care has been exercised to recreate the quality of the original construction.

In 1523 *Karmashah* undertook the sixteenth renovation of the Satrunjay temple, with the consent of the Muslim ruler Bahadurkhan of Delhi and with the help of his local ruler Rana Sangha, whom he served as a minister and who was a Jain sympathiser. Karmashah also obtained an exemption from the toll tax for the Satrunjay temple pilgrims. This temple and its main image *(murti)* of Risabhdeva are in use as a place of worship today. The Anandji Kalyanji Pedhi is currently carrying out restoration work on this edifice. *Shrenik Kasturbhai Lalbhai*, an acknowledged expert on the Jain heritage is involved in this work and has donated generously to the cost of this and many other projects.

Velaka was the finance minister for Rana Kumbha of Cittoda, Rajasthan. He had the famous temple of Cittodagadh constructed in 1448 CE and he secured exemption for the Mount Abu temples' pilgrims from toll tax.

Khema Hadalia is remembered for his generosity in feeding the whole of Gujarat, from his own resources, during an acute famine in 1493 CE. This is in keeping with the Jain teaching that wealth should not be accumulated for reasons of personal aggrandisement, but to help all living beings. The Muslim ruler of Gujarat was surprised at the generosity of this Jain merchant. He honoured him by coining the phrase: 'Ek Bania Shah, Bijo Badshah', meaning 'Bania (merchant) first and the king second' by which he meant that the merchant's generosity had raised him to a status higher than that of the king.

Around the 1590 CE, *Bhamashah*, the Jain minister of Rana Pratap, donated all his wealth to support the struggle of Mewar, Rajasthan, which was seeking to maintain its independence in the face of Akbar the Great's imperial expansion. This philanthrophy allowed Rana Pratap to keep an army in the field for twelve years, during which time he was able to recover most of Mewar from the Muslim invaders.

In 1631 CE, *Dharmadas Shah* built a temple on the Satrunjay hills which houses a fourteen foot high marble image of Adabadji (Risabhdeva). Many noted *aacaaryas*, *upaadhyaayas* and laypeople maintained Jainism's popular appeal through the composition of devotional literature (*pujaa* hymns, rituals etc.) superficially modelled on Vaisnava lines. Among those who wrote devotional compositions are: *Anandaghana*, *Vinaya Vijay*, *Yasho Vijay*, *Jnan Vimal Suri*, *Udayratna* and *Devcandra*; these works helped the Jain community to sustain a feeling of close-knit fellowship and to withstand pressures from revivalist devotional *(bhakti)* Hindu cults.

In the 19th century the British consolidated their rule in India. Bombay became the trading and commercial centre of the country. Many Jain merchants from Gujarat, among them *Amicand*, *Motishah*, *Narsi Natha and Keshavji Nayak* moved to Bombay. They used their new wealth to build temples, animal sanctuaries and other welfare institutions.

In Ahmedabad the families and descendants of wealthy Jains such as *Shantidas Sheth*, *Hemabhai* and *Premabhai* used their resources to promote general education for everyone. Their philanthropic work earned a proud reputation for the Jain community. Jain merchants flourished as textile 'kings' and, in due course made Ahmedabad 'the Manchester of India', and it attracted many creative ascetics and laypersons, among whom are numbered prominent hymn writers. Many Jain laypersons became well known in the latter half of the 19th century, creating international interest in Jains and Jainism.

Rajendrasuri (1827 to 1906 CE) At the age of twenty, he was the first person in the 19th century to be initiated as a *yati*, and at the age of forty years he became Shri Pujya *Yati*. One of his outstanding achievements was to call together an assembly of the Jain community for a public reading of the forty-five canons for the first time in many centuries. Among his own literary works is an encyclopaedic seven-volume dictionary of Prakrit of 9,200 pages and defining 60,000 terms. He organised the mass recitation of the great Jain prayer, the *Namokara Mantra*, at which the *mantra* was chanted over twelve million times. In his lifetime he officiated at the consecration of 1,023 images of *tirthankaras*, established many social welfare institutions, including Jain libraries, and the reformed the institution of the *yatis*.

Virchand Raghavji Gandhi (1864 to 1901 CE) Every Jain feels proud of Virchand Raghavji Gandhi. Gandhi is a common family name in Gujarat, but the various distinguished figures bearing the name are not related. Born in 1864 into a prestigious Gujarati family, he became a highly respected lawyer. He was active in the promotion of religious values and used his legal skills to gain exemption from tolls for the Satrunjay Hill temples, pursuing the case through the courts. He took on the Government in a case involving a proposal to build a factory near the pilgrimage site of Sammeta Sikhar in Bihar. This factory would have processed pig fat, contrary to Jain teachings not to commit acts of violence to living beings. As a result of his action, the factory project was shelved. He was politically active, participating in the National Freedom Movement against the British Raj, he represented Bombay at the Indian National Congress in Poona, and also represented Asia at an International Commerce Convention.

At the insistence of *Aacaarya* Vijayanand Suri, he represented Jainism at the Parliament of World Religions in 1893, undertaking extensive scholarly preparation for this event. He made such an impression on the international gathering that he was asked to deliver further lectures, which resulted in his staying for two more years in America, and then a year in the United Kingdom. He travelled abroad to speak about Jainism on two other occasions, reputedly he gave some 535 foreign lectures on Jainism and Indian philosophy. He gave courses on Jainism and attracted many followers outside India, and societies to promote interest in Jainism and Jain culture were founded by non-Jains in the United Kingdom and United States. He was awarded silver and gold medals for his lectures; all of which have been published and which, even today, are recognised for their substance and quality. Mahatma Gandhi held Virchand Raghavji Gandhi in great regard and corresponded regularly with him. It was a cause of great sadness that such an illustrious man died at the young age of 37 and Jains will long remember him with affection and admiration. A century after he attended the first Parliament of World Religions, he was remembered at the second Parliament in Chicago in 1993 with great respect and regard. He exemplified the best in the religious, national, political and literary life of India and Jains will always regard him with pride.

Srimad Racandra (1867 to 1901 CE)   In a short life of a mere 34 years Srimad Rajcandra achieved greatness and left behind him the memory of a very great soul and an example which many have been inspired to follow. Srimad Rajhandra was born in Vavania (Gujarat) in 1867 CE, educated in local schools and married at the age of 20 to Zabakbai, a jeweller's daughter. He was extraordinarily intelligent and early in life he had mastered at least five languages. As his father's family was devotees of the Vaisnava Hindu tradition, it was from his mother that he learned about Jainism. It was his mother's practice of traditional Jain rituals such as the twice-daily peni-tence *(pratikramana)* which attracted him to the Jain view of life and spirituality. He found Jain practice to be the best means of happiness; he became a Jain in thought and action, and he remained such to the end of his life. As a result of his obvious inner spiritual knowledge and his excel-lent oratorical skills, people flocked to him for guidance in their spiritual quest. Such was his spiritual strength that he could overcome normal human physical desires such as hunger for many days at a time, and although his physical body became emaciated, people remarked that his spirituality glowed in his face.

In addition to his skills as an orator, he was a poet, writer, translator, scriptural commentator and an impressive letter writer. Of the more than two dozen books which he wrote, *Atmasiddhi*, *Pravacanmala*, *Moksamala*, *Puspamala*, and *Bhavanabdh* have achieved considerable popularity. These books and about 800 of his letters have been published and some have been translated into foreign languages, including English.

He had immense powers of concentration and memory *(avadhaan)*. People would gather to witness his skill. An example of this was his ability to accept a hundred unconnected, random questions and then to answer them correctly in any order, merely by being given the number of the ques-tion, which is why he was known as the person with the 'hundred-fold memory' *(sataavadhaani)*. His spiritual teachings won him a wide following, including many ascetics, who call him the 'true teacher' *(krupaludeva* or *sadguru)*. They have since organised a chain of institutions called 'temples of knowledge' *(jnaana mandir)* throughout the world for the promotion of his Jain teachings.

He has become best known as the spiritual mentor of Mahatma Gandhi, who met him in 1891 after Gandhi had been in England studying law. The timing of this encounter was significant, for Gandhi was facing a personal spiritual crisis, was uncertain of his faith, and considering conversion to

Christianity. Srimad Rajcandra gave Gandhi an anchor in the values of Indian religious traditions, and it was Rajcandra's example which led Gandhi to follow the way of 'non-violence' *(ahimsaa)*, utilising it as the main weapon with which to win independence for India. Throughout his life Rajcandra expressed the truths which arose from his spiritual life, and those who were close to him knew that they were in the presence of a great soul. He died in 1901 at Rajkot (Gujarat).

Kanji Swami (1889 to 1980 CE) Born in Gujarat in 1889, Kanji Swami was initiated as a Sthanakvasi ascetic at the age of 24. The depth of knowledge and his speaking skills were such that he was honoured with the title of the 'mountain of light' *(koh-i-noor)* of Kathiawar. During his scriptural studies he was highly impressed by the 'Essence of Doctrines' *(Samaya Saara)* of Kundakunda, which led him to study the books of Banarasidas, Todarmal and Rajchandra. He felt the 'soul-oriented' Digambara path was the true path. In 1934, he proclaimed himself a Digambar layperson and began preaching Kundakunda's teaching.

Gradually, the number of his followers, both Svetambaras and Digambaras, grew to many thousands. His sermons encouraged his followers to adopt a habit of regular personal study and the distribution of Jain literature, and they impressed upon his followers the teaching that rituals and attire have no meaning without a proper understanding and the right frame of mind.

Many remarkable incidents have been associated with him, which illustrate his charismatic personality. His followers have popularised the devotional doctrine of the 'Living *Tirthankara* of Mahaavideha' (Simandhar Swami). Jain geography describes *Mahaavideha* as a continent of the Jambudvipa region, where humans live and where there is always at least one living *tirthankara* and Simandhar Swami is one of the present living *tirthankaras* on this continent.

The main centres for the propagation of Kanji Swami's teachings today are Songadh in Gujarat and Jaipur in Rajasthan, though there are outposts in Nairobi, London and the United States. Kanji Swami died in 1980 in Bombay.

Jains have remained a respected community in India. They have contributed significantly to Indian culture and heritage, and are well known for their philanthropic and welfare activities, for animals as well as people. Jain values are highly regarded and attract support from Jains as well as from the wider community.

It is impossible within the limits of this work to give an exhaustive list of all those who have supported Jain causes. Such a list would embrace many prominent figures in Indian society, and in the extensive diaspora around the world.

The Jain laity have been prominent in the economic life of India and many great industrial, commercial and financial undertakings are in Jain hands. Jain industrialists, merchants and financiers are now, as in the past, accustomed to using their wealth and influence in projects for the benefit of society and the promotion of Jain values.

DECLINE AND REVIVAL

Jainism is one of the oldest religions in the world, but like other living faiths, it has undergone many phases of growth and decline during its long history. In this chapter we will briefly describe the pattern of growth and decline in India and summarise the main factors influencing the changing fortunes of the Jain community.

Bihar was formerly the heartland of Jainism, but one does not find large numbers of indigenous Jains there today, although in recent times, some Jains have migrated to the area for reasons connected with business. There is, however, in part of Bihar a sizable number of Saraaka Jains, followers of Parsvanatha, who have remained outside the Jain mainstream, but who have recently experienced a revival. The lack of an indigenous Jain community in Bihar can be attributed to a combination of declining royal support, persecutions, and hardship caused by famines, which led to the migration of ascetics and laypersons to other parts of India. Once an area is without ascetics, it becomes very difficult to sustain a viable Jain community in the long term and as expected conversion to Hinduism became commonplace. Although, from time to time, the political situation improved, Bihar remained an area with a small Jain population, despite the presence of significant holy places.

The Jains of neighbouring Bengal and Orissa faced a situation similar to that of their co-religionists in Bihar: political turmoil resulting in a decline in the Jain population after the 8th century CE. The south of India also was a stronghold of Jainism until about the 8th century CE when political suppression was inflicted upon the Jain populations in Tamilnad, Andhra and Kerala. Karnataka remained a strong Jain centre until the 12th century CE; although here, Jain political influence went into decline. By contrast, although the situation was never entirely stable, the areas of Gujarat and Rajasthan maintained their position as strong centres of Jainism.

It is worth reminding ourselves that despite the situation described above, the superb organisation of the Jain community into the four-fold order founded by Mahavira, has kept Jainism as a living religion in practically all parts of India. The orders of ascetics and laypersons established the Jains securely in Indian society and culture, unlike the Buddhists who failed to develop such a structure and eventually disappeared from their land of origin. With its four-fold order firmly anchored amongst the people and with ascetics serving the spiritual needs of the lay orders, Jainism withstood the storm that drove Buddhism out of India.

Although the numbers of the Jain community have declined over later centuries, many non-Jains sympathise with Jain values and follow Jain practices. The teachings of Mahavira still have a relevance to the world today, indeed, some would even argue that they are more necessary today than in the past. The celebrations of the 2,500th anniversary of Mahavira's *moksa* benefited Jainism. Its values are more widely and better understood now, and there are signs that the decline in numbers of active Jains has ended. There is growing activity in the academia, publishing literature, creation of new Jain institutions, developing inter-faith relations, and a general sense of unity and purpose throughout the community.

It would be instructive to look at a schematic representation of Jain history, the factors that have affected the fortunes of the community, its strength, its decline, and its present day revival

The Main Factors in the Growth of Jainism

- Ascetics were able to exert a significant influence on merchants, the key classes of Indian society and royal dynasties.
- There is a uniformity of practice for ascetics and laity, only differing by degree.
- Jainism is inherently tolerant, as it believes in 'relative pluralism'.
- Jainism teaches equality for all irrespective of caste, creed, colour or gender.
- Jainism has exhibited the capacity to adapt to different times and environments.
- Jainism has always had respect for other faiths.
- Jainism uses the vernacular languages for scripture and sermons.
- Jainism applies 'non-violence' *(ahimsaa)* to all realms of personal and social life.
- Jains have earned a reputation for honesty, truthfulness, and loyalty; they have demonstrated their philanthropy by the provision of food, shelter, education and medical care to all in need.
- Jainism has benefited from effective and dedicated religious and secular leadership.
- Jainism developed a coherent interdependent four-fold order *(sangha)*.

The Main Factors in the Decline of Jainism

- Persecution (and fear of persecution) resulting from changes in political circumstances in the medieval period, including conversion to Hinduism among ruling elites.

- Periodic dominance of other religions and proselytising by them in India.
- Growth in the popularity of rituals at the expense of the practice of Jain values in daily life.
- Laxity in the practice of Right Conduct among ascetics and laity.
- Lack of worthy and inspiring scholars, ascetics and leaders in the medieval period.
- Lack of central infrastructure and leadership.
- Fragmentation of Jainism into sects and sub-groups, leading to a lack of common purpose and understanding among different groups of Jains.
- Lack of infrastructure for training ascetics, scholars and community leaders to the needs of the sangha in modern times.
- Lack of academic education, use of media and modern technology for the promotion of Jain values.

THE SCHISMS

It is a commonplace that living religions only survive and progress through being adaptable and undergoing change. Among the changes which religions often experience are schisms, and the Jain *sangha* is no exception to this. From what we know of the history of the Jain religion up to the time of Mahavira, it seems that no sects or sub-sects had emerged, yet later, they did emerge and, as a result, Jainism became irreconcilably divided into many sects. Why did this happen?

During the lifetime of Mahavira Jainism's extent was limited and it seems not to have penetrated beyond the boundaries of the kingdoms of Anga and Magadha, which comprise modern Bihar, Orissa and West Bengal. After the death of Mahavira, his successors and followers succeeded in extending the Jain influence throughout the whole of India, among the ruling classes as well as the people. Once this occurred, Jainism encountered a wide range of customs, languages, manners and ways of life which prevailed in different parts of the Indian sub-continent. Over time, these encounters gave rise to changes in religious practices and, more importantly, in beliefs. Ultimately, this resulted in variations in the form of Jainism which inevitably was to become a source of conflict and, with the successful spread of Jainism throughout India, the religious leaders found it increasingly difficult to foster and organise their widely-dispersed community.

The situation in which variations of practice and belief were appearing was aggravated by the lack of agreed authoritative scriptures. As the religious doctrines, principles and tenets of Jainism were not committed to writing during the lifetime of Mahavira, his religious teachings were memorised by his immediate successors and handed down from one generation to next, and were not finally canonised until the council of Valabhi in 453 or 466 CE. Even then, the decisions of the Valabhi council were not acceptable to all, as some maintained that the canon did not contain the actual teachings of Mahavira. Long before Valabhi, differences of opinion had arisen regarding the interpretation of many tenets and these disagreements had led to the establishment of separate schools of thought, which eventually crystalised into sects and sub-sects.

From Mahavira to Shayyambhava the *sangha* was led by only one *aacaarya*, but Yasobhadra introduced the system of two *aacaaryas* in 205 BCE. This seperation of the leadership may have been felt necessary due to the geographical spread of Jainism, however, it would not be unreasonable to conclude that it contributed to the development of schismatic tendencies in the community.

Early Jain literature notes seven minor schismatic 'schools', although these failed to generate substantive divisions in the community, but it was an eighth schism which became prominent in the 1st century CE and led to an irreconcilable division in Jain community. The two groups, the result of this schism, are known as Svetambaras and Digambaras, a division well documented in the historical sources, but the schism, which originated during the 4th century BCE became consolidated by the 1st century of the Common Era.

According to one account, in the fourth century BCE, *Aacaarya* Bhadrabahu realised that a long and severe famine was imminent in the kingdom of Magadha. In order to avoid its terrible effects, he and thousands of ascetics migrated from Pataliputra, the capital of Magadha, to Sravanbelgola (in the modern state of Karnataka) in southern India. Candragupta Maurya abdicated his throne in favour of his son Bindusara, joined Bhadrabahu's entourage as a-disciple, and resided with him at Sravanbelgola. Candragupta lived for twelve years after the death of his teacher and died according to the strict Jain ritual of *sallekhanaa* on the hill at Sravanbelgola; his 'holy death' is a tradition strongly supported by highly reliable epigraphic and literary evidence.

When the ascetics of the Bhadrabahu *sangha* eventually returned to Pataliputra after a twelve-year absence, they found two significant changes that had taken place among the ascetics of Magadha under the leadership of *Aacaarya* Sthulabhadra. First, the rule requiring ascetics to wear no garments had been relaxed, instead, ascetics wore a simple piece of white cloth; second, a council had been convened at Pataliputra with the intention of editing the canon of Jain literature. This council was the first of five councils, which were to undertake the work of editing the Jain canon over subsequent centuries, a process that was to be the focus of much disagreement.

The group of returned ascetics did neither accept the change to the wearing of garment, nor were they agreed upon the proposals of the Pataliputra council regarding scripture, rather they proclaimed themselves as the 'true' followers of Mahavira. Eventually, the Jain *sangha* split into two distinct sects: the Digambara and the Svetambara.

This is the traditional account of the schism, but it is not universally accepted. According to the modern German scholar Hermann Jacobi, the separation of the *sangha* took place gradually and, he maintains, there was and is little difference in their articles of faith. With the passage of time, the attitudes and approaches of the two sects began to harden and distinctive sectarian outlooks arose.

The Digambara and Svetambara Sects

There are no fundamental doctrinal differences between these two main Jain sects and both accept as canonical the major sacred text by Umasvati known as the *Tattvartha Sutra*. The differences between the two groups are described here:

Digambaras insist upon their ascetics going unclothed (sky-clad) as an absolute pre-requisite of the mendicant's path and the attainment of salvation, but the Svetambaras assert that the practice of complete nudity is not essential to attain liberation. The dispute centres upon the question of whether the possession of an item of clothing signifies *attachment* to that garment. The Digambaras assert that attachment is implied and therefore reject clothing, but the Svetambaras refer to the example of Parsvanatha's disciples, who wore clothing, to defend their view.

Digambaras believe that women lack both the physical and mental strength necessary to attain liberation; hence women must be reborn as men before such attainment is possible, but the Svetambaras hold the view that men and women are equally capable of attaining liberation; in the Svetambara tradition the nineteenth *tirthankara*, Malli(natha), was a woman.

Digambaras, believe once someone becomes omniscient, he (not she) has no need of food; Svetambaras believe that, as even an omniscient still has a body, it is necessary to continue to feed it.

Svetambaras believe that Mahavira was born of a *ksatriya* woman, Trisala, although conception took place in the womb of a Brahmin, Devananda. The 'migration' of the embryo from one woman's body to another is believed to have been effected on the order of the deity Indra, on the eighty-third day after conception, but Digambaras, dismiss the whole episode as unreliable and absurd.

Svetambaras believe that Mahavira married Princess Yasoda at a young age, and that they had a daughter named Priyadarsana, Digambaras do not accept that he was married.

The Svetambara tradition depicts images of *tirthankaras* wearing loin-cloths and jewels, the images have eyes inserted made of a variety of materials, Digambaras represent images of *tirthankaras* as unclad, unadorned and with eyes downcast in contemplative mood.

Svetambaras believe in the validity and sacredness of the collection of forty-five canonical texts, and they have been accepted over many centuries; Digambaras dispute the validity of the Svetambara canon, holding that many original and genuine texts were lost over the centuries.

Svetambaras regard the records of the great Jain personages of the past as 'biographies'; Digambaras prefer the term 'legends' for these accounts.

Svetambara ascetics live on food given freely to them by householders in the community. As they go from house to house and collect their food, they use bowls and similar vessels to contain food and may eat more than one meal in a day; ascetics, as well as observant Jain laypeople, eat only in daylight hours. In contrast, Digambara ascetics eat a single dish from just one house each day, and receive food in their cupped, upturned hands.

In principle, ascetics renounce possessions. However, the practicalities of life and religious ritual do allow some concessions: the Svetambara ascetics are allowed up to fourteen possessions including items such as a loincloth and shoulder-cloth; Digambara ascetics are allowed only two possessions: a whiskbroom made from peacock feathers and a wooden water-pot. Both sects allow ascetics to carry scriptures.

Differences between the sects over rituals, customs and manners are trivial and do not play a spiritually significant role. Until the middle of the 15th century CE all members of both sects were image worshippers, after which iconoclastic and some other influences led to the emergence of offshoots which ceased to worship images. Most scholars agree that Digambaras embrace a more severe ascetic life and are conservative with regard to doctrine. Svetambaras are more 'liberal', pragmatic and concerned with maximising the influence of Jainism throughout society. It is this attitude which has led Svetambaras to play an important role in shaping large areas of the culture, history, politics and economic development of India.

During the medieval period subdivisions arose among both sects: differences in the interpretation of religious texts, the observance of rituals, and discontent over authoritarian trends in religious leadership were among the contributory factors. While Jains were characterised by a strong spiritual discipline, political pressures and religious fervour led many towards forms of ritualism as a means of counteracting Hindu devotional (*bhakti*) movements.

In the course of time some in the community became disillusioned with ritualism and turned away from the established temples and its rituals.

They saw the conduct of the temple 'authorities' as without merit. Increasing Muslim influence brought with it iconoclastic trends and encouraged the growth of non-image worship in both Jain sects, leading to yet further internal subdivisions.

Digambara Sects

Bisapantha The followers of Bisapantha (Twenty-fold Path) support the institutions of *bhattarakas*, worship the images of the *tirthankaras* and of the heavenly beings *(ksetrapala, padmavati)* and other guardian deities. They worship these images with offerings such as saffron, flowers, fruits, sweets and incense sticks, and while performing these acts of worship, the Bisapanthis sit on the ground. They proffer the flame in the temple *(aarati)*, and distribute to other worshippers the gifts offered to the deities *(prasaada)*. The Bisapantha, according to some, is the original form of the Digambara sect and today practically all Digambara Jains from Maharashtra, Karnataka and south India, together with a large number of Digambara Jains from Rajasthan and Gujarat, are Bisapantha.

Terapantha The Terapantha (Thirteen-fold Path or Your Path) movement arose in northern India in the year 1626 CE as a result of dissatisfaction with the domination and conduct of the *bhattarakas*, and are most numerous in Uttar Pradesh, Rajasthan and Madhya Pradesh (There is also an unrelated major Svetambara sect of the same name, discussed below). In their temples, the Terapanthas install only the images of *tirthankaras*, worship images with dried materials, for example: sacred white rice and rice coloured with sweet-smelling sandalwood paste, cloves, sandalwood, almonds, dry coconuts and dates. They avoid using flowers and fruits, which are regarded as living, whereas the dried products are not; and as as a rule, they do not perform *aarati* nor distribute *prasaada* in their temples. The Terapanthas are reformers, opposed to some ritual practices, which they do not accept as authentic.

Taranapantha The Taranapantha takes its name from its founder Tarana Svami or Tarana-tarana Svami (1448 to 1515 CE) and this sub-sect is also called the Samaiya-Pantha as its followers worship sacred books *(Samaya Saara)* and not images. Tarana Svami died at Malharagarth, Vidisha in Madhya Pradesh, which is the central place of pilgrimage for the Taranapanthis.

Taranapanthis have scripture-halls in which they keep their sacred books for worship, but besides the scriptures common to all Digambaras, they regard as sacred the fourteen books written by their founder Tarana Svami. They attach great importance to inward spiritual practices, such as meditation and the study of sacred literature, and as a result of this emphasis, they practise little outward religious ritual. Tarana Svami was religiously 'liberal', even by Jain satandards, and welcomed all, including Muslims and low-castes into the sect. The Taranapanthis are few in numbers and they are mainly found in Madhya Pradesh and Maharashtra.

Gumanapantha   The Gumanapantha is a numerically small sub-sect about which very little is known, and it was founded by Pandit Gumani Rama or Gumani Rai, a son of the Jain scholar Pandit Todaramal. According to this pantha, the lighting of lamps in the Jain temples is violation of *ahimsaa*, and hence they do not perform *aarati*. Gumanapanthas revere the images in their temples but do not make offerings to them.

Totapantha   The Totapantha came into existence as a result of differences between the Bisapantha and Terapantha sub-sects. Many sincere efforts were made to strike a compromise between the Bisa (i.e. twenty) pantha and the Tera (i.e. thirteen) pantha. The surprisingly (or not surprisingly) arithmetical outcome gave the Jain world the *sadhe solaha* (i.e. sixteen and a half) pantha or 'Totapantha', whose followers believe in some doctrines of the Bisapantha and some of the Terapantha. This sub-sect is little in number and is found only in parts of Madhya Pradesh.

Kanjipantha   In recent years, a new Digambara sub-sect known as Kanjipantha, followers of Kanji Svami, has been formed and is growing in popularity, especially among the educated. Kanji Svami, a Svetambara Sthanakvasi ascetic, left the Svetambaras to become a Digambara layperson. He succeeded in popularising the ancient sacred texts of *Aacaarya* Kundakunda, which stressed an idealistic position, rather than the practical observances of daily religious life. The influence of the Kanjipantha is steadily increasing and Songadh in Gujarat and Jaipur in Rajasthan have become the sub-sect's centres of religious activity; both Digambaras and Svetambaras have been attracted to the Kanjipantha. There are Kanjipantha temples in Nairobi and in London.

Svetambara Sects

Murtipujaka   While it is not clear when the worship of images of the tirthankaras first began, it is the case that from earliest times all Svetambaras were image-worshippers; the majority of Jains are Svetambara *Murtipujaka* (image worshippers). The followers of this tradition are also known by terms such as *Deraavaasi*, *Caityavaasi* (both mean 'temple residents'), *Mandirmargi* ('temple goers') or *Pujera* ('worshippers').

They make ritual offerings including flowers and saffron paste to their images and they adorn them with rich clothes and jewelled ornaments. Rice, fruit, incense and sweet items are also offered during prayers. Both in India and outside, such edible items are not used by the Jains, but are given to the temple employees or distributed to the needy. *Murtipujak* worshippers cover their mouths when washing, anointing or touching the images and perform *aarati*. Their ascetics also cover their mouths with a *muhapatti* (mouth kerchief) while speaking; this is otherwise kept in the hand. The purpose of this practice is to avoid harm to airborne microscopic life.

Svetambaras reside in all parts of India, especially in large urban centres where they are engaged in modern businesses, though the largest populations are found in Gujarat, Maharashtra and Rajasthan. Many have migrated abroad and settled successfully in countries as diverse as the United Kingdom, Belgium, the United States, East Africa, the Far East, and even Israel.

Sthanakvasi Although now generally counted among the Svetambaras, the Sthanakvasis (hall dwellers) arose originally as reformers among the Lonka sect of Jainism. Lonkasaha, a well-read merchant of Ahmedabad, founded the Lonka sect in 1460 CE. The main reform instituted by this sect was a rejection of image worship. Later, members of the Lonka sect, led by Lavaji Rishi, disapproving of the lax way of life of Lonka ascetics, insisted upon reform based more closely upon the teachings and example of Mahavira.

A Lonka sect layman, Viraji of Surat, received initiation as a *yati* and won great admiration for the strictness of his asceticism, and many devotees of the Lonka sect followed Viraji's example. They took the name Sthanakvasis, meaning those, whose religious activities are not in temples but in places known as *sthanaks* or prayer halls. They are also known as 'searchers' *(dhundhiya)* and 'followers of ascetics' *(saadhumaargis)*. Except on the crucial point of image worship, Sthanakvasis do not greatly differ from other Svetambara *Murtipujaka* Jains.

What differences occur between the Sthanakvasi and the *Murtipujaka* Svetambaras in the observance of religious practices, are minor for example the ascetics of the Sthanakvasi always keep their mouths covered with a *muhapatti*. The Sthanakvasi admit the authenticity of only thirty-two of the forty-five scriptures of the Svetambaras; they reject the practice of pilgrimage and do not participate in the religious rituals or festivals of *Murtipujaka* Svetambaras. In practice today, many Sthanakvasi do partake in these religious activities. The Sthanakvasis are found in major business centres in India but most live in Gujarat, Punjab, Haryana, Rajasthan and Maharashtra and some have settled outside India.

Terapanthi This sub-sect arose among the Sthanakvasi. It was founded by *Muni* Bhikhanji (later on known as *Aacaarya* Bhiksu), formerly a Sthanakvasi holy man who was initiated by his guru, *Aacaarya* Raghunatha. He had differences of opinion with his guru on several aspects of Sthanakvasi ascetic practices and when these differences took a serious turn, he founded the Terapantha in 1760 CE. As Bhikhanaji stressed thirteen religious principles: five major vows, five carefulnesses and three guards, his sub-sect was named as the Tera (thirteen) pantha.

The Terapanthis are non-image worshippers and are well organised under the direction of a single *aacaarya*. In its history of little more than 200 years, the sect has had only ten *aacaarya*s from the first (founder) *Aacaarya* Bhiksu to *Aacaarya* Mahaprajna, who took office, in 1994. The ninth *Aacaarya* Tulsi was given the special title of 'head of the group of ascetics' *(ganaadhipati)*, in appreciation of his services to the sub-sect.

This practice of having a single *aacaarya* is a characteristic feature of this sub-sect. Ascetics and female ascetics of the Terapantha follow the instructions of their *aacaarya* scrupulously. They observe a remarkable annual festival known as Maryaadaa Mahotsava (festival of the restrainment) where all ascetics and lay disciples, male and female, meet together at one place and discuss the events of the past year and plans for the future.

The Terapanthis are considered reformists who believe in simplicity, for example, they do not construct monasteries for their ascetics, who inhabit part of the home of ordinary householders, instead their efforts are directed towards two activities: meditation and the literary work of translating and interpreting the scriptures. Like Sthanakvasi ascetics they also wear a *muhupatti*.

Aacaarya Tulsi promoted the *anuvrata* movement ('minor vow') that attempts to utilise the Jain spiritual teachings for the moral improvement of the whole population. Terapanthis have established a world-wide peace and 'non-violent action' organisation and a university, the Jain Vishva Bharati, which has achieved provisional recognition by the Indian government.

The Terapanthis are growing in number, and though they are present in many cities in India, they are mainly concentrated in Rajasthan. They are progressive in thought and action: recently they have developed a semi-ascetic group *(samana* and *samani)* among their followers, who are permitted to use modern transport, travel overseas, and cook in emergencies. The (male) *samanas* and (female) *samanis* visit the West regularly and undertake the propagation of Jainism and the message of their founder *Aacaarya* Tulsi.

Minor Divisions of Murtipujakas

From about a century prior to Hemcandra, we find the evidence of Svetambara divisions. These groups, called *gacchas* comprised the followers of leading ascetics. The *gacchas* evolved from the 11th to the 13th centuries, and reputedly eighty-four *gacchas* were formed; however, most *gacchas* did not survive their founders and some would have amalgamated. Today most Svetambaras of Gujarat and Rajasthan belong to the following three *gacchas*: the *Kharataragaccha, Tapaagaccha* and *Ancalagaccha*. Each *gaccha* has its own temples, ascetics and *aacaaryas*.

Kharataragaccha   There is no reliable history of the formation of this group, though epigraphic evidence suggest that it was formed before 1090 CE, the evidence is taken from the special residences for ascetics, a feature of many towns in those days. One legend claims that *Aacaarya* Jinesvara Suri defeated the temple-dwelling ascetics *(caityavaasis)* in a religious debate at the court of King Durlabharaja of Anahilavada in 1022 CE, winning thereby the title of 'person of bold character' *(kharatara)*. Another legend says that this group was started by Jinadatta Suri in 1147 CE. A third variant of the story holds that it was started by Jinavallabha Suri. This *gaccha* is very popular in Gujarat and Rajasthan. It is known for establishing socio-religious institutions, called *dadawadis* or *dadabaris* in major cities of India.

Tapaagaccha   The legend about the origin of this group is that *aacaarya* Jagacchandra Suri, had earned the epithet 'austere' *(tapa)* in 1228 CE from King Jaitrasinha of Mewar for his severe austerities. Thereafter his disciples and followers have been called *Tapaagaccha.* The members of this, the largest *gaccha*, are found all over India but largely in Gujarat, Rajasthan, Maharashtra, Punjab and Haryana.

Ancalagaccha   The ascetics of this group use a small strip of cloth *(ancala)* in place of a full *muhapatti* to cover their mouth at the time of daily penitential ritual, thus they take the name *Ancalagaccha*. Also known as the 'upholders of sacred rituals' *(vidhipaksha)*, it is said to have been formed in 1156 CE in Northern India. There are very few members of this group.

In spite of these divisions, all Jains believe in the same basic principles and philosophy, and for many years they have sought to celebrate major functions together and to promote the teachings of Mahavira. Some differences, however, remain between Svetambara and Digambara Murtipujaka groups, largely concerned with the ownership of certain temples and places of pilgrimage.

JAIN MIGRATION ABROAD

Indian sacred geography specifies two regions of the human world: the *aarya* and the *anaarya*. The *aarya* lands are the places where the higher spiritual way of life is practised, while in the *anaarya* regions, more materialistic forms of society prevail. These traditional texts regard a large part of India as *aarya* and the rest of the world as *anaarya*, but for the purpose of our discussion here, we call India as 'home' to the Jains and other countries as 'abroad'.

Jain history records how, in the past, prominent personages went abroad, often as missionaries to disseminate Jain teachings. *Aacaaryas*

Bhadrabahu and Sthulabhadra both travelled to Nepal. Kalyan Muni left India with Alexander the Great and journeyed throughout the Greek Empire. Kalakaacaarya II travelled to South East Asia, while Vajraswami visited other parts of Asia, and King Samprati sent missionaries to promote Jainism. For many centuries Jain traders have ventured abroad and acted as 'ambassadors' for Jainism through their distinctive lifestyle. The trading communities were the first emigrants, but little is known about these settlers, although some remnants of Jain culture are found in Asian lands, and in Greece, Russia and elsewhere.

A later wave of Jain migration begins in the second half of the 19th century. With economic opportunities becoming available in British colonial territories, many Jain families moved abroad, mainly to Africa, seeking to improve their standard of living. They settled in large numbers in Zanzibar, Tanganyika, Kenya, Uganda, South Africa and Fiji. Zanzibar saw the establishment of the earliest Jain community in Africa, and two beautiful temples were constructed, but fear of persecution forced many Jains to leave Zanzibar and migrate to other parts of East Africa. In time, they established substantial and characteristically elaborate temples in places like Mombasa, Nairobi and Dar-es-Salaam, and created other institutions such as *upashrayas* (meeting halls for religious observance) and *paathasaalaas* (daily religious schools for children). The temples at Mombasa and Nairobi have become major places of pilgrimage as well as tourist attractions. The Jain community is widely regarded as enterprising and hard working, their ideals of a simple life and philanthropy have led them to contribute to the education and welfare services for Jains and non-Jains alike. They have become active in trade and in practically all the important professions in the countries where they have settled.

The 20th century has seen increasing migration of Jains to the 'West', including Jain preachers and teachers, but migration from India to Africa and Asia also continued. From about the turn of the century onward, important preachers who travelled to the West included persons such as Virchand Raghavji Gandhi, Campatray Jain and J. L. Jaini. As we have already noted, Virchand Gandhi established two Jain societies in the United States and a Jain literature society in the United Kingdom (which closed for lack of resources). Campatray Jain and J. L. Jaini contributed to this society in its early days and also provided Jain literature for the public library at Bad Godesberg in Germany, support which still continues through the World Jain Mission in Aliganj, India.

There have been Jain migrants to the United Kingdom from India and East Africa, almost all in the second half of the twentieth century; eventually, communities became organised in major urban centres, including London, Leicester, Manchester and Birmingham. It is estimated that there are about 30,000 Jains in the United Kingdom, approximately 25,000 in

London, 1,000 in Leicester and 500 in each of the cities of Manchester and Birmingham. By the mid 1990s, the community could muster 28 organisations, three of which are of particular importance: the Jain Samaj Europe, the Oshwal Association of the United Kingdom and the Navnat Vanik Association (UK). Young Jains have also organised themselves and are working to promote Jain values, including vegetarianism.

Typical of Jain activity in the United Kingdom since the 1980s is the establishment of places of worship and community activities. The Oshwal Association has estabished an Oshwal Centre comprising a temple and two modern purpose-built halls with dining facilities, in an attractive setting at Potters Bar, Hertfordshire, just north of London. The Navnat Vanik Association has acquired a communal property in Harrow, close to areas where large numbers of Jains reside. The Jain Samaj Europe has established a Jain Centre in the city of Leicester. This centre is a major symbol of Jain unity, the first centre of its kind to embody co-operation among Jain groups by including in one building a Svetambara temple, a Digambara temple, a Guru Gautama *mandir*, a Sthanakvasi *upashraya* and a Shrimad Rajchandra *jnaana mandir*. Its fine Jain architecture, including elaborate interior and exterior carvings, has made it a major tourist attraction and place of pilgrimage for Jains. The Jain Samaj Europe has published books and a journal on Jainism. Jains are seeking to widen their activities through the creation of 'inter-faith' links such as the Jain-Christian Association, the Jain-Jewish Association and the Leicestershire Ahimsa Society for the Care of Nature.

Jains are increasing their involvement with academic institutions through the Jain Academy, founded in 1991. The academic year 1994 saw the launch of the first undergraduate courses offered as part of an U.K. University degree programme. Based at the De Montfort University in Leicester, students are able to pursue studies in Jain history, literature, languages, society, philosophy and religion. Jain Academy has also taken its first steps to forge international links and a 'Jain Academy Educational and Research Centre' has been set up in the Department of Philosophy at Bombay University.

Jains have been involved in the production and trade of gemstones for a long time. This has led Jains taking an active role in the modern international gem and diamond trading community, with Jain diamond dealers in London, New York, Antwerp, Tel Aviv, South Africa and India. Jain diamond traders have won major export awards both in India and Israel. Jain scholars are made welcome in these places, and these unique 'niche' business communities are actively involved in philanthropic work..

Jain Associations exist in Germany and many Jain scholars have visited and given lectures in its universities.A number of Germans have adopted Jain way of life.

Figure 2.1 The Jain Centre, Leicester, England

Jains have also migrated to Australia, and a Jain Society has been formed in Sidney. Japan has a Jain community in Kobe, with its own Jain organisation and a magnificent temple. There are Jains in Hongkong, Bangkok, Singapore, Nepal, Pakistan, Bangladesh and other places in Asia. Jains are found in the Middle East in countries such as Aden, Dubai, Egypt and Israel, but at the time of writing, restrictions in many Islamic countries prevent Jains, and members of other non-Muslim religions, openly practise their religion.

After the Second World War a large number of Jain professionals, academics, business people and students travelled to the United States of America and Canada, where many eventually settled. In the mid-1990s it was estimated that there were more than 50,000 Jains in North America. Jains have established 55 Jain societies and Jain Centres, some include temples, for social, religious, youth and womens activities, involving worship, lectures and discussions, festivals and rituals, performing arts, such as dance and drama on religious themes. To co-ordinate the activities of the various Jain centres in North America, Jains established in 1981, the Federation of Jain Associations in North America, which had more than 6,000 participants in their ninth bi-annual convention in 1997. North America has also seen academic, literary, internet and youth activities to promote Jain way of life.

The Jain migration abroad has brought Jainism to the attention of the world outside India; Jains have settled extremely well in many places, but are anxious to retain and promote their culture and way of life. There are, however, only two of the four orders of the *sangha* outside India: laymen and laywomen, because the vows of the ascetics would not permit them to use a vehicle to travel. A project a few years ago for a leading Jain ascetic to travel on foot overland to Europe had to be abandoned owing to unfore-

Plate 2.3 Pro vice-chancellor of De Montfort University, Leicester, England, receives Jain texts for the university library from officials of the Jain Academy

Plate 2.4 Dr L.M. Singhvi, High Commissioner of India in the UK, inaugurates the Jain Academy Education and Research Centre at Bombay University, December 1995. With him are Vice-Chancellors of Bombay University and the Chairman of the Jain Academy

seen circumstances. Thus, the guiding force of the orders of ascetics is absent outside India and this has provided both a challenge and an opportunity for Jains to consider the implications for the modern Jain 'diaspora' and the future forms of the *sangha*.

JAINS IN THE TWENTIETH CENTURY

The *Kalpa Sutra*, an important Jain scripture, composed several centuries before the common era, contains a prediction that Jainism would decline, only to undergo a revival 2,500 years after the time of Mahavira. Interestingly, we find that the 20th century is proving to be a period of growth for Jainism around the world. This century has also seen considerable research and publication, by Indian and foreign scholars, on Jain history, religion, culture and philosophy as well as the translation of Jain scriptures into many languages. It was also in this century, that the 'father of the Indian nation', Mahatma Gandhi, brought to international attention the principle of 'non-violence' *(ahimsaa)* during the struggle for India's independence. It is well known that he learned this basic principle from Jains. The 20th century has seen the translation of Jain scriptures into languages such as Hindi, Gujarati and English, enabling lay Jains to have direct access to the texts for the first time. The major Jain migration to the West is also a feature of the latter half of the 20th century and this has been an important factor in spreading the Jain message throughout the world.

Both male ascetics and female ascetics have played an important role in encouraging laypeople to observe the Jain way of life, and to build temples, *upashrayas* and educational institutions. It is under their guidance that the practices of meditation and religious rituals, and individual austerities such as fasting and penance have become widespread. Jain leaders have done much to make the issues of animal welfare and environmental protection into arena of public debate. Some ascetics have preached the message of Mahavira among marginal communities, whose people are largely rural, poor and with little education, and the results of such preaching can be seen in the change of lifestyle of such communities. Some of them have adopted non-violent way of life, including vegetarianism, avoiding alcohol and Jain dietary habits. The 20th century has seen many prominent *aacaaryas*, such as Buddhisagar, Vijay Vallabh Suri, Dharma Suri, Prem Suri, Ramchandra Suri, Sagaranand Suri and Anand Rushi. Their work included promotion of Jain way of life, empirical education, health, community welfare, social reforms, renovation of temples, libraries and establishment of other community welfare institutions such as the cottage industries for women and promotion of Jainism. These activities have benefited the *sangha*; many recuits to asceticism are highly educated.

Panyaasa Chandrasekhar has a large following among young educated Jains, who attend his lectures in large numbers. He has also founded a residential school for pupils from five years of age upwards, where the teaching is conducted in a traditional Indian manner as practised in the *ashrams* of the past, teaching both traditional Jain studies and modern subjects. The establishment of spiritual centres such as the Srimad *Adhyatmic* Kendra at Koba, Ahmedabad has provided aspirants training for spiritual practices.

Among the newly-built 20th century temples and *upashrayas* some are most exquisite and aesthetically delightful buildings and these have been built both in India and abroad. Some temples, have become tourist attractions. Of the modern temples, those at Satrunjay, Vallabh-Smarak in Delhi, the Velgachia temple in Calcutta, the Valkeshwar and Sarvoday temples in Bombay, the Hathising and Ajitnath temples in Ahmedabad, the Gomatagiri temple in Indore and the new temple at Pavapuri are highly regarded as masterpieces of the Indian architectural heritage. The temples built outside India include: Mombasa and Nairobi temples, the Shantinatha temple at the Jain Centre in Leicester, and in United States, temples such as those at Chicago and Los Angeles.

Literary activity has burgeoned in the 20th century. Many scholars, ascetics and laypeople have produced literature on a wide range of subjects. The scholarly work has helped dispel the misconceptions of Jain history among both Indian and foreign scholars. The Lalbhai Dalpatbhai Institute of Indology, Ahmedabad and Kailas Sagar *Jnaana* Mandir at Koba, are the main repositories of manuscripts and collections of artefacts, established in the 20th century, where the indexing of thousands of Jain manuscripts is near completion.

A large number of institutions, including major universities throughout India conduct teaching and research programs on Jainism for Prakrit and other subjects of Jain interest. Although the facilities of learning are available, the number of students taking advantage of Jain studies and research are very low, because of the lack of job oppotunites after such training.

In modern India, Jains are not only prominent in businesses but also are found in the Civil Service and the mangement of State enterprises, employed in high positions in government, the military, judiciary, police and other executive services, and Jains have also achieved high positions in politics and public life.

In the sciences, Jains have outshown in their fields and contributed in many areas such as nuclear energy, chemistry and physics, engineering and medicine. Jains hold distinguished positions in academic and research fields in western countries as well as 'at home' in India. Precise statistics about Jains' participation in various professions are difficult to ascertain. However, in 1992, the Jain Centre of Greater Boston published statistics for North American Jains, given below (in percentages):

Medicine	14.4	Business	16.0
Engineering	32.1	Finance	7.5
Management	4.4	Computers	3.5
Education	1.7	Others	20.4

These findings suggest that migrant Jains have high levels of educational and professional qualifications, and are involved in highly skilled employment.

Some monks and nuns have broken their vows and have travelled to the West for the promotion of Jainism by using vehicular transport; the major figures who have helped in disseminating Jain values are the Revered Chitrabhanu and the late *Aacaarya* Sushilkumarji. They and many other saints and scholars have been very useful to the Jains 'abroad' in preserving their culture and traditions.

A monk who remained in India, but who also broke with traditional restrictions of travelling by vehicle was the late *upadhyaaya* Amarmuni, who founded an institution in Bihar, the Veerayatan. This foundation provides facilities for the promotion of Jain values and medical and educational services to the community, and also established a museum of Jain and other culture, which has become a tourist attraction. He was rather revolutionary in his decision to initiate a woman as an *aacaaryaa*. *Aacaaryaa*, Chandana, is a serious scholar and a dynamic personality, is an accomplished public speaker and has travelled abroad, and has given her support to the creation of a museum at the Leicester Jain Centre. Her disciple *Saadhvi* Shilapi, who is in London for her doctoral studies, has been very helpful to the children and young people undertaking Jain education.

Thie 20th century has seen advances in the status and education of Jain women in many fields. There are almost two and a half times as many Jain nuns as monks, many are good scholars, speakers and leaders. In temples and *upashrayas*, women's attendance outnumbers that of men. Women now receive a higher education and professional training, and are found practically in all the professions, and in spite of the complexities of modern life, they have retained traditional Jain values within the family and the community.

Despite the above encouraging trends, all is not as Jains would wish: Jain culture is hardly taught in Indian schools, children learn their faith through *paathasaalas* and in the family, and once they go to secondary school, they are lost to the wider culture and complexities of life. If Jains wish to preserve their culture through future generations, they will have to provide an infrastructure for modern standards of education and recreation for children and young people.

Jain institutions flourished in the past and rarely faced financial problems as, like many religions, they devised schemes to ensure financial support for key institutions by asking members to donate a proportion of their income. Jain scriptures require the laypeople to offer a certain percentage, between 6 per cent and 33 per cent, of their income for community welfare and other charitable purposes, and there are moves in some quarters to revive this tradition.

Jains in the 20th century have kept abreast of the changing situation of society. They are considered a wealthy community and although they are anxious to preserve their culture and traditions, most of their time is spent in earning and in social activities. But history suggests that Jains are very adaptable to changing circumstances, and it is a challenge to the Jain leadership to adapt and prepare for the 21st century by providing the necessary vision and resources to preserve Jain identity and culture.

Belief in the self and other realities is Right Faith, their comprehension is Right Knowledge, being without attachment is Right Conduct. These together constitute the way to liberation.

(Tattvartha Sutra 1: 4)

Attachment and hatred are the seeds of karma. The wise say that karma is caused by delusion. Karma is the root of birth and death. The wise say that the cycle of birth and death is the cause of unhappiness.

*(Uttaraadhyayan*a 32: 7)

By controlling speech the soul achieves mental steadiness and, having achieved mental steadiness, the soul with control on speech becomes qualified for self-realisation.

*(Uttaraadhyayan*a 29: 54)

By controlling the mind the soul achieves the concentration of mind. The soul with the concentration of mind controls the senses.

*(Uttaraadhyayan*a 29: 53)

Chapter 3

TEACHINGS OF MAHAVIRA

THE PATH OF PURIFICATION

The teachings of Mahavira are characteristically simple, practical and ethical, but they have gradually developed into a detailed, intricate system, relating not only to the nature of the true and the ideal, but also to the practical path for their realisation. The ultimate object of the teaching of Mahavira is liberation or salvation, which can be attained through annihilating *karma* attached to the soul. It can be achieved by the practice of austerities and preventing the influx of additional *karma* through self-restraint of the body, speech and mind. Liberation of the soul is a state of perfection, of infinite bliss in an eternal abode, where there is no ageing, no disease, no cycle of birth and death and no suffering. Mahavira was very practical, possessing universal vision. His explanation of the six 'Realities' displays his deep insight into the nature of the universe, and is accepted today by many philosophers. A number of his teachings for example that spoken words can be heard throughout the universe (modern radio broadcasts); that microscopic germs are engendered in excreta, sputum, and urine; and that plants have life, are now widely accepted by science.

His teaching of the five vows of 'non-violence', truthfulness, 'non-stealing', sexual and sensual restraint, non-attachment, and his theories of 'relative pluralism', guide ethical thinkers today. His descriptions of the range of mental states and 'psychic colours' are supported today by some psychic researchers and theosophists, as what we would today term science and psychology were as important to him as spiritual knowledge. Elements of his teachings are now seen to have been centuries ahead of their time, as having a recognisable 'scientific' basis, and are relevant even to present-day concerns.

The teachings of Mahavira were preserved orally at first and only later they were commited to writing and edited at the council of Valabhi in 460 CE. While some changes may have occured, most of the original teachings of Mahavira have been recorded in the canonical literature.

The Three-fold Path

The ultimate object of human life is liberation or salvation, the purification of the soul *(moksa)*. Jainism describes the path of purification to be achieved through one's own efforts. The *Tattvartha Sutra*, one of the most sacred texts of Jainism, emphatically states in its first aphorism that Right Faith *(samyag darsana)*, Right Knowledge *(samyag jnaana)*, and Right Conduct *(samyag caritra)* together constitutes the path to the state of liberation. These are called the three jewels of Jainism. These three are not to be considered as separate but collectively form a single path, which must be present together to constitute *the path*.

In view of this firm conviction, the Jain seers over-emphasise that the three must be pursued simultaneously. By way of illustration, one could use a medical analogy: In order to bring about the cure of a disease, three things are essential, faith in the efficacy of the medicine, knowledge of its use, and its ingestion by the patient. Likewise, to achieve liberation, faith in the efficacy of the path, knowledge of it and the practising of it—these three together are indispensable. Similarly, the path to liberation is compared in Jain works to a ladder: The two sides of the ladder represent Right Faith and Right Knowledge, and the rungs of the ladder represent the (fourteen) stages of Right Conduct. It is obvious that it is possible to ascend the ladder only when all the three elements, the two sides and the rungs, are intact. As the absence of sides or rungs would make a ladder ineffective, so the absence of one element makes the spiritual ascent impossible.

The ethical code prescribed by Jainism for both householders and ascetics is based on this three-fold path of Right Faith, Right Knowledge and Right Conduct:

Right Faith

The term Right Faith has been defined in the *Tattvartha Sutra* as the true and firm conviction in the existence of the 'seven realities' of the universe. The Jain scriptures state that Right Faith should be characterised by eight essential requisites or components. These are:

- One should be free of doubt about the truth or validity of Jain tenets.
- One should be detached from worldly, materialistic things.
- One should have an appropriate regard for the body, as the body is the

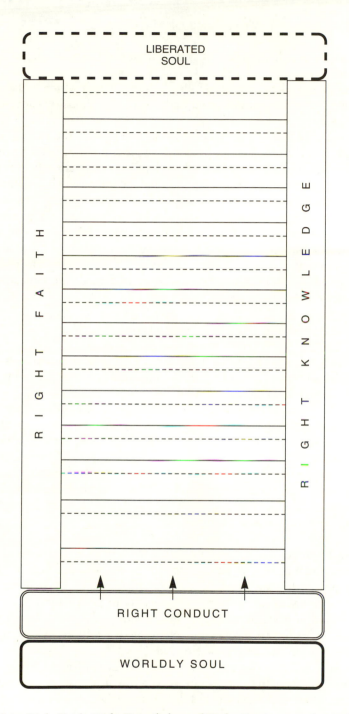

Figure 3.1   Right Faith, Right Knowledge and Right Conduct together make the 'ladder' of spiritual progress of fourteen stages

means by which one achieves salvation, but one should feel no 'attachment' to it.

- One should take care not to follow a faith or path which will not lead to liberaton; one should avoid harbouring credulous or superstitious beliefs.
- One should foster spiritual excellence, and protect the prestige of the faith from belittlement, by praising the pious and not deriding others.
- One should be steadfast in one's convictions and help others towards the path of Right Faith and Right Conduct whenever they falter.
- One should have affectionate regard and respect for the virtuous and one's co-religionists, and show due reverence towards the pious.
- In one's own conduct one should demonstrate Jain values and teachings: one should attempt to demonstrate the Jain concept of true religion both through religious observances and in the performance of charitable deeds, such as the provision of food, medicine, education and shelter to all those in need.

Right Faith should be free from erroneous beliefs such as:

- Pseudo-holiness. Some people falsely believe that practices such as bathing in certain rivers or fire walking are a means of acquiring merit for themselves or for their family.
- Pseudo-gods: Some people have faith in gods and goddesses who are credited with divine and destructive powers, but praying to such deities in order to gain favours is the false faith, leading to karmic bondage.
- Pseudo-ascetics: Some self-styled ascetics consider their teaching to be the only truth, but such ascetics should be recognised for what they are and should not be sustained in the hope of gaining favours through their magical or mysterious powers.

Jainism teaches that the mind must be freed from eight forms of pride: learning; worship; family; status by birth (or contacts and family connections); power (including physical strength); wealth or achievements; penance or religious austerities; bodily beauty or personality.

Any kind of pride disturbs the equilibrium of the mind, creating likes and dislikes, and in such cases understanding is likely to be led into error and one's 'vision' is likely to be clouded.

The Jain seers describe at length the importance of Right Faith and they enumerate the benefits that can be accrued by a person possessing right belief, and they go to the extent of declaring that asceticism without Right Faith is inferior to faith without asceticism; even a humble believer with Right Faith can attain spiritual progress.

Right Knowledge

Any knowledge which facilitates to spiritual progress is by definition Right Knowledge. Right Faith and Right Knowledge are closely related as are cause and effect, an analogy of which might be similar to a lamp and light. One may have a lamp without light, but not light without a lamp, similarly, one may have Right Faith without knowledge, but not knowledge without Right Faith.

The scriptures describe Right Knowledge as 'that knowledge which reveals the nature of things neither insufficiently, nor with exaggeration, nor falsely, but exactly as it is and with certainty'. It has also been stated that Right Knowledge consists in having full comprehension of the real nature of living beings and non-living things and that such knowledge should be beyond doubt, misunderstanding, vagueness or uncertainty.

Jain seers assert that knowledge is perfect when it does not suffer from the above three defects of insufficiency, exaggeration and falsehood, as these pervert both one's understanding and one's mental and behavioural attitudes. The Jains have developed a systemic theory of knowledge, which is described in volume 2, chapter 5.

Types of Knowledge Jain sciptures describe five forms of knowledge:

- Sensory knowledge *(mati jnaana)*: is knowledge of the world acquired by means of any or all of the five senses and the mind.
- Scriptural knowledge *(sruta jnaana)*: is derived from the reading or listening to the scriptures, and mastery of such knowledge may make one a 'scriptural omniscient'.
- Clairvoyant knowledge *(avadhi jnaana)*: is a form of direct cognition of objects without the mediation of the sensory organs. This knowledge apprehends physical objects and events, which are beyond the normal grasp of the sensory organs, and is acquired in two ways: (1) inherent in both celestial and hellish beings and acquired in case of humans and animals. Celestial beings possess a higher quality of knowledge than their hellish counterparts. (2) One can acquire clairvoyant knowledge by progressing on the spirtual path, but its degree differs according to one's spiritual progress. The soul of the *tirthankara* is born with extensive type of clairvoyant knowledge.
- 'Telepathic' knowledge *(manahparyaaya jnaana)*: is direct cognition of the mental activity of others, and can be acquired by those who are spiritually far advanced; some call it 'mind-reading' knowledge, although the terms 'telepathic' and 'mind-reading' are inadequate translations.
- Perfect knowledge or 'omniscience' *(kevala jnaana)*: is full or complete knowledge of all material and non-material objects without limitations

of time or space. It is the knowledge possessed by all the souls in their pristine state and its acquisition is the goal for a human life.

Right Knowledge has eight requirements:

- The reading, writing and pronouncing of every letter and word of the religious texts should be undertaken correctly with care and faith.
- Reading should be directed towards understanding the meaning and full significance of the words and phrases of the texts. Mere mechanical study without understanding the meaning serves no purpose.
- For Right Knowledge, both reading and understanding the meaning are essential, as they together complete the process and the purpose of knowledge.
- Study should be undertaken in quiet places regularly and at times when one is free from worries and anxieties.
- Humility and respect towards the scriptures and the teachers should be cultivated.
- If one encounters difficult expressions and ideas while studying, one should not jump to hasty conclusions that may lead to an improper understanding.
- Enthusiasm for mastering of subject is essential to sustain an interest so that one continues to study.
- One must keep an open mind and attitude so that prejudice will not hinder a proper understanding and the completeness of knowledge.

Thus, Right Knowledge is acquired by devotion to reading sacred scriptures, aimed at understanding their full meaning and significance, at appropriate regular times, imbued with zeal, a correct attitude and an open mind.

Right Conduct

After Right Faith and Right Knowledge, the third, but the most important path to the goal of liberation, is Right Conduct and Jainism attaches utmost importance to it. Right Faith and Right Knowledge equip the individual with freedom from delusion and with true knowledge of the Realities. Right Knowledge leads to Right Conduct, which is why conduct that is inconsistent with Right Knowledge, is considered to be wrong conduct. The conduct is perfected only when it is harmonised with Right Faith and Right Knowledge.

Right Conduct presupposes the presence of Right Knowledge, which, in turn, presupposes the existence of Right Faith. The Jain seers have enjoined upon those who have secured Right Faith and Right Knowledge to observe the rules of Right Conduct.

Right Conduct includes rules of discipline which:

- restrain all unethical actions of mind, speech and body;
- weaken and destroy all passionate activity;
- lead to non-attachment and purity.

Right Conduct is of two types, which depends upon the degree of practice or the rules of behaviour:

- Complete or perfect or unqualified conduct;
- Partial or imperfect or qualified conduct.

Of these two forms of Right Conduct, the former involves the practice of all the rules with zeal and a high degree of spiritual sensitivity; the latter involves the practice of the same rules with as much diligence, severity and purity as possible. Unqualified and perfect conduct is aimed at, and is observed by ascetics who have renounced worldly ties. Qualified and partial conduct is aimed at, and observed by laypersons, still engaged in the world.

The various rules of conduct prescribed for both laymen and ascetics constitute the ethics of Jainism. They are discussed later in this chapter.

JAIN ETHICS

One of the most striking characteristics of Jainism is its concern with ethics, which has led some to describe Jainism as 'ethical realism', while others have called it a religion of Right Conduct. Jain ethics see no conflict between an individuals' duty to themselves and their duty to society. The aim of the Jain path is to facilitate the evolution of the soul to its 'highest capacity' and the means to achieve this is through ethical conduct towards others.

The ultimate ideal of the Jain way of life is perfection in this life and beyond, yet Jainism does not deny mundane values but asserts the superiority of spiritual values. Worldly values are a means to the realisation of spiritual values and the activities of everyday life should be geared to the realisation of ultimate spiritual values (*dharma*), leading to liberation (*moksa*). Liberation is attainable through a gradual process of acquiring moral excellence, and Right Conduct is a very important element of the three-fold path of purification. Ethics for the Jains is the weaving of righteousness into the very fabric of one's life.

One may achieve different levels of Right Conduct in one's life: complete and partial. The complete commitment to Right Conduct entails the vigorous practice of Mahavira's teachings through the renunciation of the world and adoption of the ascetic life. For the majority who has not renounced the world, it is still possible to seek the truth and pursue the path of righteousness, although to a lesser degree. This is the path for laypersons, often referred to in Jain and other Indian texts as 'householders'. This path represents a more attainable form of social ethics. The two levels of commitment, of the ascetic and of the householder, are a characteristic feature of the Jain social structure. Laypersons have the (appropriate and moral) obligation to cherish their family; the ascetic must sever all such ties.

The ethical code of the Jains is based on five main vows for both the ascetic and the householder. These vows are unconditional and absolute for ascetics and are called major vows (*mahaavratas*), but they have been modified as minor vows (*anuvratas*) in consideration of the social obligations of householders. The vows are 'non-violence' (*ahimsaa*), truthfulness (*satya*), non-stealing (*acaurya*), celibacy (*brahmacarya*) and non-attachment (*aparigraha*). Though these vows, taken at face value, appear to be merely abstentions from certain acts, their positive implications are extensive and they permeate the entire social life of the community.

Five Main Vows

'Non-violence' (Ahimsaa)   Ahimsaa is the opposite of *himsaa*, which may be translated as 'injury' and defined as any acts, including thoughts and speech, which harm the 'vitalities' of living beings. The nature of these 'vitalities' is described later in this chapter. Harm, whether intended or not, is caused through a lack of proper care and the failure to act with due caution, but the meaning of *himsaa* is not exhausted by this definition and a more detailed examination of the concept is found later in this chapter.

Truthfulness (Satya)   The opposite of truthfulness is falsehood (*asatya*). In simple terms, *asatya* is words that result in harm to any living being, even unintentionally. This is why Jainism teaches that the utmost care must be taken in speaking. The implication of this vow is extended to prohibit spreading rumours and false doctrines; betraying confidences; gossip and backbiting; falsifying documents; and breach of trust. Other examples of falsehood would be the denial of the existence of things, which do exist, and the assertion of the existence of non-existent things; or giving false information about the position, time and nature of things.

One's speech should be pleasant, beneficial, true and unhurtful to others. It should aim at moderation rather than exaggeration, esteem rather than denigration, at distinction rather than vulgarity of expression, and should be thoughtful and expressive of sacred truths. All untruths necessarily involve violence. One should protect the vow of truthfulness by avoiding thoughtless speech, anger, greed, making others the butt of jokes or putting them in fear. Even if a person suffers through telling the truth, Jain teaching holds that truthfulness is ultimately always beneficial. Interestingly, the motto of the Republic of India: 'truth always wins' (satyam ev jayate), accords with Jain teaching.

Non-stealing (acaurya) Theft *(caurya)* is the taking of anything which is not freely given. To encourage or to teach others to commit theft, to receive stolen property, to evade the law, for example, by tax evasion or selling goods at inflated prices, to adulterate foods, medicine, fuels, and so on, and to falsify weights and measures, are all considered forms of theft and one should guard oneself against it. The vow of non-stealing is comprehensive, covering the avoidance of dishonesty in all parts of life. As material goods are external 'vitalities' for people, whoever harms them, e.g. by stealing, commits violence.

Celibacy (brahmacarya) The vow of celibacy *(brahmacarya)* literally means 'treading into the soul', but conventionally it is taken to mean abstinence from sexual activities. The vow prohibits sexual relations other than with one's spouse, and the consumption of anything likely to stimulate sexual desires. Ascetics, of course, abstain totally from sexual activity. Jain teachings also discourage excessive sensual pleasures.

Unchastity *(abrahma)* is considered to take several forms. The search for marriage partners should be limited to one's immediate family. Matchmaking by persons outside the family is contrary to Jain teaching. Unnatural sexual practices, using sexually explicit or coarse language, visiting married or unmarried adults of the opposite sex when they are alone, and relations with prostitutes (of both sexes) are all forms of unchastity. Misusing one's senses, such as reading pornography or seeing explicit films, should be avoided. Of course, such restrictions are common in many other societies too.

Non-attachment (aparigraha) Attachment to worldly things *(parigraha)* means desiring more than is needed. Even the accumulation of genuine necessities can be *parigraha*, if the amount exceeds one's reasonable needs. Other examples of *parigraha* would be greediness or envy of another's prosperity. In a similar way, if one were in a position of influence or power, such as in a voluntary or political organisation, but did not make way for another person when one should have done so, that would be a form of 'possessional' attachment.

The five vows described above, together with 'relative pluralism' form the basis of the Jain ethical code. Non-attachment and relative pluralism are described in greater detail later in this chapter.

The Ethical Code for Ascetics

Ascetics seek liberation through strict observance of the five great vows. Reverence towards all forms of life is practised rigorously by ascetics.

Possessions of Jain ascetics　Ascetics are allowed few possessions. Svetambara ascetics are permitted fourteen articles regarded as necessary both for their daily rituals and for their spiritual practices. These are: a rosary, a loin cloth, an upper cloth, a shoulder cloth, a woollen shawl, a woollen mat, a covering cloth (rather like a sheet), a 'mouth-kerchief' *(muhapatti)* to cover the mouth while speaking, a soft brush of woollen threads *(caravalaa* or *ogha)*, a staff (wooden stick) for walking, a wooden platter, a wooden or clay pot (for water) and a string with which to tie the pots together, and, finally, scriptural texts. Nuns are permitted the same fourteen articles, with one difference. The items of clothing permitted to monks are each of a single piece of cloth, but the clothing of nuns may be stitched. The soft brush, more like a short-handled mop, is a characteristic distinguishing symbol of the Jain ascetic. Its function is to enable the ascetic very gently to move aside any tiny living creature before it gets trodden on.

As for Digambara monks, only three items are permitted: a wooden pot for water, a 'brush' made of peacock feathers and scriptural texts. Strictly speaking, there are no Digambara nuns.

The ascetic state signifies absolute renunciation of the world and the sole objective is to concentrate one's activities on the attainment of liberation. Asceticism is a complete commitment to the spiritual path and it is in this state that significant efforts are made to stop the influx of *karma* and to shed previously accumulated *karma*. Only by the strict observance of ascetic precepts, austerities, bodily detachment, study and meditation, one can rid oneself of *karma* and prevent fresh *karma* becoming attached to the soul. Hence the ascetic life, with its detailed rules of conduct, is the most appropriate path to liberation.

Preventing Karmic Influx (Samvara)　Preventing the influx of karmic matter into the soul is effected by the observance of three kinds of 'guards' *(gupti)*, five kinds of 'carefulnesses' *(samiti)*, ten kinds of virtues *(dharma)*, twelve kinds of 'reflections' *(anupreksaa)*, twenty-two kinds of 'afflictional victories' *(parisaha jaya)*, and five kinds of conduct *(caritra)*.

The 'Guards'　The flow of *karma* into the soul is the result of the activities of the mind, of the body and of the speech. Ascetics must keep these channels of influx of *karmas* strictly controlled by three 'guards':

- The mind's 'guard' regulates the mind so as to achieve pure thoughts, thus avoiding mental harm to one's own soul and to other living beings.
- The body's 'guard' regulates one's bodily activities with the aim of achieving spiritual ends, for example by avoiding causing physical harm to living beings.
- The speech 'guard' controls speech by observing silences and limiting speaking to the absolute minimum necessary so as to avoid harm to other living beings.

The 'Carefulnesses'   It is possible that an ascetic may transgress vows inadvertently, hence as a precaution the 'carefulnesses' are prescribed. They are:

- 'Carefulness-in-walking' *(iryaa samiti)* regulates walking to avoid injury to living beings.
- 'Carefulness-in-speech' *(bhaasaa samiti)* regulates speech to avoid hurting the feelings of others.
- 'Carefulness-in-eating' *(esanaa samiti)* regulates eating (and drinking) to avoid the forty-two faults as described in the *Acaaranga* (see chapter 4).
- 'Carefulness-in-picking-and-placing' *(adaana niksepa samiti)*: regulates the placing of one's own possessions and other objects, for example, by picking up and setting down, to avoid harm to living beings.
- 'Carefulness-in-natural calls' *(utsarga samiti)*: regulates behaviour connected with defecation and urination to prevent harm to living beings.

Although only ascetics strictly observe these five carefulnesses, their observance is desirable to some degree in the daily life of laypeople, for example, it is expected that a devoted layperson should avoid treading on growing plants or grasses as this may harm them. One should never leave uncovered any vessel filled with liquid in case an insect falls in and drowns. One should never use a naked flame, like a candle or oil lamp, in case insects are attracted to it and are incinerated.

The Virtues (dharmas)   The soul assimilates *karma* due to the passions. The four passions of anger, pride, deception and greed must be counteracted by cultivating the ten virtues: forgiveness, humility, naturalness, contentment, truthfulness, self-restraint, austerity, renunciation, chastity and non-possession.

The 'Reflections' (anupreksaas)   To cultivate the correct religious attitude, ascetics should reflect constantly on twelve spiritual themes known as 'reflections'; ideally, these should be meditated upon repeatedly and regularly. The reflections are also termed 'contemplations' *(bhaavanaas)*. They are:

- Transitoriness *(anitya)*: Everything is subject to change or is transitory.
- Non-surrender *(asarana)*: The soul has its own destiny determined by *karma*, and there is no external agency, human or divine, which can intervene to alter the effect of *karma* and only by one's own efforts one can change one's destiny.
- The Cycle of Worldly Existence *(samsaara)*: Souls move in a cycle of

birth, death and rebirth, and cannot attain a pure state until all *karmas* are shed.

- Solitariness *(ekatva)*: All souls are alone, in the sense that each undertakes its own actions, and each alone must accept the consequences, good or bad, of those actions.
- Separateness *(anyatva)*: The external, physical world, other people, even one's own body, are not part of one's real 'self'.
- Impurity *(asuci)*: The body is material, subject to change and transitory. The bones, flesh and blood will all perish and the physical body is inferior to the true 'self'. We should not give unnecessary attention to the 'impure' body, beyond maintaining its health so that it can fulfil its proper role in facilitating spiritual progress.
- Influx *(aasrava)*: The influx of *karma* is the cause of worldly existence and is product of the passions.
- Stoppage *(samvara)*: The influx of *karma* should be stopped by the cultivation of the ten virtues.
- Shedding *(nirjaraa)*: Karmic matter should be shed or shaken off the soul by austerities and penances.
- The Universe *(loka)*: The universe is vast and humanity is insignificant and as nothing in time and space.
- The Rarity of 'Spirituality' *(bodhi durlabha)*: It is recognised that it is difficult to attain Right Faith, Right Knowledge and Right Conduct.
- Religion *(dharma)*: One should reflect upon the true nature of religion, and especially on the three-fold path of liberation as preached by the *tirthankaras*.

Victory over Affliction (Parisaha Jaya)   The path of liberation requires ascetics to bear cheerfully all the physical discomforts that might distract them or cause pain. These hardships through which the ascetics have to pass are called the 'afflictions'. There are twenty-two afflictions which ascetics are expected to bear unflinchingly. They are: hunger, thirst, cold, heat, insect bites, nakedness (for Digambara ascetics), absence of pleasure, disagreeable surroundings, sexual urges or demands by others, tiredness caused by physical activity such as walking, discomfort from sitting in one posture for a long period, discomfort from sleeping or resting on hard ground, censure or insult, injury, seeking food, failure to get food, disease, cuts and scratches from blades of grass or thorns, dirt and impurities on the body, being shown disrespect, lack of appreciation of their learning, the persistence of their own ignorance, their own lack of faith or weak belief, for example if they fail to obtain 'supernatural powers' even after great piety and austerities. The ascetics who desire to conquer all causes of pain should endure these afflictions, without any feeling of vexation.

Conduct   Ascetics are expected to observe the ascetic code of conduct:

they should practice austerities and equanimity (by which is meant even-ness of mind or temper), strive for spiritual purity, control their passions and hold to the scriptural ideal of the *jina*. If they lapse from this expected ideal, they should perform penances aimed at returning them to the proper ascetic conduct.

Shedding Karmas (Nirjaraa) The main means of shedding *karma* is through the observance of austerities; they are of two kinds: external austerities, which relate to food and physical activities, and internal auster-ities, relating to spiritual discipline. Each of these is of six kinds, discussed in detail later in this chapter.

These external and internal austerities demonstrate how rigorous is the life of self-denial which ascetics lead. They must sustain the body with only the minimum requirements of food and yet expect great strength from it in pursuit of the goal of liberation.

The *Dasavaikalika Sutra* gives descriptions of the essential qualities required of an ascetic: self-control, freedom from passions and non-attach-ment. True ascetics should live as models of righteousness, without profession or occupation as homeless mendicants.

The daily routine of an ascetic is regulated and regimented: solemnity and a strictly reserved and unobtrusive manner are the norm; singing, dancing, laughing or any form of merry-making are forbidden, and most waking time is devoted to meditation and study.

The Ethical Code for Householders

Not everyone can renounce the world, and it is neither possible nor desir-able that all should follow the path of renunciation. People have social responsibilities and it is not possible for most of them to practise the vows with the same rigour and discipline as an ascetic. In the Jain conception of moral life we find a harmonious blending of secular and spiritual. One cannot become a 'saint' overnight. One has to prepare oneself to be a good person first before entering into the life of an ascetic. The sole exceptions are the rare cases of exemplary souls, such as *tirthankaras* or great *aacaaryas*.

The ethical code for laypersons is twelve-fold: five of the vows are common to the ascetic and the householder, but in the case of the house-holder, they are the minor vows *(anuvratas)*, described earlier: 'non-violence'; truthfulness; non-stealing; sexual restraint; and non-attach-ment. In addition to the five minor vows practised by householders, there are three 'multiplicative' vows *(guna vratas)*: 'limitation of directional movements' *(diga vrata)*; 'limitation of areal movements' *(desavakasika vrata)*; and 'avoidable activities' *(anarthadanda vrata)*. The householder also practises four educative vows *(siksaa vratas)*: equanimity *(saamayika vrata)*; specific fasting *(prosadhopavaasa vrata)*; 'limiting consumables and non-consumables' *(bhogopa-bhogaparimaana vrata)* and 'hospitality', not eating before food has been offered to others *(atithi samvibhaaga vrata)*. *Gunavratas*:

- The 'directional' vow restricts unneccessary movement. The purpose is to reduce the possibility of committing violence, and this is achieved by circumscribing the area of potential injury to living beings. One may adopt the vow for a specified limited period or as a lifelong vow.
- The vow of 'limitation of areal movement' is a modified version of the vow of 'limitation of directional movement'. It restricts the movement of an individual to a house or a village or a part thereof for a period as short as forty-eight minutes or as long as several months. The rationale underlying the practice is that it creates the mental preparedness for adopting the life of an ascetic in the future.
- The vow of 'avoidable activities' prohibits an individual from professions and trades, which would lead to harmful activities or from activities, which serve no useful purpose. The five types of avoidable activities are: certain mental states such as sorrowful or hateful thoughts *(apadhyaana)*, negligent actions or addictions such as alcoholism and gambling. Avoidable activities also include watching dancing, sex displays and animal combat such as cock fighting, and others, which incite the passions. Encouraging any activity leading to the destruction of life or the giving of 'sinful' advice such as instruction in an immoral trade, is regarded as avoidable activity. Spending time and effort reading, listening to or watching pornographic material, tabloid journalism, gossip and other such trivia should be avoided.

Educative vows:

- The vow of equanimity *(saamayika)* is an important meditational practice for laypersons, as ascetics are lifelong practitioners of equanimity. Practical exercises aimed at achieving equanimity may be performed in one's own home or in a temple, in the presence of an ascetic or in an *upashraya*. The procedure for practising equanimity is described in chapter 5. During the period of *saamayika*, the householders are considered as though they were ascetics.
- The vow of specific fasting *(prosadhopavaasa)* requires fasting and observing equanimity for twelve hours or more at regular intervals in a month; it is a temporary asceticism, and a preparation for entering an ascetic order. During this fasting one avoids any unnecessary 'enhancements' of the body, such as the use of perfumes, cosmetics and the like and abstains from mundane duties.

- The vow of 'limiting consumables and non-consumables' *(bhogopa-bhogaparimaana)* forbids or limits one's use of 'consumable' goods such as food and 'non-consumable' goods such as furniture.
- The vow of 'hospitality' *(atithi samvibhaaga)* means the giving of food and similar necessities to ascetics and the needy before taking care of one's own requirements.

The Six Daily Duties

The six daily duties of householders are: equanimity *(saamayika)*, recitation of the eulogy of the twenty-four *tirthankaras (caturvisanti stava)*, reverence towards ascetics *(guru vandana)*, penitential retreat *(pratikramana)*, meditation in a relaxed posture *(kaayotsarga)*, and the renunciation of food, drink and comfort *(pratyaakhyaana)*. The study of the scriptures *(svaadhyaaya)* and the giving of donations *(daana)* to the needy are also considered to be the duties of laypersons. Chapter 5 contains further information on these duties, except for *daana*, which is described below.

Daana The duty of giving is an important element in the practice of Jain religion, for without alms-giving by the laypersons, ascetics could not be supported nor could the order be preserved. Of course, this situation applies only to India. In the rest of the world a different situation may evolve. There are specific injunctions regarding giving alms, in which ascetics take precedence as recipients. In giving alms one should consider the following five factors:

- Recipients of alms should always be treated respectfully.
- Donors should give willingly and wholeheartedly, not grudgingly.
- The alms given should be appropriate to the recipients and to their circumstances.
- The manner of giving should avoid embarrassing recipients in any way and should not make donors feel superior by their giving.
- Giving alms should not be done from the motive of personal gain for onseself or others.

There are different ways of 'giving' *(daana)* in the Jain tradition, and among these the main ways are:

- 'Giving to deserving persons' *(supaatra daana)*. An example of this would be the giving of alms, books etc. to ascetics, who are regarded as morally and spiritually superior; this giving is done with humility and devotion.
- 'Compassionate' donations *(anukampaa)* are gifts of charity to people

in need of shelter, food, medical care or education, including the welfare of animals *(jiva dayaa)*, and care of the environment.

- 'No-fear' giving *(abhaya daana)*. Jains regard one of the greatest forms of 'giving' to be the avoidance of causing anxiety or fear to any living beings, through thought, speech or action. Anybody can practise *abhaya daana* as the only 'resources' required are 'inner' strength. Those who aspire to *abhaya daana* are encouraged to practise the utmost vigilance over their conduct in order to achieve the desired situation in which all living beings feel safe and secure in their presence.

- Giving (spiritual) knowledge *(jnaana daana)*. There are many ways in which one can impart knowledge to others which will lead to their spiritual uplift and help them on the path of purification. Dissemination of Jain teachings, giving sermons, lectures, the writing of books and articles, financing publications of a spiritual nature, are all valid ways of achieving this goal.

Giving helps to nullify greed and acquisitiveness; acquisitiveness is a manifestation of violence. Paradoxically, laypeople have more restrictions placed upon them than ascetics, owing to the greater diversity of their personal circumstances and the complexity of life. Jain tradition puts a duty upon laypeople to set aside a part of their income for charitable use.

Holy Death (Sallekhanaa)

Jains are expected not only to live a disciplined life but also to die a detached death, which is peaceful, holy and faced willingly. This voluntary death is to be distinguished from suicide, which is considered by Jainism a sin. Tradition says that when faced by calamity, such as famine, disease for which there is no remedy, or very old age, pious householders should peacefully relinquish their bodies, inspired by the highest religious ideal. Both laypeople and ascetics observe the 'holy death' ritual and all should face death and leave the worldly body with a quiet detachment in peaceful meditation on religious themes. The detail of *sallekhanaa* is described in chapter 5.

General Principles of Appropriate Conduct for Householders

On the basis of the rules of Right Conduct laid down in the Jain scriptures, the prominent Jain seers have determined a number of general principles of appropriate conduct. The Svetambara text *Yoga sastra*, composed by *aacaarya* Hemcandra, presents a list of thirty-five general principles of conduct appropriate to the ideal householder.

Among Digambara texts, the work entitled the 'Rules of Conduct for

Householders' *(Sraavakaacaara)* composed by *Aacaarya* Amitgati gives a list of the eleven attributes of the ideal householder. These rules guide householders in their responsibility both for leading a proper religious life and being useful members of society, thus the householder leads a life according to Jain ideals. This ideal can be identified from the lists of qualities found in the literature.

From the *Yoga sastra* we learn that one should:

1. Be honest in earning wealth.
2. Be appreciative of the conduct of the virtuous.
3. Be apprehensive of sin.
4. Fulfil the three-fold aim of life.
5. To make spiritual progress *(dharma)*.
6. To achieve proper material ends *(artha)*.
7. To enjoy life in a proper manner *(kaama)*.
8. Follow the customs of the country in which one lives.
9. Not to denigrate other people, particularly governments.
10. Live in an appropriate place with good neighbours.
11. Aim for high moral standards.
12. Respect one's parents.
13. Marry a spouse of the same caste and traditions, avoiding excluded relationship.
14. Avoid places where disaster or troubles occur frequently.
15. Not to engage in a reprehensible occupation.
16. Live within one's means; treat wealth as a trust to be managed according to Jain tenets.
17. Dress according to one's income.
18. Develop the eight kinds of 'intelligence'.
19. Listen daily to the sacred doctrines.
20. Not to eat on a full stomach; eat at the right time observing Jain dietary regulations.
21. Be diligent in supporting ascetics, the righteous and the needy.
22. Always strive to be free of evil motives and be favourably inclined to virtue.
23. Avoid actions, which are inappropriate to the time and place; be aware of one's own strengths and weaknesses.
24. Venerate persons of high morality and discernment.
25. Support one's dependants.
26. Be far-sighted, visionary, and aim to succeed in whatever one does.
27. Be discriminating in all matters.
28. Be grateful when gratitude is called for.
29. Try to be well liked.
30. Be motivated by a sense of shame.

31. Be compassionate.
32. Be gentle in disposition.
33. Be ready to render service to others.
34. Be intent on avoiding the six adversaries of the soul.
35. Be in control over the sensory organs.

From the *Sraavakaacaara* we learn that one should:

1. Be devoid of lust, envy, deception, anger, backbiting, meanness and pride.
2. Be steadfast.
3. Be contented.
4. Not speak harshly.
5. Be compassionate.
6. Aim to be competent in all one's undertakings.
7. Be skilled in discerning what is acceptable and what to be avoided.
8. Be respectful to ascetics and prepared to submit to their teachings.
9. Be penitent for one's faults by accepting the teachings of a *jina.*
10. Be apprehensive of things which keep one attached to the world.
11. Seek to diminish one's lust for sensual things.

The Eleven Stages of Ethical Progress (*pratimaas*)

The word *pratimaa* is used to designate the ideal stages of ethical progress in a householder's life. By treading the ethical path, a layperson acquires spiritual progress. The eleven stages form a series of duties and practices, the standard and duration of which increase, culminating in a state resembling asceticism, towards the final goal of initiation as a Digambara ascetic. The eleven stages are as follows:

- Stage of Right Faith (*darsana pratimaa*): The householder must develop a perfect, intelligent and well-reasoned faith in Jainism, that is, a sound knowledge of its doctrines and their application to life.
- Stage of Vows (*vrata pratimaa*): The householder must observe the twelve vows, without transgressing them, and must observe the vow of 'holy death'; such a householder is called 'avowed' (*vrati*).
- Stage of Equanimity (*saamayika pratimaa*): The householder should practise equanimity, consisting of a three times daily, period of regular religious observance, each lasting forty-eight minutes. This observance takes the form of self-contemplation and the purification of one's ideas and emotions, accompanied by the recital of the *sutras.*
- Stage of Specific Fasting (*prosadhopavaasa pratimaa*): This involves regular fasting, as a rule, twice a fortnight in each lunar month. The

entire period of fasting has to be spent in prayer, the study of scriptures, meditation and listening to religious discourses at *upashraya* or at home.

- Stage of Renouncing Food Containing Life *(sacitta tyaaga pratimaa)*: The householder should abstain from eating those green vegetables and foodstuffs in which the Jain tradition considers there to be life, and should also refrain from serving such food to others. One should not trample upon grass or any growing plant, nor pluck fruit or flower from trees or bushes.

- Stage of Renunciation of Eating at Night *(raatri bhojana tyaaga pratimaa)*: In this stage the householder abstains from taking any kind of food or drink after sunset; the Jain tradition encourages this practice to avoid harm to minute creatures which are nocturnal and cannot be seen with the naked eye.

- Stage of Celibacy *(brahmacarya pratimaa)*: The householder in this stage observes complete celibacy, maintains sexual purity, and avoids the use of all personal decoration, which could arouse sexual desire.

- Stage of Occupational Renunciation *(aarambha samaarambha tyaaga pratimaa)*: The householder must refrain from all occupational and celebratory activities to avoid injury to living beings. Householders divide their property among their children retaining a small part for their own maintenance and giving some to charity.

- Stage of Possessory Renunciation *(parigraha tyaaga pratimaa)*: This stage sees the abandonment of all attachments. The householder gives up all kinds of worldly possessions such as: land, house, silver, gold, cattle, clothes, utensils, male and female servants, keeping just enough for the minimal requirements of food, shelter and clothing. This stage is one of acceptance of the hardships of asceticism in preparation for the final stage.

- Stage of Withdrawal *(anumati tyaaga pratimaa)*: The householder makes increased efforts towards full asceticism, a life of detachment: one becomes indifferent to personal matters such as food and drink, and to social concerns of the family and the community.

- Stage of Renouncing Food Intended for the Householder *(uddista tyaaga pratimaa)*: In this eleventh stage, the householder renounces any food or lodging that has been prepared for him, leaves the family home, goes to a forest or remote place for shelter, and adopts the rules laid down for ascetics. This is the highest stage for householders, and has two parts —'two-clothed' and 'loin-clothed'; the latter stage leads to initiation as a Digambara ascetic.

AHIMSAA, APARIGRAHA, ANEKAANTAVAADA

Ahimsaa, aparigraha and *anekaantavaada* are the distinctive principles of Jainism on which the conduct of a Jain is based.

Ahimsaa (Non-Violence)

It is difficult to translate *ahimsaa* into English, closest gloss is 'non-violence and reverence for life' or avoidance of injury. Jain ethics have given the greatest prominence to *ahimsaa,* but ' non-violence' does not explain fully its meaning. It means kindness to living beings and includes avoidance of mental, verbal and physical injury; it is reverence for life in totality. Though this principle has been recognised by practically all religions, Jainism alone has preached its full significance and application to the extent that Jainism and non-violence have become virtually synonymous. Jains always uphold that this principle represents the highest religion *(ahimsaa paramo dharamah)*, which is why among the five main vows, 'non-violence' is pre-eminent, and in Jain scriptures it is regarded as the principal vow and the other four vows are considered as extensions of this fundamental principle.

Violence is defined in Jain teachings as any action, attitude, thought or word, which results in harm to the 'vitalities', that is, all those elements necessary to sustain life. The ten vitalities are: the five senses, the three strengths of body, of speech and of mind, lifespan and respiration. Violence thus includes not only killing or physical injury but also curtailing the freedom of thought and speech of others. None should be forced to do anything against their wishes. As noted earlier, material possessions can be considered to be 'external vitalities' for a human being, hence theft is a form of violence.

We commit violence in thought before we commit it in action. Violence in thought or psychic violence *(bhaava himsaa)* is the true violence. The *Dasavaikalika Sutra* states that no sin accrues to one who walks, stands, sits, sleeps, eats and speaks with vigilance. It is said that a negligent ascetic is violent with regard to all living beings, but if the ascetic behaves vigilantly, and remains unattached, just as a lotus in water, then the ascetic is not considered to be violent, even though some violence may occur unwittingly.

Other scriptures indicate that a negligent soul afflicts its own 'self' and this remains true whether others are harmed as a result of the negligence or not. Under the influence of the passions one's judgement is impaired, one defiles the soul's pure nature by likes and dislikes. This lack of detached indifference is the real sin. Violence in thought translates into violence in action *(dravya himsaa)*, the physical violence which we see all around us.

Amitgati (11th century CE) has classified violence into 108 varieties. One can commit violence oneself *(kritaa)*, or have others commit violence *(karitaa)* or approve of violence *(anumodanaa)*. This three-fold violence becomes nine-fold, as one or more of the three agencies of mind, speech and body can commit it. This nine-fold violence becomes twenty seven-fold, as it has three stages: thinking of violent action; preparing for violence and committing violence. This twenty seven-fold violence becomes one hundred and eight-fold, as one or more of the four passions (anger, pride, deceit and greed) can inspire it. These classifications show that the Jains take a comprehensive view of physical and psychic violence and can take two forms: unintentional and intentional.

Unintentional Violence   Unintentional violence is defined as violence committed accidentally or as part of an individual's social duty and is unavoidable. It has three forms: 'domestic', 'professional', and 'defensive'.

- *Domestic Violence*   Unintentional violence is involved in the daily domestic routine of householders, such as cooking, washing, bathing, travelling, worshipping, and in their social or religious obligations. This unavoidable violence is called 'domestic' violence.
- *Professional Violence*   Certain professions, such as doctors and farmers, have to commit violence in their daily duties (e.g. doctors giving antibiotics or operating on someone). However, they should minimise violence and remain vigilant against unnecessary harm to living beings, and should regret violence. Because of their obligations, they may commit some violence, but their motive in doing so is to help other living beings.
- *Defensive Violence*   Jainism abhors violence but recognises the concept of legitimate defence, of oneself, or one's family, village, country and the like. This is a part of the duty of householders. Like those whose professions involve unavoidable violence, householders should minimise and remain vigilant and regret violence. Ascetics, however, would never knowingly commit violence under any circumstances.

Intentional Violence   Violence committed of one's own free will is called intentional violence and is avoidable. Often such violence is accompanied by intense passion and it causes greater harm to the soul of the person committing violence than to the victim. Intentional violence can be committed in thought, speech or action. Some examples are:

- Animal sacrifice, which is still common in certain traditions such as the Muslim and some sects of the Hindu religions.

- Some people maintain, mistakenly, that the demands of health require the eating of animal flesh.
- In some countries, such as India, where a vegetarian diet is the norm, some people are persuaded to eat meat because it is seen as 'fashionable' or because hosts offer them meat.
- Sound mind and physical fitness are necessary for spiritual progress, but even for nourishment one has to be vigilant in causing minimal violence to other beings. The killing of two- to five-sense creatures for food is prohibited, and one should minimise the killing of one-sense creatures. Jains are forbidden to eat meat, eggs (fertilised or unfertilised), honey, alcohol, butter, root vegetables, and vegetables with multiple seeds. The production of honey and alcohol is believed to cause harm to minute creatures. Butter and root vegetables can contain myriads of tiny living beings. Multiple-seeded vegetables and fruits contain more living beings with one-sense life-forms. Eggs are potential precursors of five-senselife. (In the West, Jains avoid meat, eggs and alcohol, but they are somewhat relaxed about others foodstuffs).
- Many sports such as hunting, shooting and fishing, the so-called 'blood sports' involve a high level of violence.
- Some industries involve violence to animals, for example, cosmetics are often tested on animals and the silk, fur and leather industries kill living creatures.
- Violence in vivisection, medical research and scientific investigations is unnecessary and avoidable.
- Open violence and conflict arise in societies through religious fanaticism, 'racial' hatred, political rivalries, greed for property or land or as a result of sexual passion.
- 'Civil' violence, crime such as robbery or burglary, and the methods used to maintain law and order can all generate violence which is avoidable.
- Exploitation, overwork or the overloading of workers and animals are forms of violence and should be avoided.

Life starts at conception and hence abortion is normally prohibited in Jainism. In a case in which a mother's life is in danger, one should use one's judgement to choose a course of action, which will minimise violence.

The use of contraception is not prohibited *per se*, but Jainism prescribes sexual restraint and that sexual activity should be reserved for procreation as over-indulgence is a form of attachment and passion, causing injury to the 'self', and hence a form of violence.

Regarding organ and tissue transplants, which are a common feature of modern medicine, Jainism permits a willing or voluntary donation to help others. The giving of one of two kidneys, for example, is permitted, if no harm results through the donation. The sale of blood or organs often involves compulsion or exploitation, for example of the poor people, and in such cases is forbiddem to the donor or recipient.

Observant Jains are exhorted not to follow professions that involve violence. Among these are: the production of wood charcoal, forestry; transport by animals, transport of animals, mining, anything involving meat products or furs, skins and the like, non-food plant products such as paper, intoxicants, trading in persons and animals, weapons and poisons, milling, work involving fire, work involving water, and prostitution.

The vow of non-violence for ascetics is absolute. They avoid all violence to living beings; they do not travel by vehicles, cook, bathe, or use modern technology; nor do they defend themselves. They have renounced everything and therefore have no country to defend, to them there are no friends or enemies, all are equal. The vow of non-violence for the householder takes account of the need for earnings, family, social and national obligations, but householders should choose a profession which involves the least violence either to human beings or to the natural world.

Mahatma Gandhi utilised the principle of non-violence successfully to win freedom for India. He declared that non-violence is the policy of the strong. It requires self-control. Self-controlled people are free from fear; they fear only causing injury or injustice. *Ahimsaa* is not cowardice. It allows the right of legitimate self-defence in the case of householders. One who stands courageous and undisturbed in the face of violence is a true follower of non-violence, regarding the enemy as a friend.

Non-violence is not mere non-injury in the negative sense. It has also a positive aspect. It implies the presence of cultivated and noble sentiments such as kindness and compassion for all living creatures, and it also implies self-sacrifice. The Buddha renounced the pleasures of the world out of compassion for all living creatures, and Jesus was filled with compassion when he said 'whoever shall strike thee on the right cheek, turn to him the other also', he demanded self-sacrifice.

Aacaarya Somadeva enumerates qualities that should be cultivated to realise the ideal of non-violence: a disposition not to cause any suffering to any living being in mind, body or speech; affection coupled with respect for those renowned for their virtues and religious austerities; the will to help the poor; and an equitable attitude. *Ahimsaa* is thus a positive virtue and it resolves itself as *jiva-dayaa*, compassion for living creatures. Jains maintain animal and bird sanctuaries *(panjaraa polas)* throughout India. In India, where most water comes from wells and streams, Jains filter the water through a thick cloth and return the strained out small living creatures to the water's source.

Some wider issues of non-violence   Some hold that there is no violence involved in taking the flesh of those animals who have met a natural death, but Jains believe that this is not the case, because the flesh of a corpse harbours micro-organisms, which are generated constantly and killed when the flesh is touched. Honey, which drops naturally from the honey-comb also, contains micro-organisms and is prohibited to Jains.

The principle of non-violence requires that violent animals should not be killed, either to save the possible destruction of lives by them or to save them from committing the great sin of violence. 'Mercy killing', euthanasia is a form of violence and is prohibited. Under no pretext can violence be justified. The Jain belief in non-violence is against all cruelty towards animals and the natural world. It is against wars, however, it allows us the right of self-defence. It guarantees freedom of thought, speech and action to all and guides us to shun violence committed in the name of religion.

Forms of non-violence Like violence, non-violence can also be expressed in different forms: psychic, verbal and physical, the last two deriving from the first. Non-attachment, truthfulness, honesty and chastity are the physically realisable forms of non-violence, and the world could be transformed if these forms of non-violence were to be widely observed.

Aparigraha (Non-attachment)

Aparigraha is the mental attitude of non-attachment to possessions, objects and attitudes, as attachment is the cause of bondage and should be avoided. For ascetics *aparigraha* is a vow of non-possession, for householders it is a vow of limited possession. The Jain seers had the psychological sense to understand the value of limits on possessions in the normal course of life and they advocated the vow of limited possession. Both the Digambaras and Svetambaras agree on the definition, but the sects vary in the number of objects allowed to ascetics. Jain ethics for laypersons do not prohibit wealth and position, provided that these are realised honestly. Regarding the vow of *aparigraha*, a limit to possessions is advised, and wealth in excess of one's vowed limit is given up and is set aside for charitable purposes.

Attachment to and the desire to procure possessions is a form of illusion, the result of a specific type of *karma (mohaniya karma)* which is an obstacle to self-realisation.

The vow of *aparigraha* also means limiting the holding of positions of responsibility of any type whether voluntary, commercial, governmental or academic. Attachment is of two types: material and psychic.

Material possessions are of various kinds, including wealth, property, livestock, servants, gold and jewels, clothes, furniture and utensils. In the modern world we would perhaps add cars, videos, dishwashers, home computers and much more. Material possessions themselves create a craving for even more. The more we get of them, the more we want, as material desires are notoriously insatiable. Happiness is not achieved through the pursuit of possessions.

Psychic 'possessions' include likes and dislikes, hatred, anger, pride, deceit, greed, sexual infatuation, grief, fear and disgust. These are the affective states corrupting the development of personality and should be sublimated.

Property earned by wrong and unrighteous means, even if it is within the self-imposed limit, is to be considered as sinful.

The vow of non-attachment has great social significance to modern society: it is not uncommon for people to be blind to the values of life while pursuing social and political ends, as for many, power and self-interest are their ultimate ends. The vow of non-attachment can lead to greater economic justice in society and improved social welfare.

Anekaantavaada (Relative Pluralism)

One of the important philosophical principles of Jainism is 'relative pluralism'. Literally, the term anekaantavaada refers to the Jain view of the many-sided nature of reality. Jain seers taught that reality could only be fully understood in a state of omniscience, and worldly beings possess only limited or partial knowledge. This view is neatly expressed in the famous story of the seven blind persons who each sought to describe an elephant. Being blind, each had to rely on the sense of touch for knowledge of the elephant. One who touched the elephant's leg thought that it was like a log; another who touched its tail thought it was like a rope; and yet another, who had touched its trunk, thought it was like a snake. All arrived at different descriptions: wall (the body), fan (the ear) and so on, but could not describe the totality. To comprehend many different points of view, all must be taken into account in order to arrive at a complete picture.

Attempting to synthesise opposing viewpoints in philosophy frequently presents problems. Jain philosophers were well aware of such problems. In order to resolve them, they developed the idea of 'relative pluralism', synthesis of two doctrines: the doctrines of 'standpoints' (nayavaada) and 'relativity' (syaadavaada). Relative pluralism is the fundamental mental attitude which sees or comprehends 'reality' differently from different viewpoints, each viewpoint (or standpoint) being a partial expression of reality. If we remember the story told of Mahavira, when he was on the middle floor of his home he was 'downstairs' according to his father who was on a floor above, and 'upstairs' from the point of view of his mother on a lower floor, but both parents were right from their differing points of view. The relativity of viewpoints (Syaadavaada) brings together such differing viewpoints into a single logical expression.

According to Jain philosophy Reality, concrete and abstract, is complex:

it is constituted of substances and their qualities which change constantly; it extends over past, present and future; it extends over the entire universe; and it is generated simultaneously, is destroyed and yet is permanent.

It has been pointed out that an object or reality cannot be fully comprehended by worldly beings, as ordinary humans cannot rise above the limitations of their senses, their apprehension of reality is partial and is valid only from a particular point of view. That is why Jainism points to the fact that reality may be comprehended from different 'angles', and the standpoints are important for understanding the theory of relative pluralism, which brings out the relativity of descriptions or accounts of the world, both concrete and abstract. In fact there can be infinite number of standpoints.

The Significance of Relative pluralism   The awareness of the existence of many standpoints makes relative pluralism necessary; the standpoints are partial expressions of truth, while relative pluralism aims at the complete truth. Relative pluralism aims to unify, co-ordinate, harmonise and synthesise individual, and even conflicting, viewpoints into a comprehensible whole. It is like music, which blends different notes to make perfect harmony.

Relative pluralism teaches tolerance, co-existence and respect for others, necessary in creating a harmonious society. Some philosophical, religious and political systems claim to interpret reality in its entirety, while containing only partial versions of the truth, but they cannot do full justice to the manifold nature of the world in which we live, as judgements about the world must necessarily vary according to the observer's perspective. Relative pluralism seeks to provide a solution to the intellectual chaos and confusion stemming from the ambiguous and metaphysical contradictions of differing philosophical systems.

The doctrine of relative pluralism frees one from spurious thinking such as the belief that any one faith is nearer to the truth than others. It is an understanding, which urges us to study different religions, opinions and schools of thought and is a basis for sound thinking. *Anekaantavaada* respects the thoughts of others and as a result one's own opinions will be accorded their worth.

AUSTERITIES

A person who intends to follow the path of self-realisation, to achieve liberation from karmic bondage, practises Right Conduct. By leading a moral and ethical life one becomes disciplined and avoids the influx of *karma*. But a disciplined life alone is not sufficient to liberate the soul as previously accumulated *karma* must also be shed. Even the self-disciplined accumulate new *karma* as a result of the activities of the mind, body, and speech, and the mild passions. To free the soul from karmic bondage one has to shed old *karma* at a faster rate than the new accumulates.

Those who aspire to liberation willingly challenge their natural instincts, controlling the demands of the senses and passions. To the casual observer, the austerities *(tapas)* appear to involve great hardship and pain, but to the spiritual aspirant the practice of these austerities is a source of great inspiration towards the goal of self-conquest.

It is through the practice of austerities that willpower is strengthened to resist the allure of worldly pleasures. Aspirants differentiate between the essentials for self-realisation and non-essentials, which keep the self in the worldly cycle; they make full use of the body as a means to progress on the path of purification. Umasvati taught that austerities are required both to stop the accumulation of new *karma* and for shedding old *karma*. The Jain path of purification encourages the aspirants to make themselves free from attachments and aversions, that is, from all the impure activities of thought, word and deed.

The Place of Austerities in Jainism

Jain scriptures define austerities as the control of desires, in the *Satkhandaagamaa* austerities are the extirpation of desire in order to strengthen the three jewels of Right Faith, Right Knowledge and Right Conduct.

The *Uttaradhyayana* praises austerities in these words: 'In the same way that a large tank, when its supply of water has been stopped, dries up because its water is consumed or evaporates, so the *karma* of an ascetic, who has gone through countless births, is annihilated by austerities, if there is no influx of new karma'. It goes on to remark: '*Tapas* are my fire, *karma* is my fuel. It is *tapas*, which bring a person honour and respect'.

The *Sthaananga* makes it clear that all *tapas* should be devoid of worldly desires, of this world or another, and the practice of austerities devoid of spirituality is referred to as *baala tapa* (literally: child(ish)-austerities). The *Pravacanasaara* says that those who are spiritually endowed, shed their *karma* much sooner than those who are not, even though the latter may perform rigorous external austerities.

Jain texts describe a number of austerities, external and internal: An external austerity involves some physical act of renunciation; an internal austerity involves controlling and directing the mind towards spiritual pursuits. As external austerities are physical acts, such as fasting, they can be undertaken even by those who do not have a spiritual disposition, yet despite this, external austerities can lead one to develop the proper detached attitude and control over one's desires.

External Austerities

There are six types of external austerities: fasting *(anasana)*; eating less than one's need *(unodari)*; choosing, for ascetics when begging, to limit which food(s) to take *(vruttisanksepa)*; abstention from one or more of the six stimulating or delicious *(rasaparityaaga)*: ghee (refined butter), milk, yoghurt (curds in India), sugar, salt and oil; avoidance of all that can lead to temptation *(samlinataa)*; and mortification of the body *(kaayakalesa)*.

- Fasting: food may be renounced for a limited period or until death. Emancipation of the body should be distinguished from fasting, which has a spiritual purpose; merely ceasing to eat *per se* is not considered an austerity, as to fast properly the correct spiritual attitude of detachment from food is essential.
- *Unodari*: The Jain scriptures prescribe a daily limit of food for an ascetic as thirty-two morsels for a monk and twenty-eight for a nun, any reduction in this quantity constitues *unodari*. *Mulaacaara* claims that this austerity helps control the senses and sleep, aids one on the path of purification, and in the performance of the six essentials (see chapter 5).
- Restriction of choice of food when begging: the ascetic decides, before setting out to beg, how many homes to visit, how to receive food, the type of food to be taken and from whom to receive food. If the ascetic finds that his conditions are fulfilled, then food is accepted; otherwise, the ascetic will go without. Sometimes the conditions are too onerous to be easily fulfilled and the ascetic has to go without food for a very long period. An illustrative example of this austerity comes from accounts of the life of Mahavira. He set a number of conditions: he would accept food only from someone, who was a princess; who was a slave; who was in chains; who had fasted for three days; who was standing astride a doorway, one leg on the inside, the other on the outside; and who had tears in her eyes. This remarkable list of restrictions meant that Mahavira had to wait five and a half months before being able to accept food from Princess Candanbala. The example of this well-known laywoman, and much-respected story, encourages many to overcome the desire for food and to emulate Candanbala.
- Abstention from taste-enhancing foods: One should eat to live and not live to eat, which means controlling one's tastes. Thus, one should therefore renounce one or more of the six foods, which enhance flavour or taste: milk, yoghurt, gee, oil, sugar and salt. Additionally one should avoid one or more of the following types of tastes: acrid, bitter, astringent, sour and sweet. The purpose is to curb the sense of taste, subduing sleep, and the unobstructed pursuit of self-study.
- Avoidance of temptations through seclusion: The ascetic should choose

a secluded place to reside, sit in solitude, and peacefully become immersed in meditation and recitation of the holy hymns, as this facilitates celibacy, self-study and meditation.

- Mortification of the body: This *tapa* involves inflicting pain on the body by adopting certain postures or by exposing the body to the weather, for example, by remaining in the sun during the summer. The purpose of this austerity is the endurance of physical hardship and to reduce attachment to bodily pleasures.

The *Mulaacaara* scripture makes it clear that external austerities should not endanger one's mental attitude, nor counter the zeal for the performance of disciplinary practices of an ethical and spiritual nature, but should rather enhance spiritual conviction. Samantabhadra also emphasises the inner aspect of austerities and says that external austerities are a means to internal austerities.

Internal Austerities

There is a six-fold classification of internal austerities: Penance *(praayascitta)*, Reverence *(vinaya)*, Service *(vaiyaavritya)*, Self-study *(svaadhyaaya)*, Detachment *(vyutsarga)* and Meditation *(dhyaana)*.

- Penance.   The *Praayascitta Samuccaya* states that without penance there cannot be any Right Conduct, without Right Conduct there can be no piety, without piety no detachment, and without detachment all vows are futile. It is said that individuals should not attempt to conceal their faults and deficiencies when seeking advice, help or justice from benevolent rulers, judges, doctors, teachers, or gurus. When advice or decisions are offered, any penance suggested should be accepted. While prescribing a spiritual penance, guru takes into account the time, place, availability of food, and an individual's capacities. There are as many penances as there are degrees of faults and therefore no one can compile an exhaustive list of penances. When prescribing a penance, a guru should keep in mind whether the sinner has transgressed under duress or wilfully, once or repeatedly, has followed the truth or not, and whether the individual attempted to resist the temptation to sin or not. Penance includes: confession *(aalocanaa)*, penitence *(pratikramana)*, both confession and penitence *(tadubhaya)*, conscientious discrimination *(viveka)*, meditation with relaxed body *(kaayotsarga)*, austerities *(tapas)*, demotion in the ascetic order *(cheda)*, expulsion *(parihara)*, re-initiation into the ascetic order *(mula)*, strengthening of the faith *(sraddhaa)*.
- Reverence.   *Vinaya* means control over the passions and the senses,

and proper humility towards those deserving reverence. All knowledge is futile without reverence. Humbleness is shown to others for five reasons: to imitate them, because of their wealth, through sexual desire, out of fear, or to achieve worldly freedom or spiritual liberation. There is a five-fold classification of reverence in order to realise spiritual liberation: faith, knowledge, conduct, austerity, and respect. Reverence as an austerity is dispelling darkness through devotion to penance and to those who are devoted to penance, while respecting those who possess knowledge, but are unable to undertake penance (e.g. cannot fast). Respectful reverence means paying proper respect in deeds, words and thoughts to those who merit our respect.

- Service. *Vaiyaavritya* means rendering service to those to whom it is due. These could be elders, ascetics or holy persons, either in person or through the agency of another. Service can be rendered when others are ill or in some other form of need, even if brought about through their own negligence. Service to the weak and sick is highly regarded as it is said to be akin to rendering service to the *tirthankaras*.
- Self-study. *Svaadhyaaya* is the study of scriptures to acquire knowledge, to learn good conduct and detachment, the practice of austerities, and penance for transgression. Self-study has five aspects: learning the scriptures and their meaning *(vaacanaa)*, asking questions of others to remove doubt or to ascertain the meaning *(pruchanaa)*, deep contemplation of scriptures which have been studied *(manana)*, repeated revision of scriptures learned *(punaraavartana)*, and dissemination through sermons *(upadesa)*.
- Detachment. *Vyutsarga* means renunciation of external and internal 'possessions': property, wealth and the like are external possessions, whereas pride, anger, deceit and greed are internal possessions.
- Meditation. *Dhyaana* helps in the realisation of the 'self' and purification of the soul. (It is described in detail later in this chapter.)

The external and internal austerities help an individual to progress towards the chosen goal of controlling desires and freeing oneself from attraction and aversion. Laypeople are encouraged to observe them according to their ability.

Austerities in Daily Practice

We shall now describe Jain fasting practices in daily use and some important ones undertaken on occasions. Fasting helps self-control, to create positive health and sound mind, but it should be practised according to one's ability. Fasting can make the body weak, infirm and withered, but it helps the mind to be spiritually active. During fasting one should practise meditation, and keep oneself engrossed in devotional activities, reading scriptures, holy recitations, and similar spiritually uplifting activities. In fasting, except the optional taking of boiled water during daylight hours, nothing is imbibed, including brushing the teeth or gargling. Ascetics drink only boiled water throughout their lives and observe strict dietary rules (see chapter 4).

While fasting, Jains drink only boiled water and, when permitted, take appropriate Jain diet (see chapter 6). Water should be filtered, boiled and cooled. In addition to reasons of health, the water is boiled to minimise violence to water-borne micro-organisms. In unboiled water micro-organisms multiply in geometric progression. When the water is boiled, although some micro-organisms are killed, the water becomes sterile and the organisms cease to multiply. As a result less number of micro-organisms are harmed when boiled water is drunk as compared to unboiled water, and also less harm is inflicted to the organisms, which would have suffered due to the contact with enzymes and acid in one's stomach.

Navakaarsi   The vow of 'forty-eight minutes' fast' means that after one has fasted overnight, one waits for forty-eight minutes after sunrise before taking any food or water, or brushing one's teeth or rinsing the mouth. (Forty-eight minutes or one-thirtieth of a day is a traditional Indian unit of time.) One recites *Navakara mantra* three times before breaking the fast. There are a number of similar fasts, which differ only in the period. They are:

Porasi   The vow of the 'three-hour fast'.
Saadha porasi   The vow of the 'four-and-half hours' fast'.
Parimuddha   The vow of the 'six-hour fast'.
Avaddha   The vow of the 'eight-hour fast'.
Cauvihaar   This vow involves abstinence from any kind of food, drink or medicine between sunset and sunrise.
Tivihaar   This vow involves taking only water at night.
Duvihaar   This vow permits taking only liquids and medicines at night.
Biyaasan   This vow permits taking food twice a day.
Ekaasan   This vow permits taking food once a day.

Ayambil   This vow permits taking food once a day, but it requires food to be bland, boiled or cooked, and devoid of enhanced taste, milk, curds, ghee, oil, and green or raw vegetables. Some aspirants undertake ayambil fast by only eating one item of food.
Upavaas   This vow involves not taking any food for a period of twenty-four hours; it has two versions: if no water is drunk, it is cauvihaar upavaas, but if some boiled water is drunk only during daylight hours, it is tivihaar upavaas.

Chatha   It is vow of continuous two-days fast, similar to *upavaas*.

Attham   It is continuous three-days fast, similar to *upavaas*.

Atthai   This is a continuous eight-days fast, similar to *upavaas*.

Many aspirants undertake this austerity during the sacred days of *paryusana*, described in chapter 5.

Maasaksamana   It is a continuous thirty-day fast, similar to *upavaas*. It is very rigorous austerity and is considered a sign of great piety.

In some cases, aspirants fast for differing periods, ranging from four days to as much as three months. In exceptional cases continuous fast have lasted longer. One such case was the fast by Sahaja Muni in Bombay in 1995, which lasted 201 days.

Vardhammana tapa   It is a vow of progressive fast, where an aspirant will observe one *ayambil* and one *upavaas*., followed by two *ayambils* and one *upavaas*, then three *ayambils* and one *upavaas*, building up to one hundred *ayambils* and one *upavaas*.

Navapada oli   It is the vow of nine continuous *ayambils*, observed twice yearly with a specific form of worship, holy recitation, meditation and other rituals in honour of the 'nine objects of veneration' *(navapad)*. Some worshippers observe nine such *olis*, over a period of four and a half years, a total of eighty-one *ayambils*.

Varsitapa   This is a year-long austerity, observed from the eighth day of the dark half of the month of *Caitra* to the third day of the bright half of the month of Vaisakh *(aksaya tritiya)* of the following year. The aspirant undertakes *upavaas* one day and *biyaasan* the next day, again *upavaas* on the third day and so on. Sometimes, during the period of this austerity, the aspirant undertakes continuously two days *upavaas* followed by one *biyaasan*, which depends upon Jain auspicious day. *Varsitapa* continues for more than a year and is broken on the day called *akshay tritiya* by accepting sugar-cane juice, which commemorates Risabhdeva, the first *tirthankara*, who fasted completely for a similar period and broke his fast by accepting sugar-cane juice from his grandson Shreyansakumar.

Upadhaan tapa.   This is a special collective group austerity, under the guidance of a senior ascetic, lasts twenty-eight, thirty-five or forty-seven days, where a celebration takes place on its conclusion. The participants observe alternate *upavaas* and *ayambil*, or a special *ekaasan*, known as *nivi*, and perform rituals unique to this occasion, together with scriptural study.

Visasthanaka tapa   It is the austerity of fast and special worhip of the twenty objects of veneration, where aspirants, observing continuous *upavaas*, worship each object for twenty days. The fifteenth object of veneration is worshipped for forty days, observing *upavaas*. Fasting may be complete or partial. The twenty objects of veneration are: *tirthankara*, *siddha*, the four-fold order, *aacaarya*, senior ascetics, preceptor, sage, knowledge, faith, reverence, conduct, celibacy, rituals, austerity, Gautama (the chief disciple of Mahavira), service, restraint, empirical knowledge, scriptural knowledge, and holy places. The scriptures affirm that all *tirthankaras* performed this austerity in their earlier lives. Guidance from spiritual superiors is helpful in observing this austerity.

Siddhi tapa This austerity lasts for forty-four days, beginning with *upavaas* for one day, followed by one *biyasan*; then two days' *upavaas*, followed by one *biyaasan*; culminating in eight days' *upavaas*, completed by the last *biyaasan*.

Apart from the fasting and austerities detailed above, Jain seers prescribe many other minor and major austerities. The austerities should be observed with the proper objective of purifying the soul by freeing oneself from attachment and aversion. External austerities are the means to aid internal ones, which explains their importance in Jainism.

JAIN YOGA AND MEDITATION

Modern science and technology have brought high standards of material comfort and welfare to people, particularly in the 'developed' countries. However, these material gains have not brought satisfaction or contentment. On the contrary, they seem to have created more greed, conflict, insecurity, unhappiness, anxiety, stress and illness. In the face of the failure of wealth and material comforts to deliver contentment, many are turning to yoga and meditation, an age-old tradition, to regain their physical and mental health.

Yoga was a way of life in ancient India. The word *yoga* is from the ancient language of Sanskrit, from *yuj* meaning 'join'. By extension of the meaning, it carries the figurative sense of 'concentration', religious or abstract contemplation. Yoga is a spiritual activity of mind, body, or speech aimed at achieving liberation or self-realisation. In theistic philosophies, its aim is to merge with the Supreme Being. The concentration of the mind onto a particular object is generally termed 'meditation'. Through the continual practice of yoga and meditation the spiritual aspirant can achieve the goals of mental peace, inner happiness, and the annihilation of karmic bondage, leading to self-realisation and enlightenment.

Mahavira's life is a superb example of the yogic path. The foundation of Mahavira's spiritual practice was meditation combined with yogic postures, leading to bodily detachment. This combined activity is known as *kaayotsarga*. Austerities, such as fasting and yogic postures, inspired and complemented his spiritual practices, which were not a special ritual, but an essential part of his life. For example, he always observed silence and carefully followed his chosen path, living totally in the present. Whatever he did, he was totally engrossed in it without either any impression of the past or imagination of the future. He was so much absorbed in meditation *(kaayotsarga)*, that he experienced neither hunger nor thirst, heat nor cold. His mind, intellect, senses, all his concerns, moved in one direction: towards the 'self' and self-realisation, and emancipation.

The aim of all spiritual practices is to achieve control over one's activities *(yogas)*: mind, body and speech. All ethics and external austerities are the means to achieve concentrated deep meditation. Meditation was very commonplace to both Jain ascetics and laypeople up to the 1st century BCE. The practice of meditation gradually became secondary, leaving few Jain exponents of the meditational techniques of Mahavira. Later, other ethical and ritual practices, and external austerities displaced it.

The Buddhist scripture *Tripitakas* asserts that the Buddha practised meditation through being initiated in *niggantha dhamma*, that is Jainism. The small image of Parsvanatha on the head of the great statue of Buddha in the Ajanta caves (7th century CE) suggests that Buddha was meditating on a symbol of Parsvanatha, and the later Chinese and Japanese forms of Buddhist meditation such as Zen Buddhism may have their roots in the spirit of Jain meditation. In the *Dhammapada* the Buddha has stated that those in whom wisdom and meditation meet are close to salvation. Patanjali (2nd century BCE) argues in the *Yoga Sutra*, that meditation is the vehicle that gradually liberates the soul and leads to salvation. The practice of meditation differs from one system to another, but all agree regarding the importance of meditation for spiritual progress.

Williams (1963) describes Jain Yoga as the spiritual practices, such as vows, 'model stages', rituals and worship of householders and ascetics.
It is to the credit of the Jain seers that they integrated yoga, meditation and other spiritual practices into the daily routine of both laity and ascetics. When the duties of equanimity *(saamayika)*, penitence *(pratikramana)* and regular veneration of images *(pujaa, caitya vandana)* are practised as part of daily life, attending special yoga and meditation classes, so popular in the modern age becomes unnecessary.

Yoga and meditation have become widespread as part of the daily practices of both Jain ascetics and laypeople. This has happened through the efforts of great 'yogis' *(mahaayogi)* such as Anandaghana (17th century), Buddhi Sagara and Srimad Rajcandra (late 19th and early 20th centuries), and Bhadrankarvijay, Sahajananda and Mahaprajna (20 century).

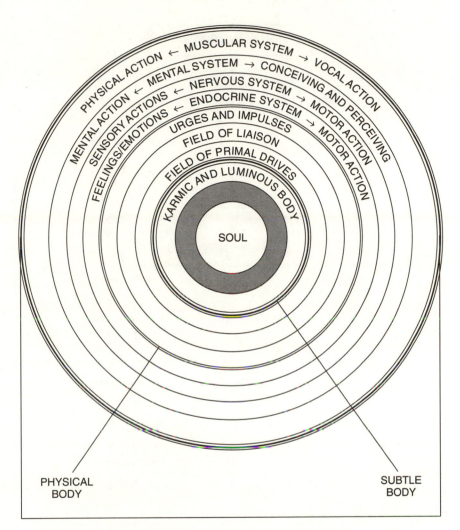

Figure 3.2 The relationship between the subtle and physical body

activate the endocrine system when they reach the physical body, stimulating the latter to secrete and distribute chemical messengers (hormones) corresponding to the nature and intensity of the impulse. Thus the hormones become the agents for executing the primal drives in the physical body.

The chemical messengers secreted by the endocrines are carried by the bloodstream and interact with the brain and the nervous system, together they constitute an integral co-ordinating system, which modern medicine

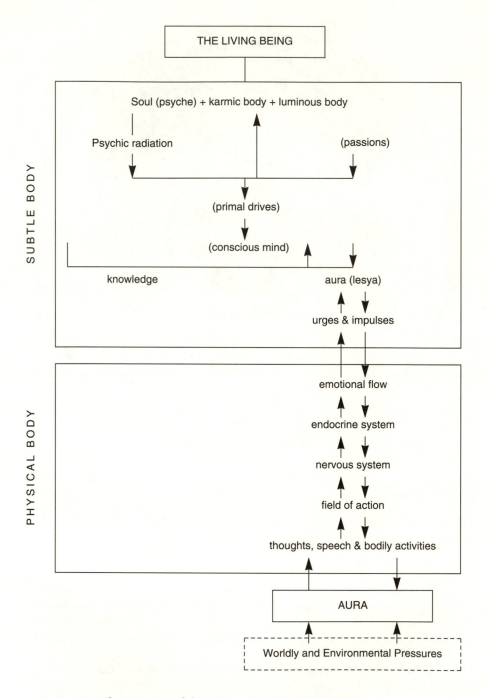

Figure 3.3   The Jain view of the relationship of body behaviour

calls the neuro-endocrine system. This system not only controls and regulates every bodily function but also profoundly influences mental states, emotions, thought, speech and behavioural patterns. Thus, the endocrines act as transformers between the most subtle spiritual 'self' and the gross body. They are gross when compared with the domain of the primal drive, but subtle when compared with the gross constituents: muscles, blood and other bodily organs. This, then, is the inter-communicating mechanism within the body, which translates the intangible and imperceptible code of the primal drive into a form crude enough to function through flesh and bones.

The pure soul radiates its characteristic infinite bliss, knowledge, perception and energy. The impure soul's radiation becomes distorted, as it must pass through the cloud of karmic body and the malevolent field of passions (where it produces primal drives).

The karmic body has eight components of which four are destructive: right faith-obscuring, right knowledge-obscuring, right conduct-obscuring, delusion-producing (insight-deluding and conduct-deluding); and four are non-destructive: feeling-producing (pleasure and pain), body-producing, lifespan-determining and status-determining.

The primal drives depend upon the karmic components and create psychic mind (conscious mind) with a distorted knowledge, and the psychic mind radiates distorted images across the field of liaison between the subtle and the gross bodies.

The physical mind acts as a vehicle for the flow of emotions, which stimulates the endocrine and nervous systems, creating the thought, speech and bodily activities.

Aura and *lesyaas*

The aura of a living organism is an amalgam of two energies: the vital energy of consciousness and the electro-magnetic energy of the material body. Mental states constitute the compelling force produced by the radiation of vital energy. Jain scriptures describe how this vital energy is responsible in effecting the physical brain and releasing the electo-magnetic material particles to produce an aura of the person. If the mental state is pure, the aura is gratifying and if the mental state is impure and full of the passions, the aura is repulsive. The aura of the saints is gratifying and is often shown as a halo aroud their heads. Although mental states are conscious and aura is material, there is an intimate relationship between the two. Aura is an image of mental states of a person.

Lesyaas (Psychic 'colours') Jain scriptures have described *lesyaas*, which are inadequately translated as psychic 'colours', and their functions. They act as a liaison between the spiritual 'self' and the physical body of a living organism. They are the built-in mechanism within the organism through which the spiritual self can exercise its power and control the functioning of the bodily organs. Psychic 'coloration' functions in both directions, centripetally, from periphery to the centre, and centrifugally, from centre to periphery. Karmic material is continually attracted from the external environment by the three-fold activities of the physical body: thought, speech and action, and this material is transferred to the sphere of the passions in a subtle form. Similarly, whatever is radiated outwards from the subtle karmic body at the centre is transferred to the gross body by the psychic colours.

'*Colorations*' The 'malevolent' *(asubha)* colorations are black, blue and grey and are the origin of evil. Cruelty, the desire to kill, the desire to lie, fraud, deceit, cheating, lust, dereliction of duties, laziness and other vices, are produced by these colorations. The endocrine glands, the adrenal gland and the gonads, work in close alliance with these colorations to produce impulses, which in turn, stimulate the body through endocrine action, expressing themselves in the form of emotion and passion.

The 'benevolent' *(subha)* colorations are yellow, red and white and are the origin of good. Perception of these bright colours curbs evil drives and transmutes the emotional state of a person. Evil thoughts are replaced by good, thus internal purification of the mental state radiates beneficial waves to influence the external environment.

How Meditation Works

Relaxation and bodily detachment are prerequisites of meditation. Meditation is the process by which one searches for the cause of misery and suffering; the gross body is the medium for the perception of suffering and its manifestation, but it is not itself the root cause. The root cause is the subtle karmic body which deludes, so that the spiritual 'self' remains unaware of its own existence. The karmic body produces vibrations, shock waves in the form of primal drives, urges and impulses, and influences the activities of the gross body, mind and speech. When all bodily activities are halted through bodily detachment, mental equillibrium is arrived at through meditation, and the vibrations, primal drives, urges and impulses become ineffective, thus meditation calms the waves produced by primal drives.

The karmic body continues transmitting vibrations and sheds karmic particles, and the true characteristics of the soul, bliss, energy, faith and knowledge start appearing. Thus meditation aid the soul in shedding the karmic body and achieving self-conquest. This is shown in figure 3.4.

Meditation is the acquisition of maximal mental steadiness. Unless the body is stable, the mind cannot be steady. The muscular system is the basis

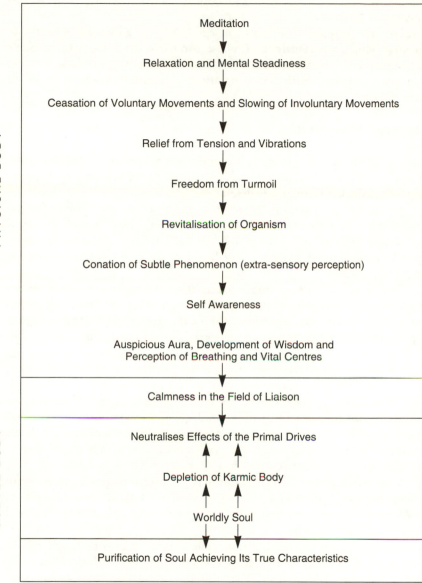

PHYSICAL BODY

SUBTLE BODY

Meditation

Relaxation and Mental Steadiness

Ceasation of Voluntary Movements and Slowing of Involuntary Movements

Relief from Tension and Vibrations

Freedom from Turmoil

Revitalisation of Organism

Conation of Subtle Phenomenon (extra-sensory perception)

Self Awareness

Auspicious Aura, Development of Wisdom and Perception of Breathing and Vital Centres

Calmness in the Field of Liaison

Neutralises Effects of the Primal Drives

Depletion of Karmic Body

Worldly Soul

Purification of Soul Achieving Its True Characteristics

Figure 3.4   Meditation and its effects

of bodily activity; relaxation and bodily detachment help achieve this steadiness of mind.

The first step in a meditational exercise is to adopt an appropriate posture, and then remain motionless for some time. Control of one's breathing, concentration on psychic and energy centres and the psychic colours, together with contemplation and autosuggestion help in meditation.

Types of Meditation

Jain scriptures describe four types of meditation: 'sorrowful' *(aarta)* 'cruel' *(raudra)*, 'virtuous' *(dharma)*, and 'pure' *(sukla)*; the first two are inauspicious and the last two are auspicious.

Sorrowful meditation Sorrowful meditation has been further classified under four sub-types: (i) contact with undesirable and unpleasant things and people; (ii) separation from the desired things and loved ones; (iii) anxiety about health and illness; (iv) hankering for sensual pleasures.

Sorrowful meditation, though agreeable in the beginning, yields unfortunate results in the end. From the point of view of colorations it is the result of the three inauspiscious psychic colours. It requires no effort but proceeds spontaneously from the previous karmic impressions. Its signs are: doubt, sorrow, fear, negligence, being argumentative, confusion, intoxication, eagerness for mundane pleasures, sleep, fatigue, hysterical behaviour, complaints, using gestures or words to attract sympathy, and fainting. Sorrowful meditation is due to attraction, aversion and infatuation and intensifies the transmigration of the soul. It is assossiated with 'malevolent' psychic colours. Usually people who engage in this form of meditation are reborn as animals. It lasts up to the sixth spiritual stage. The stages of spiritual progress are described in volume 2, chapter 4.

Cruel Meditation This meditation is more detrimental than sorrowful meditation and is classified into four sub-types (i) harbouring thoughts of violence, (ii) falsehood, (iii) theft, (iv) guarding the pleasurable material possessions and people.

The first sub-type called 'pleasurable violence' means taking delight in killing or destroying living beings oneself or through others. It includes taking pleasure in violent skills, encouraging sinful activities, and association with evil people. This cruel meditation includes the desire to kill; taking delight in hearing, seeing or recalling the miseries of sentient beings and being envious of other people's prosperity.

The second sub-type is 'pleasurable falsehood'. It means taking pleasure in using deception, deceiving the simple-minded through lies, spoken or written, and amassing wealth by deceit.

The third is 'pleasurable theft'. This form of meditation includes not only stealing but also encouraging others to steal.

The fourth is 'pleasurable guarding' of wealth and property. It includes the desire to take possession of all the benefits of the world, and thoughts of violence in attaining the objects of enjoyment. It also includes fear of losing and violent desires to protect the possessions.

It is obvious that only someone who is fully disciplined can avoid cruel meditation. Pujyapada has pointed out that the cruel meditation of a righteous person is less intense and cannot lead to hellish existence. Cruel meditation lasts up to the fifth spiritual stage.

Sometimes this meditation occurs even to ascetics on account of the force of previously accumulated *karma*. It is characterised by cruelty, harshness, deceit, hard-heartedness and mercilessness. The external signs of this meditation are red eyes, curved eyebrows, a fearful appearance, shivering of the body and sweating. Those involved in such a meditation are full of desires, hatred and infatuation and are usually reborn as hellish beings. This meditation is associated with three intense 'malevolent' psychic colours.

Virtuous Meditation   Inauspicious meditation happens spontaneously, without effort. Auspicious meditation, virtuous and pure meditation which leads to liberation, requires effort. Jain scriptures advise keeping the mind occupied with simple mantras such as *namo arham*, meaning honour to the worthy persons, so that one does not succumb to inauspicious meditation. Auspicious meditation helps to control desires, hatred and infatuation. The object of this meditation is to purify the soul.

Requirements for virtuous meditation   Whether accompanied or alone, anywhere an appropriate place is fit for meditation, if the mind is resolute. But surroundings influence the mind and places where disturbances occur should be avoided. Places that are sanctified by its association with great personages are peaceful, such as certain temples, the seashore, a forest, a mountain, or an island should be chosen. Preferably a place for meditation should be free from the disturbance due to noise or the weather. The householder can also choose a quiet corner of the home for regular meditation.

Any meditation posture is suitable for the detached, steadfast and pure person, yet postures are important. Subhacandra mentions seven postures: *padmaasana*, *ardhapadmaasana*, *vajraasana*, *viraasana*, *sukhaasana*, *kamalaasana* and *kaayotsarga*. The first two, the lotus and half-lotus positions, and the last of these seven, standing or sitting meditation, are particularly suitable for modern times.

As Patanjala yoga, a famous Indian system, gives much importance to 'spiritual breathing' (*pranaayama*), Jainism also attaches importance to control of breathing as an aid to control the mind. If performed correctly, it helps to develop certain energies and the practioner may even develop supernatural powers, but *pranaayama* performed without the objective of controlling the mind may lead to sorrowful meditation.

Conscious control over the senses is essential in controlling the mind, as when the senory organs become attenuated, they interact with the mind in a harmonious way. One can concentrate on such areas as the eyes, the ears, the tip of the nose, the mouth, the navel, the head, the heart and the point between the eyebrows.

The object of virtuous meditation   Amongst the objects upon which one can meditate are: the sentients and the insentients; their triple nature of existence, birth and destruction; worthy personages *(arhats)* and the liberated persons *(siddhas)*. One should learn to distinguish between the 'self' and the body. The self has neither friend nor foe, it is itself the object of worship and possesses infinite energy, knowledge, faith and bliss, but physical beauty, strength, wealth, attractions, aversions, material happiness, misery and longevity are temporary in nature and are due to the effects of the karmic body.

Types of virtuous meditation   The *Tattvartha Sutra* mentions four types of virtuous meditation: reflection on the teachings of the Jinas *(aajnaa vicaya)*; reflection on dissolution of the passions *(apaaya vicaya)*; reflection on karmic consequences *(vipaaka vicaya)*; and reflection on the universe *(sansthaana vicaya)*:

- Reflection on teachings of the *jinas*: This meditation is having complete faith in the nature of things as taught by the omniscients and recorded in the scriptures, as when the mind is fully occupied in the study of the scriptures this constitutes meditation.
- Reflections on dissolution of the passions: This meditation involves deep thinking on the effects of the passions (anger, pride, deceit, greed) and attractions and aversions, as their adverse effects harm the soul and counter the spiritual path. A thoroughgoing consideration of the means of overcoming wrong belief, wrong knowledge and wrong conduct constitutes this meditation.
- Reflection on karmic consequences means thinking of the effects of *karma* on living beings. All pleasure and pain is the consequence of one's own actions, which should be regulated and controlled. This meditation is aimed at understanding the causes and consequences of *karma*.
- Reflection on the universe is meditating on the nature and form of the universe with a view to attaining detachment. It includes reflection on the shape of the universe: the lower region with its seven hells and their miseries, the middle region which contains human beings and from which one can achieve liberation, and the upper region of the heavens with their many pleasures but from which liberation is not possible, and at the very apex the abode of the liberated.

The meditation of 'reflection on the universe' is of four sub-types:

- Reflection on the Body *(pindastha)*   This is meditation on the nature of the living organism and the destruction of the main eight types of *karma*, the purified self and the attributes of the liberated.
- Reflection on Words *(padastha)*   This is meditation on the syllables of certain incantations such as the *Namokara* and other mantras made up of differing syllables, and their recitations; the repetition of these mantras may lead to the attainment of supernatural powers.
- Reflection on 'Forms' *(rupastha)*   This meditation concentrates on the different 'forms' which worthy personages may take in their worldly life (e.g. such persons may be rulers, ascetics, omniscients, preachers). It may also focus on any material object or on the image of a *tirthankara* and the spiritual qualities of the enlightened, and it leads to the realisation of the ideal on which one meditates.
- Reflection on the 'Formless' *(rupaatita)*   Meditation on form implies reflection on embodied liberated souls, i.e. the enlightened ones, whereas meditation on the 'formless' implies reflection on disembodied liberated souls; ultimately this is a meditation upon one's own pure soul and it leads to self-realisation.

Supervision from a qualified teacher, constant practice and perseverance are needed to master virtuous meditation.

The benefits of virtuous meditation   The first signs that one is benefitting from this form of meditation are control over the senses, fine health, kindness, an auspicious aura, bliss and clarity of voice. It leads directly to heavenly pleasures and indirectly to liberation through merit, stopping the influx of *karma* and the shedding of previously acquired *karma*. This meditation is associated with three auspicious psychic colours. Persons engaging in this type of meditation are reborn either as heavenly or as human beings. This virtuous meditation lasts up to the thirteenth spiritual stage.

Pure meditation   In virtuous meditation consciousness of the distinction between the subject and the object of knowledge persists; whereas in pure meditation all conceptual thinking gradually ceases, and pure meditation emerges when the passions have been destroyed.

Only someone with an ideal type of constitution and full knowledge of the scriptures can engage in pure meditation, but it is believed that in the modern age such people no longer exist on this earth. Hence the notion of pure meditation is only of an academic interest. Pure meditation is the final stage before liberation and is associated with the auspicious white psychic colour.

Meditation in Hinduism and Buddhism

Yoga and meditation form an essential part of the spiritual life of Hindus. The sixth chapter of the *Bhaagavat Gita* claims activity that frees the soul from attachment and aversion is yoga. Patanjali defines yoga as the path of self-realisation through control of one's desires and control of one's mind, by physical or psychic methods. He underlines the importance of the eightfold path in realising perfect meditation resulting in the soul's union with the supreme being; this includes mortification, the singing of certain hymns, and a devoted reliance on the 'Supreme Soul', God. The following eight paths are prescribed by Patanjali for a true yogi: self control *(yama)*, observance *(niyama)*, posture *(aasana)*, spiritual breathing *(pranaayama)*, withdrawal from the sensory stimuli *(pratyaahara)*, meditation *(dhyaana)*, contemplation *(dharana)*, and profound meditation or trance *(samaadhi)*.

The study of the eight-fold path makes it clear that Patanjali's yoga is passive, and in this it is different from the *karma yoga* of the *Gita*. The passivity of Patanjali's method implies the suspension of all movement, physical as well as mental, on the part of the yogi in communion with the supreme, thus it is comparable to some aspects of the virtuous meditation of Jainism.

Buddhism also has meditation as a central practice of its spirituality. Buddhists meditate to comprehend the true nature of reality and to develop in harmony with it. Gautama, the Buddha, learned the art of meditation from Jain teachers before his enlightenment. The chanting of a mantra or sacred verses encourages mental calmness; the rhythmic ebb and flow of breath is used as a focal point to which the attention is brought back whenever it wanders; this type of meditation is called 'peaceful abiding' *(samataa)*. Those engaged in meditation can progress to the technique called 'introspection' *(vipassanaa)*, by which they hope to gain insight into reality. This is achieved by looking inward beneath the surface of consciousness. They are aware of deep underlying emotions and thoughts, but refrain from interacting with them to dampen their activity. Meditation means being totally aware of the present moment and once this is well established, meditation can be practised when standing, sitting, walking or lying down. The Buddha is portrayed as being mindful in all these states. Zen Buddhism particularly emphasises that meditation can be performed while carrying out the most basic activities of life. In the Theravada tradition in South East Asia, meditation has traditionally been viewed as largely the work of ascetics, particularly those who choose to live isolated and solitary lives in the forest, but nowadays, laypeople meditate either with ascetics or in lay meditation centres. Buddhist meditation compares favourably with some aspects of Jain virtuous meditation.

Meditational practices and their beneficial effects have been well known in India for thousands of years, but Indian meditational practices have only recently become widely appreciated in the West. Meditation helps to promote both physical and spiritual health, and in India many institutions employ meditational practices to assist the cure of illnesses and to establish the scientific basis of meditation. Jain meditation has been interwoven into the daily activities of the Jain community. It is believed that this has contributed to the lessening of certain illnesses in the Jain population.

It is outside the scope of this book to describe fully the techniques of meditation. The reader is referred to the many works published on the subject.

A person should properly practise religion before old age sets in, before ill health becomes chronic and before the senses lose their power.

(*Dasavaikalika* 8: 35)

Destroy anger through calmness, overcome ego by modesty, discard deceit by straightforwardness and defeat greed by contentment.

(*Dasavaikalika* 8: 38)

Walk carefully, stand carefully, sleep carefully, eat carefully, and speak carefully so that no sinful act is committed.

(*Dasavaikalika* 4: 31)

Persons with self-control should speak exactly as they have seen. Their speech should be to the point, unambiguous, clear, natural, free from prattle and cause no anxiety to others.

(*Dasavaikalika* 8: 48)

Chapter 4

THE JAIN COMMUNITY

THE FOURFOLD ORDER

The term *sangha* embraces the four orders of monks *(saadhus)*, nuns *(saadhvis)*, laymen *(sraavakas)* and laywomen *(sraavikaas)*, in fact the whole Jain community. The Jain *sangha* is involved in all major decisions affecting the community and has supreme authority over the individual orders. The ascetic order plays a very important part in Jainism; it observes the teachings of Mahavira rigorously. It is impossible for laymen and women to follow the teachings to the same extent, as they are involved in worldly activities and in earning their livelihood, however, they follow the teachings of Mahavira to the best of their ability.

Throughout the ages monks have been the scholars and teachers of the Jain faith. Nuns have been much less involved in scholarship but have taken a prominent part in expounding the faith to the laity. The monks have not only produced work of a religious nature but have also created scholarship of importance in science, medicine, mathematics, logic, languages and other fields of study. This tradition continues today. Lay scholarship has also developed considerably in recent times. One has to admire the genius of Mahavira and his followers for the fact that after more than 2,500 years this four-fold organisation of Jains is very much in evidence. Mahavira respected the *sangha* as if it was a *tirthankara* and the faithful do likewise. There is both respect and indirect control of one order over the other. The laity respect and learn Jain teachings from the ascetic order, and the monks and nuns respect and listen to the laymen and women.

The career of Jain monks and nuns begins with the ceremony of initiation into asceticism *(diksaa)* and by acceptance of the obligations of the five great vows, and continues unbroken to the end of their lives. The ascetic state is a permanent commitment; the discipline is strict, yet, those who leave ascetic order are few. The monks and nuns inspire the laity to establish temples, *upashrayas*, libraries and other welfare institutions for the community.

Owing to the strict vow of non-violence and reverence for life

Figures 4.1 Jain monk (Svetambara) with his permitted possessions; Svetambara female ascetic ('nun')

(ahimsaa), the ascetics will not use any form of vehicle. From the 1970s onwards some monks and nuns have violated this vow and travelled abroad to promote Jainism. Migration of Jains outside India for economic reasons means that those migrant Jains are no longer inspired by the ascetic order. Perhaps in the future some Jains abroad, or the prospective candidates for *diksaa* from India, will initiate in the West and start an ascetic order. The other alternative is for the *sangha* to send monks and nuns from India, who will then be re-initiated in the West, as re-initiation is necessary after breaking their vows.

Although the mendicant order is seen as unitary, it has for a long time been divided into many stems or groups *(gaccha, gana)*. These groups may take their names from their place of origin, from association with a particular caste, from their founders or from particular points of doctrine or ritual. The *gaccha* may be subdivided, most commonly into groups studying under particular teachers. References to these divisions of the mendicant orders are found around the 8th and 9th centuries CE and some of these exist today: the *Tapaagaccha*, *Kharataragaccha* and some other *gacchas* can trace the line of succession of their leaders back through a long history. The practice of solitary religious retreat is known in Jainism, but usually the Jain monks and nuns are to be seen as a member of a group, attached to their spiritual leader or guru. Although study, scholarship and preaching are important activities in the mendicant order, the primary aim of the monk or nun is the purification of his or her own soul, and it is to this end that all the austerities and disciplines are directed. The rigours of the mendicant life mean that relatively few people enter it, which is particularly true of the Digambaras. The total number of Digambara monks (there are no Digambara nuns in the strict sense) in the mid 1990s was estimated to be around 295, while Svetambara monks and nuns were estimated to number over ten thousand (see table 4.1)

Table 4.1 Number of *saadhus* and *saadhvis* retired for four months of the rainy season 1995

Sect	Aacaaryas	Saadhus	Saadhvis	Total
Svetambara Murtipujaka	123	1,374	4,961	6,335
Sthankavasi	8	512	2,492	3,004
Terapanthi	1	146	545	691
Digambara	33	295	250	545
Total	165	2,327	8,248	10,575

Among the Digambaras, 'semi-ascetics' (*bhattarakas*) undertake some of the religious functions, which in the Svetambara sect are carried out by monks and nuns. In the past there were 'semi-ascetics' (*yatis*) among the Svetambaras, who performed functions similar to the *bhattarakas*, and additional duties such as disseminating Jain teachings, and carrying out the ceremonial installation of images in temples. They also guided the community in a pastoral role, but today there are very few *yatis* and the institution has all but disappeared. At the end of the 20th century, with an educated laity, there are many distinguished scholars of Jain religion and practices, but the tradition of ascetic-scholarship remains strong.

In the 1980s *Aacaarya* Tulsi of the *Terapanthi* sect developed a community of *samanas* and *samani*, who take partial vows, can use a vehicle for travel, cook for themselves and use modern toilets; otherwise their lifestyle is similar to male ascetics. They have travelled to the West and play an important part in propagating Jain values.

The present Jain population in India is difficult to estimate, but is no more than one per cent of the total population; it was much larger in the past. It has succeeded in maintaining its separate identity. Jains have a distinctive outlook on life embracing ethical rules of conduct based on non-violence and reverence for all forms of life. Jain ethics, places of worship, scriptures, holy days, rituals, ascetics, history, philosophy and culture are recognisably different from their Hindu counterparts, and these differences are seen, for example, in the observance of certain widespread customs and the underlying aims of those customs. For Hindus, marriage is a religious sacrament, while Jains consider it a civil contract. Hindu culture observes a number of days of mourning for the dead, Jain teachings run counter to this. Unlike Hindu practice, in the Jain tradition a widow inherits the property of her deceased husband. Hindus consider adoption a religious matter; Jains do not. However, one can often see the influence of Hindu customs on the social life of some in the Jain community. In the case of Jains who were formerly members of Hindu castes, the persistence of these non-Jain customs may be attributed in part to their previous social, cultural and religious lives. There is no doubt of the impact of certain cultural influences on Jains from the wider Hindu community.

The Jain community in India has historically been influential. Even though numerically only a minority, the community has always had considerable prestige and produced a large number of eminent personalities. As Jains take care to maintain cordial relations with all other communities, regardless of creed and caste, they have been able to play a significant role in national life and in the many places in which they lived and still live today. In politics, emperors such as Candragupta Maurya, rulers such as Kharvel in Kalinga, Vanaraja and Kumarpala in Gujarat and Amoghavarsa in the Deccan were Jains. There have also been Jain military leaders such as the male generals Camundaraya and Gangaraja, and the female generals Jakkiyavve, Saviyavve and Bhairavadevi. In many places in India significant roles in government administration were in the hands of Jains, producing important ministers such as Bhamashah in Udaipur, Vastupala and Tejpal in Gujarat. *Aacaaryas* Simhanandi and Sudatta were instrumental in the founding of the Ganga kingdom in the 4th century CE and of the Hoysala kingdom in Karnataka in the 11th century CE, respectively.

Jains have played an important part in the past and present economic life of India. Their religious beliefs, particularly their commitment to 'non-violence' has circumscribed the types of profession or business in which they will engage. This has led to Jains having a disproportionate representation in banking and finance, accountancy and management, medicine and law and some trading and commerce. The consequence of this economic specialisation has been that the Jain community has become very wealthy. This wealth has enabled Jains to undertake extensive philanthropic projects, both in India and outside, and for the benefit of non-Jains as well as for Jains.

Despite the many successes of the Jain community, there remain problems: the common religious bond is not strong enough to prevent divisions, which have sometimes led to schisms; these divisions undermine the community. What is true of religious divisions, is equally true of social divisions: traditionally Jain social organisation is viewed as having originated in the distinctions of work and function, but later, under Hindu influence, a large number of castes and sub-castes emerged among Jains.

The modern Jain community maintains a high degree of social unity, but faces a range of new challenges, and how it responds to these challenges will determine its future, both in India and in the rest of the world.

MONKS AND NUNS, AND THEIR DAILY DUTIES

Asceticism and, in particular, the radical renunciation practised in Jainism, symbolises the principles of spiritual striving and dependence upon the self alone to achieve the ultimate objective of liberation. Jain asceticism has a multi-dimensional character: it is personal, religious and social in nature. Despite the fact that it is primarily concerned with personal spiritual progress, one cannot deny its social role in religious teaching, sermons, motivating laypersons, and protecting the integrity of the four-fold order.

Before discussing the orders of ascetics in Jainism, let us briefly consider comparable orders in other religions. Hindus, Buddhists and Christians have monks and nuns, either based in 'religious houses' or 'wandering', from early in their histories. But in general there have been two ways in which Jain ascetics differed from those of other religions. The first is in the degree of renunciation by Jain ascetics, which has always been radical. The second difference is that Jain ascetics do not separate themselves from the community as happens in some Christian 'closed orders', for example, the Carthusians. Some religions e.g. Islam, Judaism and Sikhism do not possess monastic orders.

In Hinduism men (generally women would not do this) pass through four stages of life: 'studentship' (brahmacaaryaasram), 'householdership' (grahasthaasram), 'forest-dwelling' (vanaprasthaasram) and 'renunciation' (sanyaasaasram). When family responsibilities are completed, usually about the age of fifty, one retires to the forest to lead a life of detachment in pursuit of spiritual progress, and when the aspiring ascetic is ready for renunciation, he becomes a sanyaasi. However, some aspirants become ascetics (sanyaasis) in adulthood without completing their 'household duties'. Hindu ascetics have many orders and hierchies; they wear reddish-yellow or saffron robes and live in monasteries run by individuals or public institutions. In contrast to Jain ascetics, they may use transport; wandering and begging alms are not their norms and most of them will accept donations of money. Rough estimates put the figure of Hindu *sanyaasis* and related ritualists at several millions, but forest dwelling *sanyaasis* are a rarity today.

The Buddhists have about a million ascetics, called *bhiksus*. There are a number of Buddhist nuns, but their numbers and importance have always been marginal. Ascetics wear yellow robes and live for the most part in monasteries, although they may wander and may beg alms; usually they are vegetarian, but they may eat non-vegetarian food if it is not especially cooked for them but perchance given to them as donation. After an initiation ceremony, they are trained to follow strict rules of conduct. One can be a Buddhist ascetic for a short period, in contrast to the Jain vow of renunciation, which is of a permanent nature.

There are seniors and juniors among Buddhist ascetics and authority is collective. A monk may leave the order and expulsion is possible for transgressions of the rules of conduct, but the Buddhist monastic order is not as disciplined as in Jain ascetic order.

There are many orders of Christian monks and nuns, and the following is a general impression: Initiation involves undertaking the three vows of poverty, chastity and obedience, and by adopting the way of life of Christian orders, monks and nuns are supposedly imitating the life of Jesus Christ. Members of orders are celibate and may live among the community or separated in monasteries and nunneries. The majority of Christian clergy, who today include women as well as men, are not monks and nuns. Many monks and nuns serve the community in charitable work, in caring for the sick and in teaching. The process of becoming a member of a religious order involves passing through stages, usually spending a period as a novice, before full acceptance. Monasteries and nunneries are organised under the authority of a monk or nun. While in the Middle Ages, in Europe, the religious orders wielded great influence as centres of literacy, culture, and economic and political power, the modern age has seen their influence decline sharply.

Jainism believes that over a time the physical and psychic strengths of human beings have been gradually decreasing and, as a result, one of two possible forms of asceticism, the 'Jina-model', is a rarity, and the other form, the 'order-model', is the norm today.

There is a hierarchy of Jain ascetics, regulated by the *sangha*, where the head of an order is an *aacaarya*. Where there are many *aacaaryas*, a supreme head *(gacchaadhipati* or *ganaadhipati)* may be chosen, but this is a modern development. Below the level of the *aacaarya* there are those who act as teachers to the other ascetics, the 'preceptors' *(gani, panyaasa,* or *upadhyaaya)* and the lowest member in the hierarchy is the ordinary ascetic *(muni* or *saadhu).*

Aacaarya The *aacaarya* is the spiritual leader of the *sangha*, who pursues the path of liberation as expounded by the *tirthankara*. He acquires this position through his spiritual and intellectual attainment and his potential to maintain and strengthen the order. Seniority alone has never been the sole criterion for becoming an *aacaarya*. The *aacaarya* observes five principles relating to knowledge *(jnaanaacaar)*, faith *(darsanaacaar)*, conduct *(caritraacaar)*, austerity *(tapaacaar)*, and spiritual energy *(viryaacaar)*. Ideally an *aacaarya* will fulfil thirty-six attributes:

five controls over the senses;
nine restraints for the observance of celibacy;
four restraints of the passions;
five great vows;
five observances (detailed above);
five carefulnesses in walking, speaking, eating, picking and placing, and 'bodily functions';
three guards of thought, speech and action.

Upaadhyaaya The *upaadhyaayas* are experts in scriptures. They study and teach them to other ascetics. They are required to possess 25 attributes made up of proficiency in the 11 primary canons, 12 secondary canons and having Right faith and Right conduct.

Saadhus or *munis* An ordinary ascetic strives to possess 27 (or 28) qualities, which are listed later in this chapter.

Qualifications and Restrictions for Asceticism Jainism believes that spirituality is a fundamental human characteristic, thus there are virtually no restrictions on initiation to the asceticism; those restrictions which are applied relate to the candidate's potential to fulfil the requirements of the vocation, for example, to travel, to learn, to teach. Many prominent *aacaaryas* came from non-Jain backgrounds. The only restrictions upon initiation are: candidates should not be below eight years of age; should not be infirm due to their age; should not be deaf, dumb, blind or crippled; should be mentally healthy; should not be of a present criminal disposition (reformed persons are acceptable); and may be disqualified through certain statuses e.g. debtors, slaves, eunuchs, kidnapped etc. Women candidates who are pregnant or nursing young children are not accepted.

Initiation as ascetics When candidates decide upon initiation the spiritual head assesses their suitability and, if suitable, requires them to obtain permission from their parents or guardians. If permission is refused or cannot be obtained for practical reasons, the spiritual head re-examines the resolve of the candidates and if then satisfied, initiates them into the order.

The initiation ceremony *(diksaa)* takes place in the presence of the *sangha*, where the spiritual head administers the vow of equanimity *(saamayika)* throughout life and the vow to discard all sinful activities. Before entering the order candidates are given a new name to signal the break with the past worldly life. After initiation, the novice ascetic begins training in undertaking austerities in respect of the ethical code of ascetics, and the protection of living beings, including one sense beings, and is taught to study the scriptures. Novice ascetics are also encouraged by seniors to observe fasts and other austerities for increasing spiritual energy. After due initiation and training, the spiritual head confirms the novice ascetic into the order in presence of the *sangha* by administering the three-fold vow: 'I will not commit sins with body, mind or speech; I will not see them committed and I will not encourage or appreciate such sins'.

Ascetics occasionally breach the rules of conduct. Twenty-one such transgressions are mentioned in the scriptures and the expiation or atone-ment texts *(Cheda Sutras)* prescribe minor and major penances for these transgressions. An ascetic must perform penance and in the event of severe breaches may lose a period of seniority, as he or she is regarded as having lapsed from membership of the order. In extreme cases they may be expelled and, if this happens, reinitiation is the only remedy.

Basic Virtues of an Ascetic   Jain texts describe 27 basic virtues or attrib-utes for ascetics to achieve physical control and spiritual advancement, with minor differences between the Svetambara and Digambara traditions, and it is expected that every ascetic will observe and practise these virtues. The virtues are as follows (numbers indicate how the figure of 27 is arrived at):

Five major vows of 'non-violence', truthfulness, 'non-stealing', celibacy, and 'non-attachment'.
Six 'protections' of living beings: five categories of 'one-sense' beings, and the sixth of mobile beings; Jains believe that there are minute living beings of earth, water, air, fire, and vegetable life.
Five controls over the senses.
Three disciplines of mind, speech and body.
One forgiveness.
One control over greed.
One inner purity.
One observance for restraints of five types of carefulnesses, three types of safeguards, sleep, renunciation of non-religious tales and renunciation of indiscretion.
One prohibition of eating at night.
One carefulness in cleaning belongings to avoid harm to living beings.
One endurance of afflictions.
One forbearance, even in mortal disasters.

Svetambara ascetics wear white unstitched clothes, but have no attachment to them. Digambara ascetics discard all clothes and are 'sky-clad'. Svetambara ascetics sleep on the ground or on a wooden board, resembling a low table. Digambara ascetics sleep on dried grass. There are differences between the traditions in the way ascetics accept food from devotees: Digambara ascetics eat at devotees' houses once a day in the standing posture, following the example of Mahavira. Svetambara ascetics accept appropriate simple food, which is not specially prepared for them, taken from the houses of devotees and then eaten in the *upashrayas*. The ascetics take only that food, which is needed to sustain the body, and drink only boiled water.

Ascetics walk barefoot, do not use vehicles, do not accept, possess or hoard money, stay in one place only a short time, on average a maximum of five days, except during the four months of the monsoon, when they do not travel. They preach the teachings of Mahavira to the laity during their stay, do not remove their hair with razors or scissors, but pluck it with their fingers. The aim of all these practices is to strengthen observance of the above virtues.

The worldly conduct of ascetics There are two types of conduct as described for ascetics in Jain texts: worldly conduct and spiritual or vow-related conduct. The ten rules for conduct are prescribed for inculcating humility and respect for others, especially senior ascetics. They are:

1. Seeking approval of actions.
2. Asking other ascetics if they require food or other necessities.
3. Showing food collected as alms to the senior ascetic or guru.
4. Inviting other ascetics to share food.
5. Asking the pardon of the senior ascetic or guru, using the phrase 'may my faults be forgiven'.
6. Asking permission from the senior ascetic or guru for work, or to leave the upashraya or residency.
7. Saying 'that is so' *(tahatti)* to the teacher's sermons and instructions.
8. Seeking permission before acquiring 'religious riches', i.e. studying scriptures, performing austerities and other spiritual practices.
9. Saying the words 'may I go out' *(avassahi)* while going out of temples or *upashrayas*.
10. Saying the words 'may I come in' *(nissahi)* while coming into temples or *upashrayas*.

Ascetics share belongings: bedding, food, scriptures, pupils, and provide services to seniors and to infirm ascetics.

The spiritual ethics of ascetics The second type of conduct is repre-sented by vow-related or ethical conduct.. The whole life of an ascetic is directed towards conduct leading to the halting of karmic influx and the shedding of accumulated karmas. This conduct is described in chapter 3.

Dietary regulations Ascetics scrupulously follow the rules relating to food. They will prefer to fast rather than take inappropriate food. These rules are meant to strengthen the morality of non-violence and detachment. When accepting food ascetics must be careful about a number of factors:

(1) the type and preparation of food by laypeople; (2) the attitude of laypeople offering food; (3) the ascetics' own attitude towards the food. The seers have noted twenty-six 'defects' in the first factor, sixteen 'defects' in the second and four 'defects' in the third; the details of which are described in the *Vrhatkatha Kalpa* and the *Dasavaikalika Sutra*.

The daily routine of ascetics The *Uttaradhyayana Sutra* gives details on the daily routine of ascetics. The 24 hours are divided into eight segments, four each for day and night and for convenience, we describe the general daily routine observed by ascetics, which may vary according to circumstances.

04.00	rise in the holy morning (*brahma muhurta*)
04.00–05.30	silent recital of *Namokar Mantra*, self-introspection and meditation.
05.30–06.00	service to the senior ascetics and *aacaaryas*
06.00–07.00	daily 'natural duties'
07.00–08.00	self-study and penitential retreat
08.00–09.00	careful cleaning of pots, begging for water, food and alms (Svetambara)
09.00–10.00	sermons and guidance
10.00–12.00	(a) visiting temples to pray
	(b) careful cleaning of alms, pots, clothes
	(c) begging food and alms (Digambara)
	(d) eating meals
12.00–14.00	services to seniors, self-study, meditation and rest
14.00–17.00	self-study, sermons, guidance, and receiving visitors
17.00–18.00	careful cleaning of belongings
18.00–20.00	evening penitential retreat, meditation and teaching laity
20.00–22.00	religious discourses, reflection, recitation
22.00–04.00	sleep

Svetambara ascetics carefully clean their clothes and their wooden platters twice a day (*pratilekhana* or *padilehan*) and see that no harm is done to small beings when they use these possessions.

For every breach of observances they confess to their senior, and seek atonement. Twice a year the ascetics remove their hair by plucking. They avoid intimacy with others and do not discuss worldly matters, except in the narration of stories, while teaching. They maintain minimal external contacts and concentrate on internal contemplation.

Jain Nuns

Nuns *(saadhvis)* are an important part of the four-fold order of the Jain *sangha.* Since the earliest times the ratio of female ascetics to male ascetics, i.e. of nuns to monks, has been in the region of 3 to 1. This situation continues in the present day, though in absolute terms the number of ascetics, male and female, is smaller than in the past; data from Jain texts suggests that in Mahavira's time approximately 10 precent of the Jain population were ascetics, of whom more than two-thirds were nuns.

Nuns observe the same rules as monks, including obedience to the senior nuns and gurus and to the (male) *aacaaryas.* Their daily routine virtually mirrors that of male ascetics, except for those areas of life unique to women. During a nun's menstrual period, she will not attend the temple, nor engage in study or teaching, and restricts her contacts with others; rituals, which would normally be undertaken in the company of other nuns, such as penitential retreat, are conducted alone and in silence. Jains believe that during this period, a nun (or woman) will not be able to 'communicate spiritual energy' due to the physical processes she is experiencing. Thus the recitation of mantras, to take one example, will be adversely affected by the biological state of the individual. This distorted consequence affects others, which is why nuns (and laywomen) temporarily withdraw from most activities and contacts during this short period and, for the duration of their cycle, they occupy themselves in the silent repetition of prayers, mantras and in meditation. Often female ascetics will use this time to repair clothing and to spin the wool and also embroider the eight auspicious signs on woollen cloth for *oghas,* the soft 'brushes', which are the symbols of Svetambara ascetics, and which are used to clear the ground of small living beings.

Some present day female ascetics have high academic qualifications and are proficient in scriptures, give sermons and lectures, have an excellent rapport with laywomen and with children, and are especially noted for their renderings of popular devotional songs.

It must, however, be admitted that there is disparity of status between monks and nuns among both Svetambaras and Digambaras. The Digambara nuns have a status equivalent to the eleventh stage of ethical progress (see chapter 3) and are therefore both technically and practically inferior to monks, but the Svetambaras accord higher status to nuns and believe that women are capable of liberation. Candana, the head of the order of nuns in Mahavira's time, and Rajul, who was betrothed to the *tirthankara* Neminath, are among sixteen women included in the

(a)

(b)

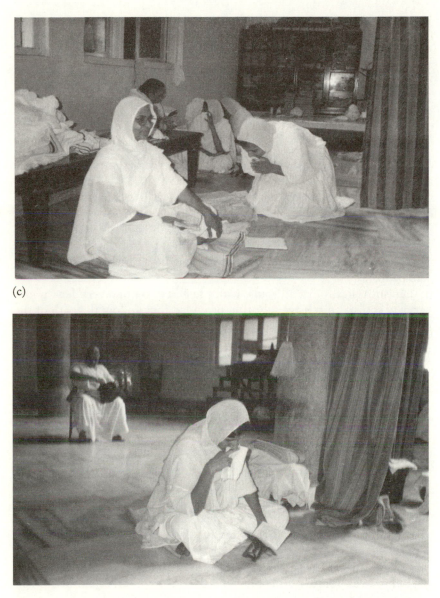

(c)

(d)

Plate 4.1 (a) Svetambara female ascetic ('nun'), helped by a lay devotee, filtering drinking water and returning filtered material to its original environment; (b & c) some of the daily activities of Svetambara nuns; (d) paying respects to a senior nun (guru vandan) and self-study

recitation for the morning penitential retreat on account of their exemplary spiritual qualities. Svetambaras believe that the nineteenth *tirthankara* Malinatha was a woman in her last life before achieving liberation. The laypeople accord a similar respect to all ascetics, regardless of gender. However, in the hierarchy of ascetics, monks are accorded a higher status.

LAYPEOPLE AND THEIR DUTIES

The *Kalpa Sutra* mentions that the four-fold Jain community of Mahavira's time comprised of 14,000 monks, 36,000 nuns, 159,000 laymen and 318,000 laywomen. Monks and nuns followed Mahavira's teachings rigorously, while laypeople followed them within the limits of their everyday duties. While persons born in a Jain community clearly have a better chance of learning the Jain path to spiritual progress, anyone who follows the teachings of Mahavira, consciously or otherwise, can be regarded as following the Jain path.

Jainism believes that all souls, with the exception of a very few 'undeserving' souls, can achieve salvation provided they follow the path of the Three Jewels, i.e. Right Faith, Right Knowledge and Right Conduct.

The ascetics refer to laypeople as *sraavaka* and *sraavikaa*, words which, in Indian scripts, consist of three letters representing the entire Jain philosophy and its goal of liberation through the Three Jewels:

sra   listening (hearing and accepting teachings, i.e. Right Faith)
va   knowledge (i.e. choosing Right Knowledge)
ka   action (i.e. performing Right Action)

An older designation for laypeople was *upaasaka*, which has the meaning of 'one who aspires to liberation'.

The Jain texts describe two types of laypeople: the actual and the ideal. The actual followers of the faith ('householders') should endeavour to turn themselves into the ideal, by observing the vows prescribed for them. Householders who do not observe any vows, even if born into Jain families, are not counted as Jain laypeople. Thus, we could construct a sequence beginning with 'ordinary people' who do not follow the Jain path, then progressing to the actual lay followers (householders), and culminating with the ideal lay followers who observe their vows. Beyond this stage are the ascetics, the enlightened ones and, finally, the liberated ones.

The traditional Jain texts, being didactic in nature, normally describe only ideal laypeople, i.e. those who follow the appropriate vows. The only literary references to 'ordinary' people come from the narrative literature.

Jain scriptures also distinguish between the '*sraavaka* by name' *(dravya sraavaka*) and the '*sraavaka* by heart' *(bhaava sraavaka)*. The former, although identified as Jain by birth, may not be living a Jain life. On the other hand, the latter has Right Faith and follows Mahavira's teachings. Both the actual and the ideal laypeople are considered *bhaava sraavakas.*

In chapter 3, we described a set of thirty-five rules of conduct and twelve vows for the householder. If a householder belonging to another faith follows these rules of conduct, he or she may be considered a Jain.

One who observes the twelve vows is considered to have reached the utmost limit of the practice for a non-ascetic; this level of observance is termed as partially restrained religion *(desavirati dharma)*. Some people progress on to an ascetic life and observe the totally restrained religion *(sarvavirati dharma)*. Digambara texts describe eleven 'model stages' leading to being an 'ideal' layperson, equivalent to *desavirati dharma*.

Daily duties of Jain Laypeople

Jain texts such as the *Dharma Sangraha*, *Sraddhaa Vidhi*, *Upadesa Prasaada*, *Sraavaka Prajnapti*, *Rantna Kaanda*, *Pujaa Pancaasaka* and *Sraavakaacaara* describe the daily duties of laypeople, and their duties for holy days, the rainy season and duties of the year and through the life. They give guidance on choosing a residence, a profession, and marriage and family issues.

The layperson is expected to carry out certain religious obligations in a uniform round of daily duties. The daily duties may be modified, depending upon time and place, and available means of worship. Svetambara laypeople follow a daily routine of morning recitations upon awakening. These are three, six, nine or twelve silent recitations of the *Namokara Mantra*, holding both hands out together, palms upwards, forming thereby the shape of the abode of the liberated *(siddha silaa)*.

Homage is paid to the liberated as examples of purification. Some may recall past pilgrimage to places such as Satrunjay, Sammeta Sikhara, Sankhesvara, Taranga, and Girnar as a form of meditation. At the same time laypeople decide upon any renunciations which might be undertaken that day. The householder, in India normally the women, sweep the floor to avoid harming any tiny creatures, filter the water and clean the utensils. Then after performing typical daily ablutions, physical and psychical *pujaa* of the *Jina* image in the home shrine is undertaken, followed by the appropriate form of renunciation and atonement for the time of day. The householder, usually woman of the house, also lights a lamp (of *ghee*) in front of the image.

The minimum renunciation undertaken by most laypeople is *navakaarsi*, the vow to avoid eating and drinking for forty-eight hours after sunrise. Some then go to the temple for worship and then seek out religious teachers, pay respects to them and listen to their sermons, perform various personal services for them, including the provision of medicines for the sick. Laypeople are expected to perform six essential duties (*aavasyakas*): 'equanimity' (*saamayika*); veneration of the twenty-four *tirthankaras* (*caturvisanti stava*); veneration of ascetics (*vandanaka*); penitential retreat (*pratikramana*); renunciation (*pratyaakhyaana*); meditation with bodily detachment (*kaayotsarga*). They would then normally proceed to their day's work.

At noon another *pujaa* is performed, then after providing food and other necessities for ascetics, householders take their midday meal. A reaffirmation of renunciation and a short meditation on the meaning of the scriptures may follow. Work then resumes until the evening meal, after which family undertakes the evening *pujaa*, normally in the temple, which includes the lamp-waving ritual and evening penitential retreat. Some self-study follows and any necessary services for ascetics are carried out. Then the layperson will normally retire to sleep meditating on the *Namokara Mantra*. Jains do not normally eat after sunset, are lacto-vegetarians and avoid root vegetables.

With regard to laypeople's professions, these must avoid violence as far as possible and be done honestly. Vijay Bhuvanbhanusuri indicates to the laypeople that earnings should be utilised as: family maintenance and welfare 50 per cent; savings (e.g. for retirement or contingency) 25per cent; and religious (or philanthropic) activities 25 per cent, but very few practise this today.

Jain laypeople have daily duties, some for ordinary days, additional ones for regular holy days and special days. There are also annual and 'lifelong' obligations. These are described in chapter 5. Digambaras have similar daily duties, with only minor variations. Sthanakvasis perform the above daily duties but do not attend temples for worship. However, in Leicester, owing to moves to greater unity among Jains, all sections of the community follow the same ritual pattern, and this tendency is seen in some other Jain centres in the West.

Lay Women The laywomen have always been the largest constituent of the four-fold order, but patriarchal mentality has led to the expression of negative and degrading remarks about women in some of the later texts. However, most Jain seers have stated that women possess the highest spiritual capacity and pronounced them the equal of men.

Among Svetambaras women are initiated as nuns, but Digambara women are initiated to a degree short of complete ascetic life. They take the vow of celibacy and are called *brahmacaarini*, and at the final stage of their spiritual progress they are called *aaryikaas*. Digambara women do not become nuns in the strict sense and are not perceived by Digambaras to be capable of liberation.

Laypeople today   The conduct of laypeople described above is an ideal, but it is generally difficult to maintain ideals. Since medieval times, a large number of changes have taken place in India; life has been getting more and more complex; and many laypeople cannot observe the ideal conduct even if they wanted to. The problem is even more acute for those Jains who have settled outside India; in an increasingly materialistic world, busy life styles and the lack of support from the ascetic orders have created a serious disadvantage to the laypeople in following the Jain path. However, most have remained vegetarians, have some sort of place of worship in the home and perform individual rituals.

Animals as Laity

Jainism advocates the equality of souls and the welfare of all living beings; Jain seers believe in the concept of spiritual advancement for animals. The *Aupapaatika Sutra* and other texts indicate that instinctive animals possessing five-sense such as elephants, frogs, snakes and lions can behave like human lay Jains, as they have:

- the instinct for the desirable and avoidance of the undesirable;
- a discriminating capacity for good and evil;
- a capacity to remember their past lives;
- the capacity to fast, perform penance and self-control, and change their behaviour;
- the capacity to hear religious sermons and receive instructions;
- the capacity to acquire sensory, scriptural and clairvoyant knowledge.

It is claimed that the holy assembly of Mahavira consisted of living beings of all forms, and his sermons were in a language, which miraculously could be understood by all. Tamed animals follow instructions; police forces use dogs extensively for a wide range of tasks; and animals are often more reliable friends than human beings. Many birds and animals do not eat at night; many are vegetarians and do not harm others; and they do not compete for the food. They live in communities; their activities are limited to natural instincts for obtaining food, sex for reproduction, sleep, and reactions to fear. If we think about their behaviour, they live a life similar to that of the human laity.

Jain scriptures contain stories of the elephant Meghaprabh, the cobra Candakaushik, a frog who worshipped, and a lion listening to the sermons in an earlier birth of Mahavira. Jains believe that animals can behave like the human laity, progress spiritually and improve their future rebirth, and the Jain scriptures claim that there are more animals, following the life of the Jain laity in the universe, than humans. Hence Jainism stresses the importance of animal welfare and shows compassion towards them; and one finds a respect for animals in practically all members of the Jain community.

JAIN SOCIETY AS DEPICTED IN THE NARRATIVE LITERATURE

In the 6th century BCE India was a very unequal society, dominated by a priestly class, although there were some people who followed the *sramana* tradition of Parsvanath and his predecessors, but they were few. Against this background Mahavira preached the equality of human beings and vigorously protested against priestly exploitation and ritualism, animal sacrifices and violence, and condemned arbitrary distinctions of caste.

The culture of the earliest Jain society is hardly described in the scriptures, but the narrative literature allows us some insight into Jain society during the five centuries or so after the time of Mahavira. This summary of early Jain society is drawn from both Jain narrative literature and on published historical research, the latter on the social and political conditions of the middle ages, largely from Gujarat and Karnataka, and the Jain sacred texts *Kalpa Sutra* and *Trisasthi Salaakaa Purusa Caritra* which contain some descriptions of social conditions and events in the time of Mahavira.

The *Kalpa Sutra* describes the life and times of King Siddhartha, his queen, his ministers and some aspects of the lives of ordinary people, where in general, life is depicted fine, with abundant essential materials. Astrologers were consulted for social and religious occassions. People bathed before worship. Rituals and prayers to the deities were a norm. It appears that people, including the king, his generals and the army, took part in a regime of regular fitness exercises, which included massages with oil and bathing.

The description of the pregnancy of Trisala, Mahavira's mother, her physical condition, cravings during pregnancy, and the care given to her allow us glimpses of the medical knowledge of the 6th century BCE.

Among the people who followed the Vedic culture, society was divided into classes *(varnas)*: *brahmin, ksatriya, vaisya* and *sudra*; these were claimed to have emerged from the body of Brahmaa, the primeral *Purusa*: the *brahmin* from his mouth, the *ksatriya* from his arms, the *vaisya* from his thighs and the *sudra* from his feet.

The *brahmins* considered themselves superior to the other classes as they performed the complex rituals and behaved as intermediaries of the gods, and convinced people that those sacrifices or ritual gifts offered, reached the gods or their ancestors.

Animal slaughter was commonplace during these rituals. The *ksatriyas* were warriors, while the *vaisyas* were traders and professionals. The *sudras* were manual workers, considered the most inferior class; women were bracketed with *sudra*, who had no rights and were considered as slaves; slaves and women were auctioned at market.

Early Jain Society

The preachings of Mahavira and his successive *aacaaryas* influenced the whole of society and his teachings were delivered simply and in the language of the common people. He taught of the equality of souls, self-reliance and responsibility for one's own actions, non-violence and reverence for life, truth, non-stealing, non-attachment, 'relative pluralism' and an easily understood spiritual path to liberation for all. He attracted many followers from all classes, men and women, who joined his four-fold order.

The early Jain narrative literature is written in the language known as Prakrit, the language of ordinary people, in contrast to the more literary language of Sanskrit, and from this literature a picture of the social conditions of the time emerges; it may be idealised, but there is no other surviving evidence with which to compare it.

Life is depicted as happy and comfortable and rulers were kind and just; the majority of kings treated their people as if they were their children. People reciprocated with goodwill, respect and obedience. Exploitation, extortion and blackmail were unheard of in these fair kingdoms, and iniquitous kings were rare. Religious tolerance and the co-existence of different religions were possible under such kings; law and order was upheld; anti-social elements were identified and brought to book, and the punishment of wrong doers was swift and severe.

Moral Life

The rulers of the time believed the caste system to be sacred and a God-given command; the rules and restrictions governing the caste system were enforced strictly and violators were severely dealt with and even exiled. Capital punishment was prevalent; murderers were sent to the gallows; and the Kings' word was final and had to be obeyed. There were some examples of gambling and prostitution, but the literature suggests a relatively high level of morality in society.

For Jains, marriage had no religious sanctity, but was a civil contract, although marriage was regarded as desirable and necessary for some religious duties and rituals; women looked after domestic affairs and children, while the man's role was to earn and perform duties outside the home. In discussing the necessity and importance of marriage, the *Aadipurana* mentions that offspring are not possible without marriage and religion is not possible without offspring.

Different forms of marriages are described in the literature: when arranging marriages, age, social status, cultural heritage, caste, community and other factors such as medical histories were taken into account. Both prospective partners had to consent to a marriage, and in the literature, references to inter-caste marriages are found. Although the practice of dowry was usual, it was not compulsory.

Polygamy was known, but not widespread. The remarriage of widows was rare. Divorce was virtually non-existent. Great emphasis was placed on the chastity of women, who would sometimes commit suicide rather than lose their chastity, e.g. through rape. The Jain literature does not contain any examples of *sati*, that is, of a widow throwing herself onto her husband's funeral pyre, as this was contrary to Jain principles.

Food, Dress and Entertainment

The Jain literature refers to food and drink rules, which differed according to the caste from which a person came. Jains were all vegetarian, but some non-Jains ate meat. Special food was eaten on festive occasions, such as a marriage, in some instances as many as thirty-two types of cooked food and thirty-three types of vegetables. Sweet foods were eaten widely, but in villages, people relied on a staple grain called *sattu*, while prisoners were given an inferior type of rice.

As one would expect, people dressed according to their means: they wore jewellery according to their status, used perfumes, applied unguents, ointments and scented powders, and chewing of betelnuts was widespread.

People took holidays from work activities: some went on pilgrimages and engaged in other worthwhile activities, gambling, drama, horse riding, playing the game of *chopat* or chess, singing, swimming, dancing, and the celebration of spring festivities were common pursuits. Some of the rich entertained themselves at establishments run by dancing 'girls'. The literate passed their spare time reading, writing, teaching, and debates. Public debates in which the elite participated were organised for the royal courts. There were exhibitions of arts and crafts, and riddles, puzzles and card games were also popular pastimes.

The World of Work

The Jain narrative literature refers to the many ways of earning one's livelihood, including agriculture, education, trade and business, arts and architecture, handicrafts, service and administration; it was the practice of

Jains to seek to minimise harm to living beings in their work.

The Jain literature describes rulers, administration, war, security, and law and order; the bureaucracy was much smaller than today, as the state was much more directly administered, and agriculture was the main means both of individual livelihood and state revenue.

Considerable wealth was earned through trade, often to distant countries, by sea and also across land routes both to neighbouring countries and further afield; although both land and sea routes carried a high risk, ventures could result in great wealth. Honesty was the most important virtue for successful business, bankruptcy in the modern sense was unknown, as people would prefer to die rather than fail to repay their debts, and their descendants could inherit debts.

The literate and learned could earn a living from scholarship in various forms, such as teaching and through the patronage of the wealthy, including royalty; and artists too depended upon patrons to a great extent. Among the lower classes of society some maintained themselves as entertainers through 'circus'-type activities such as magic, tight-rope walking, drama and conjuring tricks.

The Position of Women

Women are depicted in a wide range of roles as bride, wife, mother, widow, female ascetic, prostitute, dancer and singer.

While the literature suggests that in Indian society generally, women were respected, in some sections the birth of a daughter was, and still is, considered a misfortune; this was because, in those times, women had no opportunity for economic independence and were looked upon as a 'burden' to their parents. This contrasts with the Jain attitude, where the birth of a daughter was welcomed, though sometimes with less enthusiasm than the birth of a son. Female education was encouraged and valued, although women's 'education' mainly revolved around household affairs, like cooking and entertainment, it was also believed that an educated woman would observe customs and traditions better than an uneducated one. *Aacaarya* Haribhadra (8th century CE) supported the education of women.

In Jain society, a woman had joint responsibility with her husband in household matters, but the narrative literature cites cases of domineering wives who behaved just as they liked. Divorce was rare and instigated by husbands against their wives, generally on grounds of infidelity, but there are no cases cited of wives divorcing husbands. Families took responsibility for the care of those women who had been widowed; some widows became nuns. Orphaned children were the responsibilty of their close relatives, often in of an extended kinship network.

A woman was regarded as being unfortunate if she was infertile or did not give birth to at least one son; sometimes a husband would take an additional wife if the first failed to produce a son. But when a woman became a mother her status and importance in the family increased. Prostitution was practised in ancient times and, although looked upon as a social evil it was seen as inevitable that men would need to satisfy their sexual desire and fondness for variety. The prostitutes had their own ethic and enjoyed a higher social status than today. The women dancers entertained the royal courts.

There were many nuns who were highly respected; they walked from village to village and town to town and remained in close contact with laypeople, especially women and children. Jain women had similar duties to men in performing religious rites and rituals, and were allowed to read and study the scriptures.

JAIN SOCIETY IN THE CONTEMPORARY WORLD

The majority of India's population see themselves as part of a social organisation based upon birth whereby, in this birth-based caste system a Brahmin's son is *Brahmin* and a ksatriya's son is *ksatriya* and so on. Historically Hindu caste *(varna)* system is hierarchical and divided into many sub-groups *(jaat)*, where it was impossible to improve one's place in the hierarchy, although one could lose status through becoming polluted. This society considered women as inferior, debarring them from the initiation rites and wearing the sacred thread, a symbol of higher caste; women and manual workers *(sudras)* were not allowed to listen to sacred scriptures.

Jains (and Buddhists) belong to the *sramanic* (renunciatory) stream of Indian religious thought; historically, they have opposed the rigid birth-based caste system of the Vedic religion.

The followers of Vedic religion sacrificed animals as gifts to gods, their meat was distributed as gift *(prasaada)* to the devotees. In time, however, a movement against animal sacrifices grew, both by the *rishis*, believers in *Upanisads*, and, Parsvanatha, Mahavira and the Buddha of *sramanic* tradition. The Jain *tirthankaras* opposed social divisions based on birth and reiterated that rebirth in the society is due to one's earlier *karma*; the social divisions should be based on work to facilitate the smooth functioning of the society; different work cultures will produce different ways of life; and everyone has a potentiality to move into higher or lower social groups. All have a capacity for higher spiritual development and the status in the society depends upon one's *karma*.

Jain Social Structure

Since the time of Mahavira, people of differing *varnas* and *jaats*, from many areas, have accepted the Jain religion, making the Jain society heterogeneous. Thus, the Jains are a community, or rather a grouping of communities, as well as followers of a religion, and as they originated from different backgrounds, they organised themselves into differing groups known as *jnati* or *naat* to facilitate smooth functioning of the society. In the West, where individual mobility between religions and social groups is commonplace, the nature of Indian society, with the individual bound by group ties to his or her own community and following the same customs and worshipping the same gods, is not always understood.

Jain society is organised into more than 200 *jnati* groups, more than 100 major groups among Svetambaras and about 80 major groups among the Digambaras. The names of different groups are based upon places of origin (sometimes of ancestors many centuries before), rivers, natural surroundings, and professions. The most prominent of these groups are found among Hindus as well as both major sects of Jains, as shown in the table below. Many social sub-groups were formed based on profession, such as *Shah* (moneylender), *Bhandari* (treasurer), *Mehta* (accountant), *Gandhi* (grocer), *Kapadia* (cloth merchant) and *Jhaveri* or *Zaveri* (diamond merchant). One also finds 'sub-names' like *Sanghavi* (pilgrimage organiser) based other than on professions.

Table 4.2   The origin of Jain groups

Name	Origin	Hindu (H), Svetambara (S), or Digambara (D)	Sub-Groups
Shrimali	Srimala (Bhinmala,Rajasthan)	H/S/D	3
Agrawal	Agroha (Haryana)	H/S/D	18
Oswal	Ossiya (Rajasthan)	H/S/D	18
Porwad/Porwal	Eastern side of town	H/S/D	24
Khandelwal	Khandela (Rajasthan)	H/D	84
Parwara	Eastern side of town	H/D/S	144
Setvala	Saint-protectors, farmers (Kshetrapalas)	H/D	44
Upadhye	Priest	H/D	

Among Srimalis one finds three sub-groups: *Dasa*, *Visa* and *Ladava*, while among Oswals one finds mainly *Dasa* and *Visa*. Another aspect of Jain social organisation is the *gotra*, whereby membership of a particular *gotra* identifies one's blood relationship, the word originally meaning an enclosure for cows, but eventually it was extended to mean the family lineage. The *gotra* embodies the limit on endogamous relations, and no two people may marry if they belong to the same *gotra.*

The second quarter of the 20th century saw a move towards changing the family name as 'Jain' surname for distinct Jain identity in the official census data. This has not been universally adopted, but in some areas of northern India it is now an established practice.

Functions of Social Groups

The functions of the different social groups have always been five-fold:

- to make rules for smooth organisation of the group;
- to (s)elect trustees known as *mahaajana*, for enforcement of the rules;
- to maintain religious and social liaison with the wider Jain community;
- to aid group cohesiveness, marital and social relations, amity and the prosperity of members; and
- to settle disputes between members and to discipline any offenders who breach the rules of the group.

The groups provide facilities such as rest houses, boarding houses, educational institutions and other philanthropic services mainly for their members, although non-members are not excluded. In modern times, because of migration and social change in India, these groups are losing the importance and their functions are diminishing.

Because of their background, Jains have different socio-religious customs; rules regarding marriage and rituals such as the sacred-thread, tonsuring and worship of family deities; and hence outsiders often find little difference between Hindus and Jains. Moreover, many still follow the social customs modelled on Hindus, making the identity of Jain society difficult.

Marriage

Marriage is perhaps the most important social custom in any society. Jain philosophy places more emphasis to renunciation, but it would be a mistake to suppose Jainism is anti-marriage, on the contrary, marriage is considered as a social duty for a Jain layperson.

Jain marriage is usually within the community members with similar backgrounds, where the couple has free choice to agree to the proposal. The community not only witnesses the union but also helps in overcoming future misunderstanding. In Jain society the marriage is usually permanent, but it can be nullified by *mahaajana*, if either of the couple finds a major defect in the partner within a prescribed time; unchastity; impotence; untolerable behaviour; if the spouse absconds or is missing; or becomes an ascetic or dies. Though they are permitted, most women do not remarry; they involve themselves in religious and spiritual life, but many men remarry.

The divorce in Jain society is very rare. Intercaste marriages within different Jain communities or other religious communities are not penalised, sometimes they are accepted and blessed by the community leaders. Widow marriages are permitted in some caste groups *(setvalas)*. Pre-marital relationships bring discredit to families and are discouraged.

The Contemporary World

The heterogeneous character of the Jain community has helped Jains adjust and accommodate to other groups among whom they live, at home or abroad, without losing their cultural and religious identity. In spite of their being a minor community, Jains have influence out of proportion to their numbers in the societies in which they reside. The migration and the complexities of life have added strains on functioning of the Jain society. In the West it is a norm for both the parents to work and Jains are no exception to this; they spend less time with their children and as a result, one finds diminishing heritage of traditional culture in the young generation. Western educational institutions prepare a pupil to be independent; media and peers affect the young generation; Jains have failed to provide an infrastructure for traditional learning and leisure, and as a consequence Jain society is under severe strain. Jains find it difficult to get acceptable food in schools, canteens, restaurants and other public places. Some, because of non-availability or because of the company, have begun to accept food contrary to their acceptable norms. This has become a worrying sign to the Jain society.

Very few people in the West know the word 'Jain' or have heard of Jainism. Jains are mistaken for Hindus, although Jains work hard to establish their identity, due to lack of the infrastructure, the results are not as encouraging, as one would have wished, and Jains still face adjustment problems: socio-cultural, religious, educational and care of elderly persons.

Socio-cultural Economic gains have caused strains to Indian family life: The greater economic freedom of women has raised their expectations of a better life, and many men are unable to adjust to this novel situation, which has brought tensions to families, affecting the children. Jains spend most of their spare moments in socialising, leaving hardly any time for the welfare of their society. This is a worrying phenomenon for maintaining the values of traditional Jain society.

The modern environment has thrown up situations, which are not discussed in the scriptures, but these new inevitable problems can be resolved on the basis of the principles of non-violence, non-attachment and Jain ethics. Take family planning for example: scriptures advocate sexual restraint and celibacy, which aided the family planning, but as it is difficult to observe it in the modern complex environment, contraception may be necessary. If contraception has to be used, it should be accepted with regret as a lack of self-control.

Abortion is another problem with physical, psychic and demographic factors involved in it. The *Sthaananga Sutra* notes many forms of abortion in Indian society before Mahavira's time. Jainism does not sanction abortion, as it involves murder of a human being; Jains believe life starts on the day of conception.

Alcohol, tobacco, and drugs such as cannabis, heroin or cocaine affect health, wealth and society and produce violence. The scriptures sanction only a vegetarian diet involving minimum harm even to plant life and practically all the members of the Jain community support it.

Religious problems   Coming to the West has deprived Jains of the two orders *sangha*, monks and nuns, regular places of worship and religious activities. Many Jain centres have been established in the West, but they lack cohesive infrastructure and presence of spritual leaders. Jains have begun to discuss this problem of providing infrastructure and spiritual leadership seriously.

Educational problems   Most of the Jains coming to the West had their primary religious training in the local Jain schools in India attached to temples or *upashrayas.* Children born in the West have no such opportunity, as there is lack of teachers, traditional schools or the literature. Jains need appropriate literature specially written for the children in a Western language, style and content and facilities to learn 'mother tongues', especially Gujarati and Hindi, where most of the Jain literatue is available, and the knowledge of which is needed for cultural contacts within families, the community, their place of origin.

Problems of the elderly   In the West people are generally independent, family values are under pressure, and the elderly are cared for far less by family members. This is contrary to Indian cultural values and as a consequence earlier migrants, now grown older, have started to experience isolation. Despite the fact that their physical needs may be cared for by the state, which means the elderly people are not dependent on their family, they are suffering emotionally. Fortunately, this problem is not acute among Jains, as young Jain persons still respect their elderly, and the elderly people have adjusted to the situation, but sooner or later they would require infrastructure to pass their leisure time and their socio-religious needs.

THE FUTURE—JAINS AND JAINISM

The Demographic Situation

Over the last 200 years the majority of the Jain population in India has migrated from rural villages to towns and cities. Being largely a business and professional community, Jains found it advantageous to settle in urban areas. The younger generation has adapted to the life of larger cities to the extent that, once settled, young Jains are generally not prepared to move out to villages or small towns. The 1981 census of India showed that about two-thirds of Jains were living in urban areas, and this trend towards the urbanisation of the Jain population shows no sign of abating.

Jains are found throughout India, but the major concentrations of the population are in the western regions of the country. Maharashtra, Rajasthan, Gujarat, Madhya Pradesh, Karnataka and Uttar Pradesh are home to about eight out of ten of India's Jains, but owing to historical circumstances, there are very few Jains in Bihar, the place of Mahavira's birth and religious activity. The 1981 census figures suggest that the Jain population have fewer women than men, a ratio of 941 females to 1,000 males. These figures may have been distorted by factors which are yet to be identified and analysed.

Although the Government of India has accepted Jains as a distinct group with its own religious identity, the provisions of the Hindu Code Bill are applied to them, along with Hindus, Sikhs and Buddhists. The aim of this law is to codify for the Jain community a number of issues of civil law such as inheritance, which does not apply to religionists such as Christians, Muslims and Parsees. The effect of the application of the distinction embodied in this law, whether intended or not, is that some religions are accepted as 'authentically' Indian, while others are in some sense 'alien'. However, the Jains form a heterodox but prestigious minority in modern Indian society.

The 19th century represented a low point in Jain history, but the 20th century has seen some progress in Jain fortunes. Some attitudes and trends continue to hamper the development of Jainism, although the teachings of Jainism have the potential for wide appeal in modern times, an introverted tendency and a conservative outlook among the community has failed to match the mass popularisation of other faiths.

The *Sthaananga Sutra* indicates that the chances of being a good Jain was always rare, even in the past, due to the six 'rarities': human birth; birth in an 'arya region' (a 'holy' land); birth in a pious family; learning of the doctrines preached by omniscients; believing in the teachings of omniscients; and practising the doctrines taught by omniscients.

What is one to say of this in the scientific and materialistic age of the

20th century, when spirituality is considered by many to be even rarer than in previous eras? The *Kalpa Sutra* suggested that Jainism would pass through a difficult period about 2,500 years after Mahavira's death, but it also forecasted a greater appeal to Jain principles and way of life once this period had passed. Central Jain values: reverence for life, animal welfare, cares for the environment, and an aversion to war and violence, strike a strong chord in the contemporary world.

As, in the nineteenth century, the British had coalesced the Indic religions into Hinduism and as, Jains are not clearly distinguishable from Hindus by dress or other distinguishing marks, the total number of Jains is uncertain. The 1981 Indian census figure of just over 3 million is certainly an underestimate, as many census officers class Jains as Hindus. According to Jain sources, present Jain population of the persons born in Jain community is about 12 million in the world, a relatively small figure. But those who follow Jain principles, such as vegetarianism or a 'green' way of life is much larger and in this sense, Jainism is not a minority religion. It representats an important world-wide moral community irrespective of the number who calls them 'Jain'.

Struggle for Identity and the Future of the *Sangha*

The Jain community is engaged in a struggle for identity, as few non-Jains have ever heard of Jainism. Within the community there is sectarianism and complacency over Jain identity and many Jains are content to be regarded as 'Hindu', without stressing the unique features of Jain life. Part of the community is introverted, concentrating on the performance of ritual observances to the neglect of promoting Jain values both in their own lives and more widely. The community also relies too heavily on ascetics to perform tasks and roles, which, it could be argued, are more properly the province of laypeople. Unlike other religions, both in India and outside, Jainism lacks a coherent infrastructure for the management of community affairs, the promotion of Jain values and the education and training of community members and leaders. It is even difficult for interested outsiders to be able to find, or be supplied with, information about Jains and Jainism. Currently, most resources, mainly in the form of time and money donated by individuals in the community, are used for the construction of temples and *upashrayas*. While these are worthy objectives, there remains much to be achieved in the fields of education and training, which lack resources at present.

Jainism has been well served in the past by the four-fold order of the *sangha*, but the modern situation poses a challenge to its continuity and activities. Jain ascetics have increased in number in the 20th century and although, today many ascetics are well educated in a range of secular studies, there remains a need to develop more facilities for ascetics to increase their research in religious areas and to publish literature in modern international languages. Increasing involvement of ascetics in duties that ought to be reserved for laypeople undermines the detachment necessary for spiritual progress, and it can lead to failures in observing their ascetic vows correctly or fully and, at worst, ascetics may become egotistic or disillusioned.

Jain laypeople are becoming increasingly well educated in secular areas, but lack support for their religious education. Young people in particular need to have Jain values presented to them in the language and to the standards of their secular education, but there is little modern educational infrastructure for the teaching of Jainism to the community. The issue of language is becoming more prominent as the younger generations of Jains are educated in languages such as English. A lack of knowledge could result, in the space of several generations, in a watered-down type of Jainism in the West; perhaps the community may continue as 'Jain', but it would be devoid of Jain values. Other communities, such as the Jews, are reacting to a similar situation by investing heavily in educational resources and activities.

The other element missing from this picture of the possibilities for the future of Jainism, particularly outside India, is the absence of the four-fold *sangha* in the West. If it is the case that Jainism's survival for so long has been the result of the strengths of that order, then the future of Jainism in the West is bleak. The alternative is the creation of some new form of the ancient *sangha*, probably with a modified form of ascetic order adapted to Western conditions. What form this might take depends upon a number of circumstances, nevertheless Jain history suggests that it will be an inevitable part of the Western Jain future.

Temples and other religious buildings   A particular phenomenon of modern Britain is the 'redundant church', thousands of buildings have been demolished or converted to other uses because the Christian community was unable, for a variety of reasons, to support them any longer. In India, while some ancient temples have been restored to their former glory, such as Delwara and Ranakpur, and many new temples have been constructed, there has been considerable neglect of temples in rural areas. There is a concentration of donations in the larger centres, and without some rationalisation of the communities' handling of temple finances, for instance by the proper provision of funds for long term maintenance, much of the less spectacular but important Jain architectural heritage will decay. Some coordination on a national or regional level could allieviate this problem by making funds available for smaller temples, and the same applies equally to other religious buildings such as *upashrayas*.

All temples employ *pujaaris* (temple servants) to attend to the temple images and rituals. *Pujaaris* receive no formal training and the standard varies enormously; their knowledge of Jainism is negligible and this situation is unlikely to change without proper training and remuneration for these important personnel.

Scriptures and educational publications   Jain scriptures have been carefully preserved, but their publication and translation into modern languages is still insufficient to meet demand. In contrast to Jewish and Christian scriptures, which are widely available in translations from their original Hebrew and Greek, Jain scriptural translations are few and their quality varies greatly. There is little available which has been created specifically with children and young people in mind, but this problem is easy to solve; it requires only the provision of the financial and material resources for scholars and educators to undertake the work.

There is little doubt that there is a demand for knowledge on Jainism, both from within and without the Jain community. Jain values and practices such as vegetarianism, animal welfare, and care for the environment are reflected in the concerns of many modern people. Jain ideas need presentation in a form which can be readily understood and appreciated, not only by non-Jains, but also by those Jains who themselves feel very much part of the modern, westernised world, having been educated to a high level in universities and colleges.

This can only be achieved by increasing research and study, in schools and universities, leading to publication and the production of educational resources and opportunities to learn more on Jainism.

Look at human life in this world! It may be over either early in youth or after a hundred years. You should know that this life is an abode of very short duration. However, greedy people still remain engrossed in worldly pleasures.

(*Sutra Krutaanga* 1: 2: 3: 8)

Give up tenderness and strengthen yourself with penance; control desires, and miseries will run away; rid yoursef of faults and cut off attachment. Thus you will be happy in this worldly life.

(*Dasavaikalika* 2: 5)

Four great things are very rare in this world for a living being: birth as a human being; listening to scriptures; faith in religion; and energy to practise self-control.

(*Uttaraadhyayan*a 3: 1)

It is difficult to conquer the five senses as well as anger, pride, delusion and greed. It is even more difficult to conquer the self. Those who have conquered the self have conquered everything.

(*Uttaraadhyayan*a 9: 36)

Chapter 5

POPULAR JAINISM

REGULAR PRACTICES AND RITUALS

This chapter opens a section dedicated to what may be termed 'Popular Jainism', that is, the daily and other regular practices and rituals which are actually performed or followed by large numbers of typical Jain laypeople. These regular practices are known as *kriyaas* or *caryaas*. English speaking Jains usually refer to them as 'rituals', which are intended to lead people on a journey from the 'outer' to the 'inner' world of the self.

Every religion has some rituals but the purpose and meaning of ritual may be variously explained according to the religion in question. In Jainism ritual is regarded as part of Right Conduct. Rituals should be performed with as much understanding of the meaning as possible, with the utmost devotion and in the prescribed order as laid down in scriptures and enshrined in tradition. In this way, one may achieve the full benefits of these spiritual observances, but mere 'empty' performance of rituals, or performance out of habit or for the sake of appearances, is of little benefit to the doer. However, it must be admitted that the majority of people who attend ritual performances do so more for community motives than from a full understanding of the spiritual meaning of the rituals. This is not, however, to imply that their attendance is without value for the community, but merely recognises the situation as it is. The performance of rituals as a group or community is regarded as of greater merit than their performance by individuals alone, a practice not unknown to other religions. The performance of rituals may be unnecessary for a spiritually advanced individual, but in the earlier stages of spiritual development they aid one in devotion and worship. Group rituals help to keep the community together and provide a sense of common identity, and such gatherings for communal ritual provide a medium for popularisation of the religion.

Over the centuries, Jains have developed a series of rituals of varying frequency, e.g. daily, fortnightly, four-monthly and annual. Some essential religious observances are performed once in a lifetime. As might be expected, there is no complete uniformity of ritual observances across all

Jain sects, 'schools' and communities. The rituals among the image-
worshipping (*Deraavaasi* or *Murtipujaka*) Jains are colourful and varied
when compared with the devotions of non-image worshipping Jains (e.g.
the Sthanakvasi). In addition to the sectarian differences between
Svetambara and Digambara, the rituals may vary locally or worshippers
may introduce variations in private devotions. There are many rituals
which are observed by ascetics and laypeople alike, such as observance of
the six essential duties; other rituals are performed only by ascetics or by
laypeople.

Religious Leadership among Jains

Jainism has no priesthood. The Priests, Rabbis, Imams, and even the
Brahmin caste of the Hindu religion, have no direct counterpart in Jainism.
Though ascetics have an important role as religious teachers for laypeople,
they form in no sense priesthood, although they are respected and venerated in rituals and play an important part in guiding religious activities,
however, they perform their daily and periodic rituals. They do not act as
intercessors or mediators between the laity and any divinities; they have no
part in the administration of temples, indeed their peripatetic life precludes
this. With rare exceptions their presence is not essential to the rituals. There
are certain ritual functions, which are infrequently delegated to trained or
qualified specialists *(vidhikaarak)*. A temple which holds a consecrated
image of the Jina will need to make provision for the essential daily ritual
veneration of the image, and laypeople perform this service in the course
of their devotions, bathing and anointing the image, and making the ritual
offerings before it. Often, however, the temple will employ a temple
servant *(pujaari)* whose particular function will be to carry out these duties
to the sacred image, performing the full daily rituals. *Pujaaris* should,
preferably, be Jains, but often are not; they may well be *brahmins* but may
be of another caste. *Pujaaris* may lead the prayers and invocations on ritual
occasions.

Despite the absence of a priestly class in general, it may be mentioned
that there are many rituals, such as consecration ceremonies and purificatory rites for which a supervisory category of advanced or scholarly
laymen was developed during the middle ages, called *yatis* in the
Svetambara sect and *bhattarakas* and *pandits* among Digambaras.

Jain rituals make a framework for individual personal devotions. The
daily rituals envisage the solitary worshipper performing devotions
whether in the temple or before the image of the *tirthankara* in the home;
rituals are also performed communally. Community worship takes the
form of the singing of hymns, interspersed by the chanting of prayers. The
celebration of festivals may involve the whole community and may open

with the *Navakara Mantra*, continue with hymns, devotional singing and dancing, celebrating events in the life of a *tirthankara*, and end with the lamp-waving ritual of lights *(aarati)*. A celebration of this nature will incorporate ritual elements but it is supplementary to the formal rituals, which constitute the recommended daily or periodic religious exercises of the pious Jain. Women, as well as men, perform the rituals in the home or in the temple. Indeed the devotee seen in the temple is more likely to be a woman than a man. Although the traditional norms of Indian society do still operate to some extent in the Jain community, women, unless they are menstruating, play a large part in religious and ritual life.

The Jain rituals are meaningful and often very beautiful. They evoke devotional feelings in worshippers. The Prakrit (and here and there Sanskrit) language adds melody and dignity to the ancient prayers and has the additional advantage of uniting all devotees, whatever their daily language. On the other hand, there is a danger of excessive 'ritualism', that is, of seeing the rituals as an end in themselves, without thought to the meaning behind them. Rituals, undertaken with proper understanding, help the faithfuls to develop the right attitude towards their spiritual progress.

The Jain seers initiated certain *pujaas* and other rituals to enhance Jain worship as a counterbalance to the attractions of the colourful Hindu *bhakti* (devotional) worship, which became widespread in India from the 7th century CE. Rituals may take the form of austerities, visits to the temple, *pujaa, aarati*, and the six essential duties. We have already described Jain yoga and meditation (chapter 3) and the daily duties of Jains (chapter 4).

The Six Essential Duties

Jains should perform six daily essential duties *(aavasyakas)*. The Jain essential duties may seem to be complex and time consuming; as they take about three hours, mostly in the early morning and late evening. However, they are meant to enhance the quality of life, physically, mentally and spiritually, for the practitioner. Scholars point out that these practices date back around 2,500 years and their continuation attests to their value.

Equanimity   The detached attitude and practice of equanimity *(saamayika)* produces mental tranquility. As a ritual it is often performed three times a day, sometimes more, in the home, in a temple, *upashraya*, forest, or in the presence of an ascetic, by adopting specific yogic postures. The ritual consists of reciting a particular series of sacred *sutras* and taking a vow to sit in equanimity, self-study and meditation for forty-eight minutes. Forty-eight minutes, one-thirtieth of a day, is a traditional Indian division of time, but it is interesting to note that it is very close to the average attention span of the human mind according to modern psychologists. It ends with the recitation of a concluding series of *sutras*, an expression of desire to perform the ritual many times again and a plea for forgiveness of any transgressions committed during the performance of *saamayika*. One may continue to perform this ritual a number of times by repeating the first series of *sutras* together with self-study and meditation, and it concludes with a single recitation of the concluding *sutras*.

Veneration of the Twenty-Four   The 'veneration of the twenty-four' is called *caturvisanti-stava*, a recital in veneration of the twenty-four *tirthankaras* of each age, with the intention of developing their faith and virtues in one's own self. This recital may be performed in isolation or as part of more elaborate rituals (described later in this chapter) such as the *caitya vandana, deva pujaa, pratikramana* or other *pujaas* or *pujans*.

Veneration of Ascetics   This ritual is called *guru vandana*, by which respect for ascetics is expressed, egoism is reduced and humility cultivated. By the recitation of this ritual, ascetics are invited to accept offerings for their needs. This ritual is regarded as helpful for gaining Right Knowledge, through service to the guru and through hearing the guru's teaching.

Penitential Retreat   This ritual is called *pratikramana*. It is a ritual of confession, making atonement for transgressions committed during the past day or night. Atonement is made by meditation with bodily detachment, the recitation of hymns and *sutras* in praise of the *tirthankaras*, and asking for forgiveness for the transgressions accompanied by an expression of intention not to repeat them. Prayers for the welfare of all living beings are also offered in this ritual.

Renunciation   This ritual (described in chapter 3) is called *pratyaakhyaana*. It involves taking a vow to abandon that which is harmful to the soul and to accept that which is beneficial. The ritual of renunciation or austerities requires detachment from material things, especially those associated with sensual pleasures and helps to develop self-control and Right Conduct.

Meditation with Bodily Detachment   This ritual is called *kaayotsarga* or 'abandonment of the body', as self-contemplation can only be achieved if one forgets the body and meditates on the true self. At some time all human souls must leave their temporary physical bodies. We spend much time attending to the physical body, its needs and pleasures. The aim of *kaayotsarga* is to channel concentration away from the corporeal and onto the non-corporeal self (the soul). It is performed by standing or sitting silently in a meditative posture for variable lengths of time (forty-eight minutes or more) initiated and terminated by recitation of *Navakara Mantra*.

Yoga (postures and physical bowings), meditation and austerities necessary for spiritual progress are part of the essential duties, and donations (*daana*) are regarded by many as part and parcel of these essential duties.

The Digambara ascetics also observe these essential duties. The 10th century ascetic-scholar Somadeva advised laypeople to perform *deva pujaa*, *vandanaka*, self-study, restraints, austerities and the four-fold donation of shelter, food, medicine and books, which have encouraged the philanthropic activities for which the Jain comunities have become well known.

Rituals on special days Jains perform special rituals, penance and austerity on the 2nd, 5th, 8th, 11th, 14th and 15th day of each half of a lunar month and on the five auspicious anniversaries of the *tirthankaras*. They perform elaborate penitential retreats on the 14th day (among Sthanakvasis, the 15th day) of each lunar month, and three times a year on the 14th day of the fourth month, and annually on *samvatsari*, the holiest day in the Jain calendar (late August or early September).

Every year *paryusana*, an eight-day sacred period of forgiveness and austerities is observed. Digambaras celebrate this festival, which is known as *dasa laxani parva*, for ten days, concentrating on the ten virtues of the soul.

Annual and Lifetime Obligations

Sraavaka Prajnaapti prescribes the following eleven duties for laypersons to be performed at least once a year and duties prescribed for once in a lifetime. If it is not possible to perform these duties alone, one should perform them collectively with others.

Service to the Order One should venerate the four-fold order *(sangha pujaa)* by respectfully providing for the needs of ascetics, e.g. clothings and books, and offer gifts to laypeople in the sangha.

Reverence to Co-religionists One should show reverence to co-religionists *(saadharmika bhakti)* by inviting devoted laypeople to one's home for meals, and give help to the needy by both material and spiritual means.

Triple Pilgrimage This ritual of triple pilgrimage *(yaatratnika)* consists of participation in *pujans*, and festivals for veneration of the *tirthankaras*; participation in chariot processions and religious festivities of the temples; and participation in Jain pilgrimage to important sites such as Satrunjay, Sammet Sikhara, Girnar and Pavapuri.

Veneration by Anointing an Image (snaatra pujaa) At least once a year a devout Jain is expected to perform *snaatra pujaa*, the veneration of the Jina, in form of the re-enactment of the ritual, which tradition claims is performed by heavenly being at the time of the birth of a *tirthankara*.

Fundraising for Temples Laypeople are expected to contribute, or motivate others to contribute, funds for the maintenance, renovation and construction of temples *(deva dravya)*.

Elaborate Pujans These elaborate *pujans (mahaapujaas)* involve the decoration of images of the *tirthankaras*, and the decoration of temples and their surroundings. Recitation of elaborate sacred *sutras* form part of these *pujans*. The *pujans* are intended to encourage devotees to come to the temples for worship, although many visitors are attracted by the spectacle.

Devotion throughout the Night   This devotion *(raatri jaagaran)* involves worshippers in singing hymns and performing religious observances throughout the night at the time of designated holy days, and on the anniversary of the birth or death of prominent ascetics.

Veneration of Scriptures   This ritual *(sruta pujaa)* involves devotional *pujaa* of the scriptures by making symbolic and monetary offerings to the goddess of the scriptures, and putting the scriptures on public display.

Concluding Ritual   The concluding ritual *(udyaapan)* involves the display of the objects of worship and the making of gifts to participants in the ceremonies on the final day of auspicious religious observances. These observances include veneration of the 'nine auspicious ones' *(navapad)*, that is: the five 'supreme beings' *(parmesthis)*, *arihant, siddha, aacaarya, upaadhyaaya* and *saadhu*; the three jewels (Right knowledge, Right Faith, Right Conduct) and the austerities *(tapas)*; veneration of the 'twenty auspicious ones' *(visa-sthaanaka)*, a four hundred day ritual venerating the attributes and pious activities of twenty auspicious ones; and the vow of forty-five days of alternate fasting and eating *(upadhaan)*, together with ritual observances.

Glorification of the Order   This ritual *(tirtha prabhaavana)* is intended to promote Jainism and the Jain way of life through celebrations of occasions such as the arrival of ascetics at a paricular place, holy days or holy occasions, and consecration ceremonies.

Atonement   In this ritual of atonement *(suddhi)* one confesses faults in the presence of ascetics every fortnight, every four months, or once a year, and performs penance.

Obligations to be Performed at Least Once During a Lifetime

At least once in their lifetime, laypeople are expected to:

- Build a temple, or help to build one, which is considered a meritorious act that helps spiritual advancement. During the construction, one must take care in the choice of land, the use of materials and the utilisation of honestly acquired wealth. One should encourage the artisans, be honest with them, and bear in mind the purity and purpose of a temple building and in all dealings related to it.
- Donate a consecrated *jina* image to a temple.
- Participate in an image installation ceremony.
- Celebrate the renunciation of a son, daughter or another family member.

- Celebrate the birth, initiation or liberation of prominent ascetics.
- Commission the writing of religious works, and the publishing and public reading of the scriptures.
- Build an *upashraya*, prayer hall or *bhojansaalaa* (dining hall).
- Take the vows of the *pratimaas* ('eleven ideal stages').

The above obligations are specified in Svetambara text, *Sraavaka Prajnapti*. The Digambaras also follow a similar pattern of annual or lifetime obligations, specified in the text *Sraavakaacaara*, the conduct of laypeople.

SVETAMBARA RITUALS

The majority of Jains are Svetambar *Murtipjakas*; among them the rituals vary due to historical and regional factors. Over the centuries, with the support of ascetics, the community has remained devoted to the traditional rituals. Some Svetambara rituals are very elaborate and colourful and have been developed to counter the attraction of rituals of the Hindu 'devotional movement' *(bhakti maarga)*. In general, Svetambaras follow a pattern of rituals close to that described earlier in this chapter. This section describes worship in the temples and other public arenas.

The daily life of a pious Svetambara is interwoven with the ritual acts of the six essential duties. Every Jain learns the *Navakara Mantra* from childhood. The *Navakara Mantra* is a formula of veneration, meditation on the virtues and surrender, not petition, to the five 'supreme beings' *(panca parmesthis)*. The rolling sounds of the ancient Prakrit language used in this *mantra* echo at every Jain religious gathering, chanted in unison by the congretation. The meditative, silent recitation of this mantra may be performed at any time, in any place and by anyone. The *mantra*, transliterated into English, is as follows:

Namo arihantaanam	I venerate the enlightened souls
Namo siddhaanam	I venerate the liberated souls
Namo ayariyaanam	I venerate the religious leaders
Namo uvajjhayaanam	I venerate the religious preceptors
Namo loe savva sahunam	I venerate all ascetics in the world
Eso panca namokkaro	These five-fold venerations
Savva paavapanaasano	Destroy all sins
Mangalanam ca savvesim	Of all auspicious things
Padhamam havai mangalam	It is the most auspicious

Veneration of Jina (*deva pujaa*)

Svetambara *murtipujakas* believe that image worship is necessary for spiritual progress. Spiritual progress is a gradual process. If one reckons one's age from the time when one gains spiritual understanding, rather than from birth, then most of us are like children in spiritual terms. We have hardly begun our journey towards spiritual enlightenment. As pictures, figures and drawings are used to help children to acquire an understanding of concepts, in the same way, laypeople and ascetics alike require the help of images in the early stages of their spiritual 'journey'. The consecrated images used are of *tirthankaras* and they serve as a focus for devotion, and the lives of the *tirthankaras* represented by the images are the example which the worshipper seeks, through prayer, meditation and conduct, to emulate. Jain seers teach that worship focused upon images is necessary for the first seven of the fourteen stages of spiritual development. From the eighth stage onwards one's spirituality is sufficiently developed that one can meditate on one's soul alone.

Deva pujaa involves worship of images by: the recitation of the names of tirthankaras; the singing of hymns; listening to the recitation and the hymns; respectfully bowing to images; meditation; 'surrender', that is, adopting a spirit of detachment from worldly affairs; and making offerings to the images.

In preparation for *pujaa*, worshippers bathe themselves, put on clean clothes, 'purify' their minds by cultivating feelings of detachment, and select 'fitting' items to be offered to the images. If making monetary offerings or donations, they should take care that the money was honestly come by. In the temple rituals worshippers should observe the accepted customs, ceremonies or rites. Worship is intended to create peace of mind, develop a sense of detachment, and help in spiritual progress.

Devout Jains perform *deva pujaa* daily. If unable to perform all the rituals for any reason, they should at least try to attend the temple and pay reverence and devotion to the *jina* each day. The devout will refrain from eating anything before going to the temple for the morning rituals, in fact, will not even brush their teeth. They will not eat lunch before noon worship, and will not retire to bed before making their evening visit to the temple.

The rituals of Svetambaras can be performed for devotional purposes, for purification, as austerities or as ceremonies.

Devotional Rituals

Devotees go to the temple to perform the devotional rituals. These may be the 'veneration of temples and *jinas*' *(caitya vandan)*, the 'eight-fold worship' *(asta-prakaari pujaa)*, or the sacred lamp-waving ritual *(aarati)*.

The full ritual of the *deva pujaa* is performed in three stages:

Worship by contact with an image *(anga pujaa)*; worship before an image *(agra pujaa)*; and 'psychic' worship *(bhaava pujaa)*. Bathing and the wearing of clean clothes are obligatory for worshippers before they perform *anga pujaa*. Male worshippers wear two unstitched garments, female worshippers wear three stitched garments. For the *agra* and *bhaava pujaa* bathing beforehand is not required. Normal clean clothing may be worn. If time is short, some worshippers perform only the worship before an image and 'psychic' worship and a shortened version of the prayers.

The following account explains the basic sequence of the ritual. Whilst it remains the same in general outline, there can be considerable variation in practice. As this is usually a personal ritual, worshippers may give it their own particular order and character. There is a fairly wide choice of prayers and invocations. The worshipper enters the temple pronouncing *'nissahi'*, indicating that the worshipper has put aside all thought of outside activities on entering the temple. It is repeated when the worshipper leaves the main body of the temple to enter the inner shrine *(garbha griha)* where the principal images are situated, indicating that worshippers have ceased all thought of the mundane activities associated with the temple. It is said a third time at the conclusion of *asta-prakaari pujaa*, when the worshipper performs *bhaava pujaa (caitya vandana)*.

On entering the temple, worshippers first stand before the main *tirthankara* image and with folded hands, recite the *Navakara Mantra* or say *'namo jinanam'* ('I venerate the Jinas'), or recite hymns and then walk three times around the shrine. The circumambulation is clockwise so that the image is kept to the worshipper's right hand. During this a suitable invocation is recited. The three circuits around the image relate to the three Jewels—Right Faith, Right Knowledge and Right Conduct. Once more facing the image, a short verse of prayer is uttered. Then worshippers mark their foreheads with a 'dot' *(tilak)* of sandalwood paste, which is kept outside the main temple. The *tilak* signifies obedience to the teachings of the *jina*.

Anga Pujaa Worshippers then tie on a 'mouth-kerchief' *(mukhakosa)* or use the end of the cloth worn on the upper part of the body, to cover the mouth. This is to prevent harm to tiny living beings in the air. Then, pronouncing *'nissahi'*, the worshipper goes into the shrine and cleans away the previous day's flowers and sandalwood paste from the image using a soft brush, usually made of peacock feathers, and a moistened cloth.

Then follows the 'sacred water' or 'anointing' worship. A mixture of the 'five nectars' *(pancaamrita)*, consisting of water, milk, curds, ghee and sugar, is poured over the image from a spouted vessel. The image is then washed with clean water. This anointing recalls the bathing of the newborn *tirthankara* with milky water by the king of the heavenly beings, Indra, on Mount Meru, and a recitation relating to this is said. The image is then wiped dry with three cloths, to ensure that all moisture is removed. The symbolic washing of the image is believed to have a parallel effect upon the worshippers, dissolving karmic accretions attached to their souls. In most temples the washing of images is carried out by *pujaaris*. After the washing, the water containing the five nectars is collected in a bowl. This liquid is known as *nhaavana*. It is considered to be sacred and devotees apply it to their foreheads and eyebrows, and sprinkle it in places, which they wish to purify. It is believed that *nhaavana* helps to cure physical ailments.

The next stage of the ritual is worship with sandalwood paste *(candan pujaa)*. This involves anointing the image with sandalwood paste on the big toes, knees, wrists, shoulders, crown of the head, forehead, neck, chest and navel. Appropriate verses accompany each of these actions. Flowers are placed before the *jina* image, usually at the feet, although occasionally the image is garlanded.

In the rituals of *candana pujaa* each anointing of a different part of the image is a 'physical' prayer for a particular desired outcome.

The toes of the image are anointed out of respect for the *jina* and as a prayer in humility, detachment and *jina*-like contentment. It also expresses the desire for the welfare of all beings.

Anointing the knees is for the strength to meditate, to achieve self-realisation.

Anointing the wrists is linked to the charitable giving away of physical possessions and the passing of spiritual knowledge to others.

Anointing the shoulder is to develop humility.

Anointing the crown of the head shows veneration for the liberated soul of the *jina*.

Anointing the forehead shows respect and submission to the teachings of *jina*.

Anointing the neck expresses the desire always to speak in such a way as to promote the spiritual welfare of oneself and others.

The chest is anointed from the desire to have the *jina*-like virtues of detachment, control over the passions, friendship, compassion and equanimity.

Anointing the navel expresses the desire to experience the attributes of purified souls.

Using flowers in worship is symbolic of the fragrance created by virtuous nature and good deeds.

Agra Pujaa   This ritual is performed outside the inner shrine of the temple, where the worshipper offers waving burning incense, and then waves a *ghee* lamp before the image. Incense is used in worship, for a prayer of destroying *karma* and the passions, mirroring the way the smoke of burning incense acts. The 'lamp-waving' worship symbolises the removal of ignorance and the achievement of complete understanding.

Following the offering of incense and light, further offerings of rice, a sweet, and a fruit are performed. This completes the *asta-prakaari-pujaa*. To make these offerings, the worshipper sits at a low table and on it arranges grains of rice in the form of the traditional symbols of the Jain faith. First there is a *swastika*; the four arms symbolising the four states of embodiment (human, heavenly, animal or hellish) in which a soul may be reborn. Above this, three dots are placed symbolising Right Faith, Right Knowledge and Right Conduct. At the top of this rice 'diagram', a crescent symbolises the abode of the liberated souls and a 'dot' above the cresent symbolises the liberated souls. The sweet is placed on the swastika and the fruit on the crescent. The rice grains symbolise freedom from the rebirth; polished rice grains will not germinate. The sweet symbolises the wish to achieve a state in which one does not desire food. The fruit symbolises the desired outcome of the worship, the liberation.

Jains are not permitted to make use of anything offered to an image. Fruits, sweets, nuts, rice or other ingredients offered by worshippers may be utilised by the temple staff, if they are non-Jains. During worship some devotees wave a 'brush fan' *(caamar)* signifying their devotion, and gaze at the image of the tirthankara, reflected in a mirror; the symbolism of the reflected image signifies the purity of the soul.

Bhaava Pujaa 'Psychic' worship *(bhaava pujaa)* consists of a series of rituals, for temple veneration, which is called *caitya vandana*. In this worship hymns of praise, adoration and devotion are recited together with the performance of penance and meditation. *Caitya vandana* helps the devotee to develop spirituality and shed *karma* attached to the soul. Hence this worship should be undertaken with full concentration and understanding of the meaning of each ritual.

There are a number of paryers and rituals in the *caitya vandana*.

Veneration of the *jina*;
Asking for forgiveness for harming any living being, knowingly or unknowingly, while coming to or going from the temple;
Expression of a desire to shed *karma* acquired during those journeys;
Performance of penance with bodily detachment and meditation in the form of a *sutra* on the adoration of and devotion to the twenty-four *jinas*, or the four silent recitations of the *navakara mantra*;
Prayer of adoration and devotion to the twenty-four *jinas* of this time-cycle, and of the past and future;
Prayer to Shantinatha, the sixteenth *tirthankara*, bestower of welfare to all, and a guide on the spiritual path towards salvation;

A *sutra* of veneration to all the *jina* images throughout the universe;

A *sutra* offering respect and veneration to all the *jina* temples throughout the universe;

A *sutra* of veneration to the five 'supreme beings' *(parmesthis)*;

A *sutra* of veneration to all the saints throughout the universe;

Recitation of hymns of praise and adoration of the *tirthankaras* and their attributes;

A *sutra* containing prayers to the *jinas*, whose teachings are the most auspicious, for aid in shedding *karma* and worldly miseries;

A *sutra* of penance for allowing one's mind to be distracted during the rituals;

The mental recitation of *navkar mantra* in a standing posture with bodily detachment.

The ritual concludes with a prayer and adoration of the *tirthankaras*.

Khamaasana (beginning standing, ending touching the floor with four limbs and head)

Mukta-sukti-mudra

Yoga-mudra

Yoga-mudra

Figure 5.1 Some of the positions adopted during the ritual of *caitya vandan*

After this worship, the devotee rings the bell hanging just outside the shrine as a sign of rejoicing. On many occasions the *jina* images are decorated with silver or gold foil, or with other rich decorative materials, to recall the *tirthankaras'* previous lives as monarchs.

Normally, upon first seeing the image of the *jina*, the worshipper will engage in a contemplation of the different stages through which the *jina* passed in life, such as birth, reign as a monarch, renunciation, omniscience and liberation.

Aarati This popular waving lamp ritual involves the rotating of five ghee lamps. It is performed in mid-morning and is the last ritual at night. The five lamps symbolise five forms of knowledge: sensory, scriptural, clairvoyant, 'telepathic' and omniscient. It is a mass ritual, accompanied by melodic singing and music. *Aarati* is performed as a symbol of veneration to *jinas* and is believed to help to prevent malevolent thoughts.

Mangala Divo This ritual of rotating a single lamp follows *aarati*. *Mangala divo* symbolises everlasting knowledge passed on by the *jina*. This mass ritual includes a prayer for the welfare of all living beings. It is believed that *Aacaarya* Hemcandra initiated this ritual in the days of King Kumarpala in the 12th century CE, adopting the Hindu tradition of sharing the lamp-waving ritual with others.

Nava smarana Some staunch devotees recite daily the nine eulogies in veneration of the *tirthankaras*, *panca parmesthis*, the goddesses of learning and the guardian deities. They are: the *Navakara Mantra*, *Uvasaggaharam Stotra*, *Santikarana Stotra*, *Tijyapahutta Stotra*, *Nami Una Stotra*, *Ajita Santi*, *Bhaktaamara Stotra*, *Kalyaana Mandir Stotra*, and *Bruhacchantih Stotra*. A further description of the *Uvasaggaharam*, *Santikarana*, *Ajita Santi* and *Bruhacchantih* is given later in this chapter. The *Tijya pahutta* is a prayer to the 170 *tirthankaras* of the universe and the 16 goddesses of learning, for the destruction of the devotee's *karma*, and the avoidance of calamities due to the planets, and the actions of ghosts or evil heavenly beings. The *Nami Una Stotra* is a eulogy in praise of Parsvanatha and it is believed that devotees who recite this mantra will avoid calamity and dispel fear. The *Bhaktaamara Stotra* is a forty-four verses eulogy in praise of Risabhdeva, composed by Mantung Suri. The circumstances of the composition of this eulogy are told in chapter 2. *Kalyaana Mandir Stotra* is a eulogy in praise of Parsvanatha composed by *Aacaarya* Siddhasen Divakar Suri.

Other *pujaas*

The performance of special *pujaas* such as the *snaatra pujaa*, *panca kalyanaka pujaa*, *santi snaatra pujaa*, *antaraaya karma pujaa*, *siddha cakra pujan*, *arihanta mahapujan*, *atthai mahotsava*, *adhaara abhiseka* and

Plate 5.1 A devotee making a swastika with rice grains in a temple at Boradi, Gujarat, India

anjana salaakaa are performed on celebratory occasions. They are very colourful and vibrant ceremonies, which clearly show the popularity of Jainism as a living tradition. Devotees often gather in the temple for *bhaavanaa* to sing the hymns of praise to the *tirthankaras* prior to the lamp waving ritual at night.

Snaatra Pujaa (anointing worship) *Snaatra pujaa* is a daily ritual performed in most Jain temples. It is a re-enactment by laypeople of the birth celebration of a *tirthankara*, traditionally performed by heavenly beings on Mount Meru. It is also performed on auspicious days or for family celbrations.

Panca Kalyaanaka Pujaa This ritual entails the worship of the five auspicious occasions in the life of a *jina*: conception, birth, renunciation, omniscience and liberation. *Snaatra pujaa* precedes this ritual.

Shanti Snaatra Pujaa This special *pujaa* for universal peace and the welfare of all living beings in the universe is regarded as the most auspicious and beneficial, and is performed on the last day of any major celebratory ceremony. In this *pujaa* sacred offerings are made, either twenty-seven or one hundred and eight times before the image of Shantinatha, depending upon the time available. In this ritual worship is offered to the nine planets and to other guardian divinities. Incantations are chanted and the wish is expressed: 'May felicity, bliss, cheerfulness and holiness prevail everywhere'.

Plate 5.2 Devotees performing *caitya vandan* in the temple at Boradi, Gujarat, India

Antaraaya Karma Pujaa This ritual is performed to remove obstacles, which may be impeding the rightful outcome of meritorious actions. It is also enacted for the avoidance of unexplained disasters.

Siddha Cakra Pujan During the worship of the *Siddha Cakra*, a colourful and artistic mystical diagram known as *siddhacakra yantra* is created, in an appropriate place. It is made with wheat, green dal, black gram, Bengal gram and white and coloured rice. Holy recitations, meditation, worship and prayer are performed as symbolic representations of the five 'supreme beings', the three jewels, and austerities *(nava pad)*. Worship is also offered to the sixteen goddesses of learning and other guardian heavenly beings. Prayers for the welfare of all living beings and for universal peace are recited. Jains revere the *siddha cakra* as *mantra* in their daily worship and meditation as a representation of the essence of scriptures: the five 'supreme beings' and four essentials of Right Faith, Right Knowledge, Right Conduct and Right Austerities.

Arihanta Mahaapujan This elaborate ritual lasts three days. It invokes all the attributes of the *arihant (tirthankara)*. During this ritual the prayers to guardian heavenly beings are recited along with the prayers for the welfare of all living beings in the universe.

Atthai Mahotsava This is an eight-day religious celebration in which various *pujans* are performed daily. On this occasion, cleaning and decoration of the temples are undertaken. This celebration involves offering

Plate 5.3 Devotees bathe a Jina statue during the ritual of *siddha cakra pujan*, Leicester, England, 1985

prayers to the *jina*, with music and dances, the chanting of hymns of glorification, the recitation of devotional songs, decoration of the images *(aangi)*, and the organisation of community gatherings and the amity dinners.

Adhaara Abhiseka This ceremony is undertaken for the purification of an image, whether old or new, or any picture or engraved marble slab. It is performed by offering eighteen oblations containing various kinds of pure water, herbs and rich substances. It is a very auspicious ceremony and it is performed periodically in temples for purification.

Anjana Salaakaa This is the ceremony of consecration of an image to make it venerable for worship. It is performed at midnight by an *aacaarya* (or his deputy), who ceremoniously recites the mantras of conception, birth, renunciation, omniscience and salvation. He also applies to the eyes of the image a paste made of many rich substances, using a goldstick. It is customary for the *aacaarya* to fast for three days while performing this ceremony.

The Jain sacred literature, in languages such as Gujarati and Hindi, describe various *pujaas* composed by ascetic-scholars Virvijay, Sakalchandra, Padmavijay, Vimalsuri, Yashovijay, Buddhisagar and many others. The *Vividha Pujaa Sangraha* (a compendium of *pujaas*, 960 pages) and the *Pujan Sangraha* (296 pages), both in Gujarati language, describe the *mantras*, *sutras*, methods and protocols of the *pujaas*; texts are also available in Hindi and some other Indian languages.

Purificatory Rituals

Svetambaras perform equanimity *(saamayika)*, penitential retreat *(pratikramana)*, sacred fasting, meditation and temporary life like an ascetic *(pausadha)*, and self-study *(svaadhyaya)* as purificatory rituals. The first and last of these have been described earlier. The penitential retreat will be discussed later in this chapter and *Pausadha* is described below.

Pausadha This is an austerity observed by laypeople during which they model their behaviour on that of the ascetics. It is intended to enhance spiritual endeavour and to provide inner strength. The ritual may last from twelve to twenty-four hours, although sometimes devotees continue for longer. This austerity is undertaken on holy days, in the home or in *upashrayas*. For some, this ritual may form part of a devotee's preparation for an ascetic life.

Gurubhakti After performing image worship, devotees go to the *upashraya* to pay their respects to the ascetics, enquire after their health and invite them home to provide them with food, water and other necessities. Devotees listen to the sermons of the ascetics and take from them the vows of austerities. If there are no ascetics, they perform this ceremony by reciting *sutra*s and accept vows themselves.

Celebratory Rituals

Svetambaras celebrate a number of Jain sacred days, *pujaas* (some decribed above), and sacred festivals by performing the appropriate rituals. These are described later in this chapter.

Religious Funds

Svetambaras are very particular about the management of religious funds and maintain seperate funds for a range of purposes, which are raised by donations placed in clearly marked collection boxes and by 'bidding' *(boli* or *uchavani)* during rituals in which devotees bid for the privilege of performing rituals.

The funds are as follows:

Temple fund *(deva dravya)* is raised through devotional rituals and the temple collection box. It may only be used for the renovation and building of temples.

Ascetics' fund *(saadhu/saadhvi fund)* is raised by veneration for the ascetics and donations to meet the needs of ascetics.

Scriptural fund *(jnaana daana)* is raised by donations and is used for the publishing of scriptures and their dissemination.

Co-religionist fund (saadharmika fund) is raised by donations and is used to meet the needs of fellow members of the community.

Compassion fund (jiva dayaa/anukampaa fund) is raised by donations and is used for animal and human welfare.

General Fund (saadharana fund) is raised by donations and is used for the salaries of staff, maintenance of the buildings, administration and other expenses.

Food funds (bhojansaala/ayambilsaala fund) These two funds are raised by donations and used to supply meals for pilgrims, guests and community members. The *ayambil* fund can only be used for devotees who perform *ayambil* austerities.

PENITENTIAL RETREAT

Penitential retreat *(pratikramana)* is one of the most important and popular religious observances. It is a distinct feature of the Jain way of life, prescribed for ascetics and laypeople. It is performed: daily (in the morning and evening); once in each 'half' of a month (i.e. twice each month); once in each four month period; and once annually. The daily performance is relatively brief; the others are more elaborate and require longer time to complete.

Pratikramana means '(re)turning back', meaning a return to one's original state of purity. External environments and our daily activities, whether they are social, domestic, work related or recreational bring disturbance to the peaceful nature of the soul. Genuine bliss, which comes from within, is lost when we seek imaginary happiness from or through external things. The happiness that comes from material factors is temporary, dependent upon other persons or things, and is the cause of our passions, attraction and aversion. Happiness, which comes from within arises from the nature of the soul and is permanent, dependent only upon the self. As we cannot avoid worldly activities which disturb the soul, this daily ritual helps to shed the *karma* of our transgressions and returns us to the state of purity of the soul before we began these activities, whether mental, spoken or physical.

If *pratikramana* is not performed, the soul continues to be obscured by karmic particles and purification may become impossible. Jainism holds that no other person or divinity can assist us, we have to help ourselves, ask for forgiveness for our transgressions, perform penance, and see that such faults are not repeated.

We have evolved ethical codes of conduct in our daily life and try to act accordingly. But imperfect human beings violate the ethical code repeatedly, knowingly or unknowingly, by mind, speech or physical action, by

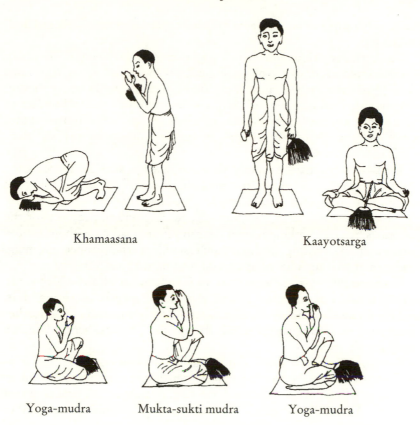

Khamaasana   Kaayotsarga

Yoga-mudra   Mukta-sukti mudra   Yoga-mudra

Figure 5.2 Some of the postures adopted during the ritual of *pratikramana*

their own actions or by motivating others to act wrongly or by applauding immoral acts. Jain seers taught that the violation of morality can be caused by any type of ill will (mental transgression); being prepared to undertake immorally ('preparatory' transgressions); partially breaking the moral code (partial violation); and acting completely immorally (total violation).

If one confesses one's transgressions, realises their wrongness, repents, performs penance and determines not to repeat such faults, one may return to one's original self. This act of 'turning back' is penitential retreat.

'To err is human' and transgressions of the moral path do occur. The Jain seers taught of intentional or accidental transgressions (*aticaara*), which arise in our daily life, such as in playing sports, in our occupations, in self-defence and other worldly activities. They classified 124 forms of inadvertent transgressions. A full account of these can be found in the

Aacaaranga Sutra or in the *Panca Pratikramana Sutra.* (available in Hindi and Gujarati).

These transgressions apply equally to ascetics and laypeople. They may be committed by physical, physiological, psychological or verbal means. Transgressions may be against Right Faith, such as: doubt or scepticism; worshipping in anticipation of gain; condemnation of the faith; belief in false deities, teachers or traditions; criticism of the *jina's* faith; activities which undermine the faith; bringing the faith into disrepute; and false piety motivated by self-interest.

Transgressions may be against Right Knowledge, such as: doubting the true knowledge of the omniscients, including seven forms of inappropriate reading of the religious texts. These are: reading at the wrong time (not at the best times, such as in the morning), reading without respect for the scriptures, reading without proper concentration, reading without proper pronunciation, reading without understanding the proper meaning, reading and reciting innaccurately, and reading without humility.

Transgressions may be against Right Conduct, and those, which apply mainly to ascetics, are carelessness in walking, speech, accepting alms, picking up and setting down objects, and bodily functions. The further transgressions of unguarded mind, speech and physical action likewise apply mainly to ascetics.

Transgressions of Right Conduct (against the twelve-fold ethical code or vows) which apply to laypeople are: manifest violence, physical or mental, to living beings; falsehood; stealing; not observing proper sexual restraint, physically or mentally; and showing attachment to worldly possessions.

Transgressions against the three 'multiplicative' vows are breaking the 'directional' vow of limiting unnecessary movement, communication or activity.

Transgressions against the four 'educative' vows involve failure to rightly observe the vows of equanimity; the temporary adoption of an ascetic lifestyle; 'limiting consumables and non-consumables'; these include transgressions as an element of certain occupations; and 'hospitality'.

There are also transgressions against the six external and six internal austerities, and transgressions which obstruct the acquisition of spiritual energy. Lastly, there are transgressions against the vow of 'holy death'.

The daily duty of *pratikramana* involves yoga, including *pranaayama* and physical postures, meditation, and the six essential duties, an all-encompassing spiritual path. This ritual also aims to promote the welfare of all living beings and world peace.

If this sacred ritual is properly performed, with understanding of its meaning and full concentration, the devotee can advance spiritually, and acquire mental peace and happiness. Ideally, *pratikramana* should be performed in the presence of an ascetic, but in their absence, a sacred text placed before the devotee may function as a consecrated substitute. This is particularly the case when this ritual is performed in the devotee's home.

Requirements for this ritual are minimal: clean clothes, a rectangular woollen cloth upon which to sit, a woollen brush *(caravalaa)*, a 'mouth-kerchief' *(muhapatti)* and a text of the *Pratikramana Sutras* (for the devotees who do not know them by heart).

All the *sutras* recited in *pratikramana* have particular meanings and purposes, as do the various yogic postures used. During that part of the ritual involving the *muhapatti*, a mental recitation is performed, expressing a desire to pronounce the *sutras* correctly and to understand their meaning; to abandon passions, attractions and aversions; to follow Right Faith, Right Knowledge and Right Conduct; to have pure thoughts; and to protect immobile and mobile living beings. Both ascetics and laypeople recite the majority of these *sutras*; a few are recited only by ascetics, fewer still exclusively by men or by women. There are *sutras* in Prakrit and Sanskrit and in at least four modern Indian languages, Gujarati, Hindi, Tamil and Kannada.

It is impossible to mention all the *sutras* in detail, however, the substance of the sacred *sutras* of penitential retreat is as follows:

1. *Navakara (Maha)Mantra* (also known as the *Panca Parmesthi Sutra*): This incantation is the most sacred *sutra* and the most commonly recited. It is the veneration mantra of obeisance to the five 'supreme beings'.
2. *Pancindiya Sutra*: This *sutra* describes the thirty-six virtues of ascetics. It is the consecration *sutra* of a sacred text prior to the performance of equanimity *(saamayika)*.
3. *Khamaasana Sutra*: This *sutra* is recited during the performance of the 'five limbs' posture (obeisance with forehead, hands and knees on the ground) with which it shares its name; it offers veneration to the *panca parmesthis*.
4. *Icchakaara Sutra*: This *sutra* respectfully enquires after the spiritual and physical welfare of the ascetics and invites them to accept food, water and other necessities.
5. *Iriyaavahiaa Sutra*: This *sutra* asks forgiveness for harm to any living being through our actions such as walking and otherwise moving.
6. *Tassauttari Sutra*: This *sutra* asks for penance to annihilate the karmic effects of sins that remain even after asking forgiveness through the *Iriyaavahiaa Sutra*.
7. *Annattha Sutra*: By this *sutra* the vow of meditation with bodily detachment is taken, allowing for exceptions in the case of the sixteen

events, including natural causes, such as sneezing, passing wind or having an accident.

8. *Logassa Sutra*: In this *sutra*, the eulogy of the twenty-four *tirthankaras* of each of the past, present and future cycles is performed. A prayer is also made to seek their help through the Three Jewels.

9. *Karemi Bhante Sutra*: This is a *sutra* for taking a vow to practise equanimity *(saamayika)* or renunciation, and to resist harmful sins of mind, speech or body, by oneself or through motivating others to sin, and to condemn and censure sins until they cease.

10. *Saamaiya vaya jutto Sutra*: This *sutra* is recited on conclusion of *saamayika*. It considers the practitioner of equanimity to be equivalent to an ascetic and desires the performance of equanimity again and again. It seeks forgiveness for thirty-two faults (ten of mind, ten of speech, and twelve of body) involved in practising *saamayika*.

11. *Jaga cintamani Sutra*: This *sutra* eulogises all the present, past and future *tirthankaras*, famous places of pilgrimage, temples and *jina* images, and offers veneration to ascetics and other omniscients.

12. *Jankinci Sutra*: This *sutra* venerates all the places of Jain pilgrimage and all the images existing in the Jain universe.

13. *Namutthunam Sutra* or *Sakrastava Sutra*: This *sutra* eulogises and offers veneration to all the present enlightened ones, and past and future liberated ones, and recites their attributes. The heavenly King Sakrendra recites it whenever the soul of a *jina* is conceived in its final human life.

14. *Jaavanti ceiaim Sutra*: This *sutra* venerates all the *jina* temples existing in the Jain universe.

15. *Jaavant kevi sahu Sutra*: This *sutra* venerates the ascetics present in the *Bharata*, *Airavata* and *Mahaavideha* regions of Jain geography.

16. *Namorhata sutra*: this *sutra* is a short form of the *navakara mantra*.

17. *Uvasagga haram Stotra*: This *sutra* is a eulogy composed by Bhadrabahu in praise of Parsvanatha, the remover of all calamities, and is a prayer to him asking for Right Faith.

18. *Jayviyaraya Sutra*: This *sutra* offers prayers before the *jinas* for the destruction of *karma* and worldly miseries, and reiterates that the teachings of *jina* are the most auspicious among all faiths.

19. *Arihanta ceiyanam Sutra* or *Caitya stava Sutra*: This *sutra* offers prayers of adoration and devotion to *jina* images in temples. It is recited as a vow before meditation with bodily detachment for obtaining Right Faith and liberation.

20. *Kallaana kandam stuti Sutra*: This *sutra* is a eulogy in four parts offering veneration to the *tirthankaras* Risabhadeva, Santinatha,

Neminatha, Parsvanatha and Mahavira in its first stanza; to all the *jinas* in its second, to scriptural knowledge in its third, and to the goddess of scriptures, Sarasvati, in its fourth stanza.

21. *Sansaara daavaanala Sutra*: This *sutra*, a eulogy of Mahavira, is a composition by Haribhadra. It offers veneration to Mahavira, all *jinas*, scriptures, and the goddesses of scripture.

22. *Pukkhara varadivaddhe Sutra*: This *sutra* venerates the *tirthankaras* as the source of the scriptural knowledge of the Three Jewels and is a prayer to them seeking Right Conduct.

23. *Siddhaanam buddhaanam Sutra*: This *sutra* venerates the liberated ones and omniscients, and all the twenty-four *tirthankaras* are eulogised and prayers are offered to them.

24. *Veyavacca garaanam Sutra*: This *sutra* venerates heavenly guardian deities who care for people with Right Faith, and the followers of the *jina's* teaching.

25. *Bhagvaanaham aadi vandana Sutra*: This *sutra* venerates the *panca parmesthis*.

26. *Devasia padikamana thaum Sutra*: This *sutra* seeks steadfastness in penitential retreat.

27. *Icchaami thaami Sutra*: This *sutra* is a vow of meditation with bodily detachment for transgressions of Right Conduct, including the twelve vows of laypeople.

28. *Naanam mi dansanam mi* or *Pancaacaara Sutra*: This *sutra* describes transgressions of the Three Jewels, austerities, and the utilisation of spiritual energy. This recital is undertaken in meditation with bodily detachment.

29. *Suguru vandana Sutra*: This *sutra* venerates ascetics and seeks forgiveness for disrespectful conduct towards them, knowingly or unknowingly.

30. *Devasiam aalou Sutra*: This *sutra* expresses self-censure for transgressions of Right Conduct, during the night or day.

31. *Saat laakh Sutra*: By this *sutra* one asks forgiveness from all living beings in the universe for any harm inflicted by oneself, or by someone whom one has motivated to do harm, or where one has 'appreciated' violence done by others.

32. *Adhaara paapa sthaanaka Sutra*: By this *sutra* one seeks forgiveness for eighteen types of sins committed by oneself, or by someone whom one has motivated to commit sin, or where one has 'appreciated' sin committed by others. The sins reiterated are: taking life, untruth, stealing, improper sexual relations, hoarding and attachment to material things, anger, pride, deceit, greed, attraction, aversion, discord, accusation, slander, excessive feelings of pleasure and of pain, defamation, lying and deception, and misguided beliefs.

33. *Savvassavi Sutra*: This *sutra* briefly expresses censure and penitence for sins in general.

34. *Icchami padikkamiu Sutra*: This *sutra* expresses the desire for penitence and forgiveness for any transgressions.

35. *Vandittu Sutra* or *Sraaddha pratikramana Sutra*: This fifty verse *sutra* is the essence of the penitential ritual. It expresses repentance for transgressions in observing the Three Jewels, the twelve vows, the three guards and the five carefulnesses during the day or night. The *sutra* eulogises the *panca parmesthis* and venerates the *jinas*, their temples and images, ascetics and scriptures. Finally, the devotee beseeches forgiveness from all and forgives all and expresses amity to every living being and enmity to none.

36. *Abbhutthiomi Sutra*: This *sutra* asks forgiveness for any impoliteness shown, intentionally or otherwise, towards ascetics.

37. *Aayariya uvaajzaae sutra*: This *sutra* asks forgiveness for offences committed against ascetics, religious leaders and teachers, the *sangha*, and all living beings. Devotees express their forgiveness to all.

38. *Sua devaya sutra*: This eulogy is a meditational prayer with bodily detachment to the god(dess) of scripture for aid in shedding *karmas*, which inhibit Right Knowledge, and is prescribed only for men.

39. *Kamala dala Sutra*: This prayer, recited by women, in meditation with bodily detachment, is a eulogy to the goddess of scripture, Sarasvati, who is depicted as seated upon a lotus.

40. *Jise khitte Sutra*: Men recite this eulogy, in meditation with bodily detachment, to the guardian deity of the region and pray for the removal of obstacles to spiritual observance.

41. *Yasyah ksetram sutra*: Women recite this eulogy, in meditation with bodily detachment, to the guardian deity of the region, but men also recite it in elaborate fortnightly, four-monthly and yearly *pratikramanas*.

42. *Jnaanadi guna Sutra*: This eulogy to the guardian heavenly beings of the world, is uttered in an elaborate penitential recitation with hymns asking for knowledge.

43. *Namostu vardddhamanay Sutra*: This eulogy, recited by men in the evening *pratikramanas*, venerates Mahavira, all the *tirthankaras* and the scriptures for their right teachings.

44. *Visaala locana Stotra*: This eulogy, recited by men during the morning *pratikramanas*, venerates Mahavira, all the *tirthankaras* and Jain scriptures.

45. *Addhaijzesu Sutra*: This *sutra* venerates all ascetics in the Jain universe.

46. *Vara kanaka Sutra*: By means of this eulogy, male devotees make obeisance to the one hundred and seventy *tirthankaras* of the Jain

universe who are venerated with rich offerings from heavenly beings.

47. *Laghu santi Sutra*: This short recital venerates *tirthankara* Shantinatha and the goddess of peace—Vijaya—for bestowing peace on the entire world. The 7th century ascetic-scholar *Aacaarya* Manadeva composed it and its recitation is said to have dispelled an epidemic; it is believed that misery is dispelled and peace appears when this *sutra* is recited or read, or water consecrated by this hymn is sprinkled.

48. *Caukkasaaya Sutra*: This *sutra* is a prayer to Parsvanatha, conqueror of the four passions, to grant spiritual uplift.

49. *Mannah jinaanam Sajzhaaya*: This *sutra* consists of five verses reminding laypeople of their daily duties.

50. *Bharahesara Sajzaaya*: By these thirteen verses, devotees remind themselves each morning of the fifty-three men and forty-seven women, ascetics and laypeople, who were celibate and pious, and whose conduct is a model for the *sangha*. Both ascetics and laypeople perform this recitation.

51. *Sakala tirtha vandanaa Stotra*: This fifteen-verse hymn was composed in Gujarati by the 17th century *Aacaarya* Jiva Vijay, and venerates all *jina* images in the universe, places of pilgrimage, present *tirthankaras* in the universe, liberated souls and ascetics on the path to liberation.

52. *Sakalaarhata Stotra*: This *sutra*, composed by Hemcandra, is a thirty-three verse sanctuary veneration in the form of an eulogy to the twenty-four *tirthankaras*, is recited in the elaborate *pratikramanas*, and offers veneration to all Jina images in holy places.

53. *Snatasyaa Stuti*: This eulogy of Mahavira, composed by Muni Balacandra, a disciple of Hemcandra in the 13th century, is recited in elaborate *pratikramanas*.

54. *Paksika aticaara Sutra*: This detailed recital seeks forgiveness for all the 124 possible transgressions in observing the five-fold conduct in every fortnightly, four-monthly and yearly *pratikramana*. It is an elaboration of the *Vandittu Sutra*, but Ascetics recite the *Pakkhi Sutra*, a detailed version relating to transgressions of their vows.

55. *Ajita santi Stava*: This is a eulogy of Ajitanatha and Shantinatha (second and sixteenth *tirthankaras*) composed by *Aacaarya* Nandisena to dispel diseases and fears, and is recited during elaborate *pratikramanas*.

56. *Bruhacchanti Stotra*: This long recitation, composed by Shanti Suri in the 11th century, is used on all auspicious occasions such as image consecrations, anointing worship and other *pujaas*, to pray for the peace, happiness and spiritual upliftment of all living beings. In this recitation prayers are offered to Parsvanatha, Shantinatha and other

tirthankaras, the sixteen goddesses of learning, the nine heavenly beings of the planets, the four heavenly beings of the regions. It prays for the peace and welfare of the *sangha*, all non-Jain persons, rulers, leaders, spiritual preachers, and for the welfare of all living beings. It reiterates that the teachings of *jina* are beneficial to all. Water consecrated by this recital is sprinkled on places to purify the surroundings and on devotees as a blessing.

57. *Santikarana Stotra*: This thirteen verse recitation, composed by Munisundar Suri, is a prayer to Shantinatha, to the sixteen goddesses of learning, and to the male and female guardian deities of each of the twenty-four *tirthankaras (saasan devas* and *devis)*. It is believed that by reciting this stotra at least three times, with full concentration, calamities and misery can be immediately averted.

Jain seers have arranged the sequence of sacred *sutras* of *pratikramana* in such a way that devotees obtain the full benefits of the performance of their daily essential duties, yoga and meditation.

Daily *Pratikramana*

In daily *pratikramana* (performed in the evening) devotees recite the *sutras* of equanimity: the *Navakara Mantra, Pancadiya, Khamaasana, Iriyaavahiaa, Tassauttari, Annatha, Logassa, Karemi bhante,* and *sutras* seeking permission from ascetics (or their substitute) to be in a state of *saamayika*. Following this, devotees mentally recite the verses concerning the *muhapatti*, while checking it, then venerate ascetics and temples, recite once more the *Karemi bhante*, the *sutra* of *saamayika*, the **first** essential duty. For the **second** duty, the *Logassa* and other *sutras* are recited in veneration of the twenty-four *tirthankaras.* For the **third** duty, devotees check the *muhapatti* and recite the *Suguru vandana Sutra*. For the **fourth** duty of *pratikramana*, devotees recite *sutras* such as the *Devasiam alou, Saat lakh, Adhaara papasthanaka, Vandittu,* and perform meditation with bodily detachment and the sequence of the *Suguru vandana.* For the **fifth** duty of *kaayotsarga*, devotees recite a series of *sutras*, interspersed with meditation, on the *Logassa* or *Navakara Mantra*, with bodily detachment.

At this point, in celebration of purification, devotees recite eulogies to the liberated ones and to the guardian deities, such as the *Siddhanam buddhanam, Sua devaya, Kamala dala* and *Jise khitte.* The **sixth** duty of *pratyaakhyaan* is performed by accepting the vows to renounce that which is harmful to the soul.

After completing these essential duties, one recites the eulogy of Mahavira and Parsvanatha followed by the short recital to peace and other *sutras* in conclusion of *samaayika*.

The morning *pratikramana* comprises a similar recitation of *sutras*, with more emphasis on eulogies and hymns, but the fortnightly, four-monthly and yearly *pratikramanas* include more elaborate *sutras* concerning transgressions, elaborate *kaayotsarga* and eulogies followed by the long recital to peace.

Although, theoretically, *pratikramana* forms the fourth of the six esssential duties, the Jain seers made it customary to include all the six duties in its performance, to ensure that devotees would observe them daily, even when short of time.

DIGAMBARA RITUALS AND RITUALS OF OTHER SECTS

This section describes the rituals of Digambara Jains, the rituals of the Sthanakvasis, Terapanthis, followers of Srimad Rajcandra, of Kanji Swami and of Dada Bhagwan. The initiation rituals for ascetics and the 'holy death' *(sallekhanaa* or *santhaaraa)* are also covered.

The Digambaras perform six essential daily duties. Majority of the Digambara rituals is variations on the essential duties. They may be classified as devotional, purificatory, expiatory, oblationary and ceremonial. Perhaps the most significant difference between Svetambara and Digambara rituals is the absence of the daily performance of *pratikramana* among Digambara laypeople.

Devotional rituals Devotional rituals include: worship, prayers, chanting, incantations and *pujaas.* There are many *pujaas*, but their sequence is similar in each case. The general sequence of *pujaa* is: physical cleanliness through bathing and putting on clean clothing; mental purity through the recital of hymns and *mantras*; going to the temple and seeking the permission of the guardian deities to enter by uttering the word *'nissahi'* three times; venerating the images; and circumambulating the shrine three times.

The third stage consists of making preparation for *pujaa* by wearing (i.e. changing into) clean 'temple clothes', followed by taking from the temple store the eight types of materials to be offered; cleaning the materials with water and arranging them on a *pujaa* tray, on which a ninth material is created by mixing together the original eight.

Each ingredient has its spiritual symbolism: *Pure water* symbolises liberation of the self and other beings from birth, old age and death. *Sandalwood paste* symbolises equanimity (sandalwood has a calming influence). *Rice grains* symbolise freedom from rebirth (polished rice grains will not germinate). *Yellow rice grains* (coloured with sandalwood paste) symbolise purity and control over the passions. *Coconut* symbolises freedom from the feeling of hunger. *Coloured coconut* (coloured with sandalwood paste) symbolises the destruction of the darkness of delusion. (this symbol replaces a lighted lamp). *Incense* symbolises the destruction (burning away) of *karma* attached to the soul. (this is 'purely' symbolic, the incense is not incinerated). *Almonds, betelnuts* and *cloves,* used in place of fruit, symbolise the fruit of liberation. *The mixture of the eight ingredients* symbolises the desire to achieve liberation. In order to avoid harm to one-sensed beings, Digambaras do not use flowers or lighted lamps or fruits in their *pujaa.*

Digambara *pujaa* begins with the devotee's placing a *pujaa* tray on a wooden stool, while an empty *pujaa* tray stands on a second stool. The empty tray is marked with a *swastika* using sandalwood paste. A small *jina* image from the shrine is carried, to the accompaniment of traditional recitations, and placed on the empty *pujaa* tray. Clean filtered water is sprinkled over the head of the image. This sacred water, called *gandhodhak,* is then taken and applied by devotees to their head and eyebrows.

This anointment of the image is called the stream of peace; although generally water is used for this purpose, other liquids such as *ghee,* milk, curd, sugar-cane juice and a liquid mixture of herbal extracts can also be employed. If liquids other than water are employed, the final anointment should be made with a jet of water, so that the image remains clean. In elaborate *pujaas,* this anointing is performed with 108 pots, each pot representing an attribute of the *panca parmesthis.* After the anointing, veneration of the *jina* is performed, accompanied by the recitation of sacred verses. Then yellow rice grains are sprinkled in all directions to purify the surroundings.

Pujaas are performed for the veneration of the vows, places of pilgrimage, *jina* temples and *jina* images, the sixteen attributes of the *tirthankara* and the ten-fold religious observances. Of the many types of *pujaas* performed, each comprises the above sequence. At each stage, there are five invocations: a main deity (or deities) of the *pujaa,* scriptures and preceptors; the liberated ones; the twenty present *tirthankaras* of *Mahaavideha* region as described in the sacred geography, the *panca parmesthis*; and the individually-named *tirthankaras.*

Following the invocation of a deity, the devotee recites a sacred *mantra,* meditating on the deity invoked. The eight-fold offering to the deities is made accompanied by the recitation of each offering in sequence.

The last stage of the *pujaa* is the recitation of the verses of veneration of the conception, birth, renunciation, omniscience and liberation of the *tirthankaras (panca kalyaanaka).* It is followed by the recitation of the 'victorious garland' *(jayamaala),* consisting of the attributes of the *jinas,* followed by the ninth offering of the mixed materials. After these offerings, devotees perform *aarati* and pray for the happiness and peace of the world by reciting the *shanti paatha*. Devotees conclude by praying to the deities invoked for the forgiveness of any faults or omissions made during this ritual.

The *pujaa* with material offerings is intended to lead to psychic *(bhaava) pujaa*. Incantations of mantras, such as the *Navakara Mantra*, and the recitation of hymns and eulogies, such as the *Bhaktamara Stotra, Kalyaana mandir Stotra*, and many others are psychic forms of *pujaas*. Incantations, eulogies and incantational repititions lead one into the deeper stages of meditation and the observance of equanimity.

Purificatory Rituals   The purificatory rituals consist of the practices of equanimity and penitential retreat; the recitation of hymns and eulogies in praise of the *tirthankaras* and torch bearers; incantational repetitions; and self-study.

Long purificatory rituals, lasting for three to ten days are known as *vidhaanas*. In recent decades they have increased in popularity. They are mass rituals and serve to increase the cohesion of the community and raise funds for temples. Nowadays, *vidhaanas* such as the 'pujaa of the nine planets', the *pujaa* for peace, and the *pujaa* for *indra dhvaja* are observed by some to alleviate individual, family and social calamities, mimicking Hindu ritual practices.

Expiatory Rituals   These rituals, *aalocanaas*, consist of confession for the transgressions of Right Conduct before a preceptor or a consecrated substitute. Devotees seek penances as prescribed in the scriptures, and try not to repeat the transgressions.

Oblationary Rituals   Digambara oblationary rituals show Hindu influence. They are intended to provide both social and individual benefits and are sometimes included in *vidhaanas*.

Ceremonial Rituals   Ceremonial rituals consist of performances of one or more day's duration involving the celebration of mythological stories, image and shrine consecration ceremonies, head-anointing ceremonies and chariot processions. They are colourful and very popular mass rituals involving thousands of people.

At the conclusion of most religious festivals, a ceremonial ritual, known as flower garlanding *(phula maala)* is observed, where devotees bid for the privilege of wearing garlands named after deities or attributes of the *jinas*. The devotional atmosphere on such occasions is enhanced by religious music, dances and chanting, which stimulates higher bidding.

Digambara non-image-worshippers generally follow the rituals of other Digambaras, with the exception of rituals associated with temples and images, instead they worship the scriptures.

Rituals of Other Sects

Sthanakvasis and Terapanthis do not venerate images and have few rituals. Their daily life is otherwise similar to the Svetambara image worshippers. They perform *pratikramana* and *saamayika* and observe *paryusana*, *ayambils*, fasting and other austerities. They also observe *paakhi*, with an elaborate *pratikramana* and other religious observances, on the final day of each half of a month.

Terapanthis celebrate *paatotsava* on the anniversary of the installation of their *aacaarya*, and *maryaadaa mahotsava*, when their ascetics and community leaders gather for a festival of restraint, penance and renewal of vows.

Over the last few decades some Jains have promoted Jain values beyond the sectarian boundaries. Jains will attend the rituals of the other sects, if invited. This trend is very prevalent among Jains in Western countries where, without much hesitation, Jains of one sect will participate in the rituals of other sects.

Followers of Srimad Rajcandra   The spiritual mentor of Mahatma Gandhi, Srimad Rajcandra, stressed the importance of ethics and self-realisation over rituals. His followers perform many of the usual Jain rituals such as *saamayika*, incantational repetitions, eulogies, recitations of confessional worship, and self-study, and they celebrate the same festivals as other Jains. They call themselves 'liberation desiring' (*mumuksus*). Rajcandra's followers celebrate *guru purnima* on the anniversary of his birth, spending the day in equanimity practices and self-study, and usually concludes with an amity dinner for the community.

Followers of Kanji Swami   The followers of Kanjiswami have a philosophy which places emphasis on the attributes of the soul. They observe similar daily rituals to the majority of the Digambara laypeople, including the performance of *vidhaanas*, *pujaas* and self-study. They also call themselves *mumuksus*.

Followers of Dada Bhagwan   Followers of Shri Ambalal Patel (1908–88 CE), known to his devotees as Dada Bhagwan, observe similar rituals to those of the Svetambara *murtipujaka*. They emphasise the ethical aspects of Jain values in their daily life and attempt to identify themselves with pure soul. They worship Simandhar Swami, a *tirthankara* in Mahaavideha a region of the universe in Jain cosmology. Their rituals are largely devotional and include hymns, equanimity practices and meditation on the attributes of the pure soul. Many of them also follow the philosophical teachings of Srimad Rajcandra.

Initiation of Monks and Nuns

The process of of becoming an ascetic, *saadhu or saadhvi*, is termed 'initiation' *(diksaa)*. The whole process of preparation, blessings, rituals and
ceremony may take several months. Aspiring ascetics are invited to
different homes and there they are offered respect and good wishes in their
pursuit of the path of *jina*.

The ritual of initiation begins with the public interrogation of aspirants
by the *aacaarya* on their motives for adopting the ascetic life. The community celebrates by taking the aspirants in grand procession around the
locality, during which, aspirants cast handfuls of mixed sacred ingredients,
including gold and silver coins, to the crowds, symbolising their renunciation of material possessions. Devotees often keep these coins as sacred
souvenirs. The procession ends with the presentation of the candidates
before the *aacaarya*, who directs his disciples to pluck hair from candidates' scalps and presents them with the garments and the necessary
equipment of an ascetic. Then the *aacaarya* administers the oath of 'all the
vows' *(sarva virati)*, by reciting the *Karemi bhante Sutra*. New ascetics are
given new names with which to start a new life.

Some Svetambara aspirants are initiated temporarily, perhaps for one or
two years, and only when the *aacaarya* is satisfied, the provisional ascetic
is granted permanent ascetic status by means of a small ritual ceremony.

Among Digambaras, laypeople are initiated in stages through the eleven
pratimaas and at the seventh stage, aspirants accept the vow of complete
celibacy and practically renounce household activities. At the eleventh
stage, they are initiated into the position of minor ascetic *(ksullaka)* with
upper and lower garments ('two-clothed'), and when he (there are no
Digambara female ascetics in the strictest sense) advances spiritually
further, he is initiated as a major ascetic *(ailaka)*, with one garment. ('loin-
clothed'). Finally the aspirant is initiated to the full ascetichood, when he
gives away all his clothes and becomes a sky-clad ascetic.

Ritual of Holy Death

Birth and death are the initial and terminal miseries of the world. Jains
believe in rebirth until liberation and celebrate both birth and death: with
birth the human acquires a body which can be used to obtain liberation,
and death is an opportunity to gain a new body.

Jainism teaches that one should not be afraid of death; the moment of
death is very significant and one should leave the body peacefully in auspicious meditation, avoiding new influx of evil *karmas* of attraction and
aversion. Jains advocate a concluding ceremony for a life, as the whole of
life is viewed as a preparation for a sacred death. This 'sacred death' ritual

(sallekhanaa) is specific to Jainism. When one feels one has made full use of the body for spiritual advancement, and that one's body is of no further use, the vow of 'holy death' has been suggested in the Jain sciptures. It has been misunderstood by many in the West, as well as a few in the East, as being a form of suicide, but Jains do not regard this practice as suicide, rather it is a ritualised leaving of the body, as the purpose of holy death is spiritual advancement. Suicide is regarded by Jains as a major sin, involving violence to human life.

Other than the completely voluntary act, there are five sets of circumstances in which the holy death ritual may be performed:

- conditions of extreme calamity (e.g. captivity and torture by an enemy);
- acute famine (where acceptable food is unobtainable);
- extreme old age (accompanied by physical and mental impairment, rendering religious observances impossible);
- terminal illness or fatal injury; and
- when imminent natural death is predicted by astrological and other prognostications.

Those proposing to undertake this ritual must have the necessary physical and psychological strength and determination.

The first condition is that the ascetic or the surrogate supervising the ritual must be satisfied of the capacity of the aspirant to undertake the ritual. Secondly, the family must give their consent.

The sacred-death ritual is generally, though not exclusively, undertaken by ascetics. The ritual must be observed without any of the transgressions mentioned in scriptures.

The story of the thirty days long holy death ritual of Ananda (the richest man of Mahavira's time) and of the Aacaarya Skandhaka, are well known in Jain literature. Two modern holy deaths are equally well known: the Digambara Aacaarya Shantisagara underwent a thirty-six-day ritual in 1955 and, a layperson, Jethabhai Javeri underwent a forty-two-day ritual in 1993 are examples which indicate the unbroken continuity, popularity and strength of the ritual.

This ritual may be observed in the home, a forest, a holy place or an upashraya. The ritual consists of the stages as given below:

- The aspirant first seeks the required permissions and takes the vow.
- The aspirant gradually renounces food, first solids, then liquids, finally renouncing water.
- Time is spent in engaging in penitential retreat, recitations of confession, condemnation and atonements, asking for forgiveness from all and forgiving all, devotional and auspicious recitations, repitions of

the rosary, scriptural studies, meditation with bodily detachment and reflections on auspicious activities.

• Besides food, one renounces physical attachments, the passions and sinful activities.

• Some accept the major vows of ascetics before the expected death.

• Silent recitations or listening to the *Navakara Mantra* are undertaken to venerate and take refuge in *panca paramesthis*.

SOCIAL RITUALS

Human beings live in societies which construct social customs, norms and rituals to bring people together and give groups a distinct outward identity and character. In this chapter we look at the social customs of Jain communities, but in India, there are regional variations in social rituals, many of which show the influence of the predominent Hindu community, and these variations in ritual have travelled with the Jains overseas.

Jain literature describes many rituals, which are essentially social in nature, the major ones are described below: these include the blessings for a viable foetus *(dhriti sanskaar* or *kholo bharavo)*; the birth celebration; the naming ceremony; the ceremony of giving solid food to a child for the first time; the commencement of learning; the 'sacred thread' ceremony; and the ceremonies for marriage and death.

Jains also perform rituals on the commencement of building a house, entry into a new house or business venture, and initiating the New Year's accounts, but there are other ceremonies, largely of a social nature: the 'sacredthread' ceremony *(raksaa bandhan)*, the lighting of lamps *(Divali)*, worship of the goddess of learning *(Sarasvati)* and offerings to heavenly beings *(yaksis* and *yaksas)*.

While some Jain social customs may show Hindu influence, there are distinctive Jain features to these rituals, such as the recital of the *Navakara Mantra*, worship using diagrams *(yantras)*, *snaatra pujaa* and the recitaton for peace.

The *ceremony of blessing for a viable foetus* is normally observed at the seventh month of conception; recitations are performed for the welfare of mother and baby; an auspicious red powder *(sindur)* is put on the scalp of the mother; and fruits, sweets and flowers are placed in her lap, as a mark of blessing and good fortune; and other gifts are also offered to the mother.

The *celebration of a birth* is performed with *pujaa*, offerings and sweets are distributed amongst the friends and relatives, and donations are made to institutions and individuals.

The *naming ceremony* normally takes place between the tenth and thirtieth day after the birth, when a paternal aunt or other similar woman relative names the child. Presents are exchanged and the occasion is celebrated with the regular *pujaa* and dinner.

The *ceremony of giving the first solid food to a child* involves the pronouncement of blessings, and is performed between the sixth and eighth month after birth.

The *ceremony of removal of hair from the scalp for the first time (baabari)* is performed in public as an offering to the 'heavenly mother' *(maataa)*, accompanied by hymns, *pujaa* and dinner.

The *ceremony of the commencement of schooling* is performed when a child first goes to school; sweets are distributed, and books and pencils are given to other school children; prayers are offered to the goddess of learning and the child is given a pencil and paper accompanied by the recitation of blessings.

The *sacred thread ceremony (yajnopavit)* consists of giving to a child a three stranded cotton thread, representing the three Jewels of Right Faith, Right Knowledge and Right Conduct, and this sacred thread is worn over the shoulder like a sash for the rest of their life as a constant reminder to follow the sacred path. Only few Jains observe this ceremony.

The *ceremony of making offerings to the 'heavenly mother' (maataa)* is performed to thank her for granting devotees' requests, such as the wish for a child or the resolution of a difficulty. Young virgin girls are invited to the ceremony, where their feet are washed and elaborate respect is paid to them, and they are treated as honoured guests because of the affection of *maataa* for young virgins. This custom is very much an infuence of Hindu society.

The *ceremony to celebrate completion of studies* is performed with community *pujaa* and dinner, and often donations are made to institutions and charities.

The 'thread' ceremony *(raksaa bandhan)* is an expression of the wish for the welfare of a brother from a sister. Sisters tie a thread *(raakhadi)* around their brother's wrist; in return, brothers are responsible for the welfare of their sisters and present them with gifts. This ceremony is said to arise from a mythological story of Vishnukumar Muni, who protected the lives of Jain ascetics who were in danger from a jealous king and, in gratitude, the women of the region tied threads around his wrist and the wrists of other men who had helped the Jains.

The *social ceremonies of Divali* are celebrated as a five-day festival with rituals on each day. This festival and the worship of the goddess of learning, which takes place on the fifth day after *Diwali*, is described in detail later in this chapter.

Marriage

In Indian culture marriage is a community event as not only two individuals, but two families are united. Until, and sometimes after, marriage, children generally live with their parents, and it is the parents' responsibility to introduce them (perhaps with the help of suitable intermediaries) to prospective marriage partners. It is quite misleading to refer to this as 'arranged marriage'—in practice, the couple has every opportunity over a long period to get to know each other, and the decision to marry belongs to them alone.

When it is agreed that a couple is suited, an *engagement ceremony* is held, to which prominent members of the community are invited; there is a ritual exchange of symbolic items and gifts and the engagement is recorded in an engagement document. This ceremony takes place in the home of the groom or in a community hall, and the date of the marriage is usually discussed at this stage.

The Jain marriage ceremony described below is based on the 'Text of Daily Duties' *(Acaara Dinkar Grantha)* compiled by Vardhamana Suri in 1411 CE, as the correct Jain rituals were lost for many centuries, and Jains appropriated a modified form of the Hindu marriage ceremony. As the prayers and *mantras* of a Jain ceremony are believed to guide the couple towards happiness, prosperity, longevity and spiritual advancement, there has been a revival of the Jain wedding ceremony. The marriage rituals are performed in Sanskrit and Ardha Magadhi.

When the date of the wedding is agreed, after consultations regarding the auspicious day and time, invitations are sent out or made in person. The number of guests invited can be very large: many relatives and many members of the community have to be included. About seven to ten days before the wedding day, the bride's family sends a delegation of close relatives to the home of the groom bearing a special invitation, written by a priest, requesting the groom's family to bring the wedding party to the marriage ceremony. The two families prepare dresses and ornaments for the bride, which she will take to her new home. The groom's family presents their gifts ritually a day or two before the ceremony, and the bride's family's gifts are presented on the wedding day. There is no dowry system in the Jain community, gifts from the bride's to the groom's family are also prescribed by the society, unless they are purely voluntary or a token gesture.

The Jain Marriage Ceremony

The marriage ceremony is conducted by a Brahmin or by any well-respected Jain. There are sixteen stages in the marriage rituals. The first three of which take place before the wedding day.

Maatruka sthaapan, the auspicious ritual at the bride's home, is an invocation of heavenly goddesses: Brahmani, Maheshvari, Kaumari, Vaisnavi, Varahi, Indrani, Chamunda and Tripura, to take up temporary abode in the bride's home to ensure the happiness and fertility of the couple, and takes place two to seven days before the wedding day.

Kulakara sthaapan, the auspicious ritual at the groom's home, is an invocation of the heavenly gods: Vimal-Vahan, Chakhsusman, Yashasvan, Abhichandra, Prasanjit, Marudev and Nabhi, to take up temporary residence in the bridegroom's home to ensure the happiness, fertility and maintenance of the family tradition.

Following these ceremonies, the skin of both bride and groom will be regularly massaged with beautifying substances such as perfumed oil, and turmeric. *Pujaas* will be performed in the temple for their well being and the ritual placing of gold chains by each family around the neck of the son or the daughter *(maalaaropana)* takes place. This immediate pre-marriage period is one of rejoicing and celebration for the families.

After the day of the wedding, ideally seven days after it, but earlier if this is not possible, a further ceremony bids farewell to the deities who took up residence in the homes of the families.

Mandapa pratisthaa, the auspicious ritual at the home or wedding hall, invokes the gods of all places to establish the sacred place *(mandapa)* within which the wedding will take place. This ceremony of the 'sacred point' *(maneka stambha)* takes place either on the day of the marriage or a few days before, at the bride's home; the *maneka stambha* is a simple wooden symbol, which evokes the blessings of the deities of the four points of the compass. Sometimes the ceremony does take place at the bridegroom's house. The *maneka stambha* is placed in the *mandapa*, a sacred place within the *cori*, an area created by creating four corner pillars with arches of leaves *(toranas)*. The marriage ceremony takes place inside the *cori*. A small low platform *(vedi)* in the centre carries the sacred fire.

Marriage procession. Bathed, dressed in his best clothes and ornaments, with a *tilak* on his forehead, the bridegroom worships the divinities and, with his relatives, begins the journey to the marriage venue. Traditionally, he would ride on a horse or elephant accompanied by musicians and singers, but nowadays, the ceremony is performed in a hall or hotel and the groom's party may travel by car. They walk ceremonially the last 100 yards or so towards the door of the hall, where the priest, who is to perform the ceremony, recites a mantra, praising Lord Adinatha, the first *Tirthankara*, emphasising the glory of the Jain path of purification, and praying for peace, contentment, health, happiness, friendship and prosperity for the couple. The bride's sister or an unmarried female relative circles ritually three times around the groom in a clockwise direction; this ritual is believed to ward off evil. The groom arrives to the entrance of the hall where he stands on a small stool and the bride's mother, with other female relatives, welcomes him with symbolic gestures or the waving of a lamp *(aarati)* and places a red cloth or garland around him, but it is a custom nowadays for the bride to welcome the groom first with a garland.

The groom enters the hall, stepping on—and breaking—two earthenware bowls placed in his path; this ritual guards the ceremony against any evil influence. He is then led into the *cori* and the groom sits on the left of the two seats. His bride, elaborately dressed and ornamented, is escorted by her maternal uncles and takes her seat facing the groom, sometimes screened from him by a small curtain.

Mangalaastaka, Auspicious prayers, are recited to Lord Mahavira and his parents, Gautama, Sthulbhadra, Lord Adinatha and his parents, and Pundarik, Bharata and other *cakravartis*, all the *vasudevas* and *prativasudevas*. Prayers are also recited to Brahmi and Candanbala, guardian deities Cakreshvari and Sidhayika, and Karpadi and Matanga for protection. After a series of prayers, the priest places a cloth garland around the couple's necks, and then the bride's parents symbolically wash the groom's feet.

Hasta melapa. The priest puts the palm of the bride's hand on the groom's palm symbolising the beginning of a lasting relationship of unity between the couple. As this ritual is the most important and must take place at the precise time deemed most auspicious. The priest recites prayers hoping that the bride and groom may become partners with similar spiritual aptitude, enjoying the same things and having a lasting unison by way of this joining of hands.

Torana pratisthaa, Vedi pratisthaa and *Agni sthaapan Torana pratisthaa* is an invocation to the goddess Laxmi to bless the couple. *Vedi pratisthaa* an invocation to the gods of the earth to protect the couple and, with the ritual of placing the sacred fire *(agni sthaapan)* in a small basin *(kunda)* is accompanied by an invocation to the fire gods to bless the couple. The priest recites a series of *mantras* and prayers for happiness, honour, children, welfare and prosperity, and he makes offerings to Laxmi and the gods of the earth and of fire.

Houm is a mantra accompanying a series of offerings of food and drink, sacrifice and material wealth, placed in the sacred fire, to the *protectors* of the eight directions: Yama, Nairuta, Varuna, Vayu, Kubera, Ishana, Naga, and Brahmaanan; the nine *planets*: the Sun, Moon, Mars, Mercury, Jupiter, Venus, Saturn, Rahu and Ketu; all the *'sur'* gods (muses); the *bhavanpati* gods, such as Asura, Naga, Supama, Vidyuta, Ocean, direction, wind, and Stanitkumars; to *vyantars* such as *pisaca, bhuta, yaksha, raksasa, kinnara, kimpurusa, mahoraga* and *maandharva*; the *star* gods such as the moon, the sun, planets, constellations and all stars; the *vaimanika* gods such as Saudharma, Isana, Sanatkumar, Mahendra, Brahma, Lanata, Shukra,

Sahastrar, Anata, Pranata, Aruna, Achyut, Graiveyak and Anuttara; the *caturnikaaya-devas*, recognised by their consort or weapon or vehicle or special strength, Indra, Samanika, Parsada, all the Lokpaalas, Anika, Prakirna; *lokaantika* and the *abhiyogika* gods; all *angels (dik-kumaris)* on the island of Rucaka; and all seas, rivers, mountains, caves and forest-gods.

The priest puts an offering in the sacred fire after each *mantra* of *ghee*, betelnut, grains of *jav* (a kind of cereal) and *tal* (a kind of oil seeds), and each begins with the words *aum arham* and ends with *swaahaa*.

The priest performs the first *abhiseka* by anointing the couple's heads with holy water *(nhaavana)* brought from the temple, then *gotraacaar* by reciting *mantras* and the genealogies of both families, and then announces the declaration of marriage. He then blesses the couple and presents them with rice, flowers, incense and sweets, which they offer in *pujaa* to the sacred fire.

In the key *caar pheraa* ceremony, the couple circles the sacred fire four times in a clockwise direction; the bride leading the first three rounds. The bride's brother presents rice grains to the bride and groom who, in turn, after each round, offer them to the priest, who makes offerings to the sacred fire, after reciting the *mantras* for each circumambulation.

In the *mantras*, various components of karmic matter attached to the soul, and their effects, are recited. The couple is reminded that physical relations are the result of deluding *karma*, which may be enjoyed, but that their goal should be liberation from this.

Plate 5.4   Jain wedding ceremony in a traditional *mandap*

In the part of the ceremony known as *kanyaa daan*, the priest offers grains of *jav*, *tal*, a small blade of grass and a drop of water to the bride's father or relative and recites a *mantra*, which the bride's father repeats, handing over his beloved daughter. The groom accepts the bride by reciting a mantra. At this point the priest recites the seven vows: to share their married life with dignity; to respect and love their families; to respect both family homes; to foster love, equality and trust; to behave so as to maintain the respect of their families; to follow the ethical path in work, pleasure and spiritual advancement; and to be mutually supportive and supportive of society and the world, and the couple agrees to each of the vows.

At this point the couple are invited to make their fourth circumambulation of the sacred fire, and led by the groom they offer grains to the fire. This *seals* the marriage bond.

The priest sprinkles a little holy powder on the heads of the bride and groom *(vaasksepa)*. Then the bride's father gives water and *tal* to the groom, who passes them to the priest who sprinkles them on the bride. With the second *abhiseka*, the priest blesses the couple saying: 'You two have been married. Now you are equal in love, experience, happiness and good conduct. You are true friends in happiness and misery, in virtues and faults. May you become equal in mind, speech and action, and in all the good virtues.'

With the unclasping of hands *(kar-mocan)*, the priest recites *mantras* and says: 'You have released your hands but your love is unbroken.' The bride's father gives a symbolic gift to the groom. The community then pronounces *blessings* of congratulations on the couple and the invoked or invited gods are reverently requested to return to their abodes.

After this, the bride and bridegroom are given a send-off by their relatives, and return to the bridegroom's home, visiting the temple on the way. It is the custom to hold a reception and dinner for the guests before the bride and groom depart, at which time individual congratulations are offered to the couple.

In many cases, Jain weddings follow Hindu customs. However, despite this adaptability, the principle of *ahimsaa* is not allowed to be compromised by any aspect of the ceremony.

Rituals of Death and Bereavement

Birth and death are natural phenomena for human beings. The soul is the one unchanging element in the living being; until the soul is purified by shedding all the *karma* attached to it, the type of being in which it is reborn depends upon its *karma*. The body is only a temporary abode for the soul and when someone is dying, this philosophy offers solace. When Jains visit someone who is dying, whether at home or in a hospital, they

sing hymns and recite the *Navakara Mantra*. A dying person would like
to receive, during this crucial period, forgiveness for any wrong commited to others during his or her life, and to forgive all who have done
wrong to him or her, and to have a peaceful death. If the dying person
cannot chant, someone else will substitute so that the dying person has
noble thoughts, and the soul leaves this world in a peaceful state.

Indeed, these simple rituals are performed not only for Jains, or even for
fellow humans, but also for all living beings: if Jains know that an animal
is dying, they will go to it and quietly recite the *Navakara Mantra*. The
most famous example of this is the story of Parsvanatha, the twenty-third
tirthankara, when he found two snakes dying in a burning log; Parsvanatha
recited the *Navakara mantra* to the snakes, which were then able to die in
peace; according to the Jain scriptures they were reborn as Dharanendra
and Padmavati, heavenly attendants of Parsvanatha.

The first ritual after a death is recitation of *Navakara Mantra*, hymns
and incantation of the *jinas* and Shantinatha, until the body begins its
journey towards the cremation ground, crematorium or undertaker's
premises. In India, a dead body is normally cremated within a day of the
death. The corpse is secured on a funeral bier and close relatives carry it to
the crematorium in public procession. The body is placed on the funeral
pyre logs of wood or sandalwood and covered with more wood; it is then
sprinkled with *ghee*, incense and flammable materials. A close relative
makes three circuits of the pyre, chanting *mantras* before lighting it. It takes
about two hours for a body to burn. After the body is consumed, the
participants in the funeral ritual return home, bathe, and purify themselves
by chanting *mantras*. It is customary that women do not take part in any
of these rites. Jainism forbids the act of *sati*, when a widow will fling herself
upon her husband's funeral pyre. Jains consider *sati* a sin, an act of violence.

For two days after the cremation the family members of the deceased
are consoled by the community with repeated periods of hymns and narrative stories, emphasising the Jain philosophy of the temporary nature of
the body and the continued life of the soul. On the third day, the ashes are
taken and thrown into a nearby sacred river, but if there is no river nearby,
they are put into a pit, thus the physical body composed of the five material
elements, returns to its origin. It is believed that the aura of the sorrowful
atmosphere of the deceased's house remains for three days, but it alleviates
with the benefit of special prayers, hymns and peace recitals, resulting in a
gradual normalisation of the bereaved family's life. The third day ends with
a visit to the temple where donations to worthy causes are made,but some
observe the period of sorrow for the deceased for up to thirteen days, when
temple worship or *pujaa* is performed in the presence of community
members and relatives.

In the albeit rare event of the death of an ascetic away from a populated area, for example in a forest, other ascetics or disciples take the body and expose it in a carefully selected spot, where there is a minimum of living beings. Animals or carrion birds may devour the body. In populated areas, the community will take responsibility for cremating the body of an ascetic on a sandalwood pyre.

Recent emigration of the Jain community abroad has made it necessary for them to modify these rituals. After death, the body is cremated and the whole community congregates to the crematorium. For three to seven days before the cremation, community members visit the bereaved's house and offer the relatives all possible support, sing hymns explaining the temporary nature of the body, and pray for peace and the permanent bliss of the soul of the deceased. The community cares for the bereaved family for their daily needs, and if somebody requires help—financial or otherwise—the community attempts to provide for them. The undertaker brings the body to the home of the deceased about an hour before the cremation. The family members, relations and close friends offer their respects to the departed by chanting hymns, and the coffin is then taken to the crematorium and placed on a platform for the final rites amidst the sounds of *'Jai Jinendra'*. The final rites constitute recitals of the meaning of *navakara* and the four refuges of the *arihant, siddha, saadhu* and the Jain faith, and the details concerning the achievements of the deceased are retold. This is followed by a silent meditation of two minutes for the peace of the soul, a sermon on the temporary nature of the worldly life and advising those present not to feel sorry for the departure of the soul, who is going to be reborn in a new body, then more hymns and asking for forgiveness, before the body is consumed in the electric oven.

The funeral participants gather in another room or outside and once again offer prayers, express sympathies and give donations for humanitarian or animal welfare causes. There are no restrictions on the participation of women in the funeral process and, in the home, rituals are identical to those practised in India.

Some people do not visit the temple after a death in their household. This is due to the influence of Hindu religious customs and Hindu views on religious purity. Digambara Jain texts, *Mulaacaara* and *Triloka Saara*, sanction this practice if it is the custom of the place, but one should use one's judgment. Svetambara texts, such as *Vyavahaara Bhaasya, Hira Prasna* and *Sen Prasna*, permit the performance of *pujaa* immediately following a death in the household, after physical purification (bathing). Again, one should use one's judgment as to whether one's state of mind is appropriate for *pujaa*.

JAIN SACRED DAYS AND FESTIVALS

Jainism has developed a sacred calendar which defines certain periods of the year as especially sacred, or relates to particular individuals or events from the religious past. Although Jainism does not deny physical pleasures, Jain sacred days and festivals are noteworthy for the muted and restrained demeanor of the participants and there is little of the extreme exuberance, enjoyment and entertainment, which often characterise Hindu festivals. The Jain festivals or sacred days are 'celebrated' by renunciation, austerities, the study of the scriptures, recitation of hymns, meditation and devotion to the *tirthankaras.* Even those who are busy with daily life, like to be free from worldly entaglements and spend time in worship and meditation. In addition to spiritual objectives, these sacred festivals serve to raise money for temples and human, animal and environmental welfare.

The Jain Calendar

The regular festivals of the Jain year follow the traditional Indian calendar. Each Indian month is divided into the bright half (when the moon is waxing) and the dark half (when the moon is waning). The year is often numbered according to the *Vikrama Samvat* era (abbreviated V.S.) which commenced in 57 BCE or, in Jain circles, according to the *Vira Samvat*, commencing with Mahavira's *moksa* in 527 BCE.

The table shows the most important dates in the Jain calendar, including the five auspicious occasions *(kalyanakas)* in the life of each *tirthankara* (conception, birth, renunciation, omniscience, and liberation), which are observed by fasting, semi-fasting or other religious activities. Although more than one commemoration may fall on the same day, they are too numerous for all to be included here. In addition, pious Jains fast partially or totally on the 2nd, 5th, 8th, 11th and 14th day of each half-month, or engage in other religious activities, as they believe that the span of the next life is decided every third day, so they show particular piety on those days.

Jain Festivals and Holy Days

Popularly celebrated sacred days and festivals are described below:

Paryusana Parva   Paryusana Parva is the most important period in the Jain calendar, an eight-day festival which falls in the months of August or September. The word *paryusana* is derived from two words meaning 'a year' and 'a coming back': it is a period of atonement and repentance for the acts of the previous year, and of austerities to help shed accumulated *karma.* During this period, some people fast for the whole eight days, some for shorter periods, the scriptures prescribe a minimum of three days, but

Jain Festivals and Holy Days

Indian Calendar	Gregorian Calendar	Bright/Dark Half	Day	Festival
Kaartika	Oct./Nov.	Bright	1	New Year, Gautama's omniscience
		Bright	5	Jnan Pancami
		Bright	8 to 15	Kaartika Atthai
		Bright	14	Four-monthly caturdasi: elaborate pratikramana
		Bright	15	End of ascetics' monsoon retreat; pilgrimage to Satrunjaya
		Dark	10	Mahavira's renunciation
Maargasirsa	Nov./Dec.	Bright	11	Maun Ekaadasi
Pausa	Dec./Jan.	Dark	13	Risabha's *moksa*
Maagha	Jan./Feb.	Both		Fifteen days devoted to celebration of 19 kalyaanakas relating to 14 tirthankaras
Phaalguna	Feb./Mar.	Bright	8 to 15	Phaalguni Atthai
		Bright	14	Four-monthly caturdasi: elaborate pratikramana
Caitra	Mar./Apr.	Bright	7 to 15	Ayaambil Oli
		Bright	13	Mahavira Jayanti
		Bright	15	Caitri purnima: pilgrimage to Satrunjaya
Vaisaakh	Apr./May	Bright	3	Aksaya Tritiyaa
		Bright	10	Mahavira's omniscience
		Dark	13	Anniversary of Shantinath's birth and *moksa*
		Dark	14	Anniversary of Shantinath's renunciation
Jyaistha	May/June	Bright	5	Sruta Panchami During this month seven kalyaanakas relating to six tirthankaras are celebrated
Asaadha	Jun./Jul.	Bright	6	Mahavira's conception
		Bright	8 to 15	Asaadhi Atthai
		Bright	14	Four-monthly caturdasi: elaborate pratikramana
Sraavana	Jul./Aug.	Bright	15	Raksaa Bandhana
		Dark	1	Vir Sahan Jayanti
		Dark	12	Beginning of Svetambara Paryusana for eight days
Bhadrapada	Aug./Sep.	Bright	4	Samvatsari
		Bright	5 to 14	Digambara Paryusana: Dasa Laxani Parva
Asvina	Sep./Oct.	Bright	7 to 15	Ayaambil Oli
		Dark	15	Divali: Mahavira's *moksa*

it is considered obligatory to fast on the last day of *paryusana*. Fasting usually involves complete abstinence from any sort of food or drink, but some people do take boiled water during the daytime.

There are regular ceremonies in the temple and meditation hall. Over the first three days, sermons are given concerning one's obligations during *paryusana*, yearly and lifelong duties. From the fourth day onwards, the *Kalpa Sutra*, which includes a detailed account of Mahavira's life, lives of other *tirthankaras* and of Mahavira's disciples, is read to the congregation. On that day, the *Kalpa Sutra* receives special reverence and may be carried in procession to the home of a member of the community who has made a generous donation in recognition of that honour, where it is worshipped all night with religious songs. On the fifth day, at a special ceremony, the auspicious dreams of Mahavira's mother before his birth are enacted. At the time of reading on the birth of Mahavira, devotees rejoice by singing and dancing and coconuts are broken and their pieces are distributed. As a symbol of the baby Mahavira, a coconut shaped silver representation put in a cradle, which is rocked by the donor, with the community singing a special cradlesong for the occassion. Then the cradle is taken in procession to the donor's house and the community members rejoice by singing devotional songs and hymns till late at night.

Listening to the *Kalpa Sutra*, taking positive steps to ensure that living beings are not killed (perhaps by paying money to butchers to cease slaughtering), showing amity to fellow Jains, forgiveness to all living beings, austerity, and visiting neighbouring temples; these are the important activities at this time. In some areas the *Antakriddasaa Sutra* is also read to motivate laypeople to perform meritorious deeds.

The final day of *paryusana*, known as *samvatsari*, is the holiest day of the Jain calendar. Jains seek forgiveness from all living creatures for any harm, which they have caused, knowingly or unknowingly, and forgive those who have harmed them *(micchami dukkadam)*. A yearly elaborate penitential retreat is performed on this day *(samvatsari pratikramana)*. It is regarded important for one's spiritual life, not to harbour any ill will beyond the space of one year. Shortly after *paryusana* it is the custom to organise an amity *(svami vaastalya)* dinner at which all Jains are welcome and dine together regardless of their social position.

Digambaras commence their *paryusana*, known as the 'sacred days of the ten spiritual qualities' *(dasalaksana parva)*, immediately after the completion of the Svetambara *paryusana*. It lasts for ten days and revolves around the exposition of ten chapters of the *Tattvartha Sutra* and discourses, delivered by the members of the community, on each of the ten spiritual qualities: forgiveness, gentleness, straightforwardness, contentment, truth, restraint, austerity, renunciation, non-attachment and chastity.

The most auspicious day is *ananta caturdashi*, the last day, which is associated with the fourteenth *tirthankara* Anantanatha. On this day people fast and *puja* is performed with fourteen flowers. On the final day people seek and grant forgiveness. An amity dinner follows it.

Divali   Divali is a most important festival in India and in Jainism. It is second only to *paryusana*, as it marks the anniversary of the liberation of Mahavira and the realisation of omniscience by his chief disciple, Gautama Indrabhuti. The festival falls in October or November. Jains celebrate the five days of Divali as *dhan teras, kaali chaudas*, Divali, New Year and *bhai beej*, both as holy days and as a community festival. Traditionally, the festival commences with the worship of the goddess Laxmi on *dhan teras*. The next day is *kaali chaudas* when the recitation of Mahavira's last sermon, the *Uttaraadhyayana Sutra*, takes place, for it was then that Mahavira commenced his last sermon which was to last until, late into the night of Divali, that he attained liberation *(moksa)*. Some Jains meditate in secluded places in order to acquire accomplishments. It is also popular to worship the wish-fulfilling deity Gantakarna Mahavira on this day. (He is not, of course, to be confused with *tirthankara* Mahavira).

Then comes the day of Divali, when Mahavira ended his worldly life and attained *moksa*. Lights are lit as a symbolic representation of knowledge to be retained. Some devout Jains fast on the day preceding Divali and on Divali itself, as did Mahavira. Some perform ritualistic *pujaas* and worship the goddess of learning, Sarasvati. The next day is the first day of the New Year, the day of the enlightenment of Gautama when people listen to nine holy *sutras (nava smaranas)*, and the epic poem *Gautama Raasa*. The fifth day of the festival is *bhai beej*, when sisters invite brothers to their homes, commemorating the invitation by Sudarshana to her brother Nandivardhana to comfort him for the loss of their brother Mahavira.

Jains also celebrate Divali as a community festival, with the lighting of lights and festive meals. At this time Jain businessmen close the old year's accounts and open new ones, with accompanying traditional rituals. They offer gifts to children, family members and employees. New Year cards are sent to friends and relatives.

Jnaana Pancami   *Jnaana Pancami* is a sacred day observed on the fifth day after Divali for the worship of scriptural knowledge; fasting, veneration of the *tirthankaras (deva vandan)*, holy recitations and meditation are performed. Books preserved in religious libraries are cleaned and worshipped.

Kaartika Purnimaa   This day is observed on the fifteenth day after Divali. After this, the Jain ascetics, who have ceased their travels during the monsoon season, may travel again. On *kaartika purnimaa* many Jains go on pilgrimage to Satrunjay. For the benefit of devotees who cannot make the journey, large paintings of Satrunjay are displayed for worship in local temples. This day is celebrated as the birthday of *Aacaarya* Hemacandra, the great scholar ascetic of the 12th century CE, and of Srimad Rajcandra, the 19th century saint.

Maun Ekaadasi   This important day of one hundred and fifty auspicious events relating to the *tirthankaras* falls in December, when devotees observe total silence, fast, meditate and listen to sermons.

Mahavira Jayanti   The birthday of Mahavira is celebrated in April, often with a grand chariot procession, public functions, and enactments of his life and message. A magnificent celebration takes place at his birthplace at Ksatriya Kunda, Vaisali in Bihar.

Ayambil Oli   The semi-fasting austerity of *ayambil oli* occurs twice a year, in April *(Caitra)* and October *(Aaso)*, for nine days. Devotees listen to the epic story of Shripal and Mayanasundari, and spend time in worship of *nava pada*, i.e. the *panca parmesthis*, the Three Jewels and austerities

Akshaya Tritiya   Following the example of Risabhdeva, some perform the austerity of *varsi tapa*, described in chapter 3, and break the fast sometime in May on the auspicious day of *akshay tritiya*, at Satrunjay or Hastinapur. Food and other necessities are offered to ascetics, which is considered a pious act on this special day.

Saanta Pancami   This Digambara festival is celebrated in May/June to commemorate the day when the first Digambara canonical scriptures were put into writing by *Aacaaryas* Puspadant and Bhutabali in 150 CE. It is observed as a day of veneration of the scriptures, emphasising the history and the importance of preservation of Jain texts and scriptures.

Raksaa Bandhan   This festival is celebrated in July/August along with discourses on the legendary story of Vishnukumar Muni, reminding us the duty of the strong to protect the weak.

Vir Sasan Jayanti   This sacred day commemorates the first sermon of Mahavira after attaining omniscience and the establishment of the four-fold order *(sangha).*

Astaanhika Mahotsava   Jains believe that there is a festival which has been observed eternally, known as *astaanhika mahotsava*, which occurs three times a year: October/November, March/April and July/August. During the eight days, fasting, narrative recitals concerning the Three Jewels and austerities take place. Ritualised worship is performed with mystical diagrams before image shrines: those observing it earn merit.

Atthai Mahotsava   This eight day festival of ritualistic *pujaas*, recitations and community gatherings can take place on any auspicious occasion such as an installation ceremony. It has been described earlier in this chapter.

Pratisthaa   This is the ceremony of installing images of the *tirthankaras* in a newly built or renovated temple. Among Svetambaras, *anjana salaakaa* is performed as a consecration ceremony before installation of the image,

while Digambaras perform the *panca kalyanaka*. The installation ceremony lasts from three to sixteen days with elaborate rituals and *pujaas*,
incuding re-enactments of the lives of the *tirthankaras*. The piety of these
occasions attracts devotees from far and wide, including ascetics who may
travel (on foot) for months to attend. Installation ceremonies attract many
donations from devotees. On each day of the ceremony there is a communal dinner. On the day of the installation ceremony at the Leicester Jain
Centre in 1988, fifteen thousand people attended.

Panca Kalyanaka Mahotsava   Digambara ritualists perform the consecration by the *panca kalyanaka* of images by re-enacting the conception,
birth, renunciation, omniscience and *moksa* of *tirthankaras*. The installation ceremony follows immediately. Representatives of other faiths and
dignitaries are invited and encouraged to attend these colourful and joyful
functions.

Dwajaarohana   On the anniversary of an installation ceremony a
specially decorated and venerated new flag is hoisted on the spire of the
temple. A long pennant-shaped flag, often red and white, is a distinguishing
emblem flying over many Jain temples in India. A special ritual containing
seventeen types of *pujaa* is undertaken on this day. The whole community
celebrates this occasion and takes part in the amity dinner.

Ratha yaatra   This ceremony involves taking the image of the
tirthankara in a 'chariot', in procession along the main roads of the city or
town, accompanied by musicians and by thousands of devotees, including
ascetics.

Sangha Yaatra   This is a barefoot pilgrimage to the holy places by
hundreds of the devotees from the four-fold order. In towns and villages,
along the way fellow Jains welcome them; ascetics among the pilgrims
preach the sermons; and wealthy pilgrims donate to local temples. During
this spiritual journey six rules should be scrupulously observed: pilgrims
should travel on foot and barefoot; they should desist from sensual and
carnal pleasures; they must eat food only once a day; they should avoid
consuming raw or green vegetables; they must sleep on a carpet on the
ground and should not sleep on a bed or a mattress; and pilgrims must
observe a vow of righteousness.

A family normally sponsors the *Sangha yatra*; the family members and
relatives take care of each pilgrim personally. One, or more, member(s) of
the family will fast in rotation on each day of the pilgrimage. *Pujaa*, recitations and rituals are performed every day and sermons are delivered by
ascetics. At the end of the pilgrimage, the sponsor gives a gift to each
pilgrim. It is the practice to award the title of Sanghavi to the pilgrimage
sponsor, who is honoured by placing a garland around the neck
(maalaaropana) and the honour of placing the garland goes to the highest
bidder who offers a donation to a temple.

Mastakaabhiseka   Every twelfth year, in Sravanbelgola, Karnataka, a colossal image of Bahubali, fifty-seven feet high (over seventeen metres) and carved from solid rock, has its head anointed. The veneration of this thousand-year-old image is of particular importance to Digambaras who revere Bahubali as the first Jain to attain *moksa* in our age. Thousands of Jains of all sects come to take part in the cerermony, which lasts several weeks. The image is a statue of Bahubali standing upright, unclothed and meditating. For the ceremony scaffolding is erected around the huge statue, to allow devotees to anoint Bahubali by pouring sacred substances over the image. The ceremony last took place in 1993.

Saadharmika Vaatsalya   At the conclusion of many of the sacred days and festivals in the Jain calendar and on many auspicious occasions, an amity dinner *(saadharmika vaatsalya)* is organised. It is also called *Navakarasi* ('dinner for one who recites the Navakara') and is considered as a pious act for the family who sponsors it.

Those who kill any living being either themselves or who have it killed by someone else or support someone else who is killing, eventually increase their own enmity.

(Sutra Krutaanga 1: 1: 3)

Deceitful persons perpetrating deceit are active only for their own comfort and happiness. They kill, cut, or dismember other living beings just for the sake of their pleasure.

(Sutra Krutaanga 1: 8: 5)

When a thief is caught while breaking into a house, he is punished for the sin committed. Similarly, all living beings have to bear the fruit of their karmas, either in this life or in the next life. No one can escape from the results of the karmas done.

*(Uttaraadhyayan*a 4: 3)

All living beings love their life. For them happiness is desirable; unhappiness is not desirable. No living being likes to be killed. Every living being is desirous of life. Every living being loves its own life.

(Aacaaranga 1: 2: 3)

Chapter 6

JAINISM IN THE MODERN WORLD

HUMAN ATTITUDES AND JAIN ETHICS

Recent centuries have witnessed revolutionary changes in many areas of human life. Standards of living, life expectancies, communications, social, economic and political values, science and technology have all undergone rapid change. The only thing that can be said with any certainty today is that the pace of such change is likely to accelerate.

The value systems of the past, whether ideological or religious, have been unable to retain the force they once had. In Western countries, identification with historic religious institutions, churches and synagogues has declined strongly in the 20th century. However, there is no evidence that the need of human beings for some form of spiritual expression has declined, but it is less clear where they can turn to find it.

Since the 18th century, and the advent of what has been termed 'The Enlightenment', there have been those who saw in technical and scientific advances, and in more open political forms, an opportunity for humanity to enjoy greater happiness. In Western nations this was interpreted in the 19th century as the fruits of 'progress', but one need only look to the history of Europe in the 20th century to see how society has been cruelly betrayed by these ideas. The most horrible and wasteful wars, the greatest suffering, famines, poverty, exploitation of people, animals and the environment have occurred in the lifetimes of people alive today (and they continue still).

Neither the political or economic systems, such as communism, socialism or capitalism, nor technological changes have stopped this exploitation, or the feelings of alienation, unhappiness and anxiety that accompany them.

No one could argue that these human problems did not exist in the past, but the difference today is that we are now more aware that humanity is capable, should it fail to show restraint, of destroying the whole world. We possess the weapons, nuclear, chemical and biological, to wipe out all life on Earth, and the environmental damage we inflict is capable of disrupting the entire world biosphere, poisoning the air, water and food upon which we all depend. This danger is the price we seem to be paying for 'progress'.

One common feeling expressed by people today is that of helplessness. The expression 'a small cog in a big machine' is often used to sum up how we feel about ourselves. Low esteem and a sense of being undervalued create stress, depression and psychosomatic illnesses, which are on the increase in modern societies.

Whatever we feel, it remains true that all individuals have an effect, however slight, on others around them in the complex networks of modern society. If we act, we influence; if we do not act, we influence; if we speak, we influence; if we do not speak, we influence; if we interfere, we influence and if we ignore, show apathy or tolerance, we influence.

The challenge presented to us is to try to identify the ideas and values, which will show us a way to deal effectively with the problems thrown up by modern living. To begin with, let us dispose of the myth that people today are in a situation of moral decline. The majority of people do recognise moral values and want to live by them. While some have thought that better education, a better standard of living and increasing democratisation would bring a more rational and moral society, the situation has turned out to be more complex than the naive view supposed.

One of the central issues addressed by the world's major religious traditions is the ethical question of how one should live. What is a 'proper' way to live; what is the purpose of our lives? Not all traditions have aimed at the same conclusions and, here, we will describe the Jain ethical position and relate it to modern life and attitudes. The message that we hope will emerge is that though Jainism is extremely ancient, its wisdom is not at all irrelevant to modern human life.

Despite the accumulation of a mass of evidence to the contrary, there are still many people who believe that they can achieve happiness through material and sensual means, and attach great importance to external things: money, property, cars, food, drink, status, and sensual and sexual gratification. They behave selfishly, concentrating their attention and care upon themselves and a circle of family and friends. One cannot achieve permanent happiness through material things. It often seems that the more we have, the more we want. Happiness dependent on external materials or agencies is transitory and does not generate that deep inner contentment which people seek, but fail to find. Greed is the cause of much misery; Mahatma Gandhi was right when he said that there are resources enough on this earth to provide for everyone's need, but not everyone's greed.

Human attitudes and behaviour in the modern world pose many challenges, and here we discuss some of the issues facing humanity, and how Jain ethics can contribute to understanding and resolving them.

If we were to interview a hundred people and ask them what they thought was the purpose or meaning of their lives, what would they answer? Probably in many cases, if not all, they would say something about happiness, as it is a goal, which most people seek in their lives. But where or how is happiness to be found? Jainism is clear on this, to answer this question, one must understand how Jainism understands people. All humans have a soul, which is the 'true' person, the 'self', and the soul is always seeking to return to its pure or pristine form, in which it will be in a state of bliss. The material world of actions and attachments precipitate the accretion of karmic particles to the soul, preventing it from enjoying its true characteristics and happiness. It is clear, therefore, that to seek happiness in attachment to material, wordly things, including human relationships, is to be deluded. Happiness is arrived at through an attitude of detachment and by behaving in accordance with this. Jainism does not deny enjoyment of the good things in life, but they should be enjoyed and used in a spirit of detachment. Chapter 3 contains further discussion on conduct and ethics in Jainism.

While human beings are conscious of their individuality, they are also social beings, dependent upon others. Selfish activities, greed and lack of thought for others may give us pleasure, but ultimately they are the real causes of our miseries; they cause violence to others and in doing so, harm us. Only by loving and respecting others, and practising tolerance, kindness, compassion and generosity, self-restraint and non-violence can we be 'true' to ourselves. In the Jain view, we may be individual souls, but our actions, which determine our destiny, tie us so closely to others that we should behave with as much concern for the welfare of others as for our own welfare.

Although many of us now live in democratic, 'free' societies, at times we have to act against our will. We have to do many things, which we may dislike. The decisions of governments and authorities are imposed on us and often we have no voice. This poses questions about our freedom. Faced with this dilemma, the Jain way is to judge how one should act in the light of the principle of *ahimsaa*; there are often ways to be found of complying with government decrees without compromising this principle.

Education is a moral act; knowledge and the ways in which it is classified and imparted are not morally neutral. Jains view education as a moral project to promote physical and mental well being and to help to bring about a good society based upon sound moral and spiritual values. Parents have an important role and responsibility in the education of their children; they cannot abdicate this responsibilty to schools or teachers. Without their active support and co-operation, children cannot learn to the best of their ability. Parents have to educate by example, practising self-restraint and demonstrating moral values to their children. Jainism makes no apology for being conservative and seeing the family as the proper building block of society.

Human life depends upon other living beings: without plants and animals, human beings could not survive, and Jainism believes that all living beings have the capacity to feel and experience pain and pleasure in differing degrees. Science has confirmed the sensitive balances of the natural world, and practically all religions teach us to safeguard life on this earth and to show compassion to living things, but clearly this compassion is often lacking. Millions of animals, large and small, are killed daily for food, but this need not happen, as we can survive without such violence. Animals suffer and die in so-called sports and through hunting, for the satisfaction of human desires.

Besides animals, the plant kingdom is also suffering from the behaviour of human beings, resulting in desertification, deforestation and similar detrimental effects on large areas of the earth, which is intensifying the environmental imbalance still further. Violence in any form is the main cause of unhappiness in the world. As a result of human dietary habits the world is becoming more and more violent every day. Although the killing of animals and destruction of the natural world happens every day, it is not essential for the human existence and its progress.

Jainism teaches that one should try to avoid harming nature in any way and live harmoniously with all life on this earth. More obvious forms of violence: crimes such as assaults, robbery, burglary, all types of dishonesty, and sexual offences are common in modern societies, causing fear and unhappiness. A society based upon Jain principles of 'non-violence and reverence for life', 'non-attachment' and 'relative pluralism' would lead to an improvement in this situation.

Modern societies are much more open about sexual matters than societies were in the past. The changed economic position of women has created a genuinely new situation. To Jains, the prevalence of family problems: single parenthood, illegitimate children, termination of pregnancies, and the many economic, health and social problems arising from sexual behaviour are avoidable. Jainism teaches sexual restraint, and there is little doubt that many of our current problems would not occur if more responsibility was exercised and attitudes were less 'liberal'. Jainism regards marriage, as an institution worthy of support and hence, divorce is very uncommon in Jain communities. As a result of Jain views on the nature of *karma*, it is also uncommon for widowed women to remarry. These women frequently devote their lives to spiritual pursuits, some even becoming ascetics.

Violence and abuse in families and apathy towards and neglect of elders are rare in Jain communities. The family problems common in much of society are minimised through devotion to Jain principles, supported by the belief in the operation of *karma*. Jains seek to be self-sufficient and take responsibilty for their own lives, avoiding over-dependence on the state or other agencies, and remain committed to the fulfilment of the duty of care and concern towards one another within families and across generations.

Jainism offers guidance on almost all the major questions of life, even in modern societies. Jains assert the positive value of life on the basis of the universal principles of non-violence and relative pluralism. Jain traditions stress the importance of individuals and of inner energy. Individual progress and the progress of society go hand in hand. Jain teachings could be summed up in the phrase 'live and help to live', and this is indicative of the high value Jainism places on each living being in the world as reverence for life should be maintained at all costs.

Jain teachings are rooted in morality, ethics and spiritual progress; they encourage people to reinforce these teachings through the practices of daily life. Jainism motivates people to inculcate the practices of reducing desires and attachment to possessions so that the violence caused by them may be minimised. If Jain teachings were followed in a proper perspective, much of the discord in society would be reduced. It is this spirit which has developed, to take one example, into the practice of vegetarianism.

With personal commitment and effort, the Jain way can achieve worthwhile rewards: happiness and inner contentment. Jainism may be an ancient religion, but its message is very relevant to the needs of the modern world.

ANIMAL WELFARE

Jains believe that the universe is populated by embodied living beings, who may have from one to five senses. All souls, which are equal when in their pristine form, occupy the body of a human, animal, plant, heavenly or hellish being, according to *karma*. In the world of transmigration, the soul creates its own body from the fine particles of matter in the universe, thus it is possible that we may acquire the particles of matter to build our bodies from one of the beings, human or animal, whom we know or whom we harm. Conversely, other beings may acquire particles from our previous bodies. Jain seers mention that there is hardly any particle of matter in this universe, which we could not have utilised to form our body at some point in the cycle of transmigration, and Lord Krishna mentions this fact in the *Gita*.

Jainism teaches that all living beings want to live and avoid suffering and death, and the more senses which a living being has, the more it is able to feel and to show its suffering, as well as experience pleasure. At the pinnacle of the hierarchy is the human being that is able to experience a spiritual life and is capable of verbal communication. Mobile beings, which have two or more senses, not only suffer or experience pleasure in proportion to their senses, but those with five senses, such as humans or animals, harbour many parasitic beings. Hence the harming or killing of animals not only leads to the suffering of the animals, but also harms the parasitic beings as well which, in turn causes a still greater influx of *karma* to the soul of the one doing harm. Therefore Jain seers have advocated compassion for all living beings and animal welfare forms a major part of this important principle.

It is important to realise that although humans are animals, they have unique characteristic not found in other animals, that is *humanity*. Human beings have a unique nature, cultures and societies; they have free will and can exercise restraint from evil actions; and they can help other living beings to live. Conversely their inhuman actions can harm other living beings, even kill them. According to the book of Genesis, humans are created in the image of God and given dominion over animals, but are stewards of the natural world. However, dominion means ruling wisely and with compassion, and not exploiting, misusing or destroying for personal benefit, therefore, human beings should not harm the beings for which they are supposed to care.

The fundamental principle of Jainism is non-violence and reverence for life *(ahimsaa)*, and Jain seers have stressed this principle in the daily lives of all Jains. Jain ascetics take the major vow of non-violence at the time of initiation, they will not harm any living being, including one-sensed beings, as far as it is humanly possible to avoid it. Laypeople observe the minor vow of non-violence and reverence for life towards mobile beings, those with two to five senses; because of worldly commitments, it is impossible for them to avoid harm to one-sensed beings, but they are vigilant to minimise the harm.

The daily duties of the ascetics include atonement and penance for the transgression of the vow of *ahimsaa*. Ascetics will be vigilant even while walking or performing any movement in order to avoid harm to minute creatures, including life in the plant kingdom, thus they will not walk on grass. Laypeople also have to be vigilant in avoiding violence, especially harm to mobile beings, e.g.animals, birds, fish and insects; they also try to minimise harm to one-sensed creatures and many will avoid activities, such as walking on grass, using flowers, cutting trees, where there is likelihood of injury to one sense creatures.

The maltreatment of animals encourages the passions and cruelty; hence it is against all the norms of a civilised society. There are many motives for the maltreatment of animals: on the social level the cause is mainly economic, such as factory farming, medical experiments and research; on an individual level, it is killing directly or indirectly for food, furs and cosmetics, the use of animals for riding, keeping them as pets, watching them perform tricks, in sports, shooting or hunting, or putting them behind bars in zoos.

Most of these practices are without justification and unnecessary for our survival. The pain and harm done to animals, their sufferings and the increase in our passions are unimaginable. Some people will argue that it is necessary to use animals for the reasons of health or for earning livelihoods. But health grounds, vanity, economic reasons, or pleasure do not justify our actions to animals. Animals possess consciousness and are aware of their surroundings, of pain and emotion, but cannot speak for themselves. They do not have the potential to become language users, but perception, memory, desire, belief, self-consciousness, intention, and a sense of future are major attributes in animals. They also possess emotions such as fear and hatred, and the capacity to experience pleasure and pain, including a sense of time. Animals become frustrated if they are not allowed to satisfy their instincts and desires. Mammals of one or two years of age possess all the above attributes.

Mammals have biological, social and psychological interests; they have family interests too and, like humans, animals live well and get satisfaction if they pursue and obtain what they prefer or what is in their interests. Deprivation of biological, social or psychological interests (e.g. the desire for food) at the expense of others cause harm and suffering. Changes of environment are also harmful to their interests, whether these cause suffering or not. Death is the ultimate deprivation of life and is irreversible. It is an irreversible loss, foreclosing every opportunity to find any satisfaction and is true whether the death is slow and agonising or quick and painless.

Although similar to young children, animals lack any conception of their long-term welfare, any formulation of categorical desires, or sense of their own mortality, yet the untimely death is harm. Death is harm independently of the pain involved in dying, whether in slaughterhouses or scientific experiments.

Putting down animals, or euthanasia, in their own interest is also harm, because it is involuntary as it would be for humans. Most animals that suffer euthanasia are psychologically alive. Paternalistic acts causing death of animals are not in their interest, whether they are painful or not painful. Hence, Jains only allow a natural death even for animals, and treat them as we would treat human beings.

Jainism teaches non-violence, reverence for life, friendship to all and malice to none, and the equality of souls. Cruelty to animals is condemned practically by all, and kindness to them should be encouraged and practised. Animals have the same right as humans to live peacefully in this universe and, in a civilised society, the interests of all are counted equitably, irrespective of race, gender or species. It is immoral to raise animals intensively for the utilisation of human beings and treat these species differently, and hence, speciesism is to be condemned as is racism or sexism. Albert Schweitzer advocated 'reverence for life' in many public discussions and felt the necessity of practising the same reverence towards all, as towards his own life. It is good to maintain and cherish life; it is evil to destroy it.

Since earliest times, human beings have exploited animals for many different reasons. They may be for meat and other animal products, sports and hunting or animal experiments. There have been many occassions when even domesticated animals and pets have been the victims of cruelty. As they cannot speak for themselves it is the duty of human beings to act for animal welfare. Animals too have a right to live on our planet peacefully without any fear of exploitation. It is impossible in this book to examine all the ways in which human acts and institutions affect animals, but we will mention some where harm can be avoided.

Food

Many people consume animal flesh on the grounds that it is tasty, nutritious, or part of one's habits and culture, and that abstaining from it would be to forgo certain pleasures of the palate, convenience, and ruin one's health. All these reasons are misguided, as balanced vegetarian food has been proved to be tasty and nutritious, it decreases morbidity and mortality and increases morality and spiritual health. Of course, it is slightly inconvenient to obtain vegetarian food in the West at present, but if more people are eating it, consumerism will force the food industries and restaurants to make it available on a wider scale. No one has the right to harm animals, which also want, like us, to live and not die. If we had been harmed, we would dislike it and there would be an outcry. Similarly, when alternative food is available, we cannot justify it for our pleasure. There is no justice in taking the life of one species for the pleasure of others.

The Meat and Farm Animal Industries

Farmers, butchers, meat packers and wholesalers have strong economic interests in raising animals, and the quality of their lives depends upon the market in food animals. The nation also has an economic interest in the maintenance and growth of the farm animal industry. Farm animals are considered the legal property of the farmers and the farmers have a right to treat their livestock as they wish, even if it means harm to them. Farmers argue that they will be ruined economically if consumers do not patronise them and become vegetarians, and that this would adversely affect the health of the nation. Animal agriculture is wrong on all counts, as the animal's lives are routinely brought to an untimely end due to human avarice, and those who support it have a moral obligation to stop buying the meat. The meat and animal farming industries are immoral trades, and those affected by the demise of these trades can find alternative employment.

Because of cruelty and harm to animals, the individual is right in withholding support to the institutions and individuals that violate the rights of others. There is nothing like humane farming, when the goal of the food industry is to deprive these unfortunate creatures of their lives and inflict pain and suffering in the name of profit. Animals, which are kept in barren cages and crates, are unable to continue their natural behaviour and suffer great stress. Hens like to peck the earth for food, to perch, to lay eggs in their nests, live in flocks, take dust baths and preen themselves, but factory farming denies the behaviour patterns of hens, chicken and other birds, including natural laying eggs. Because of the profit-based production, the birds have to lay more eggs, but as each time bird lays eggs it causes pain and harm, the behaviour of modern egg industry is unjustifiable.

Domestic Animals and Pets

Jains do not domesticate animals or keep them as pets as they believe such actions take away the liberty of animals. However, Jains do encourage the belief that pets and domestic animals should be treated with care and kindness, and unnecessary suffering or the untimely death should be avoided.

Hunting and Trapping Animals

Hunting or trapping animals for sport or commercial reasons are to be condemned. It is immoral to take pleasure in life by pursuing someone else to the death, and the pleasures derived from sport can be secured without killing animals. The commercial exploitation of wildlife assumes these animals are items to be utilised for human pleasures. It should be condemned, as the unnecessary interests of human beings deprive these unfortunate creatures of their lives and, because of these senseless actions, some wildlife is extinct or near extinction. Sport and commercial hunters do not do wildlife any favours, and their argument that they are friends of wildlife is untenable as they kill for pleasure, not for maximising the sustainable optimum of wildlife. Wildlife should be protected by the abolition of legalised hunting and trapping, and prohibiting the commerce in wild animals and their products. The fur trade, the ivory trade, commercial whaling, seal hunting, the skin and feather trade are some of the commercial reasons why humans destroy life for their own avoidable interests. One can live without any difficulty if one does not use animal products and we can have herbal cosmetics without being cruel to living beings. Jains avoid buying such articles where there is a likelihood of depriving unfortunate animals of their lives. Some nations have banned hunting of the endangered species but placed less importance on the value of plentiful animals. All animals are equal, both the rare and the plentiful, and like humans, they have a desire to live, hence the rights of these animals should be protected.

Animal Experiments

Animals are used in research contexts, in testing new drugs, and in toxicity testing; they are also used in teaching in schools and colleges, where they are dissected to understand their anatomy or physiology, but many have condemned these uses of animals as unnecessary. These practices can be avoided and relevant knowledge can be acquired or taught by other methods, such as with computer simulation or video. Jains believe that to cause the untimely death of any creature is immoral.

It is estimated that, in 1988, 3.5 million animals were killed in Britain in the processes, such as, of testing food, alcohol, cosmetics and other products. Some of these products being tested, especially cosmetics, are hardly necessary for humanlife and many of the tests are repeats of earlier experiments. The tests cause suffering and death to the species such as mice, rats, guinea-pigs, hamsters, gerbils, rabbits, cats, dogs, horses, pigs, goats, sheep, cattle, asceticeys, birds, reptiles and fish used in laboratory trials. Jains believe these tests should be abandoned; recently more tests are being abandoned, as they cannot be justified on any rational grounds of need. Only in the case of certain types of medical research, e.g. to find a cure for cancer, there is public suport for these practices. Even in genuine medical research, the results of animal experiments may not be applicable to humans as animal experiments are unreliable because differing species react to drugs in different ways, hence animal tests cannot be applied to humans with any certainty. We have seen wonder drugs being withdrawn after successful testing on animals, as animal experiments not only fail to warn of the dangers of some drugs, but can prevent the development of useful remedies when tests produce side effects which would not have occurred in humans. With a careful and cautious approach, drugs can be tested on human volunteers, and effects simulated with computers.

Millions of animals have died in cancer research but very little progress has been made, and instead of harming animals, the scientists and governments should concentrate on reducing and eliminating the cause of cancer, which is mainly due to factors like smoking, some industrial chemicals and a harmful diet.

Jains are not against medical and other research, which can be carried out by other methods without the routine use of laboratory animals, and modern technology may perhaps give better information for testing new drugs on human beings than the traditional use of animals.

Cruelty to animals and the deprivation of the life of animals can be avoided if scientists abandon tests of unnecessary and doubtful value. The achievement of scientific research is laudable and has brought many benefits for both humans and animals, but it does not justify all the means to secure them, as animals have a value and their lives are of the same importance to them as ours are to us.

The Jain Way of Animal Welfare

Jains have compassion and care for all living beings. Their concern can be seen in their daily practices, their eating habits and their compassionate and philanthropic activities. Ascetics do not take food, medication or any other product where violence is involved in obtaining and producing them. They will travel on foot, keeping their gaze to within a distance of four-feet, to avoid harm to mobile beings, and if there is no alternative path, they will clear the path with their soft woollen brush and gently remove the tiny creatures to avoid harming them. They will methodically check their clothes and other possessions before use, to see that small creatures are not harmed inadvertently, and they will clear the ground with their soft brush before sitting or lying down. They will not walk or sit on a carpet, thus avoiding inadvertent harm to small living beings, instead they sit on a small woollen mat, and keep a piece of cloth in front of their mouths, so as to avoid harm to airborne creatures with their warm breath. They motivate laypeople to show compassion and be philanthropic, and help the cause of animal welfare.

Lay Jains also have a non-violent way of life: They are vegetarians, are taught to minimise violence even to the one-sense plants by avoiding root vegetables (which contain multiple souls in one body) and green vegetables five to ten days a month. They do not take eggs, fish or chicken, and some lay Jains will avoid even medicines where violence may be involved. They prefer non-violent professions and businesses and avoid all intentional violence such as in sport, and if as part of their duty, they are involved in violence, such as doctors giving antibiotics, or soldiers fighting in legitimate self-defence, they will express regret for the violence and ask for forgiveness from the unfortunate victims.

They also will be very careful and vigilant not to even harm insects in their daily activities, such as in bathing, walking or cleaning. Normally they will not keep any pets, as they feel it is taking away the animals' liberty, and they will not exploit domesticated animals.

Philanthropic Activities

Every temple and practically all the Jain institutions and organisations accept donations for animal welfare *(jiva dayaa)* and during each mass ritual, the devotees are reminded to donate to the fund for animal welfare.

Most villages in India, inhabited by Jains, have an animal sanctuary *(panjaraa pola)* where old, infirm and disabled animals are cared for and given all the opportunities to live a natural life, and they are not put down, but are allowed to have a natural death. In cases of drought or famine, Jains raise funds to feed the animals: in the Gujarat drought of the early 1990s, Jains donated millions of rupees and personally organised drought relief work. As a result millions of animals were saved. In such severe conditions, the Government and the public look to Jains for help in saving animals.

Jains are known to save animals by paying compensation to butchers and helping them to start alternative non-violent businesses. Jains have a tradition of feeding the birds every morning and they donate generously to bird feeding places *(parabadis)* and to places for animal drinking water *(havaadaas)*. Many veterinary hospitals and dispensaries have been established with Jain help, and some Jains make arrangements to feed wild animals, insects or ants, which shows their compassion for all living beings. Material filtered out of drinking water is returned to the well, river or waterway, to allow the minute creatures to continue living in their natural environment. Jains are very generous in helping the animal welfare institutions with publication and training

Thus animal welfare is part and parcel of the daily life of Jains. They have been successful in maintaining high standards in life, good health and above average longevity, without indulging in animal products or harming animals. Their example is worth emulating.

ENVIRONMENTAL CONCERNS

Jains start the day with the morning prayers of friendship to all and malice to none. They also pray for the welfare of all living beings in the universe, which includes one-sense immobile living beings of earth, air, fire, water and vegetation, and two- to five-sense mobile ones. The Jain conviction of *parasparopagraho jivanam* teaches that all forms of life are bound together in mutuality and interdependence, but *ahimsaa* is the main theme of Jainism and is summarised in the scriptures thus:

> All the venerable ones *(arhats)* of the past, present and future discourse, counsel, proclaim, propound and prescribe thus in unison:

do not injure, abuse, oppress, enslave, insult, torment, torture or kill any creature or living being.

Jainism teaches restraint in the consumption of material things, the regulation of desires, and simplification of lifestyle; indulgent and profligate use of natural resources is seen as nothing other than a form of theft and violence. In the 'Jain Declaration on Nature' presented in 1990 to the Worldwide Fund for Nature, Dr Singhvi wrote:

> In their use of the earth's resources, Jains take their cue from 'the bee that sucks honey in the blossoms of a tree without hurting the blossom and strengthens itself'.

More than 2,500 years ago, Mahavira revived Jainism and declared that all beings of the natural world have equal potential for progress in the cycle of transmigration, and all are dependent upon one another for their mutual survival, but partial doom occurs when this interdependence is disturbed. It has been noted in the *Aacaaranga* that air, fire, water, earth and plants have comparatively unmanifest feelings, however, plants feel pain when harm is done to them or pleasure when they are properly watered and this has now been scientifically verified.

Michael Tobias, author of 'Life Force', has praised Jain culture in many ways coining some attractive, charming and realistic terms for it: he has declared the Jain ethics of non-violence and animism to be 'spiritual ecology' and 'biological ethics'. In fact, these terms indicate that Jains have not only thought of human beings alone, but for all species of the universe. Thus, higher species of living beings like birds and animals, and lower species like plants and living beings in the earth, all are postulated to have the potential equality of life. This is the result of the spiritualisation of surroundings, which Jains call 'ecology'. By formalising non-violent ethics the Jains have made all moral and ethical rules applicable to all beings of the biological realm, which is why many species have been sanctified. The different types of lotuses have been taken as identifiying emblems of the two *jinas*. It was beneath trees such as the *sal*, *asoka*, banyan and fig that many seekers reached their highest spiritual attainments. Many trees and plants such as the *tulsi*, *neem*, pipal and banyan are worshipped by Hindus.

The worship and importance of trees may have been due to the fact that they served as purifiers, not only of the external surroundings but also help inner purification. This fact can be confirmed from the scientific data on the pipal tree. It takes in 2,252 kg of impure air (carbon dioxide), assimilates and purifies it to give out 1,722 kg of pure air (oxygen mixed with nitrogen). Hence, it is presumed to be the seat of many deities, and those who meditate under it purify their inner self, as the atmosphere under the trees puts people in communion with nature. In the recitals for peace, during worship or daily penitential retreats, Jains pray for an amicable balance not only between nature and humans but also for celestials, hellish beings, plants and animals, the seasonal rains, purity of atmosphere and the absence of undersirable activity and diseases in society. The Jains believe in a pure ecology as a source of inner and outer vitality, and they provide a radiant proof that a non-violent life and behaviour could be a viable alternative for physical and psychic progress.

The Jain Declaration on Nature argues that Jain tradition enthrones ecological harmony and non-violence. The welfare of the plant world, animal welfare and vegetarianism form a partial, or total, non-violent environmental system. Accordingly, it points out that every life should be viewed as a gift of togetherness, accommodation and mutual assistance. The practice of compassion and reverence towards all living beings involves not only caring and protection for others but also sharing with and service to others, and it represents internal and external security, friendliness and forgiveness. There are many prescriptions from the Jain tradition with regard to caring for nature and the environment. The Jains have proclaimed that if one wishes to have pleasure and earn good *karma*, one must be compassionate and pacifist towards all living beings. Jain seers have advocated that one should practise only those activities, which are purposeful for Right Conduct. They also stress the need to avoid those purposeless or negligent activities, which either serve no purpose or harm the surroundings or its environmental components. Jain ethics, both for laypeople and ascetics, suggest how meticulously careful were the Jain seers to maintain the benevolent and non-polluted character of the surroundings by advising people to refrain from all possible causes of pollution, external as well as internal.

Jain ethics teach a 'give and take' balance for the benefit not only of humans but also for all living beings. Nature does not have any concept of waste, most materials designated as waste are infact useful to nature. Scientists are gradually developing 'utilisation of waste' technology, but they have not proved to be as efficient as nature. And it is due to this ineffiency that nature is overburdened. Humans should learn a lesson from nature in terms of its ability to recycle waste into useful products.

A pure environment produces a better mind, less intensity of the passions, greater happiness and an increase in compassionate spirituality. As is well known, Jains declare it as a gross offence to harm in any way any animate beings, purposely or purposelessly, as every living being has the right to live and prosper. This concept of non-violence has positive aims and has much relevance to contemporary environmental concerns.

The spiritual ecology of the Jains indicates their penetrating insight into the nature and psychology of human beings: the religious sanctions inspire people not to indulge in sinful or disturbing acts that harm the natural world, and teach compassion and reverence for all. Jainism is, thus, not fatalist but dynamic and optimistic, which is why Jainism respects all components of nature whether plants or animals; its illustrative principle of aural coloration in meditation, and its beneficial human and educational psychology are the end products of this love and respect.

Like Jainism, different religious systems have affirmed the duty of humanity to preserve the beauty of our surroundings by expressing nature as mother, water as father, and air as teacher. Men and nature hold a causal relationship of inter-dependence and inter-relatedness at the finest (micro-level) and grossest levels. Jews and Christians have been advised to be stewards of the earth, and their motto 'Thou shall not kill' is meant to be applied to all living beings. The Buddha encouraged improving the aesthetic beauty of the environment to earn merit. The Hindus have included service to nature as one of their five duties for the repayment of debts, which people receive directly or indirectly from birth. By contrast, the Jains not only declare the natural components as living but have made the care of them a part of their daily duties for spiritual progress and control over the mind. Their *karma* theory teaches them that better action achieves better results and it leads to the fact already stated, that 'better environment brings better peace of mind'. The Jain system, therefore, not only lays theoretical emphasis on environmental purity, but it inevitably inculcates the habit of practising the implementation of this theory. All its concepts — non-violence, careful eating, limitations of possessions, refraining from purposeless activity and disrespectful behaviour—preserves the purity of the environment and shows care for the natural world.

The last two hundred years have seen the state of the environment taking an undesirable turn. Industrial society, in its aim of conquering the nature for its materialistic benefit, has disturbed the environment, but the pre-modern society lived in harmony with nature. The Industrial Revolution has revolutionised human mentality towards seeking more comfort, resulting in more and more competitiveness and aggressiveness towards nature; and religious and ethical concept of benevolent equilibrium is becoming lost. At first, the consumerist culture did not discern the future catastrophe, but now, the world over, people are realising the danger with respect to the survival of the human race. This trend has resulted in the uneven distribution of natural resources and inequality among human beings, which are against humanity itself and its moral teachings.

It seems probable that had industrialisation never materialised, nature might have maintained a balance. Population growth is another challenge that has faced the world in the centuries prior to the millennium. Rather than living in harmony with nature, commercial aspirations brought industrialisation to feed and clothe the growing population and created

ecological imbalance. It is unfortunate that rather than blaming themselves
as the root cause, people blame science and technology. These problems
would have been avoided if religious injunctions had been followed.

Analysts have pointed to eight factors contributing to the current acute
environmental predicament: population, industrialisation, over-extraction
and over-use or misuse of natural resources, increase in destruction of
plants and animals due to industrialisation, food habits and modern living,
soil erosion and desertification, and municipal waste disposal.

It must, however, be pointed out that it is not only the external environment that is the problem but also the internal environment of the
human being, the mind and the passions. If the passionate mind were to be
restrained through education or religion, one could have a better society
and environment; hence, education towards minimising desires and greed,
and improving equanimity of mind is of the utmost necessity.

Population Problems

There has been a large population increase over the last two hundred years,
and an explosion of different types of industries producing a variety of
consumer goods, war materials, transport vehicles, thermal power, nuclear
power, and information systems. There is a direct, if not geometrical,
relationship between population and industries. Both not only consume
natural resources but also pollute them. They exaust nature, but as the
nature has the capacity to balance itself, the consumption of natural
resources might not have been a serious problem if the world had been
careful not to supplement them with additional industrial products such as
artificial fertilisers and harmful gases for commercial benefits. The depletion on one side and the over-production of industrial goods on the other
side is creating problems of environmental imbalance. The consequence is
polluted air, water and surface areas. The West is currently suffering more
from industrial pollution while the East is suffering from pollution due to
both population and industries. The disposal of human, domestic and
industrial wastes have compounded the problem and it is affecting the
health and wealth of human and other living beings, and is destroying many
plants and animal species everyday. The forests are being destroyed to
accommodate new population, consumerism, modern living and industry,
and chemical fertilisers, insecticides and sprays are converting the living
earth, air and water into an inert system, harmful to all.

Some of the effects of this pollution, and their remedies, will be
discussed below.

Air Pollution   Early human beings conceived of air as a deity, showing
their respect for its life-giving property to all the living beings in the
universe. Scientists, however, tell us it is a balanced mixture of some gases,

mainly nitrogen, oxygen and some other gases such as carbon dioxide etc., without which we cannot live. The balanced composition of atmospheric air is disturbed by:

- additional amounts of components such as carbon dioxide;
- its being mixed with foreign harmful components such as sulphur dioxide, carbon monoxide and hydrogen sulphate;
- reduction in the amount of natural components.

Life on planet Earth suffers in many ways through air pollution caused by industrial gases, coal or liquid fuel, power station gases, gases formed from the burning of petrol or diesel in various vehicles, gases from domestic burning of fossil or organic fuels and gases from incineration of the municipal wastes (largely containing carbon dioxide, some foul-smelling sulphurous and nitrogenous gases). Secretory and excretory volatile ingredients and other sources also mix with air. Normally, there is a natural cycle to maintain an equilibrium in the composition of air, but as the rate of pollution is greater than the rate of equilibration an imbalance occurs and the air is polluted all the time. Air pollution creates the following effects on earth and on the living beings on it:

- The 'greenhouse effect' and depletion of the ozone layer leads to the warming of the earth's atmosphere
- Deforestation due to acid rain and the felling of trees
- Diseases in humans, such as respiratory illnesses, irritating coughs and skin cancers; in animals and in other life forms due to inhalation of polluted air containing an excess of gases such as carbon dioxide, sulphur dioxide and fine solid particles such as asbestos.
- Destruction of plant life and the natural world due to acid rain caused by the mixing of acidic gases in the air, and falling as rain.
- Toxic effects (e.g. the Union Carbide tragedy in Bhopal) due to mixing of fluoride gases, hydrocarbons and nitrogen oxides in the air.

Water Pollution   Like air, water was also seen as divine in earlier times because it too supports life on earth. However, modern scientists tell us, it is a compound, made by hydrogen and oxygen, which is responsible for maintaining temperature equilibrium and many other processes in our physical systems. It also maintains agriculture and forestry. It is estimated that about two thirds of the earth's surface is covered by water.

One requires water for drinking, cooking, cleaning, industry and agriculture. The purity and quality of drinking water is the most important to us. All the sources of water are now becoming polluted through the disposal of different kinds of waste: industrial waste (including water, paper, fibres, metals etc.), washing water, toilet water, detergents, slurry liquids from livestock units, and soluble fertilisers and an overloaded sewage system. Water also becomes polluted by dam building and with solid wastes, fertilisers, insecticides and other toxic substances. Polluted water affects the lives of the living beings in many ways, for example:

- Oxygen transmission capacity in blood decreases owing to increasing amounts of nitrates;
- Wildlife and natural beauty suffer because of toxic substances in water;
- Water-borne diseases due to bacteria, soluble salts etc.

Surface Pollution   The earth's surface represents the solid earth, which has many properties for maintaining and preserving life. Generally it consists of mixtures of salts and other compounds. It has some aqueous element too for assimilation, solution or purification. The solid surface is becoming polluted from many sources such as:

- large scale excretions and secretions;
- large scale use of chemical fertilisers, pesticides, insecticides and sprays;
- large amounts of solid/semi-solid waste from municipal works;
- large amounts of solid/semi-solid waste from industrial works;
- large amounts of what is called 'Junkosis':
- the incineration of waste materials.

A good amount of the waste material on the surface is soluble. It sinks to the earth, but had it been of an appropriate quality, it would serve to purify the earth's environment. However, because of its varied nature and contents, it may be doing the reverse, adversely affecting the plant and animal life on the earth, and it reduces the fertility of the earth. Plants grown on such polluted earth contain many assimilated toxic ingredients, which humans and animals consume.

Pollutants → Food Chain → Body Chain → Danger (?)

The various assimilated components are also toxic. They kill not only the plants but also the small creatures, which beneficially serve all life on the earth. The waste or polluting ingredients undergo many physical and chemical changes on and under the surface of the earth. They dissolve in water and pollute river waters. Their foul smells pollute the air. Thus, surface pollution has the capacity to pollute all the environmental constituents.

Noise Pollution   Everybody is familiar with the noise of machines, vehicles, crowds, loud music, loudspeakers at public or individual religious rituals, social and other functions. These noises have an effect on our sensitivity of hearing. The loudest noises not only disturb our sleep but cause obstructions to blood circulation. High-pitched or high-decibel noises for long hours may cause our auditory organs to become desensitised, and one can become mentally disturbed.

Nuclear Pollution   Pollution due to radioactive wastes is a recent phenomenon of the 20th century. Disasters, nuclear bomb explosions and tragedies in atomic institutions pollute the air and affect the health of living beings.

Prevention of Environmental Pollution   Politicians, governments, voluntary organisations, religious leaders and even ordinary people are alarmed by the effects of environmental non-equilibrium. Prevention has two aspects.

What should be the aims for improving the environment? Should it be only public/human welfare or the welfare of all? Many agencies aim at only human welfare and this seems to be the western way of thinking. However, the welfare of all living beings is the Jain way of thinking, as it believes in 'live and help to live'. Caring people have been concerned with this problem for a long time and have tried to awaken public consciousness to the enormity of impending disasters and the threat to our survival. Central governments, local governments, voluntary organisations and the caring public have made some rules and regulations to improve the environment and reduce pollution. Many national and international conferences have been and are being held (last two: Rio 1992, New York 1997) to think of ways and means to safeguard the future of the planet.

Some concerned scientists have been helpful in reducing the gravity of the situation:

- Scientists have tried, in many cases, to reduce the amount of waste material by developing the recycling processes to regain useful material (paper, plastic, brickwork, cement, metals etc.).
- Scientists have also tried to reduce the harmful effects of waste by pre-treating it in such a way that its capacity to pollute becomes negligible.
- Atmospheric gases are being filtered and pre-treated to remove fine solids and harmful contents by absorption, before being released, thus reducing the temperature and the pollution of air and water, so causing less harm to living beings.
- Scientists are also trying to improve the quality of polluted air and water.

All the above are useful in preserving living beings, however, the decision-makers will not entertain a reduction in industrial growth, although they want population control and some measures to reduce pollution. It is impossible to put the clock back, but there is no alternative to minimising the use of natural resources and reducing the wastage. Many conscientious organisations are propagating principles and practices in tune with the Jain way of life. They advise using minimum quantities of water and other natural resources, proportional to natural production rates, avoiding destruction or harm to gardens and forests, and encourage waste recycling and the use of recycled products as far as possible. They also advise minimising the use of chemical fertilisers and insecticides for agriculture, and the application of organic manures to the soil. In other words, the five Jain principles of non-violence, limiting consumption, acceptable dietary habits, refraining from purposeless or harmful activities or professions, and carefulness in movement are all now being accepted.

Environmental Concerns and Jain Principles

Many scholars point out that the current problems of environmental pollution were non-existent during earlier ages of rural society. It appears very difficult to find solutions to modern problems in the teachings of the religions of the pre-industrial age. The ideal society is that which promotes the welfare of living beings at all times. In contrast to many other ethical systems, Jainism has given specific and detailed guidance.

Jains point out that environmental concerns require a specific non-violent lifestyle that has an aesthetic dimension and a practical concept of spiritual concord. A new lifestyle of spiritual ecology and environmental concern will have to be formulated and inculcated. Changing our life-style is not very difficult if we bear the following aims in mind:

- cultivation of helping attitude, detachment and universal friendship;
- cultivation of an attitude of restraint and minimal use of natural resources and consumables;
- cultivation of the habit of carefulness in eating, speaking, movements, and picking up and setting down;
- daily penitential retreat and prayer for the welfare of all living beings and for universal peace;
- cultivation of satisfaction and tolerance;
- cultivation of a non-violent life-style.
- cultivation of amity towards all co-habitants on our planet.

Governments and educational institutions can offer guidance on minimising needs and the cultivation of respect towards the natural world. We should not harm our friends and co-habitants; and if people were constantly reminded of this, they might be more vigilant in not harming the natural world. Governments and international organisations, such as the United Nations, should give assistance to those religious and voluntary organisations that are actively concerned in environmental matters, but which have few resources.

Jains all over the world have been involved in schemes to preserve and renew the local environment. It is worth quoting the ancient wisdom of the *Matsya Puraana*, which argues that 'the merit of digging ten wells equals that of making one pond; the merit of making ten ponds equals that of forming one lake; the merit of forming ten lakes equals that of producing one virtuous son, who is useful to society; but the merit of planting one tree equals that of producing ten such sons'.

As well as tree-planting, Jains have engaged in other local initiatives such as the purchase and safeguarding of unexploited swamp and mountain habitats, the creation of green areas within urban environments, and measures to preserve energy, reduce pollution, and create good personal and social environments at home.

Ecology is the inter-relationship between living organisms and their environments and any abuse or violence against this relationship is bound to react against humans. Within this ecological system shared by all living beings, Jains recognise the existence of balance as being of primary importance. Jain scriptures teach that there are a constant number of souls or living beings present in the cosmos, ranging from the smallest micro-organisms to complex life-forms such as human beings or the higher animals, although the number may vary in different destinies and species. Given this closed ecological system, the necessity of maintaining and, where appropriate, restoring, a proper proportion between its component parts is obvious.

Human beings of course have a pivotal role to play in this task of stewardship, since they are endowed with highly developed moral, analytic and creative faculties. Jainism propounds a way of life, which helps both external and internal environments, of non-violence, reverence for life, restraint and the co-operation of all to revive the balance of our ecological system. Any lasting and worthwhile contributions in restoring ecological wholeness can only be made by a partnership of interests representing all who share our common home. This was summarised beautifully in 1990 by Dr L. M. Singhvi, who became Indian High Commissioner in the United Kingdom and who is a practising Jain, when he wrote:

We are all here to offer to the world today a time-tested anchor of moral imperatives and a viable route plan for humanity's common pilgrimage for holistic environmental protection, peace and harmony in the universe.

VEGETARIANISM

Every living being has a body which requires nourishment and energy. Jain seers considered that while it is impossible for a living being to exist without food, one should obtain this with minimal possible violence even to one-sense beings of the plant world. The objective of human life is happiness, bliss and liberation, and one cannot achieve this without a sound body and mind. One should nourish the body with food, which produces minimum passions. Food from higher-sense beings produces the greater violence and passions. It has been observed that many organisms live in the bodies and secretions of animals, and hence when we use animal products, we do violence to both animals and their parasites. Jain seers have advised humans to live on vegetarian food, with a minimum of violence to plants.

History of Vegetarianism

Since earliest times humans have existed on a meatless diet: Jains, many Hindus, most Buddhists and many other communities ate nuts, fruit, green vegetables and grains as their food. Before the birth of modern organised vegetarian groups in the United Kingdom, some notable reformers, including John Wesley, the co-founder of Methodism, formed a group to promote vegetarianism. In 1809 a vegetarian coalition was established in Manchester. Many reformers promoted a meatless diet until vegetarianism became formally institutionalised. In 1847, the word 'vegetarian' was coined and a Vegetarian Society was established under the leadership of Joseph Brotherton. It flourished, and eminent among its many supporters were Dr Anne Kingsford, a leading womens' rights activist in the late 19th century, Annie Besant, long-serving President of the Theosophical Society, and George Bernard Shaw. More recently the author and broadcaster Malcolm Muggeridge, the politician Sir Stafford Cripps, and the Speaker of the House of Commons, Bernard Weatheral, have supported the Vegetarian Society. In 1980, the Young Indian Vegetarian Society was formed to promote vegetarianism in the United Kingdom. Today vegetarian societies are functioning in practically all countries of the world.

Britain is one of the countries whose population is most active in promoting animal rights, vegetarianism, veganism, anti-vivisectionism, 'beauty without cruelty' and reform of factory farming practices. Since the immigration of Indian communities from India and East Africa over recent decades, vegetarian food has become yet more widely available throughout Britain. The British Medical Association, in 1995, published fourteen years of research by two doctors on the effects of a vegetarian diet, and the findings, suggesting that vegetarianism increases longevity and decreases morbidity, have given a boost to the vegetarian movement. There have also been many notable promoters of vegetarianism in other countries, prominent among them were Richard Wagner, Albert Schweitzer, Leo Tolstoy, William Alcott, inventor of the 'corn flake' Dr John Kellogg, novelist Upton Sinclair and Greek philosophers such as Plato, Socrates and Pythagoras supported a meatless diet.

The Natural Diet of Humans

Animals can be divided into three categories according to their natural diet and corresponding anatomical and physiological systems: *Carnivores* live largely on meat and their intestines are three times longer than their bodies, have a high concentration of hydrochloric acid in their gastric juices and small salivary glands: examples are all felines and canines. *Herbivores* live on grass, leaves and plant food: examples are cows and elephants. *Frugivores* live on fruits, nuts and grain: examples include monkeys and the great apes. *Omnivores* live on a mixture of animal and plant food and are not considered a separate category.

Human beings, herbivores and frugivores have intestinal tracts about 8–12 times longer than the body, with much diluted hydrochloric acid in their gastric juices and large salivary glands. Their teeth are small and dull, with flat molars, whereas meat-eating animals have large front teeth (for tearing meat) and no flat molars. The anatomy and physiology of humans particularly facilitates the digestion of plant products. Their salivary glands assist pre-digestion, dilute hydrochloric acid aids digestion and the large intestinal tracts churn and absorb. It was only through necessity that humans began eating meat; later this became habitual. But humans cannot eat raw meat as do carnivores, as the anatomy and physiology of humans is best suited to vegetarian food.

Types of Vegetarians

The word 'vegetarian' is derived from the Latin word *'vegetare'*, which means 'to enliven'. Vegetarians in general do not eat meat, fish, poultry or eggs. *Partial vegetarians* may eat fish and chicken, but do not eat red meat such as beef, pork and lamb. *Lacto-ovo-vegetarians* take dairy products and eggs in addition to a vegetarian diet. *Lacto-vegetarians* take milk and milk products, but no eggs. Most Indian vegetarians belong to this group. *Vegans* and *Frutarians* live on fruits, grains, vegetables, but no milk or other dairy products. Jains are lacto-vegetarians, but many devout Jains do not take root vegetables.

Vegetarian Diet and Health

Plants have the ability to use the energy from sunlight, carbon dioxide from the atmosphere, water and minerals from the soil to make complex compounds such as carbohydrates, proteins and fat. Humans and animals derive their nourishment from plants or other animals, but the source of the carbohydrates, proteins or fat obtained, whether from plants or animal products, is ultimately produced by the plants from the soil with the aid of sunlight. When a human or animal dies, its body, whether buried or cremated, disintegrates into the soil. Plants use the disintegrated material to make the complex food compounds, which are, in turn, consumed by animals or humans, and are thus recycled. The dead plants also have similar recycle.

Carbohydrates include sugars, and starchy and indigestible carbohydrates, which the body breaks down as sugars. The body absorbs only simple sugars. They provide energy and any excess is stored in the body and used intermittently for various functions.

Proteins are made of carbon, hydrogen, oxygen, nitrogen and sulphur. Food proteins are broken down during digestion into relatively simple chemicals called amino acids, which are absorbed by the body for its development and maintenance of body functions. There are twenty amino acids, eight are supplied by the food, hence called 'essential' amino acids, and the remainder produced by the body. Excess proteins are not stored in the body, but excreted.

Fats are made of a variety of chemical compounds such as cholesterol, saturated and unsaturated fatty acids. Animal fats contain a relatively large proportion of saturated fatty acids. Some vegetable oils, such as corn oil, contain relatively more unsaturated fatty acids. Certain unsaturated fatty acids are not synthesised by the body and hence are essential. They are also a source of concentrated energy. Excess fat is stored in the body.

Other nutrients such as minerals and vitamins are obtained from food. Some can be synthesised by the body.

The components of food proteins are absorbed to produce the living cells and tissues of the human body, through the processes of metabolism; the carbohydrates and fats provide the energy, but if insufficient energy is provided by carbohydrates and fats, the body proteins provide energy.

A balanced diet is required for both physical and mental health. It should contain sufficient ingredients, which produce energy for the necessary functions of the body, to maintain the body tissues and to cater for the demands of growth, and repair of tissues after an accident, illness or reproduction. Diet plays an important role in maintaining the mind in sound condition and in restraining the passions. Western medical scientists and nutritionists, when discussing diet, show concern mainly for physical health. They have hardly researched the effect of diet on mental health, which is necessary to achieve the objectives of human life.

A diet containing meat, fish, chicken, eggs and alcohol, if chosen carefully, provides good physical health, but it produces passions, which are harmful to mental health and hinder spiritual progress. Many studies have revealed that due to the myth that a large amount of proteins are required for energy and strength, the western diet contains excessive amounts of flesh and eggs. The body cannot use these extra proteins and the excess is converted into nitrogen wastes that burden the kidneys. Meat has a high concentration of saturated fat. Eggs are rich in cholesterol. High levels of saturated fat and cholesterol are considered as major risk factors in heart disease and strokes. A meat diet may be low in dietary fibres, lack of which causes diseases of the gastro-intestinal tract. A large number of potentially harmful chemicals are found in meat. Factory-farmed animals are fed hormones, tranquillisers, antibiotics and many of the 2,700 drugs used in agriculture, some of which remain in the meat. Certain meat products may also contain harmful bacteria and may be diseased. Certain preservatives are also potentially harmful. Non-vegetarian food requires greater care in production and preservation compared with vegetarian food, but in spite of all possible precautions being taken, certain problems, such as the slaughtering and sale of diseased animals, are difficult to avoid.

Chemical research has shown that animal uric and uraemic toxins have effects similar to caffein and nicotine and stimulate the passions and craving for alcohol, tobacco and other stronger stimulants.

The emotions produced by worry, fear and anger in animals poison their blood and tissues with toxins. Animals experience anger and fear of impending danger and death during their transport to slaughterhouses and in the slaughter process. This fear poisons their flesh and ultimately affects the meat eater.

Nagarkatti, a surgeon at Bombay Hospital notes that research in Japan and other countries, into breast cancers, large intestine cancer, stomach cancer, prostatic cancer and cancers of other organs, has shown a relationship with dietary factors which points mainly to animal components of the diet acting as cancer-producing agents.

There is much mis-information on vegetarians. For example, they are believed to lack physical strength, which is untrue. A balanced vegetarian diet is ideal for both physical and mental health, enhancing longevity and decreasing morbidity. Vegetarians are also less aggressive than non-vegetarians. Mahatma Gandhi and many other saints have emphasised the fact that 'human nature is influenced by what we eat; we become what we eat'.

Economics of Vegetarianism

In spite of the efforts to control the human population, it is growing at a higher rate. Therefore it has become imperative to produce more food to feed the growing population as efficiently as possible on the available land.

About four-fifths of the world's agricultural land is used for feeding animals and only one-fifth for feeding humans directly. Most of the fertile land devoted to cattle, which eat cereals, root and green crops, and various grains, if substituted for crops suitable for humans, would yield far greater economic results. Statistics from the Ministry of Food, in a Government of India, yearly publication (Indian Agriculture in brief, 1966), claim that plant food, excluding vegetables, fruits and sugar, provides on average 15.8 times more calories and 11.5 times more proteins when compared with animal foods, per acre of land. About sixteen pounds of grains and soya beans are required to produce one pound of meat. This amount of grains and soya contains 21 times more calories, 8 times more proteins and 3 times more fat than one pound of meat. Statistics from the US Department of Agriculture show that 80–90 per cent of all grain produced in the United States goes for feeding animals, and millions of acres of land are used for raising livestock. If the same amount of land was used for cereals, it would produce 5 times more protein per acre; 10 times more legumes, such as lentils, peas and beans; and 15 times more protein if leafy vegetables were grown. There may be variations in the statistics in view of the fact that insufficient funds by various governments are allocated for this important research, but it is true to say that land provides more food if crops for humans are grown rather than those for animal feed. A vegetarian diet is less expensive than a non-vegetarian one, as plant food is easier and cheaper to grow and produce. Vegetarianism may even help to create employment through a switch to less intensive forms of agriculture, including organic farming.

Nutritional Values of a Vegetarian Diet

A vegetarian diet is very healthy and has sufficient nutritional value, provided it is balanced. Vegetarians in India (and now in the West) cook a variety of attractive, tasty dishes. A vegetarian diet is inadequate only if it is low in energy or contains too high a proportion of cereals and starchy foods. Vegans may require a weekly supplement of 50 mcg vitamin B12.

As we have seen earlier, ethics, religion and economics support vegetarianism. Jains are lacto-vegetarians and their health compares well with that of members of other communities. Their diet is well balanced to the requirements of their bodily needs. We will discuss this in detail in the section on Jain food habits.

Calorie requirements depend upon factors such as weight, age, sex, and activity. The World Health Organization recommends 2,800 calories for men and 2,400 calories for women per day for moderately active persons, although these figures may vary during pregnancy, lactation and child growth periods, when additional calories are required. Cereals, starches, sugars, fats and oils are major sources of energy. Fruit and vegetables also provide some energy.

Proteins are supplied by cereals like wheat, barley, maize, rice, rye, millet, fruits and leafy green vegetables, and also dairy products. The World Health Organisation recommends the protein requirement for an average male adult of 70 kg body weight to be 40 g of good quality protein per day, although many people still believe the higher figure of 100 g, set in 19th century guidelines, is valid.

The eight essential amino-acids (tryptophane, methionine, theonine, leucine, lycine, phenylamine, voline and isoleucine) can be obtained from the proteins in a balanced vegetarian diet. Two more, histidine and anginine, are important in childhood and are also available from a vegetarian diet.

Years ago proteins were divided into 'first class' (animal proteins) and 'second class' (plant proteins), but this arbitrary classification has been discarded by modern nutritionists, as it is generally accepted that no one protein source is superior to a combination of protein sources. One gram of protein provides four calories of energy.

Table 6.1   Calories and proteins from different foodstuffs

Foodstuffs	(Approx) Grams for 100 calories	Grams required for 10g proteins
Cereals	30	100
Pulses	30	40
Oilseeds	20	40
Milk	125	300
Leafy vegetables	200	250
Starchy root vegetables	100	500
Other vegetables	250	500
Fruits	100–200	1200
Animal foods	70	40
Egg	60	75

Carbohydrates are the main source of energy. One gram provides four calories of energy. The main sources are the wholegrain cereals, breads, cornmeal, root and leafy vegetables, beans, nuts, barley and rice. Excess of energy provided by carbohydrates is converted into fats. (Appendix II details the nutritional values of the major vegetarian foods, both Western and Indian, and Appendix III shows the caloric values of most Indian vegetarian foods.)

Fats produce heat and energy and the surplus is stored in the body. Vegetable fats consist mainly of poly-unsaturated fats and contain no cholesterol. They are easily digestible. One gram of fat provides nine calories of energy.

Minerals and *vitamins* are found in vegetables, fruit, milk products, some cereals and nuts. Minerals are necessary for the regulation of certain body processes and growth. Vitamins are necessary to maintain health and protection against specific disorders. The main sources of both are green vegetables such as cabbage, sprouts, green peas and watercress, carrots, cauliflowers, cheese, butter, margarine, oatmeal, yeast, lemons, oranges, blackcurrants and other fruit.

Vegetarian diet plans for reducing weight, lowering cholesterol and other diseases are available. They are very useful but if one eats a well-balanced vegetarian diet and takes regular moderate exercise, it is generally believed that one will keep in excellent health.

Meat eating should be avoided for spiritual reasons as the eastern faiths believe that demerit will be accumulated equally on whoever kills, prepares, sells and eats meat and that there is no escape for anyone who aids and abets the animal slaughter industry. The *Manusmruti* states 'All supporters of meat eating are sinners'; from the Bible, Genesis (1: 29) 'Behold, I have given you every herb-bearing seed and every tree in which the fruit of tree yielding seed, it shall be unto you for meat'; Guru Nanak, the founder of Sikhism, claims 'my disciples do not take meat and wine'. Buddha says, 'meat is food for sub-human beings.'

Thus for spiritual, health, economic, animal welfare and environmental reasons vegetarian food is preferable to that of non-vegetarian diet.

JAIN FOOD HABITS

Every living being requires air, water and food for its existence. Clean air and water are more important than the food, and they are still available without much effort on the individual's part and are provided by nature. Food, on the other hand, has to be gathered, prepared and consumed for sustenance. Animals eat to live and generally accept what is available, but humans require food for physical, mental and social well-being, and also for spiritual upliftment.

Jain seers taught the importance of food and wrote a vast amount of literature on the subject: its definition, procurement, preparation and purity, non-violent dietary habits and the effects of food on health. Most of this work concerns the dietary regulations of ascetics, but later such details as acceptable food, methods of preservation, and time limits after which food becomes unacceptable were made available for the guidance of laypeople.

Jain scholars have studied all aspects of human life. They believe in the necessity of sound physical and mental health for spiritual progress. They have stated that a healthy body and mind are necessary to undertake human functions and that food influences the body, mind and all that is associated with our lives. The modern dieticians have now accepted this fact.

Classification of Foods

Generally, the word 'food' connotes the idea of morsels of food. Jains call it *aahaara*, a combination of two words *(aa,* meaning 'from all corners', and *haar,* meaning 'receiving' or 'taking in'). It indicates materials taken in by any method for the build-up of the body, its vitality and completions by a living being. Up to ten life forces *(praanas)* and six vital completions *(paryaaptis)* are realised by the embodied soul, through the fruition of body-producing *karma.* Life forces and vital completions are described in volume 2, chapter 6.

Jain scriptures use the following terms to descibe the different methods of food intake:

aahaara: Intake of appropriate material for the growth and mainte-nance of the body.
anaahaara: Not taking food.
oja aahaara: Intake of food by the karmic and luminous body of the soul, in the process of transmigration, before the new body forma-tion.
roma aahaara: Intake of food by the skin.
kaval aahaara: Intake of food by mouth.

The classification of types, sources and methods of food intake are detailed in table 6.2.

Table 6.2   Classification of types, sources and methods of food intake

Types	Source	Methods of Intake
Morsel food	Foods, drinks	Mouth
Diffusive food	Oil, cream, etc.	Skin (by massage)
Absorbptive food	Air, sunlight	Breathing, skin
Mental or volitional	Mental activities	Passions like anger and greed
Karmic food	Karmic particles	Activities of body, speech, mind
Quasi-karmic food	Karmic particles	Quasi-passions: laughter, disgust

Thus, food includes common foods and drinks, oily substances diffused through skin, air, sunlight, and karmic particles.

Jains have laid great emphasis on the purity of food, as purity of mind depends upon the food taken. Food is also divided according to its effects upon the mind in three types:

> *Taamasika* food (emotional) induces vice and the spiritual decline of an individual, and includes meat, alcohol, honey, and root vegetables;
> *Rajasika* food (enjoyable food) are tasty dishes, prepared for sensual pleasure e.g. sweets, savoury and fried food;
> *Saatvika* food (pure, nutritious food) is obtained without any gross violence: grains, milk products, fruit, vegetables etc.

Jain sciptures describe four types of morsel food:

- *Asan*: solid, soft or liquid food by which one can satisfy hunger (grains, pulses, dairy products, vegetables, fruit, sweets, etc.);
- *Paan*: liquids (drinks, water, etc.);
- *Khaadim*: foods by which one can partially satisfy hunger (popcorn, papodam, nuts, etc.);
- *Svaadim*: foods that can enhance the taste (chutneys, pickles, ketchup and spices such as cloves, black pepper, ginger, etc.).

The above classifications are important for physical and mental health (*saatvika* food advocated for good health), and the Jain austerities, such as fasting, *cauvihaara* (renunciation of all four types of morsel food), etc. Because of the emphasis on the purity of the food and Jain way of life, Jains have a comparatively high longevity and less morbidity than non-Jains in the same societies.

Jain Diet

Jains observe non-violence and reverence for all forms of life in their food habits. They are vegetarians and are prohibited from harming any form of life, which has more than one sense. Even while procuring plant food, they are very careful in the selection, preservation and cooking so as to minimise violence to plants and other one-sense life. Their intention is not to harm any living being, but they have no alternative but to harm some one-sense life. Food is needed to sustain the body, without which they cannot progress spiritually towards liberation. Their carefulness and concern for living beings can be seen in their daily rituals, when they ask for forgiveness for hurting any form of life intentionally or unintentionally.

Foods which are procured by violent means and/or which harm the physical or mental health are prohibited. Cooked food kept overnight, even though it may be pure, nutritious and acceptable, is not a Jain food, as it can harm human health and can be a reproductive medium for the *laalia* type of micro-organisms.

Jains are lacto-vegetarians. They take milk and milk products. In India, it is customary to take the milk of a buffalo or a cow. The first right over this milk is that of a baby buffalo or a calf. In rural India, Jains are very careful in taking milk from these animals, making sure that their offsprings do not suffer. Urbanisation has forced them to accept milk from modern dairies, and due to violence involved to the cows at such dairies some Jains have become vegans.

The Jain diet is pure, nutritious and obtained without any gross violence. It sustains good physical and mental health. It consists of grains, pulses, milk, yoghurt (curds), *ghee* (refined butter), buttermilk, vegetables and fruit.

The Jain seers have advised excluding the items listed in table 6.3 from one's diet, as they are the cause of gross violence and are not conducive to physical and mental health.

Table 6.3 Prohibited food items

Prohibited Items	Reasons for Prohibition
Foods produced by gross violence	
Meat	Violence to animals and birds, as eggs, fish, poultry and other animal products are considered as meat. Many one- or more sense creatures multiply on the flesh of a dead animal. Meat harms one's physical and mental health
Alcohol	Violence to countless one-sense creatures and harm to one's physical and mental health.

Prohibited Items	Reasons for Prohibition
Honey	Violence to mobile beings like flies and bees.
Butter and cheese	Violence to countless one-sense creatures, as butter is made of groups of one sense beings. In the preparation of cheese, animal products are used.
Other harmful foods	
Ice crystals (ice cream)	Ice is made from groups of one-sense creatures.
Poisons, hard drugs, tobacco	To prevent harm to the self, one should avoid any kind of poison and refrain from smoking and taking hard drugs.
Raw pickles *(sandhaana bolaa)*	Raw pickles, preserved in brine, are a medium for the growth of countless mobile beings. Jains advise drying pickles in sunlight for three days and then preserving them in oil.
Pulses and raw dairy products	Mixtures of raw milk or milk products with pulses *(dwidal)* become media for the growth of innumerable mobile beings, hence milk or its products should be heated before mixing with pulses.
Deteriorated foods and juices	Innumerable mobile and immobile beings grow in deteriorated foods and in cooked food kept overnight. Time-expired foods, which change in taste, smell, shape or feel, harm one's physical and mental health.
Vegetables with many seeds	Eating fruit and vegetables in which the seeds nearly touch each other, such as figs, causes violence to a greater number of one-sensed creatures.
Brinjals	Contain many seeds and mobile beings in their caps. They are also harmful to one's physical and mental health.
Pulpless fruit	Indian fruit such as *jaambu, canibora, sitaafala* contain less pulp than seeds. Eating them causes violence to the seeds, which are one-sense creatures, and one derives little nutrition.
Unknown fruits	Can be poisonous and may harm health.
Udumbar fruit	Fruit such as *umbaro,* black *umbaro,* banyan, peepal and *plaksha* contain innumerable small seeds and mobile beings. They are also harmful to one's health.

Prohibited Items	Reasons for Prohibition
Root vegetables *(anantakaayas)*	Eating these causes violence to innumerable one sense living beings, as many souls live in the body of one root vegetable. Vegetables grown above the ground have one being in one seed, fruit or flower. Jain seers have identified thirty-two types of such root vegetables, such as potatoes, onions, garlic, carrots. Mushrooms and sprouted pulses are also prohibited as they have many souls in a single body.
Other Prohibitions	Scriptures include hailstones, clay, lime etc.
Eating at night	After sunset, many invisible beings which grow at night, are attracted to food. Moreover, eating at night affects one's physical and mental health.

The Jains consider that different foods vary according to the quality and quantity of violence involved in consuming them:

- maximum violence involving harm to mobile beings: meat, alcohol, honey, butter
- extensive violence to one-sense creatures and to some mobile beings: root vegetables, the five udumbar fruit
- major violence to one-sense beings and innumerable mobile beings: beans or pulses with raw milk or milk products, raw pickles
- Lesser violence to one-sense beings: grains, pulses, vegetables, fruit.

It is impossible to get perfect non-violent food. Fasting is the only way to avoid violence completely, but this is impossible to sustain indefinitely. Hence Jain seers have advised taking only pure vegetarian food. Vigilance in selecting the food inculcates them to accept foods that cause the least possible violence.

Characteristics of the Jain Diet

The characteristic of the Jain diet is to have simple, nutritious, freshly cooked vegetarian food that maintains good health and motivates the aspirer towards the spiritual path. Jain seers have observed the times of deterioration of various fresh foods and suggested not eating food after its 'expiry' time.

Foods contain immobile and mobile bacteria (and viruses), some beneficial and some harmful. Bacteria in curds and *panir* are beneficial; hence curds and *panir* are acceptable as long as they have minimum bacterial growth. Bacteria in alcohol are harmful and have much greater growth; hence alcohol is prohibited, Unless the food is chilled or cooked, bacteria begin multiplying after about forty-five minutes, and then grow in geometric progression, reaching their peak in five to six hours; then their growth stops. The same is true in, or on, human bodies.

Bacteria live for up to two days. They can multiply again whenever sources of food are available. Some bacteria are eradicated by mild to moderate heat, while some thrive in extreme heat. Surprisingly, the Jain seers took this into account and advised which foods to warm by slow heating or boiling, and then cooling immediately after heating.

Bacteria require air, water, food and the right temperature for growth. Cooked foods containing water and vegetables are good media for the growth of bacteria, but waterless foods like sugar, salt, oil, and *ghee* are poor. Hence, Jains do not keep watered, cooked food overnight. They evaporate the water with heat and dry the food, which is why raw pickles are dried in the sun for three days and then mixed with oil. Chapatis can be kept overnight or longer, if they are dried by heating. All food should be kept covered and long lasting foods like pickles are kept in air-tight jars.

Food deteriorates over time, and Jain literature prescribes time limits for different foods, taking account of the climate, but limits may be altered to take account of modern equipment. Deteriorated food is prohibited. Vegetables such as mustard, cress, and watercress are prohibited during the monsoon season and certain fruit such as mangoes are not eaten after mid-June (*aadra* constellation), due to the growth of mobile beings in them. Table 6.4 lists a few examples from the Jain literature of time limits for foods commonly used during the Indian winter, in summer the time limit could be less.

Table 6.4   Time limits for food

Watered cooked food	6 to 12 hours
Fried food	24 hours
Curds	2 days
Sweets	1 month
Flour	1 month
Sugar	1 month
Dried chapatis	1 month
Boiled water	4 to 7 hours

When the taste, smell, shape and appearance of the stored food changes, it is rendered unacceptable. Occasionally the food becomes tasty, if kept overnight, due to bacterial growth, but it is unacceptable, as there is greater violence in eating such food.

Jains have used this observation of bacterial contamination for the preserving the purity of food and, in advising on time limits for consuming foods; they show their concern and carefulness for the principle of minimal. violence and the maintenance of good physical and mental health.

Contamination of Food

Food can be contaminated by the atmosphere, storage places, utensils, clothes and handling, hence, food should be kept covered; storage places, utensils, clothes and hands should be kept clean while cooking and handling food.

When accepting food, ascetics ensure that the person who offers the food observes: *purity of mind*: giving food without any ill thinking towards the recipient; *purity of speech*: keeping pleasant and truthful speech; *purity of body*: having a clean body and clothes; and *purity of food*: food is fresh, serving utensils are clean, and kitchen and serving places are tidy.

Jain seers advise the methods for keeping foods like grains, milk, curds, refined butter, oil, sugar, spices and vegetables pure, and suggest a protocol for handling food, cleanliness for the kitchens, utensils and the individuals.

Food Habits

Jains avoid root and other prohibited vegetables, but there is some controversy among vegetarians about whether milk is an animal product. Jains believe the bacteria in milk are similar to those found in vegetables and, if milk is obtained by non-violent means and is extra to the needs of the calf, they see no harm in taking it. They will not accept eggs (fertilised or unfertilised), as their bacteria are similar to those in meat.

Jains eat two to three times a day, and their typical daily menu would be as follows:

Breakfast: Milk, tea, one or two items from *khakhara* (dried chapatis), *puri* (fried small chapatis) or other savouries.
Lunch (main meal): Chapati or *puri*, vegetables, pulses, rice, *daal*, popodam, pickles, fruit, curds or buttermilk, but there may be additional savouries, sweets and regional dishes.
Dinner (light meal): *Bhaakhari* or *dhebaraa* (kinds of chapatis), vegetables or pulses, or *khichadi* (mixture of rice and daal), *kadhi* (buttermilk sauce).

Many variations on the above dishes are served at parties, feasts or when entertaining guests. Jains prefer to eat home cooked meals.

Svetambara ascetics take meals twice a day, They accept a small quantity of food from several homes, so that donor is not inconvenienced. They will not accept any food which has been cooked especially for them, as they eat to live and not to satisfy their tastes, and the food from different houses are mixed in their bowls. They take the offered food to the *upashraya* and after showing it to their preceptor, share it with other ascetics.

Digambara ascetics take meals only once a day, and accept the food in a standing posture, from a variety of donors congregated at one home to reverently offer them. They accept the food with the palms of their hands acting as bowls.

In order to minimise violence, on every third day most Jains do not eat green vegetables. Some fast on average twice a month, and also take vows not to eat certain acceptable foods for a certain period, which aids their self-control.

Jain food is very tasty, nutritious and has a very varied repertoire of dishes. The dietary habits of Jains—eating regularly and slightly less than the capacity of one's stomach, avoiding eating at night, taking only acceptable foods and periodic fasting—keeps morbidity to a minimum.

Jains do eat manufactured or processed foods but take care that they do not contain animal products. The pressures of modern life and business activities have made many Jain laypersons somewhat relaxed about eating root vegetables and eating at night, though they see the value of not eating at night and avoiding prohibited foods.

Chapter 7

CURRENT TRENDS AND CONCLUSIONS

THE CURRENT STATE OF JAINISM

We are living in the real world, a world of technology and science, a world of communication and information, a world of media, a world of politicians and influential people, a world of real people and their struggle for existence, concern for the family, social life, their egoism, greed and struggle for power, possessions, money and fame. Most people are interested in mundane matters, pleasures and the apparent happiness obtained from material things. Because of their self-interest, people in general indulge in activities for short-term gain and do not worry about harm to other living beings, the environment, nature or, ultimately, themselves. Modern education, ever increasing 'needs' in the name of a decent standard of living, a bombardment of sensational news, advertisements and information, have changed the way people think. Except for a few, people have largely lost the values of religion, spirituality, care for others and simple pleasures. Most who practice religion are confined within the boundaries of their own faith, often developing its 'fundamentalism'.

Discipline, respect and acceptance of the teachings of religion and of educational institutions are in decline. Ever-increasing demands and the thoughtless use of natural resources have created ecological imbalances, which in the long term may threaten the health and existence of humanity. Community and religious leaders, academics, governments and authorities the world over are worried about the environment and declining values in civil society.

Jain society is not immune to these problems. In this chapter, we will discuss the current state of Jainism and its values, and suggest measures for the dissemination of Jain teachings, both for the benefit of the Jain community and the wider world.

In the early part of 20th century Jainism was hardly known outside

India, and westerners misunderstood Jainism simply as a religion of renunciation, because of its physical and dietary restrictions and austerities. Even the knowledgeable looked upon it as a religion mainly characterised by its ascetics, who sweep the ground before them as they walk; they were ignorant about its teachings and values. The general population, for the most part, is unaware of the existence of Jainism, as over the years the Jains have remained a conservative, introverted community, and little information was made available to the outside world. But its observances and ascetic practices drew the attention of some western scholars who studied its literature, art and architecture, archeological remains, tenets, practices, history and traditions. Many scholars worked on Jainism, and the sincere efforts of some of them drew the attention of others and, as a result, 'Jainology' has become an important branch of Indology and Oriental studies. The development of international Jain studies by western scholars started in earnest in 1870, and within fifty years Indologists such as Georg Buehler (1837–1898) and Herman Jacobi (1850–1937), outstanding German scholars, established the distinctive identity and the true place of Jainism among the religions. Professor Maurice Bloomfield, William Brown, Heinrich Zimmer and Joseph Campbell studied Jainism, published literature and delivered lectures on Jainism in North America; *The Heart of Jainism* by Mrs Sinclair Stevenson and *Jaina Yoga* by R. Williams were scholarly publications by British scholars; and A. Guerinot worked on Jainism in Paris. Since 1914, the literature on Jainism has been available in universities and research institutes in France, Germany, Britain and North America.

V. R. Gandhi's lecture tours in 1893 to the United States and the United Kingdom on the occasion of the first Parliament of World Religion, added impetus to the study of Jainism in the West. Mahatma Gandhi promoted *ahimsaa*, the main principle of Jainism throughout the world, and indirectly helped to promote Jain studies. Jain migration abroad, in the latter half of 20th century, awakened the interest of the West in the study of Jainism and the Jain way of life. The Jains have subsequently organised themselves and established Jain temples and centres in many parts of the world and, since the early 1970s, visits by Jain saints and scholars, and the efforts of the Jains settled in the West, have also been effective in spreading awareness of Jainism, and acceptance of Jainism as an important World Religion.

Over the last few decades, peace, pluralism, non-violence and reverence for life, animal welfare, vegetarianism, environmental concerns, a stress-free life and meditation (all Jain values) have made an impact in the minds of the civilised world. There is a growing interest among westerners in Jainism and Jain literature, but information in standard English is not readily available, thus the Jain community has a challenge to establish an infrastructure for information, study and to further the practice of Jain values both for Jains and non-Jains. Jainism can offer to the world a way to happiness, by creating a society concerned with the welfare of the entire world, including animals and the environment.

As Dr L. M. Singhvi wrote in the Jain Declaration of Nature (1990), Jainism believes 'All life is bound together by mutual support and interdependence' *(Parasparopagraho Jivaanam)*; Jainism recognises the nature of mutual dependence, which is the major principle of ecology. The above scriptural aphorism tells us that all aspects of nature are bound in a physical as well as metaphysical relationship; all the constituents of the universe are interdependent and must help one another. The principle of 'non-violence and reverence for life' *(ahimsaa)* is very important for peace and happiness, and that of 'relative pluralism' *(anekaantavaada)* is the basis of modern democracy. 'Non-attachment' *(aparigraha)*, self-restraint and the avoidance of waste are the necessities of today.

In the modern age, people in the West are much concerned with values which the Jain seers taught thousands of years ago, and they require a systematic presentation of these values; in the past, ascetics used to disseminate these values in India, from person to person, through their wanderings. Modern education, urbanisation and the migration of Jains to the West have created a new situation, and Jains will have to take advantage of information technology and the media if they wish to preserve their culture and its values amongst their own community members, and disseminate them to non-Jains.

Over the 19th and 20th centuries many notable Jains have contributed to the promotion of Jain values and their hard work has been a tremendous inspiration to the Jain community. *Aacaarya* Vallabhsuri (1870–1984) adapted the methods of Jain promotion to the current needs of society by establishing educational institutions and reform movements for the observance of Jain values, and organising welfare activities for the Jain community. Other *aacaaryas* inspired the laypeople to establish temples, translate and publish the scriptures, promote the publication of Jain literature in Gujarati and Hindi, and practise compassion towards animals and the natural world.

Srimad Rajcandra (1867–1890) modified religious observances and emphasised the real goal of Jain teachings—the liberation of the soul from karmic bondage. However, the rituals have remained popular with the majority of Jain community members, and as a result, there are some who have become ritual specialists and contributed to make religious observances popular and attractive.

The institutions of the *samanas* and *samanis* (established by *Aacaarya* Tulsi), and *veer sainiks* (established by *Panyaasa* Candrashekhar) have also been very inspirational. The establishment of Veerayatan in Bihar, where

Mahavira resided for fourteen rainy seasons, by Amar *Muni* and *Aacaaryaa* Candana, to promote Jain values through service and education, is very successful in the wider community.

The 20th century has also produced many outstanding Jain laypersons in all walks of life. In all countries, the performance of Jain students is higher than the average. The life of young Jains has remained simple, with comparatively high standards of moral conduct, but in the modern complex world, Jains will have to modify the ways of bequeathing Jain values to the younger generation, and they will also have to create an infrastructure to satisfy the needs of Jain men and women, with modern education. There are already signs of external pressures and attractions inpressing themselves, which may damage the fabric of Jain society. The infrastructure will have to address the concerns of the young on communication, social life, marriage, divorce, contraception, abortion, sensual pleasures, drugs, vegetarianism, religious education, spiritual life and welfare activities in a modern context. Jain society has been accustomed to the sacrifices of voluntary workers for its support. It worked in the past when the life was simpler and people were less busy than today, but the complexity of community work now requires time, organisation and expertise. Jains will have to train and employ competent individuals to satisfy the socio-religious needs of the community.

The Jain scriptures state that Jains are expected to donate between 10 and 33 per cent of their income to philanthropic activities, and many are generous and donate according to their ability to various charities, but individual donations need to be co-ordinated to obtain maximum results for the benefit of the community. In general, most Jain donations go to the temple funds, to the organisation of rituals and to animal welfare funds, which are all good causes, but these philanthropic activities require modification to meet the challenges of modern society. At the present time, donations to educational activities targeted at the understanding of rituals and the purpose behind them, to preserving Jain culture and to promoting Jain values, Jain academic education and research, training Jain teachers and creating employment opportunities for them, and community welfare activities are minimal. These activities are necessary to preserve Jain culture and meet the needs of the present time, and if Jains do not support them by modifying their philanthropic actions, there is a danger that within two generations the whole fabric of the Jain society could be jeopardised.

The conduct of some lay Jains has changed in ways not sanctioned by their religion, for business and social reasons. They have become relaxed in eating prohibited food, in eating at night, and in certain religious customs, but it is to the credit of their culture that practically all of them have still kept their non-violent life-style and have remained vegetarians.

The external austerities, such as fasting, are on increase over the last three decades: during *paryusana* hundreds of Jains fast for eight days or more, and thousands from one to three days. People undertake many other rituals, some regularly; but as they are performed by the majority of aspirants, without the expected protocol and understanding, they do not aid in progressing spiritually. Often people celebrate these rituals as if they were social functions. Jains will have to address this popularity and create an infrastructure for guidance for the rituals, so that the aspirants benefit spiritually.

Demographic changes are comprehensively described by Vilas Sanghave (1992). Over the last few centuries Jains have migrated from the villages of India to the cities. Being generally a business and professional community, Jain society finds it beneficial and easier to settle in the cities. The younger generation, who have settled in the cities, are not prepared to move to villages or small towns. India's 1981 census tells us that the percentages of urban and rural population amongst the Jains is 63.9 and 36.1 respectively. (Figures for all Indians are 23.7 and 76.3 respectively.) It is very surprising that few Jains live in Bihar, the land of Mahavira's birth, although recently more than a million strong *jati* of *sarakas*, who observe Jain teachings, have been located in Bihar and surrounding areas; they are very poor and require help and guidance for their progress. There are about 30,000 Jains in the United Kingdom and about 50,000 Jains in United States. The well settled, urbanised Jains have different priorities, but they have an in-built desire to preserve and disseminate Jain culture not only among their future generation, but also in wider communities. It requires vision, dedication and an adequate infrastructure to inspire these Jains to promote Jainism.

The Hindu Code Bill in India governs Jain society, but the Government has accepted its separate religious identity. It has good relations with Hindus and the other communities. Jains play an important role in the development of the economy and culture of India, out of all proportion to the number of Jains in the population. Jainism has a unique philosophy, ethical code, heritage, intellectuals, influential businesses and professions, philanthropic activities, and unselfish and dedicated ascetic orders. Jain teachings are apposite to the modern age, but Jains have been unable to transmit the teachings of the *jina* to people at large. There are many reasons for this, but they could easily be overcome if there was resoluteness in the community. However, some avoidable issues and dissent have reduced the strength of Jain society, and religious divisions, sects, sub-sects, and social divisions have further divided it; but there is more unity than disunity between these divisions. Their basic beliefs, philosophy and their goal are identical; but lack of communication, distrust and the undue importance of the past and controversies irrelevant to the modern age, further perpetuate these divisions. All the sacred centres and temples are dedicated to one, several or all the *tirthankaras*, and it is the duty of all Jains to join hands and promote the teachings of the *tirthankaras* both for Jains and for the wider community. Minor disputes can be resolved amicably if Jain principles are applied.

Marriages are usually arranged within the members of a particular sect or sub-sect. Religious educational institutions like *gurukulas* and *pathasaalaas* are specific to each sect. The members of each sect or sub-sect have their separate organisations, both on a national and regional basis. There are few that cater for all Jains, irrespective of sects or sub-sects, such as the Jain Samaj Europe, the Jain Academy, the Institute of Jainology, in United Kingdom, the Federation of Jain Associations in North America, or the Bharat Mahamandal, and Mahavira Memorial Samiti in India. In the West, people from all sects co-operate, work and usually worship together, although some sects may observe their own specific rituals separately. In general, most rituals are celebrated collectively by all Jains.

The Jain Society in the West is still a close-knit community, which organises marriages, whenever possible, within the community, irrespective of sectarian background. However, inter-caste marriages through the choice of marital partners are blessed, although reluctantly. Usually the young married couple stay within the joint family until the couple becomes financially independent, but due to western influence some have started to live separately, causing severe strain on the joint family system. Even if they live separately, relations between family members are usually good, and they do care for each other. Elderly members are usually cared for and respected by family members. The younger generation is more comfortable, understandably, with a western life-style, but is very much interested in preserving Jain culture and its way of life. The elderly have, reluctantly, adjusted to changing circumstances; they have accepted the independence of their offspring and have developed a policy of tolerance and non-interference.

Women have equality, but normally financial matters are handled by the men and domestic arrangements by women; husbands have began helping their wives in domestic work, but it is the women who usually cook. Girls are trained by their mothers to prepare food and undertake other household work; most boys escape this training.

Jain society is entertained by community celebrations, Indian cultural events and social programmes. Large numbers attend weddings and other social occasions. Jain society is very hospitable: its members like to entertain relations and friends and they often visit each other's homes; they are also welcome to stay in friend's or relative's home without any difficulty and also spend short holidays or weekends there, thus saving on the expense of costly holidays. People help each other in unfortunate circumstances such as severe illnesses or a death in the family, as victims of crime, and with family problems; as a result Jains hardly require medication or medical counselling.

For its continued existence as a respectable community, the Jains will have to ensure that internal differences are reduced to a minimum and that its members observe the dietary rules of vegetarianism and the ethics of Jainism. The behaviour of Jains will enhance their reputation and identity, and will give them an opportunity to play a positive role in promoting Jain values. But it must be emphasised that there is no alternative except to reduce internal dissent and inflexible attitudes, and create an infrastructure to promote and practise basic Jain values, if the Jain society wants to have a continued existence and its rightful place among the religions of the world. It is also essential that Jain leaders set an example by observing Jain principles, and motivate members to observe and maintain the highest standards of Jainism.

Modern trends have seen Jains migrating and establishing themselves in different parts of the world. They have established national and international organisations for the promotion of Jain values not only in the Jain community but also by encouraging academic and inter-faith relations and understanding. Jains attend many inter-faith meetings and conferences and present papers on Jainism. At the second World Parliament of Religions in Chicago, in 1994, about forty papers were presented and more than eighty delegates participated. Thus, Jain community members are labouring to promote Jain values in the West, but they are handicapped, as their ascetics cannot travel abroad due to their vows.

The Jain community in India is progressive, well settled in business and the professions. They are philanthropic in nature and will donate to a good cause. The community is blessed by an ascetic order of nearly 10,000 ascetics, who are selfless, who travel on foot, keep in close contact with the community, and have the welfare of all living beings at heart.

The ascetic order has tremendous respect from, and influence over, the laypersons, and they can influence the community to resolve their differences through mutual respect and tolerance according to the teachings of Mahavira.

Promotion of the Jain way of life can be planned together, and this joint action will require a central co-ordinating body or an international secretariat, similar to those of most successful faiths. Hence the time has arrived to have a strong, active central co-ordinating body such as the World Council of Churches, with adequate staffing and resources not only to resolve disputes or misunderstandings, but also to promote Jain values both for the Jain community and non-Jains. Such a central organisation will be effective in enhancing the welfare of the *Sangha* on religious, social, political, educational and economic areas. The Jains may have to develop some sort of western organisation to promote Jainism in the West, both for Jains and non-Jains.

Over the years Jains have remained a conservative, introverted community, but if they are to survive they may have to modify their methods of promoting Jain teachings according to time, region, resources, and the needs of their own community and wider society (of course, without changing its basic values). It is worth noting that many earlier *aacaarya*s have modified their preaching according to the needs of the day.

In the past, life was simpler, people were religious minded, and they had greater respect for the guidance and statements of spiritual leaders and elders. The modern age is an era of scientific and logical thought; people are educated, economically independent and are engrossed in worldly pleasures. Because of modern transport and communications the globe has turned into one huge community, albeit with diversities, different cultures and modes of living. Each community interacts with other communities. People require the knowledge and benefits of Jain teachings, rituals and its philosophy in scientific and logical terms, as they will not accept religion as blind faith.

Now let us examine the needs of the Jain community to meet the challenges of the present times, both in India and outside India:

Temples: It is pleasing to note that construction and renovation of many temples even in distant parts of India fulfils both historical and functional needs. Some temples such as Delwara and Ranakpur have been restored to their former glory and some beautiful new temples of cathedral size have also been constructed. But, due to demographic changes and urbanisation, some temples in rural areas have difficulty with respect to upkeep. There are some temples with abundant income and others, which are struggling; to alleviate the penury of such village temples and temples with a small number of worshippers, it has become imperative that the management of temples is overseen by a central council of temples with regional branches such as the World Council of Churches.

Places of worship need adequately trained staff, who can offer guidance on Jain history, the temples, rituals, observances, and of the practicalities of the Jain way of life.

Rituals, *Pujaas and Austerities*: These have become very popular among the Jain masses, due to their social-and religious significances. The rituals are a step towards spiritual progress and not *the path* or ultimate Right Conduct. They are religious observances and should be performed methodically according to protocols in the prescibed manner, with a proper organisation, so that devotees and younger Jains can see their benefits, and become interested in them enough to participate. Mass celebrations such as the head-anointing ceremony at Sravanbelgola installation ceremonies and chariot processions are very popular among the Jain masses and should be encouraged.

Educational: The modern age requires religious learning at all levels, for children, adolescents, university students and adults, in a language and with methods they can understand and to be taught if possible alongside their secular education. Training teachers and experts is also required. If the community wants to have quality teachers, they will have to be properly recompensed. Distance learning, the Open University and the use of modern information technology can aid the educational activities, and they should be used where possible.

Academics and Researchers: These individuals are essential to present and promote the teachings of the *Jina* to the modern world. As methodical presentation is unavailable to the needs of the present technological and scientific era, Jains require academic training to produce the scholars necessary for presentation to the world, of Jain teachings and its values. Students will only study Jainism if they are convinced of its value for their future careers, hence, the community will have to plan career-based courses in Jain studies. It will also be necessary to organise regular short courses, seminars, workshops and conferences for the teaching and practice of Jain values. The Jain Academy has made laudable efforts by convincing De Montfort University, Leicester, to start undergraduate courses in Jain Studies in 1994 and by establishing the Jain Academy Educational and Research Centre at Bombay University in 1996. Similar efforts for academic training are planned by the Jain Academy Foundation in North America, and in India by Jain Academy, Bombay.

Literature is said to be a mirror of society. Hundreds of texts in different languages have been published in last few decades. They are excellent publications, but if one wishes to promote one's culture, one must have a literature acceptable to the general public and the media. Unfortunately, Jains lag behind in this form of promotional literature, in spite of the fact that historically they possess a vast amount, more than 3 million handwritten texts (Cohen, JAINA convention 1997). Thus, Jains require a factual, analytical and research oriented literature in today's languages with standardised terms.

Social: People require guidance on social customs such as weddings, celebrations for social occassions, community service, and cremations. The community follows many customs based on Hindu rituals, which require change and modification, applying Jain methods. The guidance found in Jain literature needs to be adapted to the needs of the modern age. The literature describes the Jain marriage ceremony, but to adapt it to modern needs, priests will have to be trained to perform the ceremony. A standard cremation service for overseas Jains will have to be planned. Standard literature for other social rituals is also a necessity.

Community Welfare: The Jain community looks apparently affluent, but there are many families who are below the poverty line, requiring housing, welfare services, training and help.

Young Jains: They require special care for their needs in training, establishing businesses, employment, leadership and understanding the importance of Jain values and heritage. They have enormous energy, a modern education and the ability to present their case well, and if properly trained, they can be of great service not only as parents to their own families, but to all other community members and the wider world.

Women: They have played a leading role in preserving religion within the family and the community, have great powers of communication, and commitment to serve the community. Many of them have a modern education and increasing economic independence, but they should be trained and given opportunities to become leaders in the community.

Business and Professions: Jains are successful businessmen and professionals, but still they require guidance and help for success in a complex world. However, senior businessmen or senior professionals, or the proposed central co-ordinating body or international secretariat, can provide this. Jains should also be motivated to participate in national and regional economic institutions.

Training and Employment: Jain business houses should be motivated to organise training for deserving candidates and give employment to trained young Jains. Training grants and business opportunities from governments should also be explored for the benefit of the community, and rich businessmen and philanthropists should be motivated to consider giving loans for new businesses to promising entrepreneurs.

Institutions of Influence and Power: Talented Jains should be encouraged, trained and supported to take part in political parties, government, local authorities and institutions which can influence the life of the community. A strategy for this task may be developed by the central organisation in the interests of the community.

Philanthropic Activities: Jain history suggests that Jains were well known for providing four kinds of charity to the general public: food, medicine, education and clothing. These donations created tremendous goodwill and sympathy for Jainism; many Jains still donate to such causes although a concentrated effort is required in this direction. Co-ordinated donations and publicity may elicit sympathy from the general public, and young people, who enjoy such service activities, should be involved as voluntary help.

The Needs of the Wider World: Over the last few years, the world has become aware of the Jain values of non-violence and reverence for life, animal welfare, vegetarianism and environmental concerns. The Jain community is expected to provide information to the wider world on the above issues, and on the study and practise of the Jain way of life.

Relative pluralism is one of the important gift of Mahavira to the world. Inter-faith dialogues and pluralistic societies are in fashion in most countries of the world. As inter-faith activities are crucial for the promotion of Jainism, talented Jains should be encouraged to participate in them, as they can learn a lot from the experience of other co-religionists such as Buddhists, Christians, Jews, Muslims, and the Hindu sect of Swaminarayans.

During the last two decades, Christianity and other religions in the West have debated the issues of pluralism and a pluralistic society. Inter-faith movements are flourishing the world over. Jains should take active part in inter-faith dialogues and movements; as such participation strengthens our own faith in our own religion and it will expose Jainism to a wider world.

Many people believe in Jain values and are sympathetic to Jainism, but they should be welcomed and encouraged to practise these values with facilities and resources, as they themselves could be a great resource in the promotion of Jainism.

Promotion of Jainism: Jainism could not expand like the other major religions of the world because it placed greater emphasis on individual-spiritual progress and practices, and never possessed an organisation for promotional activities. The sphere of activities of its ascetics, teachers and preceptors were generally limited to discourses among adherents and the inherently initiated persons; Jainism neither postulated nor encouraged proselytism.

However, interestingly most of its historically important preceptors and scholars were originally non-Jains who became interested in its intellectually and spiritually benevolent principles, and who themselves, added new dimensions to the discourse. Even at the present time, it is mainly non-Jain scholars and interested parties who have been instrumental in Jainism's current world-wide popularity. However, their number is very small in comparison with the task ahead.

The community leaders and ascetics are trying to the best of their abilities and vision to promote Jain studies, practice and values. The requirements for the *sangha* and promotion to the wider community are very complex and require the efficient management of resources for temples, academic training and community welfare. Jain values are for the benefit of all the living beings of the world and hence promotional activities should be given a priority. If Jains share their values with others, Jainism will have more sympathisers, and it will help the Jains.

Promotion through Ascetics and Scholars: Jain ascetics have been the main means of promoting Jainism; they have a contact with the community which was very effective in a less complex age when life was simpler. They are still valued, appreciated and respected by all sections of the community, but in this technological world, they will have to be prepared for the needs of the present age. They also will have to master English and other foreign languages. Jainism is also lucky of having more than 9,000 female ascetics, who could be very important in promoting Jainism, if they are given adequate training.

Scholars are also impotant in promoting Jain values, but they require organisation and co-ordinated efforts to get the best out of them, and good scholars require adequate renumeration and other expenses for research.

Jains Abroad: About 100,000 Jains live outside India, but they lack spiritual guidance and teachings from their ascetics. Although a few monks and nuns have travelled to the West by breaking their traditional vows, their travels and conduct are not sanctioned by the *sangha*. Jains abroad require some form of four-fold order in the West. This is a fundamental issue and requires thorough discussions with Jain leaders and blessings from leading *aacaaryas* of all the sects; for both spiritual and socio-religious needs, overseas Jains require the establishment of such an order.

Socio-religious Needs: Migrant Jains are very keen to preserve their identity and culture, but the lack of an ascetic order in the West has deprived them of religious and spiritual guidance. They also require guidance for social occasions, family welfare and community affairs, similar to other expatriate communities settled in the West. Christians have priests and other clergy to take care of the socio-religious circumstances of the community. The Jews have Rabbis, the Muslims have Imams, the Hindus have Priests, the Sikhs have Gurus and so on, all of them responsible for the socio-religious affairs of their respective community. The Jains in the West also have socio-religious needs, and they may have to recruit personnel who have received adequate academic training in Jain literature, social customs, and family and community management. But living in the West, such individuals have to be properly remunerated so that they can be independent. Compared to the resources spent by individual families on social occasions, family and community affairs, the services of such individuals are affordable. There is an urgent need to implement this training scheme, which should be similar to the Jews' thorough training of their Rabbis, which lasts five years or more after university graduation, and for which they are properly remunerated. After the training, employment is widely available both inside the Jewish community and beyond. Similarly the Christian clergy has three years of training after graduating in divinity. The benefits of such training would be enormous to the Jain community in the complex world of today. Not only would they be able to teach the basis of Jainism and the study of the scriptures to the Jain community, but they would be a real source of much needed guidance for social customs and ceremonies, family problems and the progress of the community; they would also be able to disseminate Jain values to the wider world in a professional way.

The establishment of a Western Order of Jainism, with a modified four-fold order for the needs of the community, could be a real boost in promoting Jainism both for Jains and non-Jains. This order should be a functional necessity, and in no way can it be considered a replacement or reformation of the four-fold order established by Mahavira. *Aacaaryas* in India should be consulted; open discussion and deliberation with a series of conferences involving community members in the West are necessary before such an order is established.

In summary, Jainism is a living religion with a history extending beyond the period of twenty-third *Tirthankara* Parsvanatha (877–777 BCE). Jains are blessed to have:

A philosophy in the form of Jain values and principles;
A ready-made ethos, in the form of environmental concerns, animal welfare, equality, social welfare and a desire to improve the human reverence for life, and non-violence;
Magnificent art, architecture and heritage;
A dedicated community of ascetic orders and laity;
Philanthropists;
A desire to promote the Jain teachings and to revive its past glory;
Many sympathisers in the world.

But through pettiness and misunderstandings, activities of the Jain communities lack uniformity and a positive aim. The co-ordinated effort for the promotion of Jain values and Mahavira's teachings seems to be lacking. If Jains are not careful, they will fail to inspire the younger generation and other members of the community, and the result may be a community without Jain values.

Jainism is an ancient religion and its tradition traces the line of *tirthankaras* back through countless aeons. Yet Jainism has a basis in logic and science which makes it relevant to the modern age. It teaches love and brotherliness to all living beings; malice and hurt to none. Jainism provides a sensible, acceptable explanation of the great problems of existence — where we came from, where we are going, the nature of our immortal soul and its relation to our transitory body, and the meaning of life. Jainism provides a code of conduct that is relevant to the troubled world in which we live — a way of life which is based on its fundamental principles of 'non-violence and reverence for life', 'non-attachment' and 'relative pluralism'. Its rituals are meaningful. It is concerned with all living beings, and the current concerns of ecology, animal welfare and human behaviour are interwoven into its teachings. The social teachings of Jainism, individual freedom and equality regardless of race, gender, caste and colour strike a chord in the hearts and minds of modern men and women.

Jainism is a way of life for today and tomorrow.

APPENDIX I

MAJOR EVENTS IN THE CHRONOLOGICAL HISTORY OF JAINS

The history of Jainism can conveniently be divided into four broad periods: Jain-textual and pre-historic, ancient, medieval, and modern. The history of the first twenty-two *tirthankaras*, perhaps prior to the Ice Age, is given in the Jain texts; the periods are:

- The pre-historic period, between 15th century BCE to 8th century BCE.
- The ancient period, between 8th century BCE to 5th century CE.
- The medieval period, between 5th century CE to 14th century CE.
- The modern period, 14th century to present day.

Owing to a lack of authentic historical literature, many of the dates mentioned are approximate. Other than giving biographical information on the *tirthankaras*, Jain texts say little about history; however, in the table below, known major Jain historical events are compared with dates and events in Indian and world history. Most Indian dynasties were sympathetic to Jainism, certain of them observed Jainism as their religion or supported it actively, but persecution of the Jains was undertaken by few dynasties. For the sake of convenience, historical events are grouped together in most cases in periods of 200 years.

Date	Events in Jain History	Prominent Persons/ Places	Events/Prominent Persons in Indian History	Events/Prominent Persons in World History
4500–1500 BCE	Oral Jain texts. (Ancient written texts: events pre-4500 BCE).	Twenty-two *tirthankaras*.	Rigveda mentions *sramana* tradition, Rishabhadeva and Neminatha.	Aryans destroy Indus valley civilisation and settle in India.
1500–800 BCE			Indus Valley Civilization at Mohenjodaro artefacts of nude figures, perhaps of Jain yogis in standing postures.	Beginning of Jewish religion (worship of Yahweh) c.1200 BCE.
800–600 BCE	*Sramana* tradition, establishment of four-vows	23rd *tirthankara*, Parsvanatha (877–777 BCE).	Composition of Upanishads (800–400 BCE), Taxila university founded in NW India, attracting students from all regions.	753 BCE: traditional date of foundation of Rome. 776 BCE: First Olympic games held in Greece.
600–400 BCE	Revival of Jain tradition, establishment of five-vows and the four-fold order.	Mahavira (599–527BCE), Gautam, Sudharma and Jambu (last omniscient).	Caste system established in India with Brahmin superiority. Buddha founds Buddhism (563–483 BCE).	(1700 or) 558 BCE: Zoroaster begins prophetic work in Persia. 510 BCE: Roman Republic founded.

Date	Events in Jain History	Prominent Persons/ Places	Events/Prominent Persons in Indian History	Events/Prominent Persons in World History
400–200 BCE	Migration of Bhadrabahu to South India Composition of *Kalpasutra*.	Bhadrabahu, Sthulibhadra.	12 years of severe famine. Nandas defeated. 322 BCE: Candragupta founds Mauryan empire.	Invasion of India by Alexander the Great (305 BCE).
200–0 BCE	Kalakacharya teaches a lesson to Gardabhilla. Migration of Jain ascetics to Mathura, West and South India.	Kharvela, king of Kalinga (Orissa) adopts Jainism as state religion (150 BCE).	Vikrama defeats Saka. Vikrama era (57 BCE). Tamil kings in Ceylon.	Roman conquest of central Italy, Spain and Greece (290–46 BCE). Chin Shi Huang–Ti unites China (c.221 BCE).
1 CE–200 CE	Svetambara–Digambara split in 79 CE.	Kundakunda	Sakas establish Saka era (78 CE)	Jesus crucified in Jerusalem (c.30 CE) Julius Caesar wins Rome (c.45–47 CE).
200–400 CE	Simhanandi monk guides to establish Ganga Kingdom in (188 CE).	Umasvati (c.240–340 CE) composes *Tattvarthasutra*.	Consolidation of Kusan power. Commencement of Gupta (or Valabhi) era (c.319–320 CE).	313 CE: Christianity becomes official religion of Roman empire.

400–600 CE	Valabhi council (453–473 CE) redacts scriptures (Svetambara).	Devardhigani, Samantabhadra and Siddhasen.	Gupta period consolidation. Pallava, Calukya and Kadamba dynasties commence in south India.	Great literary era in India. Aryabhatta, Varamihara invent decimal system.
600–800 CE	Persecution of Jains by Pandyas Construction of Elora cave temples.	Mantunga composer of Bhaktamar. Aklanka, Haribhadra.	Calukyas send ambassador to China. Harsa organises religious conference (643 CE).	Muslim era (622 CE). Hiuen-Tse-sang visits India (629 CE) Bede writes his famous history of Christianity in Britain.
800–1000 CE	Royal patronage: declines in north continues in south and west India.	Bappa-Bhatti secures Kanoj patronage Silagunasuri helps Vanaraja Chavada to Gujarat throne.	Rastrakuta empire consolidated in south and parts of central and western India.	800 CE Beginning of Holy Roman Empire 853 CE First printed book in China. 935 CE text of Koran finalised.
1000–1200 CE	Construction of Delwara temples Golden period in Gujarat. Persecution in south by Cholas.	Vastupala-Tejpal, Hemcandra Kumarpala.	Rise of small Rajput kingdoms. Mahmud of Ghazni sacks and breaks power of Hindu States (1018 CE). In 1175 CE Muzzuddin Ghazni founds Muslim rule in India.	1154 CE: Gothic architecture spreads throughout Europe. 1150 CE: Hindu temple of Angkor (Cambodia) built.

Date	Events in Jain History	Prominent Persons/ Places	Events/Prominent Persons in Indian History	Events/Prominent Persons in World History
1200–1600 CE	Lack of Royal patronage. Jains confined to banking and trading. Iconoclastic zeal of some Muslim rulers. Jain influence declines in South India. Sthanakvasi sect established (1460 CE).	Hiravijaya secured decrees from Muslim rulers to build temples, celebrate festivals and allow pilgrimages. Arts developed. Manuscripts preserved and new ones prepared. Jain images distributed throughout India.	c.1215 CE: Islamic architecture spreads in India. 1398 CE: Timur invades India and sacks Delhi. 1526 CE: Babar conquers Delhi and founds Moghul Empire. 1565 CE Akbar extends empire in Deccan. 1539 CE: Death of Nanak, founder of Sikhism.	1234 CE: Moghuls destroy Chin Empire. 1275 CE: Marco Polo arrives in China. 1498 CE: Vasco da Gama: first European sea voyage to India. 1509 watch invented by Peter Henly (Nuremberg) 1538 CE: Henry VIII of England breaks with Church of Rome.
1600–1800 CE	Dark period for Jains. Confusion and political situation in India adversely affected Jains. Terapanthi sect established (1760 CE).	Jain literary activities flourished. Yashovijay, Anandghana Bhiksu.	1653 CE: Taj Mahal completed in India. 1674 CE: Sivaji creates Hindu Maratha kingdom 1690 CE: Foundation of Calcutta by English 1707 CE: Death of Aurangzeb. Decline of Moghul empire.	c.1610 Scientific revolution in Europe begins. 1616 CE: Foundation of Harvard College in North America. 1796 CE: British conquer Ceylon.

1800–1950 CE	Interest of foreign scholars in Jainism. Translation of scriptures begins.	Vallabhvijay Rajchandra. Jain migration to East Africa.	British rule grants religious freedom. Mahatma Gandhi promotes *ahimsaa*. India wins freedom (1947).	1818 CE: British defeat Maratha and become effective Rulers of India. 1864 CE: Foundation of Red Cross.
1950–1998 CE	Jain migration to the West. Translation of scriptures and other literary activities. Jain temples established in UK and North America. Jain studies and courses in universities.	Arrival of ascetics in West: Chitrabhanu, Sushilkumar. Celebration of 2,500th *nirvan* anniversary of Mahavira.	1952 CE India becomes Republic 1962 CE: Sino-Indian war 1971 CE: Indo-Pakistan war, leading to break away of East Pakistan. 1989 Indira Gandhi assassinated. Tolerance of religions in India by the state.	Communist victory in China. 1961 CE: First man in space – Gagarin (USSR). 1969 CE: First man lands on moon – Armstrong (USA). 1980 Computer revolution spreads in offices and homes. 1988–96 Concerns of ecology globally. 1998 Microscopic fossils of living creatures found in rock from Mars.

APPENDIX II

NUTRITIONAL VALUES OF VEGETARIAN FOODS

	No.	Food 100g	Water %	Energy Kcal	Protein g	Fat g	Carbohydrate as monosaccharide
Milk	1	Cow's milk, whole fluid	87	65	3.3	3.8	4.8
	2	Cream, single	80	189	2.8	18.0	4.2
	3	Yoghurt, natural	88	57	3.6	2.6	5.2
Cheese	4	Cheese, cheddar	37	412	25.4	34.5	0
	5	Cheese, cottage	79	115	15.2	4.0	4.5
Fats	6	Butter	16	745	0.5	82.5	0
	7	Lard, dripping	0	894	0	99.3	0
	8	Margarine	16	769	0.2	85.3	0
	9	Oils (vegetable), salad & cooking	0	899	0	99.9	0
Vegetables	10	Beans, canned in tomato sauce	71	92	6.0	0.4	17.3
	11	Beans, broad	90	69	7.2	0.5	9.5
	12	Beetroot, boiled	91	44	1.8	0	9.9
	13	Brussels sprouts, boiled	88	16	2.4	0	1.7
	14	Cabbage, raw	92	28	1.5	0	5.8
	15	Cabbage, boiled	94	8	0.8	0	1.3
	16	Carrots, old, cooked	91	23	0.7	0	5.4
	17	Cauliflower	93	24	3.4	0	2.8
	18	Parsnips	82	49	1.7	0	11.3
	19	Peas, fresh or quick frozen, boiled	82	49	5.0	0	7.7

	No.	Food 100g	Water %	Energy Kcal	Protein g	Fat g	Carbohydrate as monosaccharide
	20	Potatoes, boiled	80	79	1.4	0	19.7
	21	Spinach	92	21	2.7	0	2.8
	22	Sweet corn, canned	81	95	2.6	0.8	20.5
Fruit	23	Apples	85	46	0.3	0	12.0
	24	Apricots, dried	25	182	4.8	0	43.4
	25	Bananas	76	76	1.1	0	19.2
	26	Dates	22	248	2.0	0	63.9
	27	Figs, dried	23	213	3.6	0	52.9
	28	Grapefruit	89	22	0.6	0	5.3
	29	Oranges	86	35	0.8	0	8.5
	30	Pears	83	41	0.3	0	10.6
	31	Sultanas	18	249	1.7	0	64.7
Nuts	32	Almonds	5	580	20.5	53.5	4.3
	33	Coconut, grated fresh	51	608	6.6	62.0	6.4
		dessicated	0	608	6.6	62.0	6.4
	34	Peanuts, roasted	2	586	28.1	49.0	8.6
	35	Barley, pearl, dry	11	360	7.7	1.7	83.6
	36	Bread, white, enriched	36	253	8.3	1.7	54.6
	37	Bread, wholemeal	36	241	9.6	3.1	46.7
Cereals	38	Oatmeal	3	400	12.1	8.7	72.8
	39	Spaghetti	68	364	9.9	1.0	84.0
Preserves	40	Honey	17	288	0.4	0	76.4
	41	Sugar, white	trace	394	0	0	105.5

Common Indian Foods

	No.	Food 100g	Water %	Energy Kcal	Protein g	Fat g	Carbohydrate as monosaccharide
Milk products	42	Panir		348	24.1	25.1	6.3
	43	Buffalo milk		117	4.3	8.8	5.1
	44	Buttermilk		51	0.8	1.1	0.5
	45	Milk pulp (mava)		421	14.6	31.2	21.5
Cereals	46	Bajra		360	11.6	5.0	67.1
	47	Barley		355	10.4	1.9	74.0
	48	Rice		350	6.6	1.2	78.2
	49	Wheat		349	11.8	0.9	74.1
	50	Gram		361	17.1	5.3	61.2
	51	Dal (average of different types)		350	24.0	1.3	57.0
Vegetables	52	Mustard		541	22.0	39.7	23.8

	No.	Food 100g	Water %	Energy Kcal	Protein g	Fat g	Carbohydrate as monosaccharide
	53	Cress		67	4.9	0.9	9.8
	54	Tomatoes		21	1.0	0.1	3.9
	55	Gram		146	8.2	0.5	27.2
Biscuits	57	Average		177	6.8	10.1	58.1
Sweets	58	Gulab jambu		186	6.8	24.2	37.8
	59	Jalebi		494	4.4	34.3	42.0
	60	Khir		141	4.1	4.5	21.1
	61	Sweet rice		267	2.5	8.8	44.6
	62	Puran-poli		463	8.1	26.2	48.8
Savouries	63	Chevada		420	4.2	27.0	40.2
	64	Khichadi		168	4.7	7.3	21.0
	65	Upama		233	4.9	10.2	31.0
	66	Dosa		409	5.4	23.4	43.6
	67	Samosa/kachori		256	3.8	12.8	21.2
	68	Pauva		118	2.9	2.2	21.2

APPENDIX III

QUICK CALORIE RECKONER FOR COMMON INDIAN VEGETARIAN FOOD

Calories relate to 100 grams unless otherwise specified.

Cereals and cereal food

Bajra	361
Barley	336
Wheat	346
Millets	334
Maize flour	355
Maize tender	125
Weetabix, Shredded Wheat	125
Corn Flakes, Rice Crispies—1 oz	104
Popcorn	340
Ragi	328
Rice, raw milled	345
Rice, puffed	325
Rice, cooked, 3 tablespoons	70
Rice—Khichri 1 Vati (210 g)	250
Sago	351
Suji	348
Wheat flour	341
Biscuits 1 small, 16 grams	129
Chapati, thin, 16 grams	40
Chapati, small, 24 grams	80
Chapati, medium, 35 grams	119
Bread, white, 1 slice	60
Bread, white	245
Bread, brown	244
Bun	280

Oatmeal, 27 grams	110
Dosa-plain 1 med. (9 in. diameter)	130
Dosa-Masala	210
Idli-medium (3.5 in. diameter)	100
Macaroni 30 grams	115
Puri 1 (16 grams)	70
Parotha 1 (70 grams)	250
Chakali (wheat flour)	550
Chat	474
Chevra (fried)	420
Dal Vada 1	200
Dhokla	122
Gharvada	364
Pakora	200
Samosa	256
Potato Kachori	166
Potato Chips 20 grams	110
Upama	230

Pulses

Bengal-Gram (roasted, dehusked)	369
Bengal-Gram, Chana Dal	372
Black-Gram, Urad Dal	347
Green-Gram, whole (mug)	334
Red-Gram, Tuver	335
Lentil (Masur)	343
Soya Bean	432
Dal (cooked, thick consistency, 113 g)	145
Dal (cooked, medium consistency, 92 g)	92
Rasam 1 cup	12
Sambar 0.5 cup	105

Vegeatables, Leafy Vegetables

Bengal Gram, green (Channa)	66
Brussels Sprouts	15
Cabbage	45
Colocasia leaves (Arbi-ka-Patta)	56
Fenugreek leaves (Maithi)	49
Mustard leaves (Sarson)	34
Radish leaves (Moli-ka-Patta)	28
Sarli Sag	86
Spinach-Palak	26

Root vegetables

Carrot-Gajar	48

Colocasia-Arvi	97
Lotus Root-Kamal-ki-jahr	53
Onion	50
Potato	97
Sweet potato (Shakarkand)	120
Tapioca-Mara Valli Cassava	157
Turnip-Shalgam	29
Yam-Kand	79

Other Vegetables

Ash Gourd-Dudhi	10
Bitter Gourd-Karela	25
Bottle Gourd-Toriya	12
Brinjal-Baingan	24
Broad Beans-Phansi	48
Cauliflower	30
Cardamom	229
Chillies—Green	29
Chillies—Dry	246
Cloves—Dry	285
Corriander	288
French Beans—Phali	26
Garlic—Dry	145
Ginger—Fresh	67
Ladies Fingers – Bhindi	65
Mushrooms	42
Mogra	25
Papaya—Green	27
Parval	18
Peas—Matar	93
Pepper—Dry	304
Pepper—Green	98
Plantain—Green—Kela	64
Pumpkin—Kaddu	25
Tindora	21
Turmeric	349
Vegetable Marrow—Ghei	25
Water Chestnut, Fresh Singhada	115
Choli	26
Guvar	16
Green Mangoes	93
Papdi	44
Cucumber	13

Tomatoes	23
Kothmir	44

Sweets and Sugars

Badam Halva	570
Balushahi	469
Burfi 1 piece, 25 grams	100
Fruit Jelly	75
Gulab Jambu	186
Jalebi	494
Mysore Pak	357
Nankhatai	584
Penda 1 piece, 50 grams	83
Ras Gulla, 30 grams	100
Shakarpara	570
Sohan Halva	400
Suji Halva	136
Gur (Jaggery), 15 grams	57
Honey 1 teaspoon	30
Jam 1 teaspoon, 5 grams	20
Sugar 1 teaspoon, 5 grams	20
Sugar 1 cube	12

Biscuits and Cakes

Biscuits, salted 1, 3 grams	15
Biscuits, sweet 1, 4 grams	24
Cheese, tit bits 10, 3.5 grams	20
Coconut Macaroon 1, 13 grams	80
Cake, chocolate 1 slice, 45 grams	165
Cake, fruit, 1 slice, 30 grams	117

Milk and Milk Products

Milk, 1 cup	100
Milk, skimmed, 1 cup	45
Milk, condensed, 1 cup (sweetened)	320
Milk powder	496
Butter Milk, skimmed, 1 glass	25
Cheese	348
Curds (yoghurt) low fat	60
Ice Cream	205
Kheer	178
Milk cake	331
Ghee	900
Oil	900
Cream 1 tablespoon 15 g	50

| Butter | 755 |
| Margarine | 755 |

Nuts

Almond (10–12) 10 grams	65
Cashew Nuts (8–10) 10 grams	66
Coconut (dry)	662
Coconut (tender)	41
Chestnuts, fresh	150
Ground nuts	560
Walnuts (8–10 halves) 15 grams	102
Pista	626
Jardalu	53
Berries (Bor) dry	64
Peanut Butter	620
Cake, plain, 1 slice, 40 grams	146

Fruits

Apples	46
Apricot	53
Banana	76
Cape-Gooseberry (Raspberry)	53
Cherries	70
Dates (fresh)	283
Dates (dried)	317
Figs (tender – fresh)	75
Figs (dried)	320
Guavas (Peru – Jamfal)	51
Grapes	45
Grapes (dried = sultanas)	290
Jackfruits (ripe)	88
Jambu	47
Lychees	61
Lime	59
Loquat	43
Malta	36
Mandarin	44
Mangoes (green)	39
Mangoes (ripe)	50 to 80
Melon (white)	21
Melon (water melon)	16
Mulberry	53
Orange	53
Papaya	32

Peaches	50
Pineapple	46
Plums	56
Prune	75
Pommegranate (red)	77
Sapota (Cheeku)	94
Strawberry	44
Sitafal	104
Tomatoes (ripe)	112

Soups and Beverages

Clear Vegetable Soup 150 ml	12
Tomato Cream Soup 150 ml	65
Vegetable Soup 150 ml	65
Tea, lemon no sugar 1 cup	1
Tea, milk no sugar 1 cup	20
tea, milk and sugar 1 cup	75
Cocoa, 50% milk with sugar 1 cup	145
Coffee, with milk 1 cup	25
Coffee, black 1 cup	5
Coffee, milk and sugar 1 cup	75
Cola drinks 8 fl. oz	104
Fruit Juice (unsweetened) 3.5 fl. oz	75
Orange Juice 3.5 fl. oz	110
Lemon, Grapefruit squashes 3.5 fl. oz	110
Chocolate Drinks with milk 5 oz	115
Horlicks Powder 15 g	56
Lucozade 6 oz	115
Ovaltine Powder 0.5 oz	54

GLOSSARY

Aacaara	Conduct.
Aacaara dinkar grantha	Text of daily duties.
Aacaaranga sutra	Primary canon dealing with conduct.
Aacaarya	Ascetic leader; spiritual leader.
Aadipurana	Ancient Jain text.
Aadraa	Constellation in mid-June.
Aagamas	Ancient scriptures.
Aahaara	Food intake.
Aahaaraka sarira	Projectile body.
Aajnaa vicaya	Reflection on teachings of *jina*.
Aakaasa	Space.
Aalocanaa	Critical self-examination.
Aangi	The regular decoration of a *jina* image by devotees.
Aapta	Person who has attained knowledge.
Aarambha	Occupation; daily work.
Aarambha-himsa	Violence arising in an acceptable occupation.
Aarati	Waving lamps ritual before a *jina* image or worthy person.
Aarta dhyaana	Inauspicious 'sorrowful' meditation.
Aaryikaa	Digambara female ascetic.
Aasaatana	Disrespect.
Aasana Aaso	Seat; yogic posture. Twelfth month of Indian calendar vs. calendar used by Jains.
Aasrava	Influx of *karma*.
Aatmaa	Soul or the self.
Aatma-siddhi	Text dealing with self-realisation.
Aavasyakas	Essential duties.
Aayaagapata	Votive slabs.
Aayu(sya)	Life span.
Abaadha kaala	Dormant period of *karma*.
Abhavya	A soul which can never be liberated.
Abhaya daana	Actions which ensure the safety of the other lives.
Abhigraha	Resolution.
Abhiseka	Anointing ritual.

Acaurya vrata	Vow of not taking, keeping or accepting what is not given; non-stealing.
Adharma	False belief, wrong faith, wrong conduct.
Adharma (astikaaya)	The medium of rest.
Adhyaatma saara	Text concerning the practice of spirituality.
Adhyavasaaya	Primal drive.
Aghaati karma	Non-destructive or non-obscuring *karma*.
Agni sthaapan	Ritual of placing sacred fire.
Agra pujaa	Worship in front of an image.
Ahimsaa	Non-violence and reverence for life through thoughts, words and deeds.
Ailaka	Digambara 'one-clothed' major monk.
Ajiva	Non-living.
Ajivikaa	An ancient Indian philosophy.
Ajnaanavaadi	An ancient Indian philosophy.
Akriyaavaadi	An ancient Indian philosophy.
Aksaya tritiya	'Immortal third', day in vaisak month.
Amaari pravartan	Decree of 'non-killing' issued by rulers.
Anaahaara	Not taking food.
Ananta	Infinite.
Anantaanubandhi	Bondage for endless time *(karmas)*.
Anantakaaya	Body having innumerable souls, e.g. Root vegetables.
Ananugaami	Not accompanied.
Anarthadanda vrata	Vow not to perform avoidable activities.
Anasana	Fasting.
Andaja	Nourished and reared in eggs.
Anekaantavaada	'relative pluralism', taking account of multiple viewpoints.
Anga pujaa	Worship by contact with an image.
Angas	Primary canons; limbs.
Anitya	Impermanent.
Anivritti karana	Spiritual stage of desireless mind.
Anjana salaakaa	Consecration ceremony of an image.
Annupaatika sutra	Secondary canon concerning 'those who arise. spontaneously', heavenly and hellish beings.
Annuttara upapaatikadasaa	Primary canon dealing with souls reborn in uppermost heavens.
Antakriddasaa	Primary canon dealing with stories of liberated souls.
Antar muhurta	A period of up to forty-eight minutes.
Antaraala	Vestibule of a Jain temple.
Antaraaya karma	*Karma* which restricts the energy or quality of the soul.
Anu	Atom.
Anubhava	Results of *karma*; intensity of *karma*;experience.
Anugaami	Accompanied.

Anukampaa	Compassion.
Anupreksaa	Reflection; has twelve kinds.
Anuvrata	Minor vows of laypeople.
Anuyogadvar sutra	A group of post-canonical texts, an exposition of scriptures.
Anyatva	Philosophy of others in relation to the self.
Apaaya vicaya	Reflection on dissolution of passions.
Apabhramsa	An Indian language, a forerunner of gujarati.
Apa-dhyaana	Inauspicious meditation; hateful or sorrowful thoughts.
Aparigraha	'non-possession' or 'non-attachment' to worldly things.
Aparinami	Unchanging.
Aparyaaptaa	Beings with vital organs not completed.
Ap-kaaya	Beings with 'water bodies'.
Apramatta-samyati	Spiritual stage of total restraint and carefulness.
Apratipaati	Not permanent or not continuous.
Apratyaakhyaana varana	Obstructer of partial renunciation.
Apurva karana	Spiritual stage of unprecedented volition.
Apvartanaa	Reduction in the intensity and duration of karmic fruition.
Apvartanaa	Attenuation.
Arati	Not taking pleasure in sensual activities.
Ardha magadhi	The prakrit language of Jain scriptures.
Ardha padmaasana	A posture for meditation.
Arhant	Self-conqueror.
Arhat	An enlightened person or person worthy of veneration.
Arihant	Conqueror of inner enemies, e.g. Passions.
Arihanta mahaapujan	Ritualised worship of the attributes of *tirthankaras*.
Artha	Meaning: material resources.
Asadha	Ninth month of Indian calendar vs. calendar used by Jains.
Asanjnaa	Partial instinct.
Asarana	Non-surrender.
Asarira	Free from embodiment; liberated.
Asatya	Not speaking the truth.
Asi	Sword or rule of law.
Astapaahuda	A Digambara sacred text, divided into eight sections.
Asta-prakaari pujaa	Eight-fold worship.
Asteya	Vow of speaking the truth.
Asti	Means 'it is'.
Astikaaya	Having *pradesas* or body; having extension in space.
Asubha	Malevolent; inauspious.
Asuci	Impure.

Asura	Celestials of the lower world.
Asvin	Twelfth month of Indian calendar vs. calendar used by Jains.
Aticaara	Infraction of rules.
Atisay ksetra	Area of miracles and myths.
Atithi samvibhaaga	A vow of 'hospitality', taking food only after serving guests.
Atthai	Continuous fasting for eight days.
Atthai mahotsava	Continuous celebration with *pujans* for eight days.
Attham	Continuous fasting for three days.
Audaarika sarira	Gross body.
Audayijya	Realisational effects (of *karma*).
Aupaatika	Born spontaneously.
Aupasamika	Subdued.
Avadhaan	Memory.
Avadhi jnaana	'Clairvoyance', knowledge limited to material objects.
Avaktavya	Not able to be described or put into words; inexpressible.
Avasarpini	Descending time cycle.
Avassahi	'May I go out?'.
Avasthaana kaala	Time span.
Avataara	Incarnation.
Avidya	Ignorance.
Avirata samyagdristi	Non-restrained (complete) Right Faith.
Avirati	Non-restraint.
Aviveka	Lack of discrimination.
Ayambil	An austerity, eating only once a day, taking bland food.
Ayambil saalaa	A place providing bland meals for *ayambil* austerity.
Ayariya	Prakrit word for *acaarya*.
Ayogi kevali	Static omniscience.
Ayonija	Asexual or 'indirect' sexual (birth).
Baabari	Removal of hair from the scalp of a child for the first time.
Baala tapa	Austerity without understanding.
Balipata	Slab for offerings.
Bandha	Attachment of *karma* to the soul.
Bhaasaa	Speech.
Bhaasaa samiti	'Carefulness in speaking'.
Bhaava	Psychic feelings, mental attitude.
Bhaava pujaa	Psychic worship.
Bhaava sraavaka	Having the appropriate attitudes of a Jain.
Bhaavanaa	Devotional ritual in temples, usually at night.
Bhaavendriya	Psychic senses.
Bhagavati sutra	Primary canon describing questions from Gautama

	and answers from Mahavira.
Bhaktamara stotra	Eulogy for immortalisation of the devotees.
Bhakti	Devotion.
Bhakti marga	Devotional path.
Bhattaraka	Semi-ascetic head of a Digambara temple.
Bhavanvaasi	Palace dweller; celestials in the lower world.
Bhavya	One who is capable of liberation.
Bheda	Distinction.
Bhiksu	Ascetic.
Bhogabhumi	'Land of pleasures'.
Bhogopa-bhogaparimaana	Vow of limitation of consumables and non-consumables.
Bhojan	Food.
Bhojan saalaa	Place providing meals for pilgrims.
Biyaasan	Semi-fasting, having two meals a day.
Bodhi durlabha	Difficult-to-attain enlightenment.
Brahmacaari	Male celibate.
Brahmacaarini	Female celibate.
Brahmacaaryaasram	The period of life before becoming a householder.
Brahmacarya	Celibacy; chastity; control over senses.
Brahmaloka	The fifth heaven.
Brahmin or brahman	A member of priestly class.
Caamar	Brush fan.
Caar pheraa	Four rounds at the wedding ceremony.
Caitra	Sixth month of Indian calendar v.s. calendar used by Jains.
Caitya	Temple.
Caitya vandana	Ritual of temple prayers.
Cakra	Wheel.
Cakravarti	Universal emperor.
Candana pujaa	Worship with sandalwood paste.
Candra	Moon.
Candra prajnaapti	Secondary canon dealing with lunar movements.
Caranaanuyoga	Sacred text on ethics, conduct and religious practices.
Caravalaa	Woollen thread brush kept by ascetics.
Caritra	Conduct.
Caritra- mohaniya karma	Conduct-deluding *karma*.
Caritraacaara	Right Conduct.
Caturvidha sangha	Four-fold order.
Caturvisanti stava	Hymns in praise of the twenty-four *tirthankaras*.
Caughadia	Unit of periodicity.
Caumukha	Image(s) facing four entrances.
Cauvihaara	Renunciation of all four kinds of food.
Cetanaa	Consciousness.
Chaaya	Shade.
Chaayaa	Shadow.

Chatha	Continuous fasting for two days.
Cheda	Demotion.
Cheda sutra	Text dealing with monastic discipline.
Choda	Embroidered cloth with auspicious symbols.
Chyle	Lymphatic fluid.
Cikistaalaya	Hospital.
Citta	Sub-conscious mind.
Cori	A four-cornered place within which marriage takes place.
Cyavan	Path of rebirth from heavenly being to human being.
Daana	Donations; acts of giving.
Darsana	Perception; devotional viewing (e.g. of images).
Darsanaacaar	Right perception.
Darsana-mohaniya karma	Faith-deluding *karma*.
Dasavaikalika sutra	Sacred text in the form of ten lessons.
Deraavaasi	Believers in temple worship.
Desaavadhi	Partial 'clairvoyance'.
Desavikasika	Limitation of areal movement.
Desavirati	Partial vows.
Deva	*Tirthankara*; heavenly being.
Deva dravya	Temple fund.
Deva pujaa	Veneration of *jina*.
Deva vandan	Veneration of *tirthankaras*.
Dhaatu	Body primal.
Dharana	Contemplation.
Dharma	Religion; duty; medium of motion.
Dharma dhyaana	Auspicious 'virtuous' meditation.
Dharmabindu	Sacred text composed by haribhadra, dealing with the spiritual path of lay people.
Dhavalaa	A sacred text of the Digambaras.
Dhrauvya	Continuation or permanence.
Dhriti sanskaar	Blessings for a viable foetus.
Dhvajaarohan	Hoisting of a flag.
Dhyaana	Meditation; concentration.
Dhyaana-mudraa	The posture for meditation.
Digambara	Sky-clad; a major sect of Jainism.
Digambara saadhu	'sky-clad' monk.
Digavrata	Vow not to travel in certain directions.
Dik-kumari	Angel of directions.
Diksaa	Initiation into asceticism.
Dipavali or divali	Festival of lights; anniversary of Mahavira's death.
Drastivaada sutra	Twelfth primary canon, no longer extant.
Dravya	Substance; material things; wealth.
Dravya sraavaka	A Jain who exhibits the outward signs of piety.
Dravyaanuyoga	Sacred text on metaphysics, ontology and philosophy.

Dravyendriya	Physical sense organs.
Dukha	Misery.
Durgati	Inferior destiny (*tiryanca* and hellish).
Dusamaa	Miserable period.
Dvaarapaala	Door keeper.
Ekaasan	Semi-fasting: one meal during day-time.
Ekatva	Philosophy of self; singleness.
Esanaa samiti	'Carefulness-in-eating'.
Evambhuta naya	'Such-likes' standpoint.
Gaccha	Group of four-fold order.
Gana	Group of ascetics.
Ganaadhipati	Chief of ascetic group.
Ganadhara	Chief disciples of *tirthankara*; head of ascetic lineage.
Ganini	Leader of group of female ascetics.
Garbha griha	Inner shrine.
Garbhaja	*In utero*.
Gatisila	Capable of movement.
Ghee	Refined butter.
Gotra	Family name; surname.
Graha	Planet.
Guna	Attributes.
Guna sthaanas	Stages of spiritual development.
Gupti	Restraint.
Guru purnimaa	Anniversary full moon day for the veneration of a guru.
Guru vandana	Veneration of ascetics.
Haatha	Hand.
Hasta melapa	Joining hands in the marriage ceremony.
Havaadaa	A place for animals to drink water.
Heya	To be abandoned.
Houm	A sacred mantra; short version for five supreme beings.
Indriya	Sense organ.
Iryaa samiti	'carefulness-in-movements'.
Istopadesa	Beneficial preaching.
Jaat	Sub-caste.
Jai jinendra	Honour to those who have conquered themselves.
Jainendra siddhant kosha	Encyclopedia of Jain philosophy.
Jambudvipa	Continent in the middle world which includes our earth.
Jambudvipa prajnaapti	Secondary canon dealing with astronomy and cosmology.
Jarayuja	Nourished and reared by placenta and umbilical cord.
Jayadhavalaa	Digambara text commenting on scriptures.
Jina	Victor of the self.

Jina mudra	*Jina*-modelled sitting or standing posture.
Jinakalpi	*Jina*-modelled ascetic.
Jitakalpa	Conduct to conquer the self.
Jiva	Soul; living being.
Jiva dayaa	Compassion to living beings.
Jiva kanda	Sacred text on biology.
Jivaabhigama sutra	Secondary canon concerning the animate and inanimate.
Jnaacaar	Principles relating to knowledge.
Jnaana	Knowledge.
Jnaana yoga	Spiritual knowledge.
Jnaana daana	Donation for spiritual education.
Jnaana pancami	Sacred day for veneration of scriptural knowledge.
Jnaana saara	Yashovijay's text on Jain philosophy and spirituality.
Jnaatadharma kathaa	Primary canon dealing with stories of knowledge and righteousness.
Jnaati	Sub-caste.
Jneya	Knowable.
Jyotiska	Astral celestials.
Kaala	Time.
Kaama	Sensual pleasures.
Kaaya kalesa	Mortification of the body.
Kaaya-cikitsaa	Treatment of the body.
Kaayotsarga	Meditation with detached body.
Kalasvarna	Fraction.
Kalpa	Heaven or paradise.
Kalpa sutra	Svetambara sacred text describing the life of Mahavira, other *tirthankaras*, disciples of Mahavira and ascetic conduct.
Kalpaatita	Beyond paradise.
Kalpaavatamsikaa	Narrative stories describing results of good and bad actions.
Kalpavruksa	'Wish-fulfilling tree'.
Kalpopapanna	Born in paradise.
Karan	Half day time.
Karanaanuyoga	Sacred text containing scientific and technical material.
Karma	Subtle matter attached to the soul resultant of one's deeds.
Karma yoga	Spiritual activities.
Karma: anubhava	Result of *karma*.
Karma: niddhatti	Reduction in fruition and intensity of *karma*.
Karma: niseka kaala	Period of results of *karma*.
Karma: pradesa	Amount of karmic particles engulfing the soul.
Karma: sattaa	Influence of *karma*.
Karma: sthiti	Duration of karmic attachment.

Karma: upasama	Suppression of *karma*.
Karma: abaadha kaala	Dormant period of *karma*.
Karma: caritra-mohaniya	Conduct-deluding *karma*.
Karma: darsana-mohaniya	Faith-deluding *karma*.
Karma: mohaniya	Deluding *karma*.
Karma: nikaacita	Unchangeable *karma*.
Karma: phalodaya	Fruition of *karma*.
Karma: prakriti	Nature of karmic particles engulfing the soul.
Karmabhumi	'Land of action'.
Kar-mocan	Releasing hands in wedding ceremony.
Kasaaya	Passion.
Kasaayapahuda	Digambara text dealing with theory of the passions.
Kevala jnaana	Omniscience.
Kevali	Omniscient.
Khala	Waste products.
Khamaasana	'Five limbs bowing' to venerate supreme beings.
Kharatara gaccha	A Svetambara sub-sect.
Krisnaraajis	Dark masses.
Kriyaavaadi	An ancient Indian philosophy that believed in the rituals and Right Conduct.
Krupaludeva	Merciful guide; a title for srimad rajcandra.
Ksatriya	A person of the warrior class.
Ksayika	Destruction of *karma*.
Ksayopasamika	Suppressed and destroyed *karma*.
Ksetra	Area or location.
Ksina moha	Total annihilation of delusion.
Ksullaka	Digambara 'two-clothed' minor monk.
Kulakara	Guide or law giver; patriarch.
Kulakara sthaapan	Invocation of heavenly guides.
Kunda	A basin.
Laabha	Gain.
Laalia jiva	Type of micro-orgnism.
Labdhi	Manifestation of special sense experience; accomplishment.
Lesyaa	Psychic colour; 'karmic stain'.
Lobha	Greed.
Loka	People; universe where living beings exist.
Loka-akasa	The inhabited universe.
Maagha	Fourth month of Indian calendar vs. calendar used by Jains.
Maalaaropana	Auspicious garlanding.
Maana	Egoism.
Maasaksamana	Fasting for one continuous month.
Maataa	Heavenly mother.
Maatruka sthaapan	Invocation of heavenly goddesses.
Madhya loka	Middle world.
Mahaadhavala	Sacred text commenting on Digambara scriptures.

Mahaajana	Reputed persons.
Mahaasati	Sthanakvasi nun.
Mahaavideha	Vast region of *jambudvipa*.
Mahavira jayanti	Birth anniversary of Mahavira.
Mahotsava	Elaborate celebration.
Mana	Mind.
Manahparyaaya jnaana	Telepathic knowledge; knowledge of mind and its modes.
Manana	Reflection.
Mandapa	Sacred place within which an auspicious event takes place.
Maneka stambha	Sacred wooden symbolic piece used in marriage ceremony.
Mangala divo	Ritual of waving an auspicious lamp.
Mangalaastaka	Auspicious prayers.
Manovarganaa	Particles constituting mind.
Manusya	Human.
Marga	Pathway.
Maryaadaa mahotsava	Annual gathering of terapanthi *sangha*.
Mati jnaana	Sensory knowledge.
Micchami dukkadam	Asking for forgiveness and granting forgiveness.
Misra	Mixed.
Mithyaatva	Wrong faith.
Mithyadrsti	Incorrect view of reality.
Moksa	Liberation.
Muhapatti	'Mouth-kerchief', a cloth piece kept in front of mouth to avoid harn to tiny living beings of air.
Muhurta	Period of forty-eight minutes.
Mukhakosa	Large 'mouth-kerchief' resembling a scarf.
Muktaa sukti mudra	Special sutra recital posture in temple or penitential retreat.
Mula sutra	Sacred text of basic teachings.
Mumuksu	Desirous of *moksa*.
Muni	Male ascetic.
Murti	Image; idol.
Murtipujaka	Image worshipper.
Naat	Sub-caste.
Naigama naya	Universal standpoint.
Naksatra	Constellation.
Namo arham	Veneration to the worthy being.
Namo jinanam	Veneration to the *jinas*.
Nandhyavarta	Place with 52 *jina* temples where heavenly beings worship.
Nandi sutra	Sacred text dealing with theory of knowledge, cognition and sources of valid knowledge.
Naraka	Hellish being.
Nasti	It is not.

Nava smarana	Nine eulogies.
Navakaara (namokara) mantra	A sacred mantra of surrender, obeisance and veneration to the five supreme beings.
Navakaarasi	A vow of fasting for forty-eight minutes after sunrise; Amity dinner for the Jain community.
Navapada oli	Semi-fasting with veneration of the nine auspicious things.
Nayavaada	Standpointism.
Nhaavana	Sacred liquid obtained from the ritual bathing of *jina*.
Nigoda	Simplest micro-organism.
Nirayaavalikaa	Narrative stories describing results of good and bad actions.
Nirgrantha	Detached person; Jain ascetic.
Nirjaraa	Shedding of *karma*.
Nirvrutti	Physical part of sensory organ.
Niscaya-naya	Non-conventional view.
Nissahi	'May I come in?'.
Niyama	Observance.
Niyama saara	Sacred text dealing with rules of Jain conduct.
No-kasaaya	Subsidiary passions.
Nyaayavtaar (visaarada)	A scholar of logic.
Oja-aahaara	First intake of food by the newly conceived soul.
Paakhi	A holy day for spiritual observances.
Paapa	Demerit.
Paapaanubandhi	Demerit-causing.
Paataala	Vast receptacles in *lavana-samudra*.
Paathasaalaa	Religious school for children.
Padastha	Reflection on words.
Padilehan	A ritual of carefully cleaning clothes or wooden platters.
Panca kalyanaka pujaa	Ritual worship of five auspicious events in the life of *jina*.
Pancaamrita	'Five nectars'.
Pancanga	Indian calendar.
Pancastikaaya	Kundakunda's sacred text on metaphysics and ethics.
Pandit	Scholar.
Panjaraa pola	Animal sanctuary.
Panyaasa	A male ascetic who is expert in scriptures.
Parabadi	Feeding place for birds.
Paramaanu	Indivisible unit of matter; ultimate particle.
Paramaatmaa	Supreme being; liberated soul.
Paramadhaami	Evil celestials.
Paranaamika	Changing.
Parasparopagraho jivanam	Living beings are mutually interdependent for the welfare of each other.

Parihara	Expulsion.
Parinaama	Result; change of modes.
Parisaha	Physical affliction.
Parisaha jaya	Victory over physical affliction.
Parmesthi	Supreme beings.
Paroksa	Indirect.
Paryaaptaa	Beings with completed vital organs.
Paryaapti	Capacity for completion of vital organs.
Paryaaya	Modes.
Paryusana	Eight sacred days of spiritual activities and austerities.
Phalguna	Fifth month of Indian calendar vs. calendar used by Jains.
Phula maala	Garland of flowers.
Pindastha	Reflection on body.
Potaja	Born as babies without umbilical cord.
Praana	Life forces.
Praayascitta	Penance.
Pradesa	Space-points.
Prajnaa	Wisdom.
Prajnaapanaa sutra	Secondary canon enunciating *bhagavati sutra*.
Prakirnaka	Miscellaneous texts.
Pralaya	Destruction or deluge of the world.
Pramaada	Negligence.
Pramaana	Logical validity.
Pramatta samyati	Stage of total restraint with occasional carelessness.
Pranaayama	Spiritual breathing.
Prasaada	Gift from deity.
Prasamarati	Umasvati's text on Jain philosophy and Right Conduct.
Prasna vyaakarana	Primary canon on philosophy, conduct and society.
Prathamaanuyoga	Sacred text containing biographical and historical material.
Pratikramana	Penitential retreat.
Pratilekhana	A ritual of carefully cleaning clothes or wooden platters.
Pratimaa	Image.
Pratyaahara	Withdrawal from the senses.
Pratyaakhyaana	Partial renunciation.
Pratyaakhyaana varana	'Obstructers of partial renunciation'.
Pratyaksa	Direct.
Pratyeka	Individual.
Preksa dhyaana	Type of Jain meditation.
Prithvi-kaaya	Living beings with body made of earth.
Prosadhopavaasa	Periodic specific fasting and temporary life like an ascetic.

Pruchanaa	Asking questions.
Pudgala	Smallest particle of matter.
Pujaa	Ritual of worship.
Pujaari	Temple servant who performs temple rites.
Pujan	Elaborate *pujaa*.
Punaravartana	Revision.
Punya	Merit.
Punyaanubandhi	Merit-causing.
Purvas	Pre-canons.
Puspaculikaa	Narrative stories on the results of good and bad actions.
Puspikaa	Narrative stories on the results of good and bad actions.
Raajaprasniya	Secondary canon on arts and science, soul and body.
Raajasika bhojan	Tasty food.
Raasi	Progression.
Raatri bhojana	Eating at night.
Raatri jaagrana	Awakening at night for devotional ritual.
Rajju	A vast measurement of length; geometry.
Raksaa bandhan	Sacred thread ceremony.
Rasa	Sap; juice; tasty food.
Rasa-ayan	Rejuvenating juice; chemistry.
Rasaparityaaga	Renunciation of tasty foods.
Ratha yaatra	Chariot procession.
Ratti	Smallest unit of weight.
Raudra dhyaana	Inauspicious 'cruel meditation'.
Ravi	Sun.
Rujusutra naya	Pinpointed standpoint.
Ruksa	Coarse; negative.
Rupaatita	Reflection on the 'formless'.
Rupastha	Reflection on 'forms'.
Saadhaarana	General; common.
Saadhanaa	Spiritual activity.
Saadharmika bhakti	Service to co-religionist.
Saadhu	Male ascetic.
Saadhvi	Female ascetic.
Saagara	A very large unit of time.
Saamayika	Equanimity; a forty-eight minute ritual of equanimity.
Saatvika bhojan	Nutritious food.
Sabda	Sound; word.
Sabda naya	Verbal standpoint.
Sacitta	Material with existence of living beings.
Sad darsana sammucaya	Sacred text dealing with six realities.
Sadgati	Superior destiny.
Sakalendriya	Beings with all the sense organs.

Salaakaa purusa	Torch bearers.
Sallekhanaa	Holy death.
Samaadhi	Profound deep meditation; trance.
Samabhirudha naya	Etymological standpoint.
Samana	Male semi-ascetic.
Samani	Female semi-ascetic.
Samataa	Equanimity.
Samavaayanga	Primary canon, a compendium of summaries of other texts.
Samaya	Unit of time.
Samaya saara	Kundakunda's text dealing with Jain philosophy.
Sambandha	Relation.
Samlinataa	Avoidance of all that can lead to temptation.
Sammurchim	Asexual or 'indirect' sexual birth.
Samsaara	Empirical world.
Samsaari	Worldly soul.
Samsaya	Doubt.
Samudrik sastra	Texts on palmistry and omens.
Samvara	Prevention of influx of *karma*.
Samvatsari	Holiest day in Jain calendar; annual day for forgiveness.
Samyag caritra	Right Conduct.
Samyag darsana	Right Faith.
Samyag jnaana	Right Knowledge.
Samyaktava	Right Faith; right perception.
Sangha	Four-fold community of Jains.
Sangha pujaa	Veneration of the four-fold order.
Sangraha naya	Synthetic standpoint.
Sanjnaa	Instinct.
Sanjvalana	'Producers of apathy and attachment'.
Sankraamana	Transition.
Sansarga	Association.
Sansthana vicaya	Reflection on the universe.
Sarasvati	Goddess of learning.
Sarira	Body.
Sarvajna	Omniscient.
Sasvaadan samyagdristi	Stages of residual faith.
Sataavadhaani	Person with hundred-fold memory.
Satkandadaagama	Digambara sacred text dealing with *karma* and the fourteen stages of spiritual development.
Satya	Truth.
Savavirati	Total restraint.
Sayogi kevali	Dynamic omniscient; embodied omniscient.
Shul	Acute pain.
Siddha	Liberated soul.
Siddha silaa	Place where liberated souls live.
Siddhi	Accomplishment.

Siddhi tapa	Austerity for attaining accomplishments.
Siksaavrata	Educative vows.
Sila	Character.
Sindur	Auspicious red powder worn by a married woman.
Skandha	Aggregate of matter particles.
Skandha desa	Aggregate occupying space.
Skandha pradesa	Aggregate occupying limited space.
Snaatra pujaa	A ritual enacting the birth celebration of the *jina*.
Snigdha	Sticky; positive.
Sraavaka	*Jain* layman.
Sraavaka prajnaapti	Text dealing with duties of lay people.
Sraavakaacaara	Text dealing with conduct of lay people.
Sraavikaa	*Jain* laywoman.
Sraddhaa	Faith.
Sramana	Non-vedic culture such as Jain or buddhist.
Srivatsa	A diamond-shaped emblem on the chest of *jina*.
Sruta jnaana	Sciptural knowledge.
Sthaanaka	Hall for spiritual activities; *upashraya*.
Sthaananga	Primary canon, an encyclopaedic compilation on a wide range of subjects.
Sthaavara	Immobile.
Sthanakvasi	Hall dweller; a sect of Jainism, non-image-worshipper.
Sthavira	Resident senior (elderly) ascetic.
Sthula	Gross.
Stotra	Eulogy.
Subha	Benevolent; auspicious.
Suddhi	Purification.
Sudra	A manual worker or member of lower class.
Sukha	Bliss.
Sukla dhyaana	Auspicious 'pure' meditation.
Suksama	Fine.
Suksama samparay	Spiritual stage of the control of subtle passions.
Supaatra daana	Giving to a worthy person or cause.
Surya	Sun.
Surya prajnaapti	Secondary canon concerning time cycles.
Susamaa	Joyous; blissful.
Sutra krutaanga	Primary canon concerning heretical views.
Svaadhyaaya	Self-study.
Svacchosvaasa	Respiration.
Svamivaastalya	Welfare of co-religionist; amity dinner.
Svetambara	'White-clothed'; a major sect of Jainism.
Syaadavaada	Statement or standpoint in some respects.
Taamasika bhojan	Passionate food.
Taapa	Heat.
Taapasa	Performer of austerities.
Tablaa	An Indian musical instrument (drum).

Tadubhaya	Both confession and penitence.
Tahatti	'That is so'.
Taijasa sarira	Luminous body.
Tama	Darkness.
Tapa	Austerity.
Tapaa gaccha	A sub-sect of Svetambara.
Tapaacaara	Principles relating to austerities.
Tattvartha sutra	Sacred text, a treatise on reality.
Tejas-kaaya	Fire-bodied.
Terapanthi	A sect of Jainism, non-image-worshippers.
Tilak	A sacred mark on forehead, usually of sandlewood paste.
Tirtha prabhaavana	Glorification of the four-fold order.
Tirthankara	*Jina*; founder of four-fold order *(tirtha)*.
Tiryanca	Animals, birds, fish, bacteria, viruses and plants.
Tithi	Date.
Torana	An arch of leaves or embroidered cloth.
Trasa	Mobile.
Trasa nali	'Channel' in the occupied universe for mobile beings.
Triloka prajnaapti	Secondary canon dealing with cosmology.
Tyaaga	Renunciation.
Uchavani	Bidding.
Udiranaa	Prematuration.
Udvartanaa	Augmentation.
Udyapaan	Concluding ritual.
Udyota	Light.
Unodari	Eating less than one's fill.
Upaadeya	Worth attaining.
Upaadhyaaya	Ascetic teacher; scriptural teacher.
Upaangas	Secondary canons.
Upaasaka	Devotee.
Upaasakadasaa	Primary canon dealing with accounts of lay devotees.
Upadesa	Teaching others (through sermons).
Upadhaan	A communal austerity of fasting, meditation and devotion.
Upapaat	Spontaneous.
Upashraya	Monastery; a place for performing spiritual activities.
Upavaas	Fasting.
Upayoga	Conscious spiritual activity; carefulness in activities.
Upkarana	Protective physical cover of an organ.
Upsant moha	Suppressed delusion.
Utpaada	Origination.
Utsarga samiti	'Carefulness in natural calls'.

Utsarpini	Ascending time-cycle.
Uttaraadhyayana sutra	Sacred text, last sermon of Mahavira.
Vaacanaa	Learning scriptures and their meaning.
Vaaha	Largest unit of weight.
Vaasksepa	Sacred powder.
Vaayu-kaaya	Air-bodied.
Vacana	Speech.
Vaikriya sarira	Transformational body.
Vaimaanikas	Heavenly beings with celestial cars.
Vaisak	Seventh month of Indian calendar vs. calendar used by Jains.
Vaisnava	A Hindu sect.
Vaisya	A member of the business community.
Vaiyaavritya	Respectful service for physical welfare of the ascetic.
Vaktavya	Describable.
Vanaspati-kaaya	Vegetable-bodied.
Vandanaka	Veneration.
Vardhamaana tapa	Ritual of progressive fasting.
Varna	Caste; class.
Varsi tapa	Year long austerity, following the example of Risabhdeva.
Vedi	A low platform with sacred fire used in marriage ceremony.
Vidhikaarak	Specialist conductor of rituals.
Vikala	Deficient.
Vikalendriya	Being with deficient sense organs.
Vinaya	Reverence.
Vipaaka sutra	Primary canon, stories illustrating the law of *karma*.
Vipaaka vicaya	Reflection on the end results of *karma*.
Viryaacaar	Principles relating to spiritual energy.
Visa-sthaanaka tapa	Austerity for veneration of the twenty auspicious things.
Viveka	Conscious discrimination.
Vrisnidasaa	Secondary canon on neminatha, krishna and balarama.
Vyaakhyaa prajnaapti	Also called *bhagavati sutra*; primary canon containing questions put by gautam to Mahavira and their replies.
Vyaghat	Obstacle.
Vyantara	Peripatetic type of celestials.
Vyavahaara naya	Practical standpoint.
Vyaya	Disappearance.
Vyutsarga	Renunciation of egoism.
Yaatratnika	A ritual of *pujans*, veneration of *jinas* and pilgrimage.

Yajnopavit	Sacred thread ceremony.
Yaksas and yaksis	Male and female heavenly attendants of *jina*.
Yama	Self-control.
Yati	Svetambara semi-ascetic.
Yoga	Spiritual activities; conjunction of planets.
Yoga sastra	Sacred text dealing with spiritual activities.
Yogi	A person involved in spiritual activities.
Yojana	A unit of measurement of length.
Yoni	A place for conception.
Yonija	Uterine birth.
Yuga	Era; five years.
Yuga pradhaana	A person who influences the era.

BIBLIOGRAPHY AND SOURCES FOR REFERENCES IN ENGLISH

*indicates books suitable for general readership or readers new to Jainism.

Amarendravijay (1993) *Science Discovers Eternal Wisdom*, Gandhidham: Jain Sahitya Academy. (An introduction to Jain thought from the point of view of Western science)

Andhare Shridhar (1992) *Treasures from L.D.Museum*, Ahmedabad: L.D. Museum (Serves as an introduction to Jain art and is extensively illustrated)

*Atmanandji (1993) *Aspirant's Guide*, Koba: Shrimad Rajchandra Adhyatmik Sadhana Kendra. (An introduction to Jain ethics and values)

Bhargava, D. (1968) *Jain Ethics*, Delhi: Motilal Banarsidass.

Bhaskar, B. (1993) *Jainism and Mahavira*, Delhi: Digamber Jain Sahitya Sanskriti Sanraksan Samiti.

Bhattacharya, B. (1974) *Jain Iconography*, Delhi: Motilal Banarsidass. (Detailed illustrated guide to Jain images, including a history of their development)

Bhattacharya, N. (1976) *Jain Philosophy*, *Historical Outline*, New Delhi: Munshiram Manoharlal.

*Bhuvanbhanusuri (1987) *A Handbook of Jainology*, Mehsana: Visva Kalyan Prakashan Trust. (An introduction to Jain conduct)

Bothra, S. (1987) *Ahimsa*, Jaipur: Prakrit Bharati Academy.

Burgess, J. (1971) *The Temples of Santrunjaya*, Calcutta: Jain Bhavan (originally published 1869).

Button, J. (1989) *How To Be Green*, London: Century Publishing.

*Caillat, C., Upadhye, A. and Patil, B. (1974) *Jainism*, Delhi: Macmillan Company of India. (Three short essays giving an introduction to Jainism)

Carrithers, M. and Humphrey, C. (eds) (1991) *The Assembly of Listeners*, Cambridge: Cambridge University Press. (Collection of edited papers from a conference held at the University of Cambridge)

Chakravarti, A. (1971) *Samayasara of Sri Kundakunda*, Delhi: Bharatiya Jnanapitha. (English translation of a sacred text on Jain philosophy with an introduction)

Chatterjee, A. (1978) *Comprehensive History of Jainism, Volume I*, Calcutta: Firma KLM. (Traces the history of Jains and Jainism up to 1000 CE)

— (1984) *A Comprehensive History of Jainism, Volume II*, Calcutta: Firma KLM. (Traces the history of Jains and Jainism up to 1600 CE)

*Chitrabhanu (1979) *The Psychology of Enlightenment*, New York: Dodd, Mead and Company. (A guide to practical meditation on the seven energy centres, written by a former Jain ascetic, who now devotes himself to teaching Jainism in the USA)

— (1978) *Ten Days Journey into the Self*, New York: Jain Meditation International Centre. (A useful introduction to Jain values)

*Chitrabhanu, P. (1993) *Jain Symbols, Ceremonies and Practices*, New York: Jain Meditation International Centre.

Clarke, P. (ed.) (1978) *The Worlds Religions*, London: The Reader's Digest Association.

Devendramuni (1983) *Source Book in Jain Philosophy*, Udaipur: Sri Tarak Guru Jain Granthalaya. (A detailed and scholarly account of Jain philosophy by a Jain monk)

Dixit, K. (1971) *Jain Ontology*, Ahmedabad: L.D. Institute of Indology.

Doshi Saryu (1981) *Homage to Shravana Belgola*, Bombay: Marg Publications.

— (1985) *Masterpieces of Jain Painting*, Bombay: Marg Publications. (A scholarly account of Jain paintings, containing many fine coloured illustrations)

*Dundas, P. (1992) *The Jains*, London: Routledge. (A very readable account of Jains, Jain society and Jain philosophy written by a university academic)

Dwivedi, R. (ed.) (1975) *Contribution of Jainism to Indian Culture*, Delhi: Motilal Banarasidass.

Fischer, E. and Jain, J. (1977) *Art and Rituals, 2500 Years of Jainism in India*, New Delhi: Stirling Publishers (A general introduction to Jain festivals, practices of the four-fold order and to the place of art in Jainism)

Folkert, K. (1993) *Scripture and Community*, Harvard University Press

George, D., Richard, T. (ed) (1968) *Ethics in Society*, London: Macmillan.

Ghosh, A. (ed) (1974–75) *Jaina Art and Architecture*, Vols 1–3, New Delhi: Bharatiya Jnanpith. (A broad ranging and detailed account of Jain art and architecture, a standard work).

Godlovitch, R., Godlovitch, S., Godlovitch, H. and Godlovitch, J. (1971) *Animals, Men and Morals*, London: Victor Gollancz.

Gopalan, S. (1973) *Outlines of Jainism*, New Delhi: Wiley Eastern. (An introduction to Jain philosophy, based on lectures given by the author in Madras University)

Hemchandra (1970) *Pramana Mimansa*, Varanasi: Tara Publications (trans. S. Mukherjee).

Hemming, J. (1969) *Individual Morality*, London: Thomas Nelson and Sons.

Henshaw, D. (1989) *Animal Warfare*, London: Fontana.

Hutchings, M. and Caver, M. (1970) *Men's Dominion: Our Violation of the Animal World*, London: Rupert Hart-Davis.

Jacobi, H.(1968) *Jaina Sutras* Part 1 and Part 2, New York: Dover Publications. (Part 1 contains *Acaranga Sutra* and *Kalpa Sutra*; Part 2 contains the *Uttaradhyanan Sutra* and *Sutrakritanga Sutra*; reprints of translations with introductions by great nineteenth-century scholars)

Jain, B. (1992) *Jaina Logic*, Madras: Madras University. (A collection of papers from a seminar)

Jain, C. (1974) *Fundamentals of Jainism*, Meerut: Veer Nirvan Bharti. (A useful book originally published in 1916 as *The Practical Path*)

Jain, D. (1992) *Basic Tenets of Jainism*, New Delhi: Vir Sewa Mandir.

Jain, G. (1975) *Cosmology Old and New*, Delhi: Bharatiya Jnanpith.

Jain, H. and Upadhye, A. (1951) *Mahavira, his Times and his Philosophy of Life*, New Delhi: Bharatiya Jnanpith. (A booklet of sixty pages containing two essays)

Jain, J. (1961) *The Doctrines of Jainism*, Bombay: Vallabhsuri Smarak Nidhi. (An attempt to describe the heart of Jain Philosophy)

*— (1983) *Religion and Culture of the Jains*, New Delhi: Bharatiya Jnanpith. (A general and readable book on all aspects of Jainism)

— (1964) *The Jaina Sources of the History of Ancient India*, Delhi: Munshiram Manoharlal Publishers.

— (1951) *Jainism: Oldest Living Religion*, Varanasi: Parsvanath Vidhyashram.

Jain, J. and Fischer, E. (1978) *Jain Iconography, The Tirthankaras and Objects of Meditation* (2 volumes). (Vol. 1 contains *The Tirthankaras* in *Jain Scriptures, Art and Rituals*; Vol. 2 , *Objects of Meditation* and *the Pantheon*)

Jain, K. (1974) *Lord Mahavira and his Times*, Delhi: Motilal Banarsidass. (Places Mahavira in the cultural and social context of his time)

— (1992) *Researches in Jainology* (Hindi–English) Khatoli: Kailascandra Smriti Nyaas.

Jain, L. (1994) *Labdhisaar*, Katani: M.K. Jain Trust. (An account of the attainment of Right Faith and the purification of the soul as it passes through succeeding stages of spiritual development)

— (1992) *The Tao of Jain Sciences*, Delhi: Arihant International. (A scholarly text on Jain sciences)

— (1982) *Basic Arithmetics*, Jaipur: Prakrit Bharati Sanstha.

— (1984) *Astronomy and Astrology*, Jaipur: Prakrit Bharati Sanstha.

Jain, N. (1993) *Jain System in Nutshell*, Satna: N.S. Siksha Kosh.

— (1996) *Scientific Contents in Prakrit Canons*, Varanasi: Parsvanatha Vidya Pitha.

Jain, S.C. (1978) *Structure and Functions of Soul in Jainism*, New Delhi: Bharatiya Jnanpith.

Jaini, J. (1979) *Outlines of Jainism*, Indore: J.L. Jaini Trust.

*Jaini, P. (1979) *The Jaina Path of Purification*, Berkeley: University of California Press. (An account of Jainism by a noted scholar from the University of California, written with a Western readership in mind)

Jenkins, S. (1992) *Animal Rights and Human Wrongs*, Harpenden: Lennard Publishing.

*Jindal, K. (1988) *An Epitome of Jainism*, New Delhi: Munshiram Manoharlal Publishers. (A brief account of Jain sacred texts including *Dravya Samgraha, Tattvartha Sutra, Panchastikaaya Saara, Gommatsaara Jiva kaand* and *Karma Kaand, Samayasaara, Niyamasaara, Parikshamukham* and Jain Cosmology)

Johnson, W. (1995) *Harmless Souls*, Delhi: Motilal Banarasidass. (An academic from the University of Wales gives a scholarly account of *karma* in Jain philosophy, probably accessible for a general readership too)

*Kalghatgi, T. (1988) *Study of Jainism*, Jaipur: Prakrit Bharati Academy.

— (1961) *Some Problems in Jaina Psychology*, Dharwar: Karnatak University.

Kapashi, V. (1984) *In Search of Ultimate*, Harrow: V.K. Publications.

Khushalchandramuni (1990) *Jain Tirtha Dashanavali* (Gujarati–English), Palitana: Jain Tirtha Darshan Bhavan.

Laidlaw, James (1995) *Riches and Renunciation*, Oxford: Clarendon Press (A report on recent research by a British anthropologist into the religion, economy and society of Jains in contemporary India).

Lalvani, G. (ed.) (1991) *Jainthology*, Calcutta: Jain Bhavan.

— (1973–85) *Bhagavati Sutra*, Calcutta: Jain Bhavan (4 vols).

— (1974) *Uttaradhyanan Sutra*, Calcutta: Jain Bhavan.

Lalvani, K. (1979) *Kalpa Sutra of Badrabahu Swami*, Delhi: Motilal Banarsidass.

Lalvani, K. (1988) *Uvavaiya Suttam* Jaipur: Prakrit Bharati Academy.

Lishk, S. (1987) *Jaina Astronomy*, Delhi: Vidya Sagara Publications.

Mahaprajna (1979) *Ramblings of Ascetic*, New Delhi: Books for Today (trans. Goswamik).

Malvania (ed.) (1977) *Mahavira and His Teachings*, Ahmedabad: Navjivan Press.

Mardia, K. (1990) *The Scientific Foundation of Jainism*, Delhi: Motilal Banarsidass. (A scholarly attempt at an account of Jain thought in relation to the concepts of modern Western science written by an academic from Leeds University)

*Marett, P. (1985) *Jainism Explained* Leicester: Jain Samaj Europe. (An introduction to Jainism by a British university academic written in direct, uncomplicated language for a wide readership)

Mills, H. and McLaine, M. (eds) (1988) *My God*, London: Pelham Books.

Mukherjee, S. (1985) *Illuminator of Jain Tenets*, Ladnun: Jain Visva Bharati (trans. of Tattvartha Sutra).

Neal, P. (1992) *The Acid Rain Effect*, London: B.T. Batsford.

Nevaskar, B. (1971) *Capitalists without Capitalism, the Jains of India and the Quakers of the West*, Westport: Greenwood Publications.

Nirvansagar Muni (ed.) (1986) *Pratikraman Sutra* (Hindi–English) Koba: Mahavir Aradhana Kendra.

Pal, P. (1994) *Jain Art from India*, New York: Thames and Hudson.

Pandey, V. (1976) (ed) *The World of Jainism*, Bombay: (Self-publicaton).

Patel, D.(1960) *The Self Realisation*, Agasa: Rajachandra Mumukshu Mandal (trans. of Atma-Siddhi).

Pujyapada Acharya (1960) *Sarvarthasiddhi*, Calcutta: Vira Sasana Sangha (English trans. by S. Jain).

Radhakrishnan, S. (1929–31) *Indian Philosophy*, London: Allen and Unwin (2 vols.).

Rao, S. (1922) *Jainism in South India*, Part 2, Delhi: Satguru Publications.

Rosenfield, C. (1981) *Gurudev Shree Chitrabhanu, a Man with a Vision*, New York: Jain Meditation International Center.

*Roy, A. (1984) *History of the Jains*, New Delhi: Gitanjali Publishing House.

Sancheti and Bhandari (1995) *First Steps to Jainism* (2 vols), Jodhpur: Sumcheti Trust.

*Sangave, V. (1980) *Jaina Community, a Social Survey*, Bombay: Popular Prakashan.

(A social history of Jains in India from the earliest times to the present day)

*— (1990) *Aspects of Jain Religion*, Delhi: Bharatiya Jnanpith. (A clearly written introductory book for general readers)

— (1992) *Jain Society Through Ages*, Delhi: R.K. Jain Charitable Trust.

Schubring, W. (1974) *The Doctrine of the Jains*, Delhi: Motilal Banarsidass. (Translation of a German work published in 1934)

Shah, C. (1989) *Jainism in North India*, Delhi: Nav Bharat Printing Press

*Shah, D. (1965) *Jain Dharma Saara*, Adoni: Jain Marg Aradhak Samiti. (A detailed synopsis covering most aspects of Jainism)

Shah, R. (1995) *Jina-Vachana*, Bombay: Jain Yuvaksangh. (200 quotations in Prakrit, English, Hindi and Gujarati from the sacred texts)

Shah, U. (1974) 'Jainism', *New Encyclopaedia Britannica*, Chicago: Encyclopedia Britannica.

— (1978) *Treasures of Jaina Bhandaras*, Ahmedabad: L.D. Institute of Indology.

Shah, U. and Dhaky, M. (1975) *Aspects of Jaina Art and Architecture*, Ahmedabad: Committe for Celebration of 2500th Anniversary of Mahavira.

Shastri, I. (1990) *Jaina Epistemology*, Varanasi: P.V. Research Institute.

Sivaramamurti, C. (1983) *Panorama of Jain Art*, New Delhi: Times of India Publications.

Sikdar, J. (1974) *Jain Biology*, Ahmedabad: L.D. Institute.

— (1960) *Studies in Bhagvati Sutra*, Muzafarpur: Vaisali Inst.

— (1991) *Concepts of Matter and Reality*, Varanasi: P.V. Research Institute.

Singh, R. (1993) *Jain Perspective in Philosophy and Religion*, Varanasi: Parsvanatha Sodhapitha.

Singhi, K. (1990) *The Philosophy of Jainism*, Calcutta: Punthi Pustaka.

Singhi, N. (1987) *Ideal, Ideology and Practice: Studies in Jainism*, Jaipur: Printwell Publishers.

Sogani, K. (1967) *Ethical Doctrines in Jainism*, Sholapur: Jaina Sanskriti Sanrakshaka Sangha.

Stevenson, S. (1970) *The Heart of Jainism*, New Delhi: Munshi Ram Manoharlal. (First published by Oxford University Press in 1915, systemic account written from the point of view of a Christian missionary)

Tatia, N. (1994) *That Which Is*, HarperCollins.

Tiwari, K. (1983) *Comparative Religion*, Delhi: Motilal Banardidass.

Tiwari, M. (1983) *Elements of Jaina Iconography*, Varanasi: Indological Book House.

Tobias, M. (1991) *Life Force: The World of Jainism*, Berkeley: Asian Humanities Press.

*Tukol, T. (1980) *Compendium of Jainism*, Dharwad: Karnataka University.

Upadhye, A. *et al.* (1983) *Lord Mahavira and his Teachings*, Bombay: Shree Vallabhsuri Smarak Nidhi. (A collection of essays on Jain teachings which seeks to show their relevance to the modern world)

Warren, H. (1983) *Jainism in Western Garb, as a Solution to Life's Great Problems*, Bombay: Shree Vallubhsuri Smaraka Trust. (First published in 1912, frequently reprinted, contains an account of Jain teachings)

Williams, R. (1983) *Jaina Yoga*, Delhi: Motilal Banarsidass. (First published in 1963 by Oxford University Press, contains an account of the rituals and spiritual practices of the lay person)

Winne-Tyson, J. (1979) *Food for the Future*, London: Sentour Press.

Wright, M. (1991) (ed.) *Our Backyard*, London: Hodder and Stoughton.

*Yashovijay Muni (1995) *Tirthankar Bhagawan Mahavira*, Bombay: Jain Chitrakaka Nidarshan. (First published in 1976. A masterly illustrated account of Mahavira's life. Contains 48 coloured photographs and many line drawings. Written in Hindi, Gujarati and English)

Zaveri, J. (1991) *Microcosmology, Atom in Jain Philosophy and Modern Science*, Ladnum: Jain Vishva Bharati

— (1992) *Neuroscience and Karma*, Ladnum: Jain Visva Bharati.

BIBLIOGRAPHY AND SOURCES FOR REFERENCES IN INDIAN LANGUAGES

Amarendravijay (1971) *Vijnan ane adhyatma* (Gujarati), Vadodara: Atmajagruti Trust.

Amitayashavijay (1982) *Sraavaka Pajnapti* (Gujarati), Ahmedabad: Zaveri Park, Adisvar Jain Trust.

Arunvijay (1991) *Karma Ki Gati Nyari* (Hindi), Bombay: Mahavir Vidhyarthi Kalyan Kendra.

Atmanandji (1988) *Arvachin Jain Jyotirdharo* (Gujarati), Koba: Satsrut Seva Sadhana Kendra.

Baraia, G. (1987) *Jain Siddhanta Praveshika* (Gujarati), Songadh: Digambar Jain Svadhyaya Mandir Trust.

Bhadrabahuvijay (1990) *Jain Dharma* (Gujarati), Mehsana: Visva Kalyan Prakashan Trust.

Bharill, H. (1987) *Karmabaddha Paryay* (Hindi), Jaipur: Todarmal Smarak Trust.

Bhuvanbhanusuri (1975) *Jain Dharma Nu Vijnan* (Gujarati), Surat: Kirti Prakashan.

— (1987b) *Jain Dharma Ka Parichaya* (Gujarati), Mehsana: Visva Kalyan Prakashan Trust.

Chandrasekharvijay (1985) *Sutrartha, Tattva Jnana, Katha and Jivan Ghadatar Praveshika* (Gujarati), Ahmedabad: Kamal Prakashan Trust.

Devluck, N. (ed.) (1985) *Jain Ratna Chintamani* (Gujarati), Bhavnagar: Arihant Prakashan.

Doshi, C. (1979) *Pancha Pratikraman Sutra* (Hindi), Bombay: Jain Sahitya Vikas Mandal.

Duggadh, H. (1979) *Madhya Asia aur Panjab Main Jain Dharma* (Hindi), Delhi: Sahitya Prakashan Mandir.

Hemratnavijay (1990) *Chalo Jinalaye Jaie* (Gujarati), Ahmedabad: Arhad Dharm Prabhavak Trust.

Jain, S. (1981) *Jain Aradhanani Vaijnanikata* (Gujarati), Bhavnagar: Samanvaya Prakashan.

Kadiwala, B. (1981) *Jivanni Sarva Shrestha Kala Navkar* (Gujarati), Navsari: Adhyatma Dhyan Kendra.

Kalapurnasuri (1980) *Tattvajnan Praveshika* (Hindi), Anjar: Nahavir Tattvajnan Prakashak Mandal.

Kishansingh, K. (1985) *Kriya Kosha* (Hindi), Agas: Rajchandra Ashram.

Khushalchandramuni (1990) *Jain Tirtha Dashanavali* (Gujarati–English), Palitana: Jain Tirtha Darshan Bhavan.

Mahaprajna (1974) *Dasaveiyalam* (Hindi), Ladnun: Jain Visva Bharati.

— (1980) *Chetana No Urdharohana* (Gujarati), Ahmedabad: Anekant Bharati Prakashan.

— (1981) *Karmavada* (Gujarati), Ahmedabad: Anekant Bharati Prakashan.

— (1986a) *Suya Gado* (Hindi), Ladnun: Jain Visva Bharati.

— (1986b) *Jivan Vijnana* (Gujarati), Ladnun: Jain Visva Bharati.

— (1990) *Chitta Ane Mana* (Gujarati), Ahmedabad: Anekant Bharati Prakashan.

— (1991) *Jain Darshan Aur Sanskriti* (Hindi), Ladnun: Jain Visva Bharati.

Malavinia, D. (1966) *Agam Yug Ka Jain Darshana* (Hindi), Agra: Sanmati Jnan Pith.

Mallisenasuri (1979) *Syadvada Manjari* (Sanskrit–Hindi) Agasa: Rajchandra Ashram.

Modi, D. (1977) *Sanksipt Jain Darshan* (Gujarati), Bombay: Modi Publishers.

— (1991) *Jain Ahar* (Gujarati), Bombay: Modi Memorial Trust.

Modi, M. (1988) *Shrimad Rajchandra* (Gujarati), Agasa: Rajchandra Ashram.

Muktiprabhavijay (1979) *Shravake Shun Karvu Joie* (Gujarati), Ahmedabad: Jayantilal Atmaram.

Nathmalmuni (ed.) (1976) *Thanan* (Hindi), Ladnun: Jain Visva Bharati.

Nirvansagar Muni (ed.) (1986) *Pratikraman Sutra* (Hindi–English), Koba: Mahavir Aradhana Kendra.

Prabhakarvijay (1968) *Vijnan Ane Jain Darshan* (Gujarati), Ahmedabad: Ramanlal Sakarchand.

Upadhyaya (1915) *Dhyan Dipika* (Gujarati), Bombay: Premji Hirji Shah.

Sanghamitra Sadhvi (1986) *Jain Dharma Ke Prabbavaka Acharya* (Hindi), Ladnun: Jain Vishva Bharati.

Saumyajyotishri Sadhvi (1990) *Visvadarshan Jayajyota* (Gujarati), Sisodara: Panchashaka Prakashan Samiti.

Shah, J. (1979) (ed.) *Vividha Puja Sangraha* (Gujarati), Ahmedabad: Jain Prakashan Mandir.

— (1983) *Pujan Sangraha* (Gujarati), Ahmedabad: (Self-publication).

Shah, R. (1985–92) *Jina Tattva* (Gujarati), Bombay: Jain Yuvak Sangh (5 vols).

— (1992) *Prabhavaka Sthaviro* (Gujarati), Bombay: Jain Yuvak Sangh (3 vols).

— (1995) *Jina-Vachana*, Bombay: Jain Yuvaksangh.

Shastri, N. (1974) *Tirthankar Mahavir Aur Unki Acharya Parampara* (Hindi), Budhana: Shantisagar Chhani Granthmala.

Umasvati (1989) (ed. Subhasya) *Tattvarthadhigama Sutra* (Hindi), Agasa: Rajchandra Ashram.

— (1985) (ed. Bhadraguptavijay) *Prashamrati* (Gujarati), Mehsana: Visva Kalyan Prakashan Trust.

— (1986) (ed. M. Kapadia) *Prashamrati* (Gujarati), Bombay: Mahavir Jain Vidhyalaya.

Vaid, P. (1980) *Tirtha Darshan* (Gujarati and Hindi), Madras: Mahavir Jain Kalyan Sangha.

Varni Jinendra (1984–87) *Jainendra Siddhanta Kosha* (Hindi), New Delhi: Bharatiya Jnanpith.

— (1986) *Shantipath-Darshan* (Gujarati), Koba: Adhyatmik Sadhana Kendra (Tr. S. Vohora).

Vidhyavijay Muni (1983) *Jain Dharma* (Gujarati), Dhansura: Vidhyavijayji Smarak Granthamala.

Vijaybhuvanvhanusuri (1978) *Jain Dharma No Parichaya* (Gujarati), Bombay: Divya Darshan Prakashan Trust.

Vijaydevasura Sangh (ed.) (1981) *Pancha Pratitraman Sutra* (Gujarati), Bombay: Sangh Publication.

Vohora, S. (1990a) *Kalpasutra Katha Saar* (Gujarati), Ahmedabad: Self-publication.

— (1990b) (ed.) *Jiva Srustinu Parijnan* (Gujarati), Ahmedabad: Self-publication.

— (1990c) (ed.) *Guna Pantrisi* (Gujarati), Ahmedabad: Self-publication.

Yashovijay Muni (1976) *Tirthankar Bhagawan Mahavira* (Hindi, Gujarati and English), Bombay: Jain Chitrakaka Nidarshan.

— (1992) *Sangrahani Ratna* (Gujarati), Vadodara: M. M. Jain Jnan Mandir.

Yashovijay Upadhyaya (1976) *Jnaana Saara* (Gujarati), Mehsana: Vishvakalyan Trust (ed. Bhadraguptavijay).

INDEX